The Flatbush Journal of Jewish Law and Thought

Volume 20 / Winter 2015

A publication of
Hakirah, Inc.
www.Hakirah.org

Ḥakirah

The Flatbush Journal of Jewish Law and Thought

Volume 20 / Winter 2015

JEWISH LAW

זכור

הלכה

Introduction

Different branches of Judaism can be distinguished by the degree to which they identify either with the rational or with the mystical schools within Jewish philosophy. In this edition, we focus on these two distinct types of thought but also examine how they are often found in tandem, merged in the minds and works of great thinkers. "Paḥad Yitzḥak: A Joyful Song of Affirmation" studies the classic work of Rav Yitzḥak Hutner which combines the Brisker approach with the mysticism of Maharal and Ḥassidic Masters to "produce a theological/psychological system that incorporates elements of many strands of Jewish thought" that "form the essential elements of an optimistic, humanistic message." In "Kabbalah—Escape from Reality or Affirmation of Life?" the author responds to a well-argued article that claims that Jewish mysticism poses dangers to contemporary Jewish society with the counter argument that "Jewish mysticism in the hands of an ethical genius such as a Rav Kook… invigorates rather than vitiates our existence."

Two articles in a special section on free choice argue that the rationalism of science complements man's search for answers that are in the realm of the mystical. In "God, Man, Chaos and Control: How God Might Control the Universe" the author posits that modern scientific theory can be used to explain the mechanism by which G-d allows for free choice. The author writes, "As our scientific knowledge grows, we have faced criticism and concern from some religious thinkers who believe that science is an affront to religion. However, an educated approach to these big questions reveals that not only is there a history of using scientific lenses to better understand religion, an advanced knowledge of the complexities of our world magnifies the awesomeness of God." Another essay, entitled "The Jewish Idea of Freedom," maintains that the Jewish concept of freedom, rooted in creation and man's free choice, is the first such concept in human history "and still the most radical." The author goes on to explain how, in the modern era, the Jewish idea of freedom was reborn in the political sphere through the 17th-century revolution in political thought that preceded the American Revolution. But more surprisingly, he demonstrates "the contribution of biblical and rabbinic thought to the contemporaneous scientific revolution."

The importance of understanding the difference between scientific principles and mystical ideas is investigated in "Misinterpreting Rabbi Judah Ha-Levi," where the author shows that charges of racism against R. Yehudah Ha-Levi are based on confusing the concept of "*inyan Eloki*" with modern genetics. The misinterpretation of the views of R. Yehuda

Ha-Levi is central to another article, "What Must a Jew Believe? Dogma and Inadvertent Heresy, Revisited," where the author notes that Ha-Levi accepts the view that Jewish identity is defined by belief in certain key principles. "In fact, not only staunch rationalists like Rambam, but also 'anti-rationalists' like Ha-Levi, Naḥmanides, and Maharal expounded what they saw to be the principles of Judaism."

Tradition and Innovation is the focus of other articles in this volume. In our History of Halakhah section, in an essay entitled "A Short History of the Jewish Fixed Calendar," the author presents evidence against the traditional view that the Jewish calendar was fixed 1800 years ago, detailing how the discovery of new documents in the Cairo Genizah seemingly disproves this belief, and demonstrates the changes that he believes occurred in different eras until the calendar came into its present form. A Jewish Law article, "Torah Authority," examines the sources of authority that allow the Rabbis to legislate the calendar as well as other decrees. Similarly, "The Mysterious Origin of Lag Ba-Omer" claims that the holiday was a late innovation, not an age-old tradition related to Rabbi Akiva and Rav Shimon ben Yochai. And interestingly, Rav Shimon Ben Yochai is the subject of a Hebrew article with regard to his *shitta* on *shiurim,* which suggests that he was an innovator of standardization. In contrast, another article in the History of Halakhah section, "Redacting Tosafot on the Talmud: Part Two – Editing Methods," demonstrates the extreme degree to which R. Eliezer was a faithful "transmitter of the rich Tosafist tradition." In our History section, "Christian-Hebraism in England: William Wotten and the First Translation of the Mishnah into English" exposes us to the interesting phenomenon of the serious gentile scholarship of Jewish sources that flourished in England for several centuries.

Finally, we are saddened but inspired by *divrei hesped* for Rav Eitam Henkin, *H"YD*, who represents the broad scope of learning that *Ḥakirah* tries to encompass and who combined in himself the best qualities of the different schools of thought within Orthodox Judaism.

Special thanks to all those who worked hard to make this edition of *Ḥakirah* a reality, including Ari Bornstein and Nina Ackerman Indig, copy-editing; Mindy Schaper, typesetting; Tuvia Ganz, cover design and production; and Chaim Lam, design and maintenance of our Web page, www.Hakirah.org.

It is our continuing hope that the articles in this journal will stimulate thought, study and discussion, and inspire other members of the public to contribute their own insights. The articles we print thus reflect a wide range of opinion and do not necessarily reflect the views of our Editorial Board. ☙

Instructions for Contributors

Ḥakirah, The Flatbush Journal of Jewish Law and Thought, publishes original, interesting, well-researched and well-organized manuscripts that provide new or profound insights into areas of Jewish *halakhah* and *hashkafah.*

Manuscripts should be in Microsoft Word format and sent as an email attachment to HakirahFlatbush@msn.com. Short references—for example, to a Biblical verse or to a page within the Talmud—should be embedded directly into the text of the manuscript. Longer references should be inserted electronically as footnotes, rather than endnotes.

The author's name should not appear on the manuscript, as it is the Journal's policy to forward the articles for evaluation without disclosing the author's identity. On a separate cover sheet include your name, a short bio, an abstract of your article, your telephone number, fax number, and e-mail address.

After reviewing and accepting your manuscript, we are likely to request clarification of certain points. A revised electronic copy of your manuscript will then be required.

To encourage a wide variety of contributors, the Journal accepts articles employing the Hebrew transliteration style of either *Encyclopedia Judaica* or *ArtScroll.* If you have no preference we suggest you follow the pronunciation rules used by the *Encyclopedia Judaica.* Words in languages other than English should always be italicized, unless the foreign words have become part of the English language.

For more information about writing an article for *Ḥakirah* see <www.Hakirah.org\HakirahGuideToWriting.pdf>. ☙

LETTERS TO THE EDITOR

Supporting Israel

LIKE TODAY'S RAPIDLY shifting sands of the Middle East, the factors—laid out so beautifully in Heshey Zelcer's seminal article, "Who Will Support the State of Israel?"[1] —that have been in place for the last several decades are rapidly eroding in front of our very eyes.

One may reasonably make the argument that these factors have almost entirely been washed away in a sea of moral ambiguity and cultural relativism, which are endemic to 21st-century American culture. It is quite difficult for many Americans to even be able to acknowledge that Iran is an evil regime, or that evil even exists in the world. It is equally difficult for them to even utter a value judgement.[2]

And most Jews, who have been so eager and willing to assimilate into the welcoming and nourishing soil of this great nation, have rapidly adopted many of these cultural mores. Many Jews, with the exception of most in the Orthodox and modern-Orthodox communities, have traded in the religion of Judaism for that of liberalism, long ago, and have willfully blinded themselves to the immediate threat that this nuclear deal with Iran may cause to their Israeli brothers and sisters.[3]

This past summer, a dramatic sea change occurred. Many of us who are active in the pro-Israel political community witnessed, with an increasing sense of horror, the way that the Obama administration handled the negotiations with Iran. We watched as the highest office in the land enthusiastically promoted a deal that, without a doubt, emboldened the Islamic Republic, the number one threat in the region to Israel, to the Middle East, and arguably to the world. We watched, again, as the President made an end run around the Constitution,[4] and went

---

[1] *Ḥakirah*, Vol. 19 <http://www.hakirah.org/Vol19Zelcer.pdf>.

[2] In fact, most Americans, when making a value judgement, qualify it by saying, "I don't want to make a value judgement but…."

[3] I regret to add that for many, or perhaps most American Jews, the cultural distance has become so great, that they no longer consider the Jewish residents of Israel their "brothers and sisters." They choose to identify with a "community of choice" rather than that of "ascription." For example, a close relative of mine identifies herself not as a Jew, but as an intellectual, a writer, and an atheist.

[4] The Constitution specifically calls for a vote of 2/3 of the Senate to ratify a treaty. This deal, which has huge international implications for generations to come, cannot be regarded as anything short of a treaty.

directly to the United Nations Security Council[5] to have the deal enshrined in international law, and managed to make a show of getting the deal through Congress, while it was filibustered, and a vote was never even allowed to take place.

We watched and some of us, but far too few of us, acted.

This deal, the Joint Comprehensive Plan of Acton (JCPOA), undoubtedly makes the Middle East an infinitely more dangerous neighborhood in which to live.

Equally horrifying was the fact that the American Jewish community was blatantly (and quite loudly) divided over this issue, and that, although most polls showed that well over half of the American public were against the Iranian nuclear deal,[6] many American Jews were actually in the forefront of the movement to back the JCPOA.

Many organizations, such as J Street and Americans for Peace Now, have allowed themselves to be used as a shill by the Obama administration, and were out in full force advocating for the deal. An astounding example of this was a series of ads placed in newspapers around the country, with the Hebrew words *Todah Rabah* (thank you very much) to individual Members of Congress who voted to endorse this outrageously generous Iranian nuclear deal. In this ad, Members of Congress were specifically named, depending on which area of the country they were from, and singled out for gratitude. These were paid for by a new 501C4 organization, with the ironic name of "No Nukes for Iran Project."

It was so difficult to watch how many American Jewish Members of Congress loudly professed their sacrosanct love of Israel, while stating how gut-wrenchingly difficult and profoundly personal the decision on the Iranian deal was, while lending their signatures to this horrible deal—a deal that will have disastrous implications for the people of Israel, and throughout the world for generations to come.[7]

They must have known it had dire implications, or it would not have posed such a moral dilemma for them to lend their signatures to it. If, in fact, the deal was able to get rid of the Iranian nuclear threat, as its proponents had vociferously argued, it should not have posed any such moral dilemma.

The fact that the United States

---

[5] Foreign Policy, July 15th 2015. "Obama Turns to U.N. to Outmaneuver Congress," John Hudson and Colum Lynch. <http://foreignpolicy.com/2015/07/15/obama-turns-to-u-n-to-outmaneuver-congress-iran-nuclear-deal/>.

[6] For example, the Pew Research Center, on September 8th, 2015, found that just 21 percent of the American public approve of the agreement. <http://www.people-press.org/2015/09/08/support-for-iran-nuclear-agreement-falls/>. There seemed to be a marked decline of support, the more the American public found out about the details of the agreement.

[7] Take for example, Rep. Debbie Wasserman Schultz's remarks on *Meet the Press*.

had led the way in international negotiations together with the other members of the P5 plus 1 countries (Russia, China, France, Britain and Germany), to forge a deal that will enable the Iranians to have a nuclear bomb if they just wait 10 to 15 years, clearly demonstrates that Israel can no longer rely on American support for Israel.

First of all, there should be absolutely no doubt that the JCPOA is inimical to Israel's long-term survival. What is 10 to 15 years in the life of a nation? It is but a blink of an eye. In a matter of months, upon "Implementation Day," Iranian assets that had been frozen will be released, giving the Iranian economy an immediate boost of more than 100 billion dollars. Beyond that, the international sanctions that have been in place since 1996, when the Iran Libya Sanctions Act (ILSA) was passed, will be lifted, giving the Iranian economy a huge boost.

The 3.4 billion dollars in foreign aid that Israel gets annually pales in comparison to these staggering numbers.[8]

The Tehran Imam Khomeini International Airport is bustling, and Iran is planning to expand the airport with a $2.8b project.[9] This is primarily due to the excessive greed of European companies, hungry to do business with the oil-rich Islamic Republic which has a population of 77.45 million consumers, eager to purchase modern products.

It should be noted that there is a clause within the JCPOA that states that any business contract that is signed when the sanctions are lifted can endure if sanctions are re-imposed, and that the mere act of re-imposing sanctions gives Iran grounds to withdraw for the entire deal (so much for the Obama administration's much vaunted talk of "snap back sanctions").

Approximately $30 billion of Iran's economy goes towards its military and paramilitary operations.[10] We are talking about a staggering influx of money that will go to the Iranian Revolutionary Guard Corps, and to operations such as Hamas, Hezbollah, Islamic Jihad, the Yemenis Houtis, and to Bashir Assad's Syria. Iran has long been known as the Central bank of operations for all of these, and many other such terrorist groups.

On July 15th, the day after announcing that the P5 plus 1 and Iran have reached an agreement, President Obama held a White House Press Conference in which he was asked a question about

---

[8] Most of which comes back into the American economy for defense spending

[9] Airport-technology.com, September 28, 2015. "French firms in talks to build second terminal at Iran's Imam Khomeini Airport" <http://www.airport-technology.com/news/news french-firms-in-talks-to-build-second-terminal-at-irans-imam-khomeini-airport-4679885>.

[10] Politifact, April 9th 2015. Jon Greenberg. <http://www.politifact.com/truth-o-meter/statements/2015/apr/09/barack-obama/obama-iran-spends-30-billion-defense-us-about-600-/>.

whether Iran will use money it receives from sanctions relief towards funding terror, and his response was: 'I think it is a mistake to characterize our belief that they will just spend it on daycare centers, and roads, and paying down debt."[11] In other words, with a quick turn of the phrase, the President was utterly dismissive of the quite serious concerns about arming some of the world's most nefarious groups, which are dedicated to murdering civilians, and most particularly Jewish and Israeli lives.

We witnessed the farcical nature of this deal when Iran collected its own samples of soil from Parchin, a military site long suspected as a location where the Iranians were working on the weaponization of the nuclear project.[12] If the International Atomic Energy Administration (IAEA) would yield such a critical aspect of the inspections, when the capacity for deception is so great, why would the United States, and the other P5 plus 1 nations, let alone the IAEA, allow for such a process?

Could it be the same capacity that enabled the Red Cross to visit Theresienstadt in June of 1944 and be taken in by the "beautification project" that the Nazis had made before the visit?

The words of Jonathan Swift come to mind, "There are none so blind as those who will not see. The most deluded people are those who choose to ignore what they already know."[13]

And where was the outcry from the Jewish community when this was taking shape?

This summer, while all of this was still very much in play, and a few of us were working quite vociferously to stop the Iranian nuclear deal in any way we could, I spoke to a good friend who works for the national combined United Jewish Appeal-Federation. I asked if we could possibly organize a massive rally in Washington, reminiscent of what was done in the days of the Soviet Jewry movement, and that friend regretfully told me "No…The American Jewish community is much too divided over this issue."

There are many lessons to be learned from this painful summer of 2015. It certainly demonstrates that the "powers that be" within the organized Jewish community in America did much too little, and much too late. This is a lesson that we had thought our people had learned, at a very painful price, in the 1930s and 1940s.

During World War II, many in

---

[11] White House, July 15th 2015. "Press Conference by the President." https://www.whitehouse.gov/the-press-office/2015/07/15/press-conference-president

[12] CNN, August 5th, 2015. "Iran attempting to clean up suspected nuclear site at Parchin." Jim Sciutto and Deirdre Walsh. <http://www.cnn.com/2015/08/05/politics/iran-nuclear-site-parchin/>.

[13] David Wyman, "Abandonment of the Jews."

the American Jewish community argued that the most important thing we could do was "trust in the powers that be" and defeat Hitler "through the war effort."[14]

"Never again" is an easy slogan to say. However, actually acting upon it has proven to be as difficult for the majority of Jews living in America in 2015 as it was for the Jews living in America in 1939.

In fact, I have much more sympathy for the American Jewish community of the 1930s and '40s than for those living in 2015. Most Jews in the 1930s were relatively new immigrants to the United States, and were a bit "green." Many of them did not have the secular education we have. They spoke English with a Yiddish or European accent. They did not feel comfortable lobbying the halls of Congress.

Today, most of us do not have such an excuse. A significant number of Jews living in America have college and post-graduate educations. Not only should we feel comfortable walking the halls of Congress, but many of us occupy the offices of Congress and other branches of our government.

However, the fact that many of our people have been blessed to have received quality educations might be part of the problem. Our universities have become hotbeds of anti-Semitism and of anti-Zionism.

Some of this stems from the way that Middle Eastern Studies programs have been taught. In order to understand this phenomenon, we have to go back to 1965, during the height of the Cold War, when folks in Washington rightfully understood that some of our American students were woefully ill-equipped to compete with the Soviet threat because they lacked a knowledge of foreign languages and cultures.

Congress therefore passed Title VI of the Higher Education Act.[15] The purpose of this act was to establish various regional studies departments, i.e. African Studies, Asian Studies, Latin Studies, Soviet Studies and Middle Eastern Studies at several of our nation's college campuses. The original intent of this legislation was to establish a generation of well-educated university graduates who could compete with the Soviet threat, to help to serve our national security interests.

However, the original legislative intent of this bill was turned on its head in 1978 with the publication of a single book. The book, entitled "Orientalism," was a simple, single factor treatise, written by Edward Said, the late professor of English and Comparative Literature at Columbia University.

"Orientalism" cemented a revolution that had been brewing on the college campuses since the radical years of the 1960s. Said's argument was essentially built upon the popular post-colonial narrative, saying

---

[14] Et al.

[15] U.S. Department of Education, "International Education Programs Services" http://www2.ed.gov/about/offices/list/ope/iegps/history.html

that the domination of much of the third world by America and the European powers had left a negative influence on the natives of these lands and cultures, and is the source of America's resentment.[16]

However, Said's contention went so far as to say that no one can speak with any authority or any authenticity about the field of Middle East Studies, unless he is a native of the region. That means excellent scholars like Bernard Lewis and Efraim Karsh have been thrown by the wayside. Only scholars with thorough anti-Israel and anti-Semitic agendas, such as Rashid Khalidi[17] and Joseph Mossad[18] of Columbia University, Hatem Bazian[19] of University of California at Berkeley, and John Esposito[20] of Georgetown University, have dominated the teachings of our Middle Eastern Studies programs, ever since Said's treatise originally appeared.

What happens within these classrooms is nothing short of an intellectual travesty that turns scholarship into a form of mere propaganda, as a paltry substitute for a good, solid education. For example, at Berkeley, Hatem Bazian is the director of that university's "Islamophobia and Research Documentation Project." He is also the founder of the radical groups "Students for Justice in Palestine" and "American Muslims for Palestine."

Bazian, a lecturer at Berkeley's Title VI–funded Near Eastern Studies Center, recently hosted a seminar for students featuring Omar Barghouti, co-founder of the BDS movement (the movement to boycott, divest from, and sanction the State of Israel).[21] These professors, and the majority of others who teach in most of our taxpayer-funded Title VI programs, are proponents of the BDS movement.

Irrespective of the sort of gross human rights violations that occur all around the globe, from the slaughter of 250,000 lives in an internecine Muslim war in Syria, to the hanging of homosexuals, dissidents and bloggers in Iran, to the stoning of women who have been

---

[16] Said, Edward. "Orientalism," 1978, Random House, Inc. New York, NY.

[17] *inFocus*, "Rashid Khalidi, Campus Watch, & Middle East Studies," Cinnamon Stillwell, Winter 2008 <http://www.meforum.org/2411/rashid-khalidi-campus-watch-middle-east-studies>.

[18] FrongPageMagazine.com, "Will Columbia Tenure Joseph Massad?" Winfield Meyers, April 15, 2009 http://www.meforum.org/2122/will-columbia-tenure-joseph-massad

[19] Fight Hatred Blog, "Profiles in Hate: Hatem Bazian," November 5, 2011, http://www.campus-watch.org/article/id/11850

[20] "John Esposito: Defending Radical Islam," http://www.investigativeproject.org/documents/misc/304.pdf

[21] "Berkeley, Bazian, and Barghouti Promote BDS," FrontPageMagazine.com By: Cinnamon Stillwell, September 30, 2015 <http://www.frontpagemag.com/fpm/260280/berkeley-bazian-and-barghouti-promote-bds-cinnamon-stillwell>.

raped in Saudi Arabia, or the wanton murder of all but the most radical Sunni men and the sexual enslavement of women by the Islamic State, our nation's college campuses have singled out one and only one state for moral opprobrium—the State of Israel.

Parents of many college students have complained to me that when they try to speak to their college-aged children about the Israeli perspective, they are usually shot down. Why would these students believe what their mother or father has to say about the matter, when their professors, the "experts," are teaching them something altogether different?

What is even more egregious is that, according to Title VI of the Higher Education Opportunity Act, in order for our nation's Title VI programs to receive funding, they are required to conduct teacher-training workshops for teachers of students from kindergarten through 12th grade. That means there is a trickledown propaganda effect to some of our nation's most vulnerable and impressionable youngsters.

We at EMET have examined some of the materials that have been passed out to the teachers in these outreach centers, and what our nation's youngsters have been learning is a steady diet of anti-Israel propaganda. For example, Audrey Shabbas,' "The Arab World Studies Notebook," which is put out by AWAIR: The Arab Word and Islamic Resources and School Services and the Middle East Policy Council. The entire book is replete with strong anti-Israel bias.

Take, for example, the poem "Identity Card" by Mahmoud Darwish, which students are encouraged to memorize, a segment of which reads:

Record!
I am an Arab
You have stolen the orchards
of my ancestors
And the land which I cultivated
Along with my children
And you left nothing for us
Except for these rocks
So will the State take them
As it has been said?!

This poem, unfortunately, is not an aberration. It is, rather, emblematic of the sort of unbalanced and politically biased one-sided education that many of America's students have been exposed to, even before they arrive on the college campus.

Is it any wonder that college campuses have become hostile environments for Jewish students? According to the AMCHA Initiative, during the 2014-2015 academic year, swastikas had been found scrawled on walls of more than 30 campuses. [22] Many college campuses around the United States have demonstrations, which include "Israel Apartheid Walls," "reenactments," where students dress up as

---

22 AMCHA Initiative, "Swastika Tracker." <http://www.amchainitiative.org/swastika-tracker/>.

Israeli soldiers who are "brutalizing" students dressed up as Palestinians, "mock checkpoints," and more.

Many Jewish students who lack a strong background in Judaism have become ashamed of their Jewish identity. It is no wonder that Natan Sharansky warned approximately ten years ago that US Jewry is in danger of "Jews of silence." He noted then that "90% of Jewish students are not willing to stand up for Israel," and "in America, Jews feel very comfortable," he said, "but there are islands of anti-Semitism—the American college campus."[23]

And I am not only concerned about the America Jewish community. I am concerned about the average American students, who graduate from these fine, ivy-covered campuses, and later on become thought leaders in journalism or policy makers in our government.

No wonder there is such an erosion of support for the State of Israel in those segments of the American Jewish community that have not received a solid Jewish education, and who lack a strong sense of Jewish identity and of the history of what our people have gone through within the last century.

It is therefore incumbent upon us, the fraction of a fraction of American Jews who have a strong sense of Jewish identity, who have a knowledge of Jewish history or at least of the dramatic events our people went through within the last century, and a strong commitment to the continuation of the modern State of Israel which was resurrected within our ancient Jewish homeland, and feel comfortable enough in both the Jewish and secular worlds, to be able to make the case for Israel in the halls of Congress and the administration.

Sarah N. Stern
Founder and President, EMET
Endowment for Middle East Truth

IT IS WITH GREAT INTEREST that I read the recent issue of *Ḥakirah* Vol. 19. I also enjoyed reading your article on support for the State of Israel. Your account of Haredi attitudes did not include serious theological obstacles they would have to overcome in order to support the Zionist state. These obstacles do not seem to go away as I discovered last year when my book on Jewish opposition to Zionism was published in Israel and I did a book tour there. Even the subtitle given to the Hebrew edition was telling, *A History of Continuing Struggle.* This is an aspect of Jewish attitudes to Zionism and Israel that deserves attention, particularly in a scholarly journal of this caliber.

Wishing you further success with *Ḥakirah.*

Yakov M. Rabkin
Professor of History
University of Montreal

[23] 'Columbia Unbecoming' A Wake-Up Call for 'Jews of Silence,' Israel National News, February 8, 2005 http://www.israelnationalnews.com/News/News.aspx/76575#.Vh1pmPlViko

Heshey Zelcer Responds:

I thank Sarah Stern for her kind words. She adds much detail and pathos to the problems we face in winning the public relations battle on behalf of the State of Israel. Ms. Stern and EMET deserve our unqualified praise and support.

I agree with Professor Rabkin that certain *ḥaredim* have theological obstacles that "do not seem to go away." It is for this very reason that the article appealed, not to all *ḥaredim*, but to the vast majority of them, described as "Practical Ḥaredim," who are concerned for the safety of our brothers and sisters in Israel, who love to visit our country, but who have not yet openly identified with it. It is easier to motivate those who appreciate the State of Israel than to change the mind of the small minority who, unfortunately, are not pro-Israel.

Silk Screen Sefer Torah

THE ARTICLE BY Yisrael Kleinhendler which discusses the halakhic ramifications of a silk screen Sefer Torah is both informative and enjoyable, but it must be classed as an attempt to "give 150 arguments for the claim that a *sheretz* is pure." This is in no way meant to be a criticism of the author, as the ability to give such arguments is a requirement for membership in the Sanhedrin (Sanhedrin 17a). However, the *sheretz* remains a *sheretz*. That is to say, there are times when even the most powerful deductive reasoning cannot overcome the force of *pshuto shel mikra* (as opposed to a kabala m'Sinai regarding the meaning of a word or phrase, which can indeed override its plain meaning).

The author cites a number of *poskim*, including some of the greatest of earlier generations, who argued that printing is a form of writing. He then lists the objections that were raised against them, and shows how the method he describes meets those objections. I suggest, though, that beyond the specific objections that were raised, the primary reason their opinion was not accepted is simply that the overwhelming majority of people consider writing and printing to be two different activities. And the mitzva is to "write" a Sefer Torah, as stated in Devarim 31:19, "...write for yourselves this song...." While deduction, based on the principle that "the Torah is not written in excerpts" (Rambam, *Hil. Tefilin, Mezuzot, v'Sefer Torah*, 7:1), can lead to the conclusion that "this song" means "the entire Sefer Torah which contains this song," it cannot obscure the difference between writing and printing.

To belabor the point a bit more, consider the following social experiment: Show randomly selected people video clips of a *sofer* silk-screening a Sefer Torah, a person scribbling notes with a pen, a *sofer* writing a Sefer Torah in the usual way, an artist using a 3-inch-wide paint brush to sign his name in the corner of a larger-than-life mural, someone else using a computer printer, a baker squeezing icing onto a cake to form the words "Mazal Tov!" and another person using a rubber stamp. Ask each subject to identify those video clips that show someone writing. Without a doubt, almost everyone will identify as writing all of those cases—and only those cases—in which the letters are formed one at a time.

David Hoffman
Jerusalem

Yisrael Kleinhendler responds:

I thank David Hoffman for taking interest in my article, and I would like to respond to the points he made.

David equates permitting a silk screen Sefer Torah to purifying a *sheretz*. I find this comparison to be inappropriate. In addition to Rabbi Yitzchak Abadi approving silk screen Sifrei Torah, many other prominent halachic authorities permitted its use as well. These include Rabbi Shlomo Yitzchak Zilberman, Rabbi Chaim Kreiswirth, Rabbi Tuvia Goldstein, Rabbi Chaim Pinchas Scheinberg, Rabbi Zalman Nechemia Goldberg, and Rabbi Dovid Feinstein, to name a few. Is it being suggested that they actually purified the *sheretz*?

Regarding *pshuto shel mikrah*, there is no contradiction. The Torah says, "write" and this is writing. The early *acharonim* considered their method of "printing" to be writing as well. Also we do not *pasken* halachos based on *pshuto shel mikrah* or social experiments. Rather we follow the interpretation of *chazal*, and the rules they laid out for us in regard to *psak halachah*. The Tzedukim *paskened* halachos based on *pshuto shel mikrah*. That's why they wore tefillin on their hands and between their eyes (*Megillah* 24b).

David writes, "I suggest, though, that beyond the specific objections that were raised, the primary reason their opinion was not accepted is simply that the overwhelming majority of people consider writing and printing to be two different activities." The quote, "overwhelming majority," seems to be a bit of an overstatement, as the majority of *acharonim* actually permitted the printing press Sefer Torah. Also, what's the basis to suggest that those who objected to the process stated one reason but really meant another? Is there a source or other evidence to support this thesis? I would like to reiterate that the silk screen process is not similar to the printing press process, even though they are both coined "printing."

Finally, I don't understand how the above-mentioned Rambam is relevant to our topic.

Responsa of R. Shimon Duran

IN HIS ARTICLE in *Ḥakirah* Vol.19, Samuel Morell outlines the dispute between R. Duran and the Rivash over the use of *neter* by women washing their hair prior to use of the mikveh. In part, the dispute hangs on whether *neter* and *qalida* are identical or whether they are two distinct materials as R. Duran argues in permitting use of the latter. In support of his argument it appears that R. Duran feels that *qalida* merely causes hair to become wavy whereas *neter* causes detachment which may subsequently interfere with direct contact with water in the *mikveh.*

It is interesting to note that modern chemistry, based on Mendeleef's Periodic Table, assigns the symbol "Na," based on the Latin *natrium,* to the element Sodium, and "K," based on the Latin *kalium*, to the element Potassium. The Latin is clearly based on the Arabic/Hebrew. This has significance insofar as soaps made with sodium hydroxide (hard soaps) are distinctly more aggressive from those made with potassium hydroxide (soft soaps), lending some credence to R. Duran's argument.

David Cymerman
Toronto

The Jewish Calendar

I ENJOYED THE ESSAY "A Statistical Analysis of the Conjunction of Tishrei," *Ḥakirah* Vol. 19, very much, as the Jewish calendar is my special area of interest.

Still there is a serious flaw in the reasoning, which makes the thesis of the article, in my opinion, moot.

In short: the data on 400 years of conjunction are too small of a sampling to be statistically meaningful. I explain:

On page 229 the authors write, "Because the Molad of a month is based on a calculation that repeatedly adds the same number, it seems intuitively reasonable that it is equally likely that the Molad of Tishrei would occur in any day of the week." This is certainly true, but only because 29/6/793 and 7/0/0 (the length of a week) have no common denominator. If the length between 2 Molad would be, say, 28/0/0, every Rosh Chodesh would be on the same day of the week.

The next sentence, "However, because of the fluctuation of the inter-conjunction time from month to month, it is by no means obvious how the actual conjunction times are distributed among the days of the week," needs to be more closely examined.

This fluctuation, as you know from Fig. 1 on page 228, has 2 components: a fluctuation from month to month, and a fluctuation from cycle to cycle, each cycle varying in length from 13 to 16 months.

I will show you now that a 400-year period of data is giving you only a maximum of 4.76 good data which is statistically insufficient.

If, for argument's sake, all the cycles were of the same length and their length would be 13 months, then it would take 12 years to have the same pattern of monthly time differences for a Tishrei-to-Tishrei stretch again. This gives to 33 similar 12 month patterns (and similar Tishreis) in a 400-year time frame.

If you divide this by the 7 days of the week, this gives you 4.76 samplings of Monday, same for Tuesday, Wednesday etc.

If all the cycles are of the same length of 16 months, it would take 15 years to have the same pattern of monthly time differences for a Tishrei-to-Tishrei stretch again, or about 27 similar 12 months pattern (and similar Tishreis) in a 400-year period. If again you divide 27 by the 7 days of the week, you have 3.8 good data for Monday, Tuesday, Wednesday etc.

In reality, since these cycles continuously change their length, you cannot really compare one 12-month Tishrei-to-Tishrei period to another, and any statistically valuable information can be gleaned only if you are dealing with a much larger number of years.

Your own data prove my argument without any doubt: in the 70-year period from 1946 to 2015, the Sundays are lagging behind by 10%, in the 400-year period the Sundays are ahead by 17%.

I am actually surprised that you hoped to see any differences between the different days of the week. There is no causal or mathematical connection at all between the inter-conjunction time of any month and the days of the week, as there is really no astronomical meaning to a 7-day week.

Yehuda Rosenblatt
Toronto

IT IS MY OPINION that the statistical issue discussed in the article of Epstein, Wilamowsky, Dickman, and Weiss, *Ḥakirah*, Summer 2015, is not a genuine statistical issue and therefore the statistical method that they used to analyze their data is inappropriate. The fundamental concepts of the theory of statistics are "universe" and "random sample." The former is defined as a set of similar objects (or individuals) where each one of these belongs to exactly one of several well-defined categories. The proportions of objects in the various categories are assumed to be unknown, and the goal of the statistical investigator is to draw an inference about these proportions, such as estimating their numerical values. A common example of such a universe is a population of voters who are categorized as favoring particular candidates up for election, where the polling statisticians want to determine the unknown proportions of voters favoring the various candidates. This is done by selecting a random sample of individuals, that is, voters, and using the observed proportions favoring the candidates to draw inferences about the true proportions. In general, statistical theory is concerned with the drawing of inferences about an unknown characteristic of a universe on the basis of a random sample. In the article of Epstein et al, the universe is never precisely defined and the so-called sample is not a random sample.

The objects in the implicit universe in the paper are a set of years, and the "categories" to which the years belong are the seven days of the week in which the Tishrei conjunctions fall. (By analogy to the voting example, the years and days represent the voters and their preferred candidates, respectively.) The article reports the values of the corresponding seven proportions for the years 1700–2099. While referring to these years as a sample, the authors have not specified the "universe" from which the sample is taken.

The universe must be either finite or infinite, that is, must consist of either a finite set of years containing the given four centuries, or, if not, must consist of an infinite set of years containing the four centuries. In the case of a finite universe, the categories to which the years belong and their proportions can be determined by the same algorithm as that used to calculate those for the four centuries. Therefore the proportions of the categories in the universe are effectively known, and so there is no need for sampling and using statistical methods. In the case of an infinite universe, for example, the set of all years starting with 1700, it is mathematically impossible to draw a finite sample at random. To illustrate this, suppose that we wish to draw a finite random sample from this universe, for example, a sample of one year. Let there be a number *p* between 0 and 1 representing the probability of drawing the year 1700 (or any other particular year). If the sample is random, then every other year must have the same probability *p* of being selected. It follows from the axioms of probability that the probability of randomly selecting either 1700 or 1701 is 2 times *p*, and of selecting 1700, 1701, or 1702 is 3 times *p*. By extension the probability of selecting at least one of a given set of *n* years is *np*. Since *n* is arbitrary, it may be taken to be as large as desired, so that if we take it so large that *np* exceeds 1, then it cannot represent a genuine probability because the sum of the probabilities of all items in a universe cannot exceed 1.

The conclusion is: If the universe consists of a finite number of years, then the proportions are effectively known and the data should not be analyzed by statistical methods. If it consists of an infinite number of years, then it is impossible, under the laws of probability, to draw a random sample. In either case the terms in the article, "probability," Uniform distribution," and "likely," are meaningless.

The following comment is unrelated to the previous discussion and concerns an error in the application of the chi-square test. It will be understood by those with some knowledge of basic statistics, and is included here only because it is my opinion that a technical error published in a journal as influential as *Ḥakirah,* if uncorrected, can tarnish the integrity of the journal. Appendix 2 reports the p-value of 0.054 for the chi-square statistic. The null hypothesis is that the proportions are equal, and the alternative is that they are not all equal. In conventional statistical practice the null hypothesis is rejected if the p-value is 0.05 or less, and according to others, 0.01 or less; otherwise it is accepted. Since the p-value here, namely, 0.054, is larger than 0.05, the null hypothesis cannot be rejected, and so one is left with the conclusion that we must accept the null hypothesis of equal proportions (uniform distribution). The authors' claim that "there is less than 6% chance that the data is Uniformly Distributed" is meaningless.

Simeon M. Berman
Emeritus Professor of
Mathematics at the Courant
Institute of Mathematical Sciences,
New York University, New York

The authors respond:

We thank Prof. Berman and Yehuda Rosenblatt for their technical comments on our article "A Statistical Analysis of the Conjunction of the Time of Tishrei." Both letters expressed concern about our "sample" of 400 consecutive years of data, i.e., 1700–2099. The latter objected that we "overstated" the number of data points because

> In short: the data on 400 years of conjunction are too small of a sampling to be statistically meaningful.

The former critiqued that:

> While referring to these years as a sample, the authors have not specified the "universe" from which the sample is taken… In either case the terms in the article, "probability," "uniform distribution," and "likely," are meaningless.

and added,

> In conventional statistical practice the null hypothesis is rejected if the p-value is 0.05 or less, and according to others, 0.01 or less; otherwise it is accepted. Since the p-value here, namely, 0.054, is larger than 0.05, the null hypothesis cannot be rejected, and so one is left with the conclusion that we must accept the null hypothesis of equal proportions (uniform distribution). The authors' claim that "there is less than 6% chance that the data is Uniformly Distributed" is meaningless.

We begin by pointing out that the word "sample" appears in our paper only once on p. 235 (Appendix 2). Our paper is not a rigorous Mathematical proof of Rambam's position but rather an attempt to understand how Rambam could possibly have come with his "novel" and unattributed explanation of "Lo ADU Rosh"? We do not ascribe to Rambam any statistical knowledge of techniques unknown in the 12th century, but do know that Rambam was an expert in calculating *molads* and True Conjunctions. We therefore assume that in formulating his theory he would have analyzed recent data of both of these values in his time. That is exactly what we did when we initially looked at the most recent 70 years of data (we picked the starting point to coincide with Mandlebaum's initial cycle, Figure 1). What we found, supported Rambam's assertion for DU but not necessarily for ADU. (Interestingly, see Adjler's article in this current *Ḥakirah* edition which provides evidence that the A of ADU was not in the original formulation of the fixed calendar). Had Rambam seen similar results for a modest review of data from his era (it would have taken him far longer to do these calculations) he would undoubtedly have expanded the number of years in his study to see if the trend held up. That is exactly what we did. We chose 400 years because it was the most readily available data. The 400-year results supported every point Rambam made. Our suggestion is then that absent any other rationally offered explanation of Rambam's position had his data in any way resembled our data (we have no proof that it did but have no reason to assume it didn't) it would offer a logically sound underpinning for his assertion. All this was said in the paper without resorting to any statistical testing or sampling.

With respect to our

- use of X^2 in Appendix 2 – while the set of years chosen may not be technically random, we have no reason to believe that they are not representative of the situation at the time of Rambam.
- use of 6% – the choice of the $\alpha = 0.10$ is not uncommon.

ᘓ

Paḥad Yitzḥak: A Joyful Song of Affirmation[1]

By: YAAKOV ELMAN

In his own lifetime Rav Yitzhak Hutner זצ"ל (1906–1980) was considered something of a paradox and he was certainly an anomaly; he was a Lithuanian rosh yeshiva who in his personal life, at least in his later years, adopted ḥasidic garb. But he was an anomaly and paradox in a number of other ways. Known as the "Varshaver *illuy*" even in his youth, and a masterful *lamdan* at a relatively young age, he published his first *sefer* with the approbations of the Gedolei Hador at age 26. At the same time he was also a poet and master of prose, an original thinker who produced a theological/psychological system that incorporates elements of many strands of Jewish thought, enriched with insights both from his own preternatural understanding of human nature and behavior, and from that of other sources. Perhaps most of all, he was a consummate educator, who quickly assessed the capabilities and the needs of his students, and nurtured them.

As an educator, he enlivened his yeshiva, Yeshiva Rabbenu Chaim Berlin, by introducing Hasidic/Musar elements into it, with discourses (*ma'amarim*) along the lines of a ḥasidic *tish* or *farbrengen*, and significantly, reminiscent of those of Slobodka, discourses that were devoted to matters of "laws of dispositions and the duties of the heart" (הלכות דעות וחובות הלבבות) and interspersed with *niggunim*. This style of presentation was typical of the Hasidic courts of his youth, but of Slobodka as well—a yeshiva in which Rav Hutner spent eight formative years, from age 15 onward. His discourses were eventually edited and collected into the volumes of his *magnum opus*, *Paḥad Yitzḥak* (1964–1982). Aside from an early, youthful

1 A different version of this paper was first presented at the Orthodox Forum 2015 on March 16, 2015. My thanks go to Rabbis Kenneth Hain and Shlomo Zuckier for inviting my participation and permitting me to publish this version, to Rabbi Joel Wolowelsky for suggesting its publication in *Ḥakirah*, to Rabbi Asher Benzion Buchman for encouraging me to do so, and to Mr. Heshey Zelcer with the staff of *Ḥakirah* for their professionalism and patience.

Yaakov Elman, a long-time resident of Flatbush, is Herbert S. and Naomi Denenberg Professor of Talmudic Studies at Yeshiva University. He has authored or edited eight volumes, and dozens of articles on Jewish Biblical exegesis, intellectual history and ḥasidic thought.

work, *Torat ha-Nazir*, these volumes remain, more than thirty years after his passing, his major legacy, one that is still as unique today as it was in his own time.

However, perhaps the most remarkable—and paradoxical—aspect of his work is that he dealt with very modern philosophical problems, employing his own terminology. In order to express the essence of these concerns in language that would be accessible to a non-ḥasidic yeshiva audience, Rav Hutner created a nomenclature uniquely his own, often based on references from the Siddur or Ḥazal. But once the existential—and existentialist—referents are made clear, his work becomes a compelling narrative of the encounter of a twentieth-century "prince of Torah" with the modern world and its concerns, concerns that continue, and indeed, have only intensified, in the generation that has passed since their publication. Rav Hutner sounded the eternal verities of a G-d-created Torah in the workings of G-d's other creation, the human psyche. And thus within the pages of *Paḥad Yitzḥak* one will find disquisitions on the difference between the psychologies of generalists versus specialists, the tensions of the individual within human society, other problems of identity and personality, of change and renewal, the problem of mortality and other aspects of the human condition, and much more. It is this attention to the existential side of Jewish thought that makes for such compelling reading.

Steven Schwartzchild's pioneering study—about which Rav Hutner himself expressed approval—pointed to the sources of his thought in Slobodka Musar,[2] *ḥasidut*, and modern philosophy; Hillel Goldberg, in line with his own interests, emphasized the Musar aspect. The three most recent studies of *Paḥad Yitzḥak* in Hebrew emphasize the parallels in modern philosophy, with Nietzsche, Rosenzweig, Heidegger and Levinas prominent among the moderns. Naturally, Rav Nathan Zvi Finkel, the "Elder of Slobodka," is mentioned as well. In contrast, the influence of Reb Zadok ha-Kohen of Lublin, which Schwartzchild pointed out, has been somewhat stinted.[3] But it is clear that the wine of ḥasidic thought was poured into the methodological containers of Brisk.

---

2 One of the many desiderata in regard to the study of *Paḥad Yitzḥak* is a comparison of its thought with that of the Alter of Slobodka, Rav Nathan Zvi Finkel's *Or ha-Tzafun*.

3 However, though Reb Zadok is mentioned only nine times in Kasirer's dissertation, his concern with the ḥasidic roots of *Paḥad Yitzḥak* is manifest throughout.

The existential aspects of Rav Hutner's work have been duly noted by Steven S. Schwarzchild, Hillel Goldberg, and, more recently, Tsippi Abrahamov[4] and Shmuel Vigoda.[5] And in 2009 Shlomo Kasirer submitted a dissertation on Rav Hutner's philosophy of repentance to the Jewish Philosophy Department of Bar Ilan University.[6] However, with the exception of Goldberg, who himself has written a valuable dissertation on Rav Yisrael Salanter,[7] the handful of articles (and the one dissertation) that have appeared have been written by professionals in the field of modern philosophy, and this perhaps gives a certain overly "academic" tinge to the analysis.[8]

---

4 Tsippi Abrahamov, "Ma'avaq be-Yetser ha-Ra' o Hedvat Yetsirah?: Al Ra'ayon ha-Teshuvah be-Mishnat ha-Rav Yitzḥak Hutner," *Da'at* 44 (5760), pp. 95–122.

5 Shmuel Vigoda, "Be-Havlei ha-Zeman: Ha-Adam veha-Zeman be-Haguto shel ha-Rav Yitzḥak Hutner," in Binyamin Ish-Shalom, ed., *Be-Darkhei Shalom: Iyyunim be-Hagut Yehudit Mugashim le-Shalom Rosenberg*, Jerusalem: Beit Morasha of Jerusalem Press, 2007, pp. 399–427. For scans of these articles, and much more over the years, my thanks go to Mr. Zvi Erenyi of Gottesman Library, who has facilitated my research in this and many other endeavors for more than a quarter-century.

6 Shlomo Kasirer, "Ha-Teshuva be-Haguto shel ha-Rav Yitzḥak Hutner: Al Reqa' Meqorotav ba-Ḥasidut, bi-Tenu'at ha-Musar uve-Hagut ha-Me'ah ha-Esrim," Ramat Gan: Bar Ilan University, Kislev, 5769. My thanks go to my former student Rabbi Dovid Bashevkin for alerting me to Kasirer's work and supplying me with a copy.

7 *Israel Salanter, Text, Structure, Idea: The Ethics and Theology of an Early Psychologist of the Unconscious*, New York: Ktav, 1982. His *Between Berlin and Slobodka: Jewish Transition Figures from Eastern Europe*, Hoboken: Ktav, 1989 is also of importance in this context. More recently, another unpublished academic work has come to my attention, and here I wish to tender my thanks to Prof. Jonathan Meir of Ben Gurion University, to Mr. Menachem Butler of New York, and to Mr. Alon Shalev himself, for providing me with a copy of his masters' thesis, presented in 2013, "Qavim Merkaziyyim li-Demuto ule-Haguto shel ha-Rav Yitzhak Hutner al pi Sifrei Paḥad Yitzḥak," presented Elul 5773. Prof. Meir informs me that Mr. Shalev is now working with Prof. Benjamin Brown of Hebrew University; I have no doubt that the dissertation that Mr. Shalev will produce under Prof. Brown's direction will add substantially to our understanding of *Paḥad Yitzḥak*.

8 Again, there are two exceptions: See also the adaptation/translations of Rabbi Pinchas Stolper, *Purim in a New Light: Mystery, Grandeur and Depth*, Lakewood, NJ: David Dov Publications, 2003, *Chanukah in a New Light: Grandeur, Heroism and Depth*, Lakewood, NJ: David Dov Foundation, 2005, and *Shabbos in a New Light: Majesty, Mystery, Meaning*, Lakewood, NJ: David Dov Foundation, 2009, and Leibel Rutta, *Reshimot Lev: Pesaḥ, Sukkot, Ḥanukah, Purim*, Brooklyn, 1997, 2000 (2 volumes). Rabbi Rutta himself, of course, would not claim to have analyzed the thought of *Paḥad Yitzḥak*, but his references, and especially those of A.H.,

The world of *Paḥad Yitzḥak* is a joyful one: a dynamic world filled with creativity, renewal and innovation, one that celebrates the products of the individual and the individual human mind at its creative best, that is, in the study of G-d's Torah. It is also a world that does not denigrate the use of those intellectual tools when employed to enhance human life. Nor are those tools limited to rational discourse and logic; intuition and emotional engagement, and in particular the pleasures that accompany them, are essential parts of Talmud Torah. In short, it is the world of Slobodka but with a Hutnerian flavor, a world that proclaims not only the greatness of G-d, but also the greatness of His Creation, and, in particular, the summit of that Creation, humankind. It is thus a world in which the individual can—and *must*—contribute something of his or her own unique selfhood, for that is what we were created for.

It is also a world of poetic beauty and metaphor: the Maharal does not teach us, he "implants" knowledge in us; the GRA does not instruct, we "discover the pearl hidden beneath his words." These metaphors are not mere literary flourishes, but reflect Rav Hutner's inner world, a world that he wishes to share with us. It is a world mysterious but knowable; the controlling metaphors reveal the inner workings of the world and of the human mind and psyche. It is a world of parallels and analogies, analogies that connect the parallels, a world of macrocosm and microcosm. It is also a world of paradox, and those too must be reconciled; a world of *din*, but a world of *ḥesed*. The metaphor of implanting reflects the Maharal's own view of the world, which is a world of potential that must be actualized by humans, as a plant grows from a seed. The world is mysterious, but can be understood, and, once understood, will be seen for all its beauty, as is the pearl. That is one of the sources of the dynamism of the Maharal's system, and that same dynamism characterizes the world of Rav Hutner.

---

scattered throughout, give us an insight into the view of *Paḥad Yitzḥak* by those not alert to its ḥasidic antecedents. See also the popular articles of Rabbi Yaakov Feitman, a close *talmid*, especially his profile in *Mishpacha* 338, November 24, 2010, and that of Matis Greenblatt, "Rabbi Yitzchak Hutner: The Vision Before His Eyes" in *Jewish Action*, summer 5761/2001, pp. 1–7. I might also mention an excellent article of that type by Yeshaya Steinberger in *Musaf "Shabbat"* of *Maqor Rishon*, November 26, 2010.

Last but hardly least, let me note the *ma'amarim* by Rav Hutner's *talmid* and son-in-law, Rav Yonatan D. David, in a volume entitled *Quntres Pesaḥ*, which continues the thought of *Paḥad Yitzḥak* in the same style as the original, and often takes *Paḥad Yitzḥak* as its point of departure, but, as we might expect, does not analyze his father-in-law's work from an "outside" perspective.

From the Maharal and from Reb Zadok ha-Kohen of Lublin he took not only that controlling metaphor, but a number of important exegetical principles by which he could transfer knowledge gained from one world to another; from the world outside to the world inside; from the Torah to the world and to the human psyche; from society to the individual and from the individual to society. Israel and the Torah are one, a principle he would have learned from Reb Zadok but also from the Alter of Slobodka; and from *hasidut* and Kabbalah: G-d made things parallel ("one opposite the other"), the world is a Book of Revelation, one of G-d's Two Books, each of which is a commentary on the other. Again, the dynamism inheres in the *search* for truth, which must be uncovered; thus it was from Creation, where first there was darkness before light was created, enslavement preceded the liberation of the Exodus, and for us, both as individuals and as societies, confusion and error pave the way for true understanding.

I

This view of humankind, its purpose, history and future is built on a number of bundled concepts: individualism, autonomy, creativity, all of which foster innovation and renewal. In an earlier article, I traced the role of autonomy within this conception of humankind, which Rav Hutner roots in the statement of Rabbenu Yonah that "truth is one of the foundations of the soul."[9] That truth cannot be denied, but must also conform to G-d's Torah; the occasional tension between them fuels the creativity that in turn enables the renewal of both the individual (as in repentance) and of society. In this article I will concentrate (though not exclusively) on the means of *attaining* that renewal. Before I do, however, let me point to one

---

9 See *Pahad Yitzhak* Rosh Hashanah 15.6-7, and my "Autonomy and Its Discontents: A Meditation on *Pahad Yitzhak*," *Tradition* 42 (2014), pp. 7–40, especially pp. 25–27; see also Rabbenu Yonah, *Sha'arei Teshuvah* 3.184. I would like to stress here what I did not in that article: this striving for the truth of the soul mirrors the search for authenticity of Przysucha and Kotzk; see Michael Rosen, *The Quest for Authenticity: The Thought of Reb Simhah Bunim*, Jerusalem/New York, 2008, p. 16. Rav Hutner's maternal uncle was a Kotzker. Second, at least part of the solution of the problem of the grant of human free-will and autonomy and the consequent violation of the Divine Will is to be found in the Izbica doctrine that "all is in the hands of Heaven," *including* "the fear of Heaven," that is free-will; see *Ma'amarei Pahad Yitzhak* Sukkot 99.16–18, and Joseph Weiss, "A Late Jewish Utopia of Religious Freedom," in Joseph Weiss, *Studies in Eastern European Jewish Mysticism & Hasidism*, ed. by David Goldstein, London: Littman Library of Jewish Civilization, 1997, pp. 209–248 and Morris M. Faierstein, *All Is in the Hands of Heaven: The Teachings of Rabbi Mordechai Joseph Leiner of Izbica*, Hoboken: Ktav, 1989.

of the hallmarks of *Paḥad Yitzḥak*: its insistence that truth is defined by its reflecting reality, a point to which we will return below. Here is Rav Hutner's discussion of the meaning of truth from *Paḥad Yitzḥak*, *Quntras Birkat Avot* (Sukkot, 5713), 15.2 (Shabbat/Sukkot volume, pp. 198-199).

> ב...אמת והפוכה מתיחסות הן לדעתו של אדם. אם ציור המציאות בדעתו של אדם מתאים למציאות, הרי זה דעת אמת; אם ציור המציאות בדעתו של אדם אינו מתאים למציאות, הרי זו דעת שקר או דעת מוטעית. השתלשלותה של הדעת בתוך המציאות באה היא בתלתא בבי. היא נפעלת מן המציאות, פועלת על המציאות, ובאופן זה היא מקשרת את המציאות הפועלת עם המציאות הנפעלת. כשהדעת היא דעת אמת, כלומר שהמציאות הפועלת מתאימה עם ציור המציאות של הדעת, אז יעלה הקשר יפה והמציאת הנפעלת תתחבר ותתלכד עם המציאות הפועלת. ולהיפך כשהדעת היא דעת מוטעית, וציור והמציאות של הדעת לא תתאים לעצם המציאות, הרי זה ניתוק השרשרת, והמציאות הנפעלת על ידי הדעת תהיה בודדה, באין לה הזדווגות עם עצם המציאות הפועלת....

> 2...Truth and its reverse relate to a person's intellect. If the image (ציור) of reality in the mind (דעת) conforms to reality, this then is a true opinion (דעת אמת); if the image of reality in the mind of a person does not conform to reality, this is then a false opinion (דעת שקר) or a mistaken one (דעת מוטעית). The "enchaining" (השתלשלותה) of the mind (הדעת) within reality comes in three forms (lit., "cases"). [Either] it is acted on by reality, [or] it acts upon reality, and in this guise connects the reality that acts with the reality that is acted upon. When the opinion is a true opinion, that is, the reality that acts conforms to the image of the mind, then the connection is good, and the reality that is acted upon is connected and overlaps with the reality that acts upon [it]. And in reverse, when the opinion is a mistaken one, and the image of reality in the mind does not conform to the essential reality (עצם המציאות), this then constitutes a breaking of the chain, and the reality that is worked upon by the mind is isolated, without a connection (הזדווגות) with the essential reality that works [upon the mind].

By stressing the importance of the correspondence of an intellectual apprehension of the world with reality in assessing the truth of that apprehension even in regard to Divine promises, as evidenced by his concern with the problem of theodicy,[10] Rav Hutner is valorizing a modern, scientific approach to understanding that reality. Lest anyone suspect that Rav Hutner is proposing a "double truth" theory, note that in *Ma'amarei*

---

10 See n. 18 below, and the text it covers.

Paḥad Yitzḥak on Sukkot, both aspects of truth are juxtaposed in successive paragraphs of *ma'amar* 65, paragraphs 3 and 4. Truth must conform both to the truth in one's soul *and* to outer reality. Ultimately, one's personal truth must correspond to the outer truth as well, but it must be remembered that this outer truth is also the truth of the Creator of that outer world, and thus the truth of the Torah.

To return to our discussion of the system as a whole, let us begin with the individual, for he stands at the center of Creation. In a revealing comment in *Ma'amarei Paḥad Yitzḥak* on Sukkot (99.15), Rav Hutner transforms a common staple of medieval philosophical and kabbalistic thought into an important observation on the individual and his place in the world:

> ...ידועה האימרה: "האדם הוא עולם קטן". ועדיף, ויותר נכון לומר שהעולם הוא אדם גדול. מרכז מחשבת הבריאה הוא האדם, והעולם אינו אלא "שפיגעל" (ראי) בהקבלה לעניניו של האדם. כל מה שנמצא בעולם מוכרח שימצא לו קו מקביל בקומת האדם....
>
> There is a well-known expression: "Man is a microcosm ('small world'), [that is, his *Gestalt* reflects the world of which he is part]."[11] It is preferable, and more correct to say that the world is a macrocosm ['large man', i.e., a reflection of man's *Gestalt*]. Man is the center of the intent of Creation; the world is nothing more than a "mirror" that is parallel to the character and concerns (עניניו) of a human being: all that exists in the world must find a parallel line within the *Gestalt* of man....

Rav Hutner once commented that if his mind were to be compared to a building, the first floor would be the influence of the Alter of Slobodka and the top floor would be that of Rav Kook.[12] We may add that the basement would be the thought of that strand of Polish *ḥasidut* represented by his maternal uncle, who was a Kotzker Hasid, and the subbasement would be the thought of the Maharal mi-Prague, who had such a great influence on Hasidic thought early and late, and on Rav Kook as well. Elsewhere I hope to trace these connections and assess them; here I only mention them.

---

11 This is of course more than a "well-known expression"; it belongs to that nebulous realm shared by medieval philosophy and Kabbalah, and may indeed refer to the structure of the upper worlds; for a parallel in the writings of the Maharal, see Yoram Yakobson, "Tzelem Elokim u-Ma'amado ke-Meqor Ra'ato shel Adam lefi ha-Maharal mi-Prague," *Daat* 19 (5747), p. 103–136, esp. pp. 106-107, 114.

12 See the remembrances of Rav Z.Y. Neriyah, "Shemesh u-Ma'or," *Bi-Sedeh ha-Re'iyah*, Kefar Ḥabad, 5651, pp. 419–438.

But there is no contradiction between these sources on this matter: from the Maharal to Peshischa (Przysucha), Kotzk, Izhbitz (Izbica), and Reb Zadok of Lublin, the status of the individual and his role in creation are stressed and celebrated. Nor should this be a surprise: all these sources are rooted in Ḥazal, in this case a plangent Mishnah, Sanhedrin 4:5.

> ...נברא אדם יחידי ללמדך שכל המאבד נפש אחד מישראל מעלה עליו הכתוב כאילו איבד עולם מלא וכל המקיים נפש אחת מישראל מעלה עליו הכתוב כאילו קיים עולם מלא ומפני שלום הבריות שלא יאמר אדם לחבירו אבא גדול מאביך ושלא יהו מינין אומרים הרבה רשויות בשמים ולהגיד גדולתו של הקדוש ברוך הוא שאדם טובע כמה מטבעות בחותם אחד וכולן דומין זה לזה ומלך מלכי המלכים הקדוש ברוך הוא טבע כל אדם בחותמו של אדם הראשון ואין אחד מהן דומה לחבירו לפיכך כל אחד ואחד חייב לומר בשבילי נברא העולם....

> Man was created singular in order to teach you that whoever destroys a single Jewish soul Scripture considers it as though he destroyed the whole world, and whoever preserves a single Jewish soul Scripture considers it as though he had preserved a whole world. Moreover, [he was created singular] for the sake of peace among men, that one might not say to his fellow: My father was greater than yours, and that the heretic might not say: There are many ruling powers in heaven; again, to proclaim the greatness of the Holy One, blessed be He, for if a man strikes many coins from one mold, they all resemble one another, but the supreme King of kings, the Holy One, blessed be He, fashioned every man in the stamp of the First Man, and yet not one of them resembles his fellow. Therefore every single person is obliged to say: The world was created for my sake.

While this rabbinic statement is found already in mSanh 4:5 and thus some discussion is found in the commentaries, it appears three times in the works of Reb Zadok.[13] However, as we shall see, Rav Hutner developed the idea in a different direction, one with an existential quality that perhaps owes something to the *Zeitgeist* of the twentieth century, and whose development is facilitated by a "Brisker" analytic approach, but also by the Maharal's dialectal approach. *Paḥad Yitzḥak* may be seen as an application of the Brisker system of analysis to questions of Jewish theology and human psychology, not only in a descriptive sense but also in a

---

13 *Peri Zaddiq* Shemot, Sheqalim 1, *Peri Zaddiq* Devarim, Rosh Ḥodesh Elul 1, and *Sihat Mal'akhei ha-Sha*ret, ch. 3, p. 38a; see also *Tzidqat ha-Tzaddiq*, n. 154, p. 51b, regarding the requirement for a person to have faith in himself, and see my "Autonomy and Its Discontents, p. 15, n. 32 and text. It also appears in *ma'amarim* written by students of the Alter of Slobodka, see *Or ha-Tzafun*, Bereshit, Jerusalem: Haskel, 5719, p. 13 (in "Zeh Sefer Toldot Adam").

generative one. Rav Hutner expects to find—and often does—a binary dynamic within human and human-divine interaction that this dynamic assumes such large a role in his work. In this case, note that the individuality of the human being is not only an observed fact, but one that has a "faithful [Torah] source" (*maqor ne'eman*). Individualism alone can be destructive, and therefore requires a Torah source to give it validity. Having found one, he goes on to delineate the practical consequences of this biological fact.

Here, first, is Reb Zadok, from *Sihat Mal'akhei ha-Sharet*, chapter 3:

> כי כלל גדול בידינו (שבת ע"ז ב) כל מה שברא הקדוש ברוך הוא לצורך בראו והכל לצורך האדם כדתנן (סנהדרין ל"ז א) כל אחד ואחד חייב לומר בשבילי נברא העולם ובברכות (ו' ב) כל העולם כולו לא נברא אלא בשביל זה ושם (נ"ח א) וברא כל אלו לשמשני. וגם הוא מבואר מסברא שאין ממדת אומן בשר ודם חכם גם כן לעשות דבר לבטלה וליגע לריק ואילו היה די באחד לא יעשה שנים. כל שכן הבורא יתברך בהכרח שכולם צריכים ובוראם יודע צורכם של כל פרט ופרט והצורך הוא לאיזה תשמיש מה. ועל כרחך שהתשמיש שישמש תבנית גשם זה לא ישמש תבנית זולתו:
> וכח השימוש הנה הוא כח רוחניי כאילו תאמר דרך משל תשמיש הכדורי או עגולי להתגלגל מה שאין כן בעל הקצוות אין לו כח המתנועע מעצמו והוא ינוח במקום שיפול הנה כוחות המתנועעי והמנוחי הם כוחות רוחניים ובלתי נתפשים בגשם שהרי כבר מצינו תנועה ומנוחה בנפש גם כן. וכללות הבריאה עגולות או כדוריות ויש להם כח התנועי וכן הנפש ומחשבת המוח לא ישקוט ולא ינוח אם לא במותו אז נקרא בפי חז"ל ובלשונם הצחה דנח נפשיה שקנה כח המנוחה:
> וכיוצא באלה כל מיני שינויי הברואים כאשר נתבונן על טיב השינוי ההוא בענין צורך הבריאה אשר בעבורו חייבה הבריאה בתבנית כך וכך לצורך השלמת כח ההוא על ידי הגשם ההוא הנה אותו הכח הנרצה הוא כח פרטי עומד בפני עצמו בזולת הגשם. ואין צריך לומר בהבדליהם הרוחנים כמו הקשיות לדוממים והבדלי הקשיות והחיזוק בינם וההזנה והצמיחה לצומחים והבדלי איכות הזנתם והחיות ושארי כוחות הבעלי חיים להחיים וכיוצא באלה. וכן הבדלי גווניהם שיש לכל גוון סגולה וענין מיוחד כידוע קצת לחכמי הטבע המעמיקים. ובוראן יודען על בוריין וכן חכמי האמת ז"ל המשתמשים ברוח הקודש בידיעות המצטרכות להם להשלמת הנפשות אל הענין אשר הוסדו. [כמו שתמצא בדברי חז"ל בקיאות בחכמת הטבע מופלאת מאוד בעיני כל חכמי הטבע מאין זה להם כי לא למדו מעולם בבתי מדרשיהם חכמות טבעיות אבל ידעו זה על ידי ידיעתם בסודות הבריאה מסוד ה' ליראיו וכמו שנתבאר אצלינו במקום אחר]:

For we have an important rule: "Everything that the Holy One, blessed be He, created He created for a purpose" (Shab 77b), and it was all created [to fulfill] human needs, as we learn: "Everyone must say: 'The world was created for my sake'" (Sanh 37a), and "the entire world was created for this one" (Ber 6b), and there too: "and He created all these to serve me" (ibid., 58a). This can also be understood by logical deduction, for a wise human artisan does not make any [feature of his manufacture] in vain and for no purpose, and if one were sufficient he would not make two [of the part when only one was necessary for the item's functioning]. All the more so in relation to the Creator, may His Name be blessed, it is necessary [to suppose] that each and every one [of His creations] is needed, and the Creator recognizes the function (lit., "need") of each and every individual—and the need for some particular purpose [that he serves]. And you must [understand] that the utility of one material being is not the same as another though similar one.

And the [essential] utility is a spiritual one, as though you would say, for example, that the quality of a circle or oval to roll is not the same as that of a geometrical figure with angles, which has no power to move on its own, but rather rests on the place it falls. [Similarly,] the powers of that which rolls or that which remains put are, [so to speak,] spiritual powers that cannot be apprehended by material beings, for, behold, we have found powers of movement and rest in the soul as well. In general, created beings are "oval" or "round" and have the power of motion (in the soul and in the thought of the mind as well)—they do not rest until death, as our Sages, may their memory be blessed, have put it in their euphemism [regarding death]: "his soul rested"—that [the deceased] acquired the power of rest.

And in similar fashion in regard to differences among beings, when we observe the nature of these differences in terms of their function in Creation, that is, whose utility was required by their creation in such and such a form, in order to fulfill some material function, that individual is required for a specific function; that is, the required power (הכח הנרצה) exists by itself, independent of materiality (בזולת הגשם). And there is no need to emphasize that the same applies to spiritual differences as we may draw an analogy to things that are inanimate and plants in terms of nurture and growth, and, again, in regard to the differences between the quality of their nurture, their liveliness and other powers of living beings [that contribute] to their life, and similar matters, and animals and other animate beings; [we may say the same in regard to] the individual powers and needs of each, as is known to some extent to those versed in the natural sciences. Their Creator [of course] knows [these matters] completely, and the sages of Truth, may their memory be blessed, those who have divine inspiration in regard to matters that relate to the perfection of their souls [in the matter] for which they were created. [As you will find in the words of Ḥazal a wondrous knowledge of natural science that astonishes those versed in such matters—how do they know such things, since they never studied natural sciences in their study halls, but they knew such things by their knowledge of the secrets of Creation, [as is written,] "G-d's secret is for those who fear him" (Ps 25:14), as has been explained by us elsewhere].

Thus, each person has a function in G-d's Creation simply by being born; as Reb Zadok notes in *Tzidqat ha-Tzaddiq* 154, everyone must believe in oneself, just as one must believe in G-d. However, *Paḥad Yitzḥak* introduces a new element: the centrality of the individual human being is contrasted with another aspect of the human condition—the world continues on its own way even after we pass from it, as Rav Hutner explains in *Paḥad Yitzḥak* Shavuot 21.4.

> ד...יחידותו של אדם מחייבת אותו לומר "בשבילי נברא העולם." ובודאי במצבו של אדם הראשון בשעת יצירתו, היתה הכרה זו ש"בשבילי נברא עולם", גלויה לפניו בכל מלוא-פשיטותה. אבל לאחר שהניח עליו הקב"ה כפו ומיעטו, ונגזרה עליו מיתה, הרי הכרה זו ש"בשביל[י] נברא עולם", אינה באה לו לאדם אלא על ידי עמידה בנסיון. שהלא בפשוטם של דברים, הופעת המיתה נראית כסותרת את ההכרה של "בשבילי נברא עולם". שהרי העולם נשאר קיים ועומד, גם לאחר חליפתו ומיתתו של אדם. ורק מתוך האמונה, שסוף גזירת-המיתה היא גזירה דעבידא ובטלא, ...ואדרבה, המות היא הופעת זמנית, וחק-חיים היא חק-נצח,-- רק מתוך אמונה זו. מוכשר הוא האדם להחיות בנפשו את ההכרה כי "בשבילי נברא עולם".

> 4....Man's individuality obligates him to say: "the world was created for my sake." And certainly in first Adam's situation when he was created [before death was decreed against him], this recognition was revealed in all its stark simplicity (מלוא-פשיטותה). But after the Holy One, Blessed Be He, placed His hand on him and diminished him, and death was decreed against him, this recognition that "the world was created for my sake" comes only through withstanding the trial [of realizing that death contradicts this recognition]. For in the plain sense of things, the appearance of death seems to contradict the recognition that "the world was created for my sake," since the world continues to exist even after a person's death and passing from the world. And it is only through the faith that the decree of death will be annulled [at the Resurrection of the Dead]..., and [that], indeed, death is a temporary phenomenon, and the measure of life is an eternal measure—only through this faith is a man prepared to enliven in his soul the recognition that "the world was created for my sake."

Please note: "Man's individuality (*yeḥiduto*) obligates him (*meḥayyev oto*) to say: 'the world was created for my sake.'" Man's singularity *obligates* him; his individuality is not merely acknowledged or tolerated, but becomes a *positive value*. By his use of halakhic language—the language of obligation,

Rav Hutner signals Halakhah's approval of man's individual nature. Moreover, in 21:3 he asserts that the difference between human society and groups of animals (flocks, herds, and species) is precisely Man's individuality.

> גם בחינת היחוד וגם בחינת האיחוד מושרשות הן בחידוש מידת היחידות ביצירתו של אדם. בלעדיה של יחידות זו אין כאן לא "יחוד" ולא "איחוד". ואין כאן אלא קיבוצים, קיבוצים, של עדרים, עדרים, אשר כל "קיומם אינם באיש אלא במין" (לשון חכמים קדמונים).
>
> Both the aspect of individuality and that of the collectivity are rooted in the introduction (חידוש) of this facet of individuality [promulgated] with the creation of Adam. Without this individuality, there is no "individuality" (יחוד), nor any "collective society" (איחוד), but rather various groups of flocks, flocks whose "existence is not [by means of] individuals but rather the species" (as enunciated by the early scholars).[14]

Here again we see Rav Hutner's emphasis on the individual, and, in this case, his role in society, while Reb Zadok deals with his role in creation. But the contrast is greater: for Rav Hutner, death is a *challenge* and possible refutation of this view of humankind, and only the belief in eternal life will enable us to continue to believe in our unique role in creation. Reb Zadok views life and death as antonyms that must be understood in tandem: life cannot be understood apart from death, nor death apart from life. Both are joined by the view that despite the challenge or contradiction, light and darkness, life and death, constitute a whole, and each is a necessary part of that whole.

This is an important proviso, for even during the glory days of Slobodka, the Alter, Rav Nathan Zvi Finkel, was accused of naiveté, and a competing vision of the "lowliness of man" emerged from the Alter of Novaredok, Rav Yoisef Yoisel Horowitz, a vision strengthened by the likes of Hitler and Stalin, who destroyed Rav Hutner's family and homeland, that sensitive, alive and alert Warsaw Jewry of which he was an magnificent exemplar, and, by Fatah, which kidnapped him and held him captive for a month, along with a planeload of passengers. Slobodka did not remain unaffected by the bloody events that marked the twentieth century, both for humanity and especially for the Jewish people. Benjamin

---

14 See Maimonides, *Guide of the Perplexed*, III:17, fifth theory, where he denies providence to individual animals. See Moses Maimonides, *The Guide of the Perplexed*, trans. Shlomo Pines, Chicago: University of Chicago Press, 1963, p. 471; *Moreh Nevukhim*, trans. Yosef Kapaḥ, Jerusalem: Mosad Harav Kook, 1972, p. 313.

Brown has shown that the Alter's successors withdrew somewhat from the Alter's glorious vision.[15] Despite the communal and personal catastrophes he faced, however, Rav Hutner did not withdraw from the Alter's view of humanity, and *Paḥad Yitzḥak*, which began to be published nearly two decades after the end of the Second World War, stands as a magnificent continuation of Slobodka "before the fall."

II

To assess the personal dimensions of his achievement, consider the following. From his earliest years as a self-reflective individual, Rav Hutner kept a diary, one from which his daughter drew on and quotes frequently in her biography of him. But from 5707 to 5714 no entries survive. In *Sefer Zikaron*, p. 36, n. 139, his daughter notes: "In these years there appears a void (*ḥalal*) in these original impressions (*yediot meqoriyyot*), from 5707 to 5714. However, these years were years of qualitative and quantitative growth and development for the yeshiva." These were also the years when the full dimensions of the destruction of Polish Jewry became apparent, and the yeshiva itself accepted at least one survivor of Auschwitz, David Weiss Halivni. It is difficult to disconnect the silence from the destruction. At the heart of *Paḥad Yitzḥak*, that measured theological assessment of G-d's universe and man's place in it—an assessment filled (*à la* Slobodka) with gratitude for G-d's grace and hope for the future (hence the repeated emphasis on the Messianic times)—there is that void into which his family and friends, and the cradle of his consciousness—vanished. And it is from that vantage point that we must view Rav Hutner's struggles to understand what had happened to the Jews of Europe, to the Jews of Poland, and, what had happened to him personally in the loss of his family.[16] We are informed that he was a first-born son, but not of any siblings. If there were any, they did not escape. What survivor's guilt underlies the insights of *Paḥad Yitzḥak* into life, death, and the recognition that we as persons will vanish even as the world continues!

---

15 See Binyamin Brown, "Gadlut ha-Adam ve-Haqtanato: Temurot be-Shittat ha-Musar shel Yeshivat Slobodka," in Immanuel Etkes, *Yeshivot u-Vatei Midrash*, Jerusalem: Merkaz Zalman Shazar, 2006, pp. 243–272.

16 See Gamliel Smalo, "Radiqaliyyut Filosofit be-Olam ha-Yeshivot: Rav Yitzhak Hutner al ha-Shoah," *Ḥakirah* 19 (2015), pp. 35–56 [Hebrew numbering], and Lawrence Kaplan, "A Righteous Judgment on a Righteous People: Rav Yitzhak Hutner's Implicit Theology of the Holocaust," *Ḥakirah* 10 (2010), pp. 101–115, both of which advance our understanding of this issue. The topic requires more detailed treatment than is possible here; I hope to deal with it on another occasion.

It would be a mistake, however, to view this as a debate between Slobodka and Nevaradok as one over the nature of man alone; it is rather a debate over how to achieve a certain educational goal: to produce humans who would be a credit to themselves, their society, and their Maker. Some people react better to the carrot, some to the stick.

It is also a debate over priority, over the exact mixture and proportion of desirable qualities to encourage and develop. Is obedience the goal, or creativity? Here I must admit that I write as a convinced Slobodkan, but I do not deny that some people, perhaps many people, would be better served by Nevaradok. The question is: how to produce creative, autonomous individuals who are also moral, sensitive beings who will become exemplary *bnei Torah*? And here, without casting aspersions, I think the answer is clear: fearfulness, a feeling of one's unworthiness, and the consequent timidity do not produce creative individuals.

However, as noted above and as Brown emphasized, this debate did not take place in a vacuum, but against the landscape of deteriorating Jewish life in Europe before and after World War I, which caused massive dislocation of most Jewish communities of central and Eastern Europe, and then with the destruction of European Jewry. As my son Zev David, a therapist who has had experience treating the syndrome, has observed, world Jewry can be seen, under the shadow of that destruction, to be suffering a sort of communal Post-Traumatic Stress Syndrome, which may go far in explaining some of the more bizarre developments of recent years. The effects of PTSD have been found to extend beyond those who underwent trauma to multi-generational trauma transmission.[17] Indeed, I might add, this phenomenon may go far in explaining some of the directions of Jewish life and thought throughout history.

Nevertheless, as noted, Rav Hutner held fast to his own version of that optimistic Slobodkan vision, despite his own experiences and those of his contemporaries; moreover, no one who has had even a glancing acquaintance with him could ever dream of accusing him of naiveté, and I would contend that he produced a vision of potential human achievement that mirrors the complex interaction of reason, evaluation and judgment, emotion and intuition, individualism, autonomy, initiative and self-fashioning that unite to produce the creative human being.[18]

---

17 Such experiences can apparently affect the victim's DNA; see Rachel Yehuda, *et al.*, "Holocaust Exposure Intergenerational Effects on *FKPB5* Methylation," in *Biological Psychiatry: A Journal of Psychiatric Neuroscience and Therapeutics* (forthcoming). My thanks to my son for this reference.

18 See Shlomo Kasirer, pp. 186-187.

III

The primary method of attaining these goals is by means of the intellect, and so let us begin with judgment; here is *Paḥad Yitzḥak* Shabbat 1.4:

ד. המוציא אוכלין בכלי פחות מכשיעור פטור אף על הכלי, מפני שהכלי טפלה לאוכלין. כלומר, אף על פי דגוף פעולת ההוצאה של הכלי נגדרת היא בכל גדרי מלאכת הוצאה דחילול שבת, מכל מקום כיון דבשעת הוצאת הכלי היתה פעולת הוצאה זו טפלה לפעולה אחרת, הרי זה מוציא את פעולת הוצאת הכלי מכלל "מלאכת מחשבת". וממילא אין היא סותרת את שביתתה של השבת. ונכונים אנו בזה לקראת ההארה המחודשת של המאמר הזה: אין ענין זה של טפל ועיקר דין פרטי בין המון הלכותיה של שבת, אלא שענין זה של טפל ועיקר מהוה היא את המהלך הפנימי של שביתת שבת בראשית. לשם הבהרת דברים אלו, עלינו לחזור לששת ימי בראשית שלפני השבת. בששת ימי בראשית פעלו עשרה המאמרות. בכחם של המאמרות הללו נאצלו, נבראו, נוצרו ונעשו כל חוקי ההנהגה של עצם *טבע* כל העולמות. אבל בכל העשרה מאמרות של ששת ימי בראשית לא הוזכר עדין ענין הקדושה כל עיקר. ורק עם הופעתה של שבת נזכרה בראשונה מציאות הקדושה. כלליות ענין הקדושה בכאן פירושה הוא, כי בעוד שעד עכשו בששת ימי בראשית יצא לפועל *גופם* של העולמות, הנה עכשו עם הופעתם של השבת יצא מן ההעלם אל הגילוי *התכלית והמטרה* של קיום העולמות, "אם לא בריתי יומם ולילה חוקות שמים וארץ לא שמתי". הברית היא התכלית והמטרה של חוקות שמים וארץ.

4. One who takes food less than the amount that would make him liable for violating the Sabbath [law against carrying from one domain to another] in a container is also not guilty for carrying the container, because the container is only an accessory to the food [and he had not carried enough food to make him liable], that is to say, even though the essential act of taking out the container is defined by all the rules [forbidding] transferring [from one domain to another] that make the carrier liable for violating the Sabbath, nevertheless, since at the time of the transfer the container was only an accessory to another act, [that is, the forbidden one of transfer of the food], this aspect of the action takes the act of transferring the container out of the category of "intentional labor" [which defines acts that violate the Sabbath]. And thus [that act] does not contradict the [commandment of] resting on the Sabbath. [With our understanding of this rule] we are prepared [to understand] the particular insight [to which] this *ma'amar* [is dedicated]: This matter of essence and accessory is not a particular rule governing only this situation among the many other rules governing Sabbath rest, but rather this rule of essence and accessory constitutes the inner process governing the rules of resting on the Sabbath [instituted at] Creation. In order to clarify these matters, we must return to those six days that preceded the Sabbath of the week of Creation. During those six days the Ten

Statements [by which G-d created the Universe] operated. By dint of these sayings the laws governing the essential *nature* of the all the worlds were emanated, created, fashioned and made. However, [despite the operation of] the Ten Statements of the six days of Creation, the matter of sanctity was not yet mentioned at all. Only with the appearance of the Sabbath is the existence of sanctity mentioned for the first time. The general matter of sanctity here means that though until that point in the six days of Creation the substance of the worlds had become actual (*in actu*), only now, with the appearance of the Sabbath, did *the purpose and goal* of the existence of the universe issue from hiddenness (העלם) to its revelation. "If I had not created day and night, I would not have put in place the laws of heaven and earth" (Jer 33:25). The covenant is the purpose and goal of the laws of heaven and earth [playing on the likeness of *bariti*, "I created" and *beriti*, "my covenant"].

This covenant Rav Hutner equates with the Ten Commandments, representing the Giving of the Torah, which serves to lower the natural, created world to a secondary or accessory status, *tafel.*

זו היא עצמיות מציאותה של שביתת שבת בראשית, שמצד הופעת אורה של קדושת שבת, ירדה בחינת הטבע של העולמות וגופם למדרגת כלי וטפל—היא היא שביתתה של שבת בראשית.

This is the essence of the existence of the rest of the Sabbath of creation, for because of the appearance of the light of the sanctity of the Sabbath the importance of the nature of the worlds and their substance was relegated to the level of [merely] a vessel and accessory—that is [what] the rest of the Sabbath of creation [represents].

And, as he goes on to say in paragraph 5, the precipitating factor in all this is no less than the human intellect, *ha-da'at.*

ה. אבל הרי כל קביעת משקל הערכין של עיקר וטפל, אי אפשר לו שייעשה רק בכוחה של הדעת. רק הדעת היא השוקלת ומעריכה.

5. However, the determination of the weight of the values of essential and accessory cannot be accomplished without the power of the intellect.[19] Only the intellect weighs and evaluates.[20]

Rav Hutner selects the use of the intellect to exemplify the essence and meaning of the Sabbath, which, though the intellect can be equated with Torah study, nevertheless has a different valence when it is expressed as *da'at* rather than as *talmud Torah*. Indeed, Rav Hutner adds a second chapter to his first *ma'amar* on Shabbat, a chapter comprising no fewer than 6.5 pages *in celebration of the uniqueness* of the human intellect and *its creativity*.

ז. וממשיכים אנו את הקו הלאה. מתוך מה שנתבאר לנו בפרק ראשון של מאמר זה נלמד כי לגבי שביתת שבת יוצא הוא המאמר של "נעשה אדם"—הוא מאמר של יצירת כוח הדעת. והרי נתבאר לנו כי מהות שביתתה של שבת היא הנמכת ערכו של גוף העולמות עד כדי התבטלות לאורם של העולמות. ומכיון שהנמכה זו נעשית היא רק בכוחה של הדעת, הרי ממילא יוצא מזה שאי אפשר לומר שכוח הדעת נעשה לטפל. מאחר שכוח השביתה מתקיימת בכוחה של הדעת. הרי ברור הוא שלא תתכן שביתה בכוח הדעת עצמו. והנה בכוחה של הדעת להכיר גם את גופו של עולם וגם את אורו, ולקבוע את ערכם ההדדי כמו טפל לגבי עיקר, ומתוך כך להשיג את התבטלות פעולתם של עשרת המאמרות כלפי אורם של עשרת הדברות. ומכיון שהתבטלות זו היא שביתתה של שבת, הרי נמצא בדוקא בשעה שמאמרי-בראשית שובתים, דוקא אז מתאדר כוח הדעת בכל הנשגביות שבו. וממילא יוצא מזה כי דוקא *בשעה שהכל שובת הדעת יוצרת*. מאמר "נעשה אדם" הוא מאמר הבריאה של כוח הדעת. ועל כן אנו אומרים כי דוקא שביתתה של שבת המבטלת את "עיקריות" עולם הטבע שנוצר במאמרות-בראשית, היא היא המוציאה לאור את עיקריות כוח הדעת הנוצר במאמר "נעשה אדם". וזה הוא מה

19 See Rav Y.D. David, *Quntras Pesaḥ* 13.5: "כי הדעת כוללת גם הכרת האמת וגם הבחנה היפוכו—"אם אין דעת הבדלה מנין". ופעולה זאת של הבחנת האור מן החושך הוא ענין הדעת המתייחס אל משה". For the intellect includes both [an appreciation of] the necessity of the truth and a discernment of its opposite—"If there is no *da'at*, wherefrom discernment?" (Yerushalmi Berakhot 5:2). And this action of distinguishing light from darkness is the matter of *da'at* which relates to Moses." See there for the meaning of the reference to Moses.

20 As we shall see below, Rav Hutner also employs the term *sekhel* for the intellect, but the emphasis there (*Paḥad Yitzḥak* Shavuot 17.8) is on the intellect's creative power, while here he emphasizes weighing and evaluation, for which he employs *da'at*. Whether this distinction is carried throughout *Paḥad Yitzḥak* requires more research. What is clear, however, is that *da'at* is not used in its kabbalistic sense, as contrasted with *ḥokhmah* and *binah*, as Reb Zadok does; and *sekhel*, which he does use, does not have that kabbalistic valence, but refers to "mere" human intellect. In contrast, Reb Zadok emphasizes insights that are "beyond man's intellect" (*lema'aleh me-hasagat ha-sekhel*) dozens of times in his writings.

שאמרנו כי לגבי קדושתה של שבת יוצא הוא המאמר של "נעשה אדם" מכללם של שאר מאמרות.

7. We [now] continue the line [of reasoning] further. From what was explained to us in the first chapter [of this *ma'amar*], that in regard to the Sabbath rest [of the week of Creation] the [Divine] statement of "Let us make man" is not in the same category (lit., "goes out of the general rule") of the other [Divine] statements. "Let us make man" is the command regarding the creation of intellect. And so we become aware (lit., "it is explained to us") that the quality of Sabbath rest involves the lowering of the value of the substance of the worlds [created at Creation] to the point of nullification of the light of those worlds. And because this lowering was accomplished only by means of the powers of the intellect, it is thus impossible to maintain that the powers of the intellect can become mere accessories [to a greater end]. Since the generality of the Sabbath rest exists by means of the powers of the intellect, it is clear that there can be no cessation in the powers of the intellect *per se.* And since it is within the powers of the intellect to recognize both substance of the world and also its light, and to establish their mutual value as accessories contrasted to essentials, and from this to apprehend the nullification of the workings of the Ten Statements [of Creation] in comparison to the light of the Ten Commandments. And since this nullification constitutes [an essential ingredient] of the Sabbath rest, it thus comes out that precisely at the moment that the [Divine] statement [of Creation] ceases, precisely then is the power of the intellect exalted in all its sublimity. Sabbath rest is created by the power of the intellect, with the inevitable consequence (וממילא יוצא מזה) that *when all ceases, then the intellect creates.* The [Divine] statement of "Let us make man" is the statement of the creation of the intellect, and so we say that precisely the Sabbath rest that nullifies the "primacy" of the natural world (עולם הטבע) that was created with the statements of Genesis—is what brings to light the primacy of the powers of the intellect that was created by the statement "Let us make man." And this is what we said that in regard to the sanctity of Sabbath the statement of "Let us make man" is no longer in the category of the other statements [of Creation].[21]

ט...וממילא גם בתוכו של האדם עצמו בטלים הם שאר הכוחות של האדם לגבי כוח המיוחד שבאדם, דהיינו לכוח הדעת שהיא ה"אדם שבאדם".

21 On man's power to remake himself by means of repentance, see Kasirer, pp. 140–146, and see below.

9. And thus also within the inner being of man himself all other human abilities are null as compared to this unique power within a person, that is, the intellect, which constitutes the inner core of humanity (lit., the "man within man").[22]

In this Rav Hutner applies the Rambam's understanding of the human intellect as reflecting the "image of G-d."[23]

יד....ונמצא דעיקר ברכת השבת הוא דוקא בזה שיום השבת הוא הזמן המיוחד והמקודש להוספת מהות האדם. והוספת מהות האדם זו משמעותה כפולה: הוספת ה"מיוחד לאדם" בתוך כלליות האדם עצמו, והוספת אדם בכלליות העולם.

14...And thus the essence of the blessing of the Sabbath is precisely in this: that the Sabbath day is the unique and sanctified day for the addition to man's (essential) quality. And this addition to man's essential quality has a double meaning: the addition of that which is "unique to man" within the general category of man's qualities, and the addition of man into the generality of the world.

טו. והננו נועצים את חתימת המאמר בפתיחתו: טועמיה חיים זכו. ועמדנו על שנתיחסה הזכיה בחיים להרגשת טעמה של שבת. לפי כל המבואר לעיל למדים אנו טוב טעם ודעת ביחס זה. רואים אנו בפרשת בראשית, שאף על פי שענין החיות בכלל נתפרש גם לפני יצירת האדם, מכל מקום תיבת "חיים" לא נזכרה עד שעת בריאתו של נשמת אדם .... רואים אנו מכאן כי אותה החיות הנגדרת בתיבת "חיים" מיוחד היא אך ורק לאדם. על ענין זה המתפרש להדיא בפרשת בראשית עצמה העמידו חכמים את מטבע התפילה "טועמיה חיים זכו". "חיים" דוקא. כלומר, מכיון שאותה החיות הנגדרת בתיבת "חיים" מיוחדת היא אך ורק למהות אדם, והרי שורש ברכתה של שבת הוא הוספת-מהות-אדם, ממילא נמצא כי ההרגשה בטעם השבת היא היא הזיכוי באותו סוג חיות הנגדרת דוקא בתיבת "חיים". ומתחלף הוא הענין לפי הנושאים. הזכיה לחיים מתיחסת היא להרגשת הטעם של השבת *עצמה*, בעוד ש"גדולה בחרו" מתיחסת היא לאהבה *דבריה* של שבת. הם הם הדברים. הרגשת תוספת-מהות-האדם היא היא "טועמיה", והלא תוספת-מהות-האדם היא היא עצמיותה של ברכת שבת, ואילו "בחירת הגדולה" משתייכת להבחנת עיקר וטפל, והערכת גדלות וקטנות של שבת, כמו שנתבאר באות ה' שהבחנות והערכות אלה הם *תולדותיה* של תוספת הדעת הנוצרת בשבת. ועל כן "בחירת הגדולה" מתיחסת היא לאהבת *דבריה* של שבת, בעוד שהזכיה ב"חיים" מתיחסת היא להרגשת הטעם של השבת *עצמה*. טועמיה חיים זכו וגם האוהבים דבריה גדולה בחרו.

15. We thus join the conclusion of this *ma'amar* to its opening: "those who taste [the Sabbath] merit life" (a line from the Sabbath Musaf Amidah). We have come to understand the relationship of meriting

---

22 Note that Rav Hutner employs the term *da'at* rather than *sekhel* here. In kabbalistic terms, *da'at* would rank higher than *sekhel.*

23 *Guide* I, 2.

> life with the apprehension (lit., "the feeling") of the taste of the Sabbath. From all that was explained above we learn the proper understanding of this relationship. We have seen from the Creation account that even though the matter of life in general precedes the creation of man, nevertheless the word "life" is not mentioned until the creation of man's soul[24]….We see that that life that is defined by the word "life" is unique to man. The root of the blessing of the Sabbath is that additional-quality-of-man, and thus that feeling of the taste of the Sabbath is precisely in that category of life designated by the word "life" which varies with the context. Meriting life relates to the apprehension of the taste of the Sabbath itself, while (the phrase) "they chose greatness" relates to the "love of her *words*"—of the Sabbath. This is the same equation (הם הם הדברים). The feeling of the addition-to-the-quality-of-man on the Sabbath is "those who taste her." And this addition-to-the-quality-of-man represents the essence of the blessing of the Sabbath. The (phrase) regarding "choosing greatness" belongs to the distinction between essential and secondary, and the valuation of greater and lesser in regard to the Sabbath, as was explained in paragraph 5—that these distinctions and valuations are the *consequences* of the increase (alternatively: enhancement) of the intellect that is created on the Sabbath. And therefore "the choice of greatness" relates to the love of *her words* of the Sabbath, while meriting "life" relates to the feeling of the taste of Sabbath itself. "Those who taste her merit life, and those who love her words choose greatness."

This then is Rav Hutner's summation of the lesson of this long—10-page—*ma'amar.* The Sabbath rest enhances man's intellect and sharpens his ability to make fine distinctions in Halakhah, such as the example he opens with regarding moving foodstuffs less than the minimum amount required to constitute a violation of *hilkhot Shabbat.*

For Rav Hutner, the human intellect is the crowning point of Creation, and at its apex stands human creativity, which is an expression of an individual's uniqueness (*Paḥad Yitzḥak* Shavuot 17.8). That uniqueness and creativity is actualized in *talmud Torah*, which requires autonomy for its achievement, as we have seen (*Paḥad Yitzḥak* Shavuot 15.6, repeated from Hanukah 6.6).

But taking a cue from Maimonides, Rav Hutner, in contrast to Reb Zadok, not only assigns the intellect a role unique to humans, but defines

24 Here again Rav Hutner employs the principle that the Torah's placement of terminology is itself significant, a principle employed extensively by the Ramban and ḥasidic writers.

the essence of humanness in terms of the workings of the intellect, emphasizing as well the uniqueness of each individual (*Paḥad Yitzḥak*, Shavuot 17.8).

ח. והנה כשאנו אומרים שסגולת היחידות טבועה היא בשכלו של כל אדם, ממילא נשמע מזה, כי עיקר מהותו של השכל הוא בהיותו מחודש בהחלט, מפני שאם לא היה כל שכל ושכל הנמצא בעולם מחודש במהותו, הרי אי אפשר היה לו לשמש בכתר היחידות. כי מבלי תאר היחידות בעל כרחו שהיה בו משום "היינו-הך" עם עוד שכל אחר הנמצא בעולם, ועצם האפשרות של היחידות בשכלו של אדם, באה היא לו רק מפני שיש בכל שכל ושכל דבר מחודש מה שאין בשכל חברו. ונמצינו למדים, דמהותו של כל שכל ושכל הוא במציאות החידוש הנמצא בו. ומפני כן אמרו "אין בית המדרש בלא חידוש". כלומר, הבית המדרש הוא מקום פעולתו של השכל, ופעולתו של השכל היא בהתאם למהותו. ועל כן עיקר פעולתו של השכל הוא ה"חידוש". החידוש במהלך פעולתו של השכל הוא בגדר פסיק רישא, עד כדי כך שאמרו "אין בית המדרש בלא חידוש". אין השכל מוצא את עצמו במילוי ענינו, אלא בשעת יצירה. עיקרו של כח השכל, כח הולדה הוא. ורק זה הוא מהלך יגיעת השכל. כשהשכל עסוק בעיונו, הרי אין התעסקות זו, אלא רדיפה אחר התחדשות הפנים של הדבר הנידון. לפני העיון היה הנידון נראה בפנים אחרים, מאשר לאחר העיון. חידוש-פנים זה, הוא הוא ההולדה אשר בכח השכל, וחידוש-פנים של הנידון הבא על ידי השתקעות השכל בנידון--הוא הוא עמילות השכל. וכשאתה אומר "שכל בלי כח עמילות", הרי זה כאילו היית אומר "אבהות בלי כח הולדה".

8. Now, when we say that [a person's] unique quality inheres (טבועה) in the intellect of each person, we infer from this that the essence (lit., "quality") of an intellect is that it is absolutely unique מחודש) (בהחלט, for were it not that each and every intellect in this world were unique in its essence (lit., "quality"), it would not be possible for it to symbolize (lit., "serve as") the crown of [human] uniqueness"). For without the attribute (תאר) of uniqueness, one intellect would be identical to another, while the potential for uniqueness (as inherent) in a person's intellect comes precisely from [the fact] that every intellect has something unique about it that is different from another's. We learn from this that the [unique] quality of each and every intellect inheres in the creative capacity (במציאות החידוש) that is found in it. And it is because of this that they said: "There is no *bet midrash* without any innovation."[25] That is to say, the *bet midrash* is the place for the workings of the intellect, and the working of the intellect is in accordance with its essence (lit., "quality"). Therefore, the essential [product and proof] working of the intellect is the "*ḥiddush*" [=an innovation in Torah learning]. (Producing a) "*ḥiddush*" in the course of the workings of the intellect is inevitable, to the point that it is

25 Hag 3a.

said that "there is no *bet midrash* without a *ḥiddush*." The intellect finds its proper fulfillment in the full meaning of the word only at the time when it creates (lit., "of creation"). The essential quality of the intellect is the power to conceive. This alone is the intellect's mode of operation (מהלך יגיעת השכל). During its [work of] analysis, the intellect's activity [may be perceived] as the urgent search (רדיפה) for a new perception (התחדשות פנים) of the thing being analyzed: [that is,] before the analysis takes place, the object of the analysis was seen in a different light (פנים) than it is after the analysis. This new aspect (חידוש פנים) is the conception (ההולדה) brought about by the power of the intellect. And this new aspect brought about by the intellect's occupation with the matter at hand—is precisely the labor of the intellect (עמלות השכל). And when you say "intellect without the power of (intellectual) labor," it is as though you said: "Fatherhood without the power of conception" (אבהות בלי כח ההולדה)![26]

Please note that *Paḥad Yitzḥak*'s "labor of the intellect" (*amelut ha-sekhel*) may be seen as an amalgam of the Lithuanian *amelut ba-Torah* and the ḥasidic *avodah be-gashmiyyut* (conventionally rendered as "worship through corporeality").[27] Here though the *avodah* is not so much worship as another prime mitzvah, *talmud Torah*; in essence, what Rav Hutner has done is extend Reb Zadok's notion of the Sabbath's rendering of *oneg Shabbat*, which includes bodily pleasures (to whatever limited extent), as a mitzvah, to both a full-fledged concept and one that explains the function of *talmud Torah* as well.

IV

And so, let us look at *Paḥad Yitzḥak*, Shavuot, 15.6-7.

ו. אמנם לא יהיה ענין זה שלם אם לא נעתיק בכאן את לשונו של ספר פחד יצחק, קונטרס וזאת חנוכה, מאמר ו'-- -- -- החידוש אשר מצינו בענינו של תלמוד תורה, כי לעולם ילמד אדם מה שלבו חפץ. והלא פשוט הוא כי אין מקומה של הכרעה זו אלא בלימוד התורה...אשר בו התעסקות במקום שלבו חפץ הוא הכרעתו של הדין עצמו. והסברת הדברים היא, כי כל שייכותו של אדם עם מציאות שחוצה לו, הרי

26 See Rav Moshe Mordechai Epstein, *Levush Mordechai al Bava Metzi'a/Bava Batra*, Jerusalem: Makhon Yerushalayim, 5774, p. 14a, where Rav Epstein refers to הידיעה בלי הוספת לקח ופלפול הוא כגוף בלי נשמה, "knowledge without the addition of [further] analytic understanding is like a body without a soul." Rav Epstein (1866-1934), was, of course, long-time *rosh yeshiva* at Slobodka and brother-in-law of the Alter.

27 See Norman Lamm, *The Religious Thought of Hasidism: Text and Commentary*, Hoboken: Ktav, 1999, pp. 371–386, and *passim*.

היא בדרך של חבור. כל החושים פועלים את פעולתם בדרך חבור. חוש המשוש פועל הוא את פעולתו על ידי החבור בכחה של הנגיעה. גוף הדבר נוגע הוא בגוף האדם. חוש הראות פועל הוא את פעולתו על ידי החבור אל כחם של קוי אור. חוש השמיעה פועל הוא את פעולתו על ידי החבור בכחם של גלי הקול. ועלינו לדעת כי הוא הדין והיא המדה גם בנוגע להשגת השכל. אי אפשר לשכל לבוא לכלל השגה כי אם על ידי חבור עם ענינו של המושג. חבור זה של השכל עם ענינו של המושג נעשה הוא בכחו של התענוג הטמון בהשגה. כחו של השכל בלי פעולת התענוג הוא כמו כחה של העין מבלי פעולת האור, וכמו כחה של האוזן מבלי פעולת האויר. ואשר על כן כשהעין מתענגת על מראות של יופי, או כשהאוזן מתענגת על קולות של מתיקות, הרי התענוג הזה הוא דבר נוסף על פעולתו של כח הראיה או השמיעה; ואילו בשעה שהשכל מתענג על ההשגה, הרי התענוג הוא נפשה של תנועת ההשגה, אשר בלעדו ינוח השכל כאבן דומם. ועל כן חפץ הלב הכרעה היא רק בתלמוד תורה. משום דמצות תלמודה של תורה מתקיימת היא בכחה של ההשגה וההשכלה. וכל תוספת תענוג בשעת השגה—הרי היא ממילא תוספת השגה. ולא עוד אלא שרואים אנו כי רק ביחס לתלמוד תורה נתקנה ברכת תחנונים על ערבות הדברים, שהרי לא מצינו דוגמתה של ברכת "והערב נא" בנוגע לשום מצוה מלבד תלמוד תורה. והם הם הדברים. כי התענוג בהשגת דברי תורה נכנס הוא בכלל גוף המצוה, ואילו בשאר מצוות אינו אלא עטרה של ראשם. עכ"ל של ספר פחד יצחק, קונטרס וזאת חנוכה.

ז. ונמצינו למדים כי אף על פי שניתן כתר תורה בראשו של כח השכל להשתלט על שאר כחות הנפש, מכל מקום גופו של שלטון זה מותנה הוא בפעולתו של כח התענוג. וטעם הדבר הוא משום דשלטון השכל על כחות הנפש ומדותיה, עיקר הגדרתו הוא כי פעולת השכל יש לה כח ממשלה, ואשר על כן אין ממשלה זו מתחלת אלא לאחר שבא השכל ליד פעולה,אבל כח התענוג שהוא הוא המביא את השכל לידי פעולה, לא נכנס לעולם בכללם של כחות הנפש הנמצאים בתחום שלטונו של השכל.

6. However, this matter will not be complete[ly explained] if we do not repeat a passage from *Paḥad Yitzḥak* on Hanukah, Ma'amar 6—the innovative aspect that we find in regard to *talmud Torah* [in contrast to other mitzvot] [is this: In regard to *talmud Torah* we have the rule] that a person should study what his heart desires. It is clear (פשוט) that this decision relates to the study of Torah…in which involvement (התעסקות) in matters that his heart desires is the decisive point (הכרעה) of the law (דין) itself. The explanation of this matter is that all of man's relation to reality outside of himself (השתייכותו עם מציאות שחוצה לו) is by means of connection (חיבור). All the senses work by means of connection. The sense of touch works by means of a connection to touch. The substance [of the thing touched] (גוף הדבר) touches a man's body. The sense of sight works by means of its connection with light rays; hearing works by means of its connection to sound waves. And it is incumbent on us to know that the same is true in regard to intellectual apprehension. It is impossible

for the intellect to come to comprehension [of any matter] except by means of connection with the thing apprehended. This connection of the intellect with the matter to be comprehended is accomplished by means of the pleasure (תענוג) that is embodied (טמון) in the matter to be comprehended. The power of the intellect without the working of pleasure is like the power of the eye [to see] without the stimulation of light (פעולת האור), or the power of the ear [to hear] without the stimulation of air (פעולת האויר). However, when the eye is pleased by a beautiful sight, or the ear by sweet sounds, the pleasure is something added to the essential action of the power of sight or hearing, while when the intellect is pleased by its apprehension [of something], that pleasure is the very soul of the action of apprehension, which, without it, the intellect [may be compared] to a dumb stone. Therefore, the heart's desire [to understand] is a decision relevant only in matters of [the mitzvah of] *talmud Torah*, for the mitzvah of the study of Torah exists only by the power of apprehension and understanding. And [thus] any enhancement of the pleasure [of learning] at the moment of comprehension—is thus an enhancement of the apprehension [itself]. Not only that, but we see that it is only in relation to *talmud Torah* that a blessing [that includes] a request for the pleasure of the words [of Torah] was ordained, for we do not find an example of the blessing of "Ha'arev Na" ("Please make it pleasant") in regard to any mitzvah aside from *talmud Torah.* And that is the point (והם הם הדברים), for the pleasure at apprehending the words of Torah enters into the very substance of the mitzvah, while in regard to other mitzvoth it is [merely] a crown at its head—thus far the quotation from *Paḥad Yitzḥak* on Hanukah.

7. The upshot is that even though we give the intellect the crown of Torah to rule over the other powers of the soul, nevertheless, the essence of this sovereignty is predicated on the workings of the capacity (כח) for [intellectual] pleasure. And the reason for this is that the sovereignty of the intellect over the powers of the soul and its characteristics (מדותיה), its essential definition (עיקר הגדרתו) inheres in [the fact that] the powers of the intellect have the quality of dominion, [but] this dominion comes into being only after the intellect is energized (שבא השכל ליד פעולה)—and it is this pleasure that brings the intellect into play, [and without it] the powers of the soul that are located in the realm of the intellect's dominion never enter [into operation] at all (בכללם).

This is a remarkable analysis on several grounds. First, Rav Hutner assigns pleasure a role in the workings of the premier mitzvah, and moreover, he compares the role of desire and pleasure in Torah learning to the workings of the senses,[28] and thus understands that desire as a *natural* outgrowth of the pleasure to be attained in the course of Torah study. In this way he also emphasizes the role of human autonomy within the domain of *talmud Torah*, as he assigns it a role within the process of repentance (see below). But perhaps the most remarkable of all is the fact that pleasure here is viewed positively, and, indeed, *the joy of intellectual discovery in the very essence of talmud Torah; without it, one has not fulfilled the mitzvah of talmud Torah.* The importance of pleasure in Slobodkan thought is well attested,[29] but Rav Hutner's application of this importance to an essential role in Talmud Torah is his own innovation.

The personal importance of creativity Rav Hutner expressed in a letter in 1933.

> I am now becoming steeped in studies. . . . Study in its various guises absorbs me, and yet I know that the essence of my personality is the life of my soul and not the life of my mind. . . . For me to live a life of the soul means to live a life of soul-creativity. For myself, I cannot imagine any realm of life of the spirit to be without creativity. But this is the rub: I am not able to be creative in the life of the soul without first taking important strides—creative ones—in study and *mada*. And so, I am stuck between the insistent claims of the soul, which penetrate to my depths, and between the command of my personality to overcome these claims temporarily (as I pursue my studies) to build for greater soul-creativity at a later time.[30]

The stress on creativity and the joy of intellectual cognition in *Paḥad Yitzḥak* thus expressed a deeply felt need on the part of its author, one that will resonate with other creative individuals. While the *ma'amarim* in *Paḥad Yitzḥak* were addressed, first and foremost, to a yeshiva audience, it holds a message for the wider society of whose tradition it is part: stagnation is as much a danger as unbridled innovation.

---

28 Note the parallel to Reb Zadok's use of geometry to explain the workings of the soul (see above).

29 See *Or ha-Tzafun* II, "Memadei Ta'anugot ha-Adam," Jerusalem: Havaad le-Hotza'at Ma'amarei Maran ha-Sava mi-Slobodka ztl, 5728 (1967/8), pp. 190–193, esp. pp. 192-193, Dov Katz, *Tenuat ha-Musar: Toldoteha, Isheha, ve-Shitoteha*, vol. 3, Tel Aviv: Tziyyoni, 1967, pp. 199–207 ("Ha-Ta'anugim ve-Simḥat ha-Ḥayyim"), and Binyamin Brown, "Gadlut ha-Adam ve-Haqtanato: Temrot be-Shittat ha-Musar shel Yeshivat Slobodka," pp. 248–250. See now his short book, *Tenu'at ha-Musar ha-Lita'it*, Moshav Ben-Shemen: Modan/Misrad ha-Bitaḥon, 2014, esp. pp. 84–96 on Slobodka.

30 See Goldberg, p. 27.

How do we differentiate the two? Here another *ma'amar*, this one from *Ma'amarei Paḥad Yitzḥak* Sukkot 27, will help us. In it Rav Hutner discusses the difference between a Torah scholar who has *da'at*, and one who does not.

ג. התחלת הדברים היא בביאור דברי חז"ל על "ויקרא אל משה" (ויקרא א, א), שהיה צריך משה לקריאה מיוחדת לבא אל המשכן. "מכאן לתלמיד חכם שאין בו דעה שנבלה טובה הימנו" (ויקרא רבא א, ט). בודאי במה שנקטו בלשון "נבלה טובה הימנו" הוא משום שדבר חי שמת הוא יותר גרוע מאשר לא היה בו חיים מעולם. והוא הגריעותא בנבלה. אולם בתלמיד חכם הוא הוא עוד יותר גרוע מזה. כלומר, שטוב לתלמיד חכם שאין בו דעת אילו לא נעשה לתלמיד חכם לכתחלה.
ד. אלא שעלינו לפרש בשפה ברורה מהו תלמיד חכם ומהו "תלמיד חכם שיש בו דעת". מה היא המעלה של "יש בו דעת" שבלעדה יותר טוב לתלמיד חכם אילו נשאר עם הארץ.
ה. סדר העבודה מתחלק לשני מהלכים. א) מצוות ממש ב) דברי רשות. הראשון הוא שכבר מבורר שהוא רצון השם וכבוד שמים. השני הוא שעדיין תלוי ועומד, והאדם בעצמו צריך לבררו ולחשוב מחשבות איך למצות [מ"ם פתוחה] ככל היותר כבוד שמים מתוך פעולותיו (ווי אויסקצוקוועטשן דאס גרעסטע מאס כבוד שמים), מכל המצבים והענינים שניתנו לאדם להשתמש בהם לצרכו. כמו שאמרו "כל מעשיך יהיו לשם שמים" (אבות פרק ב). ויהיו דברינו להלן בהחילוק בין סוגי הדעת הדרושים להוראה בשני ענפים אלו.
ו. בהקבלה לחילוק זה הוא החילוק בדרגה על תלמיד חכם סתם ותלמיד חכם שיש בו דעת. הדעת דתלמיד חכם היא בזה שעל ידי לימודו בגופי תורה ממש, חדורה בו החיות איך לנצל עניני האי עלמא ודברי רשות לריבוי כבוד שמים במדה היותר גדולה. ואילו תלמיד חכם שאין בו דעת—הוא שקנה קנין בגופי תורה ממש מבלי היכולת להרכיבם לסניפי דברי רשות. אין כוח ההוראה שלו מתפשט על תחום דברי רשות. בלשון דאמרי אינשי, היינו אומרים: תלמיד חכם הוא בד' חלקי שולחן ערוך; ותלמיד חכם בדעת הוא גם "שולחן ערוך החמישי".

3. The beginning of these matters inheres in the explanation of the words of Ḥazal on "He called to Moshe" (Lev 1:1), that is, that Moshe required a special invitation to come to the Mishkan: "From here [we learn] that a Torah scholar who has no *de'ah*—even a *neveilah* is better than he" (Lev. Rabba 1:9). Certainly, Ḥazal's choice of metaphor—"a *neveilah* is better than he"—relates to the fact that a living being that has died is greatly inferior to one that never had life at all—so much for [our understanding of] the inferiority of a *neveilah*. But a Torah scholar [of this sort] is even more inferior. That is to say, it would have been better for a Torah scholar who has no *da'at* had he not become a Torah scholar at all!
4. However, we must clearly explain what a "Torah scholar" is and what a "Torah scholar who has *da'at*" is, and what the advantage of "who has *da'at*" is, to the point that it would have been better for a

> Torah scholar to have remained an *am ha-aretz* [if he remains without *da'at*].
> 5. The order of Divine service may be divided into two paths: a) the mitzvot themselves, b) matters of personal choice. The first category is clearly one [that reflects] the Will of Hashem and [an increase of] the honor of Heaven [i.e., a *kiddush Hashem*]. The second category is in suspension, and each person must clarify and consider how to extract the greatest accrual of Heavenly honor through his actions in all the matters and situations available to an individual to make use of for his needs. As Ḥazal said: "All your deeds should be for the sake of Heaven" (Avot, chapter 2). Our explanation below will refer to the requisite distinction between these two types of knowledge of instruction.
> 6. The distinction between an ordinary Torah scholar and one who has *da'at* is in parallel to this distinction. The *da'at* of [that latter] Torah scholar inheres in this: by means of his study of the essentials of Torah he becomes imbued with the knowledge of how to utilize the matters of this world and of personal choice for the increase in the honor of Heaven in the greatest measure. In contrast, a Torah scholar who has no *da'at*—[that is,] one who acquired the essentials of Torah without the capability of harnessing them to those matters of personal choice; his powers of Torah instruction do not extend to the realm of matters of personal choice. As the popular saying goes: He is a Torah scholar in the four sections of *Shulḥan Arukh*, while a "Torah scholar with *da'at* has also mastered the 'Fifth [Section] of *Shulḥan Arukh*.'"

Rav Hutner here adverts to a popular Yiddish saying that I shall explicate by means of another one: "*Sekhel iz an eidler zach*"—"common sense is a rare thing." Matters that relate to human relations, specifically, to the increase of the honor of Heaven within the highly complex realm of human relations, require a sharply honed sense of the norms, expectations and needs of the society within which the Torah scholar lives and works, beyond those of the conventional four sections of *Shulḥan Arukh*. A Torah scholar who represents that honor must always take that role into account in his dealings with people, and if he does not—a *neveilah* is better than he.

Talmud Torah also requires evaluation and judgment, as we saw in *Paḥad Yitzḥak* Shabbat. Halakhah is tempered by a sense of proportion in evaluating its stringencies. *Hefsed merubbeh, piqqu'aḥ nefesh, ein gozerin gezerah al ha-tzibbur ela im ken rov ha-tzibbur yekholin la'amod bah*, and other principles of halakhic decision-making are all intended to fulfill this requirement, and all require good judgment not only of Halakhah, but of the "carrying capacity"—the amount of extra effort and expense and danger the *tzibbur* can tolerate. And that requires intimate knowledge of, and the capacity to take into account, the *tzibbur*'s limitations.

The ultimate purpose of Torah study, as of the mitzvot in general, is thus to increase the honor of Heaven, and this must be kept in mind even as the student of Torah enjoys the pleasures of the creative use of his intellect and the expression of individuality inherent in Torah study. And woe betide any Torah scholar who somehow fails in that task and thus does not increase, or even worse, diminishes that honor. In the end the expression of one's creativity and the joy of intellectual labor must contribute to the task of preparing the way for the creation of a Torah society that will be a *kiddush Hashem*. But if we succeed, even partially, we will have fulfilled both ourselves as individuals and our designated role in society, and with it, brought the Redemption that much closer!

V

Humans' powers of evaluation and judgment, creativity, renewal and self-(re)fashioning are no more evident than in the process of *teshuvah*, as described by Rav Hutner in *Paḥad Yitzḥak*, which has been investigated by Shlomo Kasirer in his dissertation. In describing this Hutnerian approach, Kasirer focuses on *Paḥad Yitzḥak*, Yom Kippur 19.3-4. Paragraph 4 traces the implications of the Maharal's interpretation of Yoma 86b:

> אמר רבי יצחק, אמרי במערבא משמיה דרבה בר מרי: בא וראה שלא כמדת הקדוש ברוך הוא מדת בשר ודם. מדת בשר ודם, מקניט את חבירו בדברים - ספק מתפייס הימנו ספק אין מתפייס הימנו, ואם תאמר מתפייס הימנו - ספק מתפייס בדברים ספק אין מתפייס בדברים. אבל הקדוש ברוך הוא, אדם עובר עבירה בסתר - מתפייס ממנו בדברים, שנאמר קחו עמכם דברים ושובו אל ה', ולא עוד אלא שמחזיק לו טובה, שנאמר וקח טוב, ולא עוד אלא שמעלה עליו הכתוב כאילו הקריב פרים, שנאמר ונשלמה פרים שפתינו. שמא תאמר פרי חובה - תלמוד לומר ארפא משובתם אהבם נדבה.
>
> R. Isaac said: In the West [Israel] they said in the name of Rabbah b. Mari: Come and see how different from the character of one of flesh and blood is the action of the Holy One, blessed be He. As to the character of one of flesh and blood, if one angers his fellow, it is a matter of doubt whether he [the latter] will be pacified by him or not. And even if you would say [that] he can be pacified, it is doubtful whether he will be pacified by mere words. But with the Holy One, blessed be He, if a man commits a sin in secret, He is pacified by mere words, as it is said: Take with you words, and return unto the Lord (Hos 14:3). Still more: He even accounts it to him as a good deed, as it is said: And accept that which is good. Still more: Scripture

> accounts it to him as if he had offered up bullocks, as it is said: So will we render for bullocks the offerings of our lips. Perhaps you will say [the reference is to] obligatory bullocks. Therefore it is said: I will heal their backsliding, I will love them freely (Hos 14:5).

The Maharal is astounded that one who sins and thus throws off the yoke of mitzvot still has an obligation to repent, and, moreover, his repentance is considered by G-d as equivalent to a free-will offering.[31] After noting that this interpretation "pierces the heavens" and that "it is impossible to exaggerate the magnitude of this *hiddush* and its profundity," Rav Hutner lays out the paradox it embodies: while one who performs a mitzvah is deemed as one who merely fulfills his obligations, one who repents after sinning and performs a mitzvah is deemed as one who has gone *beyond his obligation* and has volunteered a free-will offering, Rav Hutner explains:

> ד....מכיון דעבודת התשובה היא עבודה של התחדשות ושינוי מן הקודם, הרי השינוי והתחדשות הקיום יוצרים הם את התחדשות ההתחייבות. הקיום וההתחייבות של אותו קיום בבת אחת הם חלים. כאילו הקיום הוא הוא שיוצר את ההתחייבות, ואין כאן התחייבות הקודמת לקיום. וכל זה הוא כי מכיוון שהקיום הוא מחודש, הרי הוא נחשב התחלה, ואין שום דבר קודם להתחלה....ובזה אנו אומרים שאותה נקודת התחלה שהתשובה מחזירה לה את בעליה היא התחלה ממש המפקיעה את בעליה מכל ענין קדום ממנה. וכל קיום שאין לו התחלה של התחייבות הרי הוא בודאי קיום נדבה. וזה הוא שהנבואה אומרת על בעלי תשובה 'אוהבם נדבה'....
>
> ו....אם הפרישה מן החטא היא בתורת תשובה, בעל כרחך שיש כאן דעת של שינוי ודעת של התחדשות, ודעת של ניתוח בין העבר להוה. וכל שיש כאן ניתוח ומקום חתך, ממילא נוצרה בכאן נקודת התחלה, ונקודת-התחלה זו מפקיעה היא כל התחייבות קודמת, כמו שגילתה לנו הנבואה במאמרה "אוהבם נדבה", וכל פרשת התשובה מתרוממת ומתעלית מריצוי של חובה לעודף ריצוי של נדבה.

> 4....Since the [spiritual] work of repentance is one of renewal and change from what precedes (התחדשות ושינוי מן הקודם), this change and renewal of the fulfillment [of the mitzvah of repentance] create the renewal of obligation [which has been nullified by the previous sin—YE] which came into being at the same time, as though the fulfillment [of the mitzvah of repentance] is what *creates* [italics mine—YE] the obligation [as though] there had been no previous obligation [which had been nullified by the sin]....In this [respect] we say that that point of beginning to which repentance returns him [=the one who repents] is truly a beginning that frees (מפקיע) him from every issue that preceded. And any fulfillment [of a mitzvah]

---

31 *Netiv ha-Teshuvah*, p. 155.

> that has nothing to precede it is certainly deemed an offering, and that is why the prophecy says of one who repents "I love them freely (lit., 'as a freewill offering')….
> 6….If this separation from (his previous) sinning comes by means of repentance, inevitably there is an awareness of change and an awareness of renewal, and an awareness of a break from the past to the present. And insofar that there is that break and a place of separation (מקום חתך), ineluctably there is a point of a (new) beginning, and this frees (מפקיע) [the sinner] from any previous obligation, as the prophecy reveals to us with the phrase "I love them as a free-will offering." And this process of repentance is elevated (מתרוממת ומתעלית) from the (mere) status of obligation to that of a free-will offering.

As Kasirer explains:

> After [the sinner] has thrown off G-d's yoke, and thus has explicitly announced that he is no longer under the yoke of [the] mitzvah [that he has transgressed], from then on the obligation [to perform mitzvot] no longer serves as an authoritative motivation for fulfilling the mitzvot. For that reason, [the sinner's] decision to repent is thus an original movement (תנועה ראשונית)—a voluntary gesture, the expression of the free-will offering of the heart. Thus, the fulfillment of mitzvot after repentance is conceived as the expression of good will that issues from total freedom….The motivation of a *ba'al teshuvah* not to repeat his sin is different from that of the "usual" G-d-fearing individual [who has not sinned]. The refraining from sinning again of the former is tied to his repentance, which opened up an absolutely new chapter in his life, [different] from the obedience to an obligation that had existed before (Yom Kippur 19.6; Rosh Hashanah 29.6)….[32] The *ba'al teshuvah* accepts the yoke of the mitzvot autonomously, in contrast to the righteous person [who has not

---

32 As Kasirer notes, here Rav Hutner "neutralizes" the kabbalistic intent of the Maharal, for whom "the concept of returning to the beginning functions…in a Neo-Platonic sense: an ontological return to G-d," while Rav Hutner interprets the concept of return to the beginning in only a practical sense, as a conscious sign of the ability to break the bond of the past and turn a new page. This example may serve as an additional example of [Steven S.] Schwartzschild's observation regarding the rationalization of mysticism in Rav Hutner's work (Kasirer, p. 142). However, it should be noted that Rav Hutner may well have modeled his policy on that of the Maharal, who almost always does the same. The result has been an ongoing debate over whether there are kabbalistic elements in the

> sinned], whose acceptance of the mitzvot has a heteronomic character. More precisely: in the *ba'al teshuvah* autonomy and heteronomy converge [for the heteronomy spoken of here is not Kantian, and does not relate to the substance of the Law, which remains totally divine, but only as a decision of acceptance]. In this concept Rav Hutner's immanent goal comes to expression, along with the intention to mix the obligation that comes from without with the free-will decision that comes from within. Similarly, the view of repentance as a present without a past is based on the original meaning of continual becoming (ההתהוות המתמדת), which expresses in a complete manner the present....[33]

As Kasirer rightly stresses, this stress on "continual becoming" has a goal: the unification of a person's character and abilities in order to employ even his "evil inclination" for good, which we, for our part, may identify with the ḥasidic *avodah be-gashmiyut* ("worship through corporeality"), along with intense Torah study, as we noted above.[34] The theoretical grounding of the place of renewal within one's spiritual life is set out in *Paḥad Yitzḥak*, Pesaḥ 76.14-5, but its length and complexity cannot be presented here; instead, here is Kasirer's reworked and condensed version:

> Rav Hutner emphasizes the ideal situation of repentance rather than discoursing on the parameters of sin. However, in the few places he deals with sin, evil is described as an outgrowth of the failure of the forces of renewal in coming to expression.[35] In this way he interprets the statement of Ḥazal that "a person's evil inclination gathers strength over him and is renewed every day, and were it not for the help that the Holy One, blessed be He, provides, he would not overcome it, as it is said: 'The wicked watch the righteous, and seek to slay him' (Qid 30b)."[36] The entire goal of the evil inclination is to enable the existence of free will by setting the person before two equally powerful choices. Therefore, in essence there is no place for the strengthening of the creation of the evil inclination to the point

---

Maharal's thought, and if there are, to what extent. Indeed, the same debate could be carried out in regard to *Paḥad Yitzḥak*.

33 Kasirer, pp. 141-142. The translation is mine.

34 See Norman Lamm, *The Religious Thought of Hasidism: Text and Commentary*, New York: Yeshiva University Press, 1999, pp. 371–385.

35 For a similar thought see Rav Yonatan David, *Quntras Pesaḥ* 4.7: והכלל הוא שיצירה או רעיון שהתחיל לצאת לדרך ולא נתממש קורין לו "נפל". The rule is that a creation or thought that is about to come forth but is not actualized is called a "stillbirth."

36 As Kasirer notes, this is a combination of two statements in Qid 30b, that of R. Yitzhak and that of R. Shimon b. Levi.

of making a person unable to cope with it without divine help. Moreover, the phrase "a person's evil inclination is **renewed** against him every day," does not fit the nature of evil, for the power of renewal is a power of the good, and is nurtured by an expectation of the future of which it is said, "In the future the Holy One, blessed be He, will renew the world," and this future, which approaches and comes into being, extinguishes the power of evil. If so, what then is the meaning of evil's power of renewal? The answer is that indeed, by itself, evil has no independent power of renewal, but its powers are nurtured in a parasitical fashion by the powers of the renewal of the good which do not come to expression in a positive and holy manner. Since evil receives its nourishment as a product of the weakening of the good, the person himself, by means of his free will, creates the powers of renewal for evil. That is the meaning of the verse "the wicked look to the righteous," that is, evil looks for [the opportunity when] the powers of renewal of the good will fall into its possession from the righteous person's table ([*Paḥad Yitzḥak*,] Pesaḥ 76, 15). The upshot is that evil has no basic and original power of its own, but such powers are a defective by-product of the life-force that has not found its expression in an ordered manner. These words remind one of the modern humanistic concept that sees the origin of the human problematic is a defective life that does not bring the person's powers and abilities to full fruition.[37]

Another aspect of this question is brought out in *Ma'amarei Paḥad Yitzḥak* Sukkot 65.7:

ז. מעתה יתבאר לפנינו קטרוגה של מדת האמת לפני הקב"ה בשעת בריאת האדם שטענה "אל יברא שכולו שקרים". וכנגד קטרוג זה נאמר "ותשלך אמת ארצה", ורק על ידי השלכת מדת האמת ארצה נתאפשרה בריאת האדם. ואל לנו להתפס לקטנות הדעת בהבנת דברי חז"ל אלו, שהחשש שאדם יוכל להכשל באמירת שקר הוא שמוליד טענת "אל יברא". אלא שכך הוא מובנה של טענת "אמת": מדת האמת מחייבת נאמנות ותלות על המקור. ומכיון שמהות האדם מונחת בכוח הבחירה שלו, ובמדה שאדם הוא בעל בחירה יכול לעשות עצמו אמצעי מבלי להשאר נאמן למקורו, (ולא רק בבחירת הרע, אלא בעצם עובדת היותו בוחר, יש בו עצמאות), לכן באה מדת האמת וטוענת נגד בחירה זו: "אל יברא".

And now the charge of the characteristic of Truth before the Holy One, blessed be He, at the time of the creation of humanity can be explained: [Truth] argued "Let him not be created since he is all falsehood." And against this charge it is said: "He flung truth to the earth" [Genesis Rabba 8.4, Dan 8:12]. And it was only through this flinging of truth to the earth that the creation of humanity was made

37 Kasirer, pp. 138-139.

possible. Let us not be small-minded in our understanding of the words of our Sages, may their memory be blessed, that [it is only] because of the concern that humanity may stumble in uttering falsehood that brought forth the argument that "let him not be created." Rather, this is the argument of the "Truth": the characteristic of truth requires faithfulness to and dependency on the Source. And since the essence of humanity lies in his power of free-will, to the degree to which a person is a creature of free-will he is able to make himself independent without remaining faithful to his Source, (and not just in choosing evil, but from the mere fact of his possessing free-will, he has this independence), that is why Truth comes and argues against this choice: "Let him not be created."

In light of all this we may understand Rav Hutner's declaration that there are people whose stature is not diminished by their sin(s), though there are also people whose stature is diminished. Here are parts of *Paḥad Yitzhak* Yom Kippur 11:

נפלא הוא הענין העומד כאן לדיון, כי על כן נושא הדיון הזה את חזונו על סוגי מדת סליחתו יתברך, כפי שהם משתקפים בנפשו של אדם הזוכה לסליחה. ונתחיל ונאמר. על כחה של מדת התשובה אמרו חכמים: גדולה תשובה שמקרבת את הגאולה שנאמר ובא לציון גואל ולשבי פשע ביעקב. גאולה בסמיכות לשבי פשע. וכתב על זה המהר"ל: והיינו דמצינו דיום כיפור דשנת היובל הוא זמן גאולה תתנו לארץ, גאולה תהיה, זמן שעבדים משתחררים ושבים לבתיהם, שבו שדות ונחלות חוזרות לבעליהן, בזמן שהכל שבים למצבם הראשון. יום-כיפור שהוא זמן התשובה, בו מתקיימת המצוה של גאולה תהיה לכם. וברור הוא דכונתו של המהר"ל בהוספה היא להורות לנו שלא נחשוב כי הצירוף הזה של תשובה לגאולה, לא נאמר אלא בגאולה דאחרית הימים, וכפשוטו של הפסוק דשבי פשע ביעקב. ובכדי להוציא שורש גדול לצירוף זה של תשובה לגאולה. ואף על גב דכל יום כיפור הרי הוא מיוחד לתשובה, וצירוף זה של גאולה לתשובה אינו מתקיים אלא ביום-כיפור של יובל. מכל מקום, דעת לנבון נקל, כי כל האורות של יום-כיפור של יובל אינם אלא קיבוץ אורות של כל מועדי יום כיפור של היובל. וכל יום כיפור ויום-כיפור של כל שנות היובל מוסר את אורו ליום-כיפור של היובל. והסך הכל של האורות הללו מוליד הוא את השלהבת הקודש של כל מיני הקדושה של יום-כיפור של שנת היובל. ואם אנו רואים את הצירוף של תשובה לגאולה מופיע במלא הדרו ביום כיפור של שנת החמישים, בעל כרחך שכל יום כיפור לחוד יונק הוא את כחו מן הצירוף הזה של תשובת גאולה, אלא שאין הצירוף הזה מתבלט עד שנת החמישים, שרק אז בשנת החמישים מסתכמים כל חמישים ימי-הכיפור ליחידה אחת. אבל בעצם יונק הוא כל יום-כיפור לחוד את כחו מצירוף זה של גאולה לתשובה.

1. The matter that stands before us for discussion is wondrous, for the subject of this discussion is the vision of the types of [G-d's] characteristic of forgiveness, may He be blessed, as they are reflected

in the soul of one who merits forgiveness. And so we will begin. On the power of the characteristic of repentance our Sages have said: Great is the power of repentance that brings the Redemption closer, as it is said: "And a redeemer shall come to Zion, and to the repentant of the sin of Jacob"—Redemption together with repentance. And the Maharal has written on this: That is, we find that the Yom Kippur of the Jubilee year is the time of "give redemption to the land," "there shall be redemption," a time when slaves are freed and return to their houses, when fields and estates return to their [original] owners, at the time when everyone returns to their original status. Yom Kippur, which is the time of repentance, is the time in which the mitzvah of "there shall be a redemption for you" is fulfilled. It is clear that the Maharal's intention with this addition [to the Sages' words] is to teach us that we should not think that this combination of repentance and redemption was meant only for the Redemption of Messianic times, as the simple meaning of the verse "to those who repent in Jacob" would seem to indicate. In order to preclude such an understanding, the Maharal wrote that even in regard to the laws of the Torah is this combination of repentance and redemption to be found at this time, even though every Yom Kippur is specially dedicated to repentance, and this combination of repentance and redemption is fulfilled only on the Yom Kippur of the Jubilee year. Nevertheless, understanding is easy for the discerning, [and we must understand] that all the lights of the Jubilee Yom Kippur are only the gathering of the lights of the festivals of the Yom Kippur[s] of the Jubilee. And each and every Yom Kippur of all the years of the Jubilee [cycle] contributes its light to the Yom Kippur of the Jubilee. And the sum total of these lights kindles the holy flame of all the types of holiness inherent in the Yom Kippur of the Jubilee year. And if we see the joining of repentance and redemption appear in its full glory in the Yom Kippur of the fiftieth year, we must understand that each individual Yom Kippur receives its nourishment from this joining of repentance and redemption, but this joining is not discerned until the fiftieth year, for only in the fiftieth year do all the Yom Kippurs sum up to one unit. But in essence each individual Yom Kippur gains its power from the joining of repentance and redemption.

ג. ...העמוד הזה [של טיבו של תשובה] נתגלה לנו מתורתו של הגר"א. הנה המקרא אומר על דוד המלך שהוא הגבר הוקם על. ופירשו חכמים בזה שהוא הקים עולה של תשובה. וכתב הגר"א דעולה של תשובה בכאן הכונה היא מלשון עלייה, כלומר, דוד הקים עליתה של תשובה. והענין הוא, שאדם הראשון לאחר שחטא, קיים בעצמו סדר נורא של ק"ל שנה בתשובה. ומכל מקום לא הוחזר לגן עדן, ובני ישראל לאחר תשובתם על חטא העגל לא קיבלו שוב את הלוחות

הראשונות. שאול, גם אחרי אמרו חטאתי נקרעה ממנו המלכות, ללא חזור אליו עוד. ואילו דוד, לאחר תשובתו, חזרה אליו המלכות, כמו שהיתה מקודם. והיינו מה שהקים עולה של תשובה, דהיינו שהקים עלייתה של תשובה. תשובה למקומה הראשון, בלי שום הורדה.

ד. בכדי לדלות את משמעותה של מרגניתא זו נקדים את החק שחז"ל השרישו בנו, כי יש אדם שגבוה מעונותיו, ויש אדם שעונותיו גבוהים ממנו. חז"ל הורו לנו ענין זה במאמרם על הפסוק "אשרי נשוי פשע". פסוק זה נדרש הוא אצל חז"ל ש"נשוי" פשע הוא מלשון התנשאות, כגון אדם הנושא משא על ראשו שהמשא מרומם ומתנשא עליו. ובלשונם ז"ל אמרו "אשרי אדם שגבוה מעונותיו". מה הוא, איפוא, תוכן מעלתו של אדם המתנשא ומתרומם על גבי עונותיו? משום שנקודת-התמצית של הענין היא עדינה מאוד, לכן כדאי להשתמש בכאן במשל פשוט דוקא. הנה בחצר המלך, בין משרתיו, נמצאים הם בודאי כמה וכמה חילוקי מדרגות. ישנם כאלה שנתמנו על תפקיד קל בעל ערך פחות, וישנם כאלה שנתמנו על תפקיד מסובך שכל מעמדו של המלך תלוי בו. ישנם חסרונות וישנם יתרונות מכל אחד מסוגי המשרתים הללו. גם לשר היותר גדול יש לו בחינות לטוב שלו וברע שלו, וכמו כן ישנן בחינות כאלו לעבד היותר שפל. אבל הבדל הערך העיקרי שיש בין השר ובין העבד, הוא במקום הנגיעה של פעולתם. שפעולתו של השר, בין בחסרונו ובין ביתרונו גם הטוב שלו וגם הרע שלו נוגעים בעיקרי הנהגת המלכות, בעוד שהעבד, גם חסרונו וגם יתרונו נוגעים הם בפרט קטן של קרן זוית בחצר המלכות. ונמצא, שמלבד החילוק אם נידון בטוב או ברע לפי מעשיו, יש עוד חילוק, באיזו נקודה נוגעת היא גם טובתו וגם רעתו, גם יתרונו וגם חסרונו.

ה. והוא הדין והיא המדה גם בעולם הנשמות. אין לנו שום מושג ושום ידיעה במטמניות הללו. אבל ברור לנו, שישנן נשמות, שמעשי בעליהן בין לטוב ובין לרע נוגעות במקום יותר עליון ויותר עיקרי מאשר נשמות זולתם. מלבד הבחינה של כל אחד אם מעשיו טובים או רעים, ישנה עוד בחינה של מקום הנגיעה של מעשיו, ובעוד שטמונים הם ממנו השינויים בין איש ובין רעהו, הנה עוד יותר נעלם ממנו החילוק בין סוגי החטאים, איזו חטאים נוגעים הם רק במשקל טוב ורע שע"י כל אחד, ואיזו חטאים נוגעים הם גם במשקל נקודת מקום הנגיעה של כל אחד להרמה או להורדה. וכל החשבונות והשינויים הללו נכללים הם בהדי כבשי דרחמנא והוא הוא מדרגתו של האדם העומד למעלה מעונותיו. דהיינו שלמרות חומר הרע הנמצא בחטאו, במשקל טוב ורע שלו, מכל מקום עונותיו לא גרמו לו הורדה ממקום נגיעתו. והדברים נוקבים עד כדי כך, עד שחכמים המציאו מקום לומר "אשרי" אפילו בשאול תחתית. שהלא יתכן שאדם נענש על חטאו בעונש של שאול תחתית, מכל מקום כל זה הוא בתחום משקלו של טוב ורע, אבל מכיון שעל ידי עונש זה מקום-נגיעתו לא הורד, הרי הוא גבוה מעונותיו. וחכמים אומרים על אדם זה הנמצא במעמקי-שאול "אשרי". אשרי נשוי פשע, אשרי אדם שגבוה מעונותיו.

3...This pillar [of the nature of repentance] was [also] revealed to us through the teaching of the GRA. Behold, Scripture says of King David that he is the man "raised by the yoke." And the Sages interpreted this [to mean] that he raised the yoke of repentance. And the GRA wrote that the meaning of the yoke of repentance here refers to [the derivation of *ol*, "yoke"] from [a root] denoting "elevation" (עלייה), that is, David raised the elevation of repentance. The matter is [as follows]: Adam after he sinned arranged for himself a terrible regimen of 130 years of repentance. And nevertheless, he was not returned to the Garden of Eden; likewise, the Israelites, after they repented of the sin of the Golden Calf, did not receive back the original Tablets [of the Ten Commandments]. [Again,] Saul, [even] after he admitted "I sinned"—the kingship was still torn from him, with no return. However, as to David, after his repentance, the kingship was restored to him, as it was before. And that is the meaning that he raised the yoke of repentance, that is, that he raised the importance of repentance, repentance [in the sense of return] to its original place, without diminution.

4. In order to draw out the meaning of this pearl we must preface it with the law that our Sages implanted in us, that there is a man who is greater (lit., "higher") than his sins, and there is a man whose sins are greater than he. Our Sages taught us this in their statement regarding the verse "Happy is he who is forgiven (where the Hebrew means, literally, "raised from sin"). This verse is expounded by our Sages that [the phrase] נשוי פשע is derived from the root of "elevation," as a man carries a burden on his head where the burden is higher and more elevated than he, and, as though they said, may their memory be blessed, "Happy is the man who is greater than his sins." What then, is the nature (lit., "content") of the degree of this man who is elevated above his sins? Since the essential point of this is subtle indeed, it is fitting to employ a metaphor that is particularly simple. Thus, in a king's court, his many servants are divided by degree: some have been appointed to fulfill a simple task of a minor nature, and some have been appointed to fulfill a complicated task upon which the very standing of the king depends. Each one of these classes of the king's servants has abilities and deficiencies. Even the greatest minister has pluses and minuses, and so too those who are of the lowest order. But the essential difference between a minister and a servant is to be found in the nature of their task (lit., "the place of their attachment to their activities [for the king]"). For the function of the minister, whether by his abilities or deficiencies, for his good or bad qualities, touches upon the essential governance of the state, while the function of the servant, whether by his disability or ability, touches only upon a small corner of the [king's] court. The upshot is that, aside from the difference in the standards of judgment of the minister or the servant, the consequences, for good or evil, depend on the minister or servant's authority and function.

5. And this applies likewise to the world of souls. We have no knowledge or concept of these hidden matters. But it is [nevertheless] clear to us, that there are souls whose owners' deeds, whether for good or ill, touch upon a place that is higher and more essential than the souls of others. [Thus,] aside from the aspect [of judgment] as to whether an individual's deeds are good or bad, there is another aspect that derives from the point of contact of his deeds. And though the differences between a person and his fellow are hidden from us, the difference between the various categories of sin are even more hidden from us, which sins touch on the weighing of good and bad that applies to everyone, and which sins touch upon the point of contact of each individual in regard to elevation [of status] or diminution [thereof]. And all these calculations and differences are in the keeping of the Merciful One—and this is the status of one who stands higher than his sins. That is, despite the heinousness of the evil that is to be found in his sin, in the weighing of good and evil, nevertheless his sins have not caused a diminution in his point of contact. These matters are so penetrating that our Sages provided a place for [this status] so as to say "Happy [is he]" who may be [consigned] to the lowest point of Sheol. For it is possible that a person may be consigned to the lowest point of Sheol as punishment for his sin, nevertheless, this is from the aspect of the weighing of good and evil, but inasmuch as this punishment does not touch upon point of contact [in regard to his function], which is not diminished, he remains above his sins. And [thus] the Sages say of this person consigned to the lowest point of Sheol, "happy"—happy is he who is *nasui pesha'*, happy is a man who is above his sins.

ו. וממשיכים אנו את הקו הלאה לתוך עולמה של תשובה, ואנו אומרים: כל ההבטחות על פעולת התשובה המוחקת והכובשת את הרע ואת החטא לא ניתנו אלא בגבול המשקל של טוב ורע. כלומר, שמעשיו הרעים לא יחשבו ויתכפרו, ואפילו הזדונות יתהפכו לזכיות, ואפילו יזכה להארת פנים, ושיהא מרוצה לפני המקום. וכל זה כתוצאה מתשובתו—מכל מקום אין זה מכריח כלל וכלל, שגם במשקל הבחינה של מקום הנגיעה שלו פעלה התשובה. ואין כאן שום ברירות, שיוחזר לו מקום הנגיעה שהיתה לו מקודם. את החטא בודאי שהתשובה עוקרת למפרע, אבל אותו מקום הנגיעה שהיה חלקו לפני החטא, זה כבר חלף ועבר לבלי שוב.

6. And we [now] extend the line further into the world of repentance, and we say: All the promises regarding the effect of repentance, which wipes out and crushes the evil and the sin, apply only within the bounds of the weighing of good and evil. That is to say, his evil deeds will not be considered and will be atoned for, and even the intentional sins will be accounted as merits, and even [if] he merits the shining of the Face, that he will be in a state of approval before

the Omnipresent, and all this as a result of his repentance—nevertheless, all this does not inevitably require that repentance will be effective in regard to the aspect of his point of contact that he had had before. That sin repentance certainly uproots in advance, but that point of contact that was his portion before the sin—that has already passed from him, never to return.
Nevertheless,

ט. ונכונים אנו עכשיו לחזור לדברי מהר"ל, שהורה לנו שיש יחוד בסליחות יום-כיפור לגבי הסליחות שתשובה פועלת בשאר ימות השנה. ויחוד זה הוא מפני שתשובת יום-כיפור היא בדרך גאולה כדחזינן ביום כיפור של יובל. ועמדנו בצמאון להבהרת הבדל בין התוכן של שני סוגי תשובה הללו. ואמנם לאחר שנקלט בנו שפע האור של המאמר הזה, הצמאון נהפך לרויה. כי הלא כל ההבדל הזה נובע הוא מיום-כיפור של יובל. ומכיון דעיקר הבליטה בענינו של יום-כיפור דיובל הוא החזרה והשיבה למקום הראשון אשר ממנו יצאו, עבדים נפטרים לבתיהם, ושדות ונחלות חוזרות לבעליהן, וזה הוא הגאולה הניתנת לארץ, הרי בודאי שהסליחה והכפרה של יום כיפור זה באות הן על דרך השיבה והחזרה למקום הראשון, הרי שבתשובה זו של יום-כיפור הפועלת סליחה, הרי היא מחזירה גם את נקודת-נגיעה הקודמת. שאין לך שיבה למשפחתו ולנחלתו גדולה מזו. והלא כבר למדנו שמה שנעשה ביום-כיפור של יובל בכלל, הוא הוא שנעשה בכל יום-כיפור בפרט. וכאן הוא המקום שבו צירף המהר"ל תשובה לגאולה. וגילה לנו כי סליחה דיום-כיפור היא סליחה בדרך גאולה. ישמע חכם ויוסף לקח, ומלבו יוציא מלים, להכניס את האור הזה לתוך חדרי-לבבו.

9. We are now prepared to return to the Maharal, who taught us about the special quality of the forgiveness of Yom Kippur, in contrast to the forgiveness that repentance achieves during the rest of the year. This special quality is because the repentance of Yom Kippur is by means of redemption, as we see regarding the Yom Kippur of the Jubilee year. And we stood, thirstily, to [hear] the clarification of the difference between these two types of repentance. However, since the abundance of light of this *ma'amar* has been absorbed into us, the thirst has turned to overabundance. For [we have seen that], indeed, this entire difference flows from the [unique quality] of the Yom Kippur of the Jubilee year. And since the entire significance of the Yom Kippur of the Jubilee year inheres in the return to one's origins, slaves return to their houses, and fields and inheritance return to their owners, and this is the redemption that is given to the land, then certainly the forgiveness and atonement of this Yom Kippur come by means of return to the origin, then indeed the repentance of this Yom Kippur, which provides forgiveness, must then return [the repentant] to his previous contact-point, for there is no greater return to one's family and estate. We have already learned that what is accomplished on the Jubilee Yom Kippur in general is

what is accomplished on each Yom Kippur. And here is the place in which the Maharal combined repentance and redemption. He thus revealed to us that the forgiveness of Yom Kippur is a forgiveness accomplished by means of redemption. Let the wise hear and add [additional] lessons [to it], and from his heart will come forth words, in order to allow this light to enter the chambers of his heart.

In an enlightening comparison between the conceptions of repentance in the works of Rav Y. B. Soloveitchik and Rav Hutner in his dissertation, Shlomo Kasirer observes that:

> In the view of Rav Hutner, as in the view of Rav Y.B. Soloveitchik..., *haratah* (regret) aids in the accomplishment of the psychic separation between the past and the present. However, while for Rav Soloveitchik the emphasis is on the separation from the past, for Rav Hutner the emphasis is on the turn to the future....

> And in this context he quotes *Pahad Yitzhak* Yom Kippur 19.7:

> ז... ה'להבא' הזה היא דפיקת הנפש המכה על האדם ואומרת לו 'גזורו'. נפרד הוא היום מן האתמול. שוב אינני אותו האיש שהייתי. ה'להבא' הזה היא פעולת ניתוח בנפש. ה'להבא' הזה הוא מקום החתך בנפשו של המתהפך מדרך לדרך. מקום חתך זה הוא הוא המקפל בתוכו את דעת השינוי ואת דעת ההתחדשות (יו"כ יט, ז).

> The [Rambam's stress on acceptance of a new lifestyle in the future]—*'lehaba'* ("to come") is the soul's knocking [on the door] of the person['s psyche] and saying to him: Cut [yourself off from your past]. Today is separate from yesterday. "I am no longer the person I was yesterday." This "to come" is the action in the soul of cutting off. This "to come" is precisely the place of the cutting off in the soul of the one who turns from one path to another. The placement of this cut is where he combines within himself the intention of change and the intention of renewal.

And in a footnote he refers to a similar statement in *Pahad Yitzhak* Rosh Hashanah 29.6:

> תכנו הנפשי של הקבלה להבא הוא ההכרה הפנימית הברורה כי על ידי הפרישה מן החטא אני מעמידים חתך בחיינו, ואנו מפלגים את חיינו לחצאים. חלק אחד של חיינו הוא לפני התשובה, ומן התשובה ואילך מתחיל החלק השני בחיינו.

> The psychic content of acceptance for the future is the clear inner recognition that by this separation from the sin we are establishing a division in our lives, and we are dividing our lives into two. One part

> of our lives is [that] before repentance, and from that repentance onward begins the second part of our lives.[38]

We have thus examined a number of *motifs* that find their place in the system that unfolds in the pages of *Paḥad Yitẓhak*, whose underlying theme stems from Slobodka: *gadlut ha-adam*, the greatness of man, his intellect and human creativity, which is also an index of human individuality and the self-fashioning that accompanies repentance. Along with these, there is also the theme of renewal, in which a person recreates himself through the process of repentance. All these *motifs* coalesce to form the essential elements of an optimistic, humanistic message, one that provides a strong underpinning for the maintenance of Jewish tradition in an increasingly hostile world. ☙

---

38 Kasirer, p. 161.

Kabbalah—Escape from Reality or Affirmation of Life?

A Response to Lippman Bodoff, "Jewish Mysticism: Medieval Roots, Contemporary Dangers and Prospective Challenges"[1]

By: BEZALEL NAOR

Lippman Bodoff's bold new credo is packed into the following explosive statement:

> I believe, therefore, that the new ascetic-mystical spirituality of Ashkenazi Jewry arose not as an inevitable organic development from within rabbinic culture, but as a result of on-going Christian persecution and pressure, and a resulting sense of vulnerability and hopelessness of any redemption through history. If so, the progeny of that historical trauma, represented in Jewish mystical movements and their many forms of escapist, separatist, anti-rationalist, esoteric, and ascent religiosity, which have engulfed Judaism in the last one thousand years, culminating in Hasidism for the past two hundred and fifty years, is subject to reexamination and question in the radically new situation of Jews and Judaism in the twenty-first century... Today's scholars have a right and even a duty to consider whether at least some of these ascetic and mystical ideas and practices, having arisen as responses to historical trauma, may no longer be relevant,

---

1 <http://www.edah.org/backend/coldfusion/search/document.cfm?title=Jewish+Mysticism:+Medieval+Roots,+Contemporary+Dangers+and+Prospective+Challenges&hyperlink=Bodoff3_1.htm&type=JournalArticle&category=Orthodoxy+and+Modernity&authortitle&firstname=Lippman&lastname=Bodoff&pubsource=not+available&authorid=531&pdfattachment=Bodoff3_1.pdf>

Bezalel Naor is the author of several works of Jewish Thought, with a concentration on Kabbalah, Hasidism and Rav Kook. His most recent books are: *Kana'uteh de-Pinḥas* (2013), an analysis of the critique of the *Leshem Shevo ve-Aḥlamah* by Rabbi Pinhas Hakohen Lintop of Birzh; *Maḥol la-Tsaddikim* (2015), an exploration of the controversy between Rabbi M.H. Luzzatto and Rabbi Eizik of Homel concerning the purpose of creation; and a new edition of Rav Kook's seminal work, *Orot* (2015).

and may perhaps even be dangerous to Judaism today.

Without doubt, Bodoff's article is one of the most original essays to enter public Jewish discourse in the past several years. Whether one subscribes to its historic thesis and contemporary ramifications or not (and the present writer has serious reservations in both regards), Bodoff's article is a must-read for any committed student of Kabbalah. Having said that, let me proceed to my response to Bodoff's analysis of Jewish Mysticism.

What is most refreshing to a student of Jewish Mysticism or Kabbalah who reads Lippman Bodoff's article is the shifting of focus from Provence to *Ashkenaz*. Since the meteoric appearance of Gershom Scholem's *Das Buch Bahir* in Leipzig in 1923, academic students of Kabbalah have been primed that the esoteric wisdom originated in Provence. Bodoff has moved the cradle of Kabbalah from the sunny Mediterranean clime of Provence to the dark, dour surroundings of the German Rhineland. In so doing, the essayist has effected not only a geographic shift but a major shift in terms of worldview.

What, the reader may ask, is refreshing about this perspective? Well, for one, if pursued properly, it would acknowledge the influence of the *Ḥasidei Ashkenaz*, those Rhenish pietists, on the development of the *Zohar*. True, the *Zohar* (not undeservedly referred to on occasion as "the Bible of Jewish Mysticism"), which surfaces in Castile at the end of the thirteenth century, is deeply indebted to the earlier *Bahir*, but it might appear that traces of Rabbi El'azar of Worm's angelology are to be found in the *Zohar*.[2] (I throw out the *Roke'aḥ*'s angelology as merely one of the many

---

2 I make this bold assertion fully cognizant of the earlier layer of *Hekhalot* literature that undergirds most of the works of Rabbi El'azar of Worms. See Isaiah Tishby, *Commentary on Talmudic Aggadoth by Rabbi Azriel of Gerona*. Jerusalem: Magnes, 1982, p. 38. The correlation of the angelology of the *Zohar* to that of Rabbi El'azar of Worms might be made easier if in Rabbi Reuben Margaliot's encyclopedia *Mal'akhei 'Elyon* the obsolete references to *Sefer Raziel ha-Mal'akh* (Amsterdam, 1701) were updated to *Sodei Razayya* by Rabbi El'azar of Worms. For a survey of *Sodei Razayya*, see Joseph Dan, *History of Jewish Mysticism and Esotericism, The Middle Ages*, Vol. VI. Jerusalem: Zalman Shazar Center for Jewish History, 2011, pp. 493–558.
Moshe Idel writes (perhaps tentatively) that the angelology of Ashkenaz that made its way southward to Sefarad was not that of Ḥasidei Ashkenaz, but that of a rather obscure figure, Rabbi Nehemiah ben Solomon of Erfurt (Rabbi Tröstlin the Prophet), a younger contemporary of Rabbi El'azar of Worms. See M. Idel, *The Angelic World: Apotheosis and Theophany* (Hebrew). Tel-Aviv: Yedioth Aḥronoth, 2008. Idel identified material of Rabbi Nehemiah in *Sefer Raziel*; see

influences of *Ashkenaz* upon the *Zohar*'s mysticism.)[3]

The Angelic World, p. 147. (Thanks to Prof. Yosef Yitzhak Lifshitz who brought Prof. Idel's work on angelology to my attention.)

Elsewhere, I noted a striking similarity between *Hilkhot ha-Kisse* of Rabbi El'azar of Worms and Rabbi Ezra of Gerona's Commentary to Song of Songs 3:10. Cf. *Sodei Razayya* II, ed. Aaron Eisenbach, Jerusalem, 2004, pp. 33, 37 to *Kitvei Ramban*, ed. C.B. Chavel, Vol. II. Jerusalem: Mossad Harav Kook, 1968, p. 494, s.v. *merkavo argaman*. See *Hassagot ha-Rabad le-Mishneh Torah,* ed. Bezalel Naor. Jerusalem: Zur-Ot, 1985. Intro., pp. 23-24, n. 5.

3 The late Israel Ta-Shma was convinced that there are residues of Ashkenazic halakha in the *Zohar*; see I. Ta-Shma, *Ha-Nigleh she-ba-Nistar* (Tel-Aviv, 1995). More recently, Moshe Idel has briefly sketched the profound influence the *Ḥasidei Ashkenaz* or Rhineland Pietists (specifically Rabbi El'azar of Worms) exerted upon the development of Spanish Kabbalah. See Idel's Introduction to *The Hebrew Writings of the Author of Tiqqunei Zohar and Ra'aya Mehemna* (Hebrew), ed. Efraim Gottlieb. Jerusalem: Israel Academy of Sciences and Humanities, 2003, pp. 12–15.

One cannot be but impressed—as was Idel—by the deferential tone assumed by the leader of Catalonian Jewry in the second half of the thirteenth century, Rabbi Solomon ben Abraham Ibn Adret (Rashba), when referring to the spiritual prowess of the German Jewish mystics. How ironic that in the very responsum to the Jewish community of Avila (*She'elot u-Teshuvot Rashba*, Part 1, no. 548) that impugns the so-called "Prophet of Avila," Rashba lauds the extrasensory accomplishments of Abraham of Cologne (who reportedly acted as a medium for Elijah the Prophet). That the acknowledged leader of Spanish Jewry, in the very process of debunking his own countrymen's forays into the *terra incognita* of preterrational consciousness, would so romanticize the prophetic ability of Ashkenazic Jewry, is indeed remarkable. By the same token, while speaking *ad hominem*, the fact that Rashba sponsored Rabbenu Asher ben Yeḥiel (Rosh), a German refugee rabbi (disciple of Rabbi Meir of Rothenburg), to assume the rabbinate of Toledo, also bespeaks enormous respect for the *Ḥakhmei Ashkenaz*. See A.H. Freimann, *Ha-Rosh, Rabbenu Asher ben Rabbi Yeḥiel ve-Tse'etsa'av*. Jerusalem: Mossad Harav Kook, 1986, pp. 28, 158.

Inter alia, in a recent newspaper interview, Haym Soloveitchik observed that generally, halakhic texts moved from North to South, from Ashkenaz to Sefarad, and not vice versa. The one notable exception was Maimonides' code meriting *Hagahot Maimoniyot*, the glosses penned by a disciple of Rabbi Meir (Maharam) of Rothenburg.

> In the volume that already appeared [=Collected Essays, Vol. 1], I address the "one way street" that you mention. For example, the Rosh moved from Germany to Spain in the beginning of the fourteenth century. His Pesakim and the Tur, the work of his son, made their way swiftly to Ashkenaz, but the Hiddushei HaRamban or those of the Rashba never did. The same caravans or boats which brought the

And by the way, there are now scholars who contend that Scholem got the *Bahir* wrong when he conceived it as a Provencal creation. Of late, we are told that the *Bahir* too has its roots in Ashkenaz.[4] So, Bodoff has hit the mark in repositioning the origins of the Kabbalah.

What comes next is highly tendentious, to say the least. Bodoff would have us believe that Jewish Mysticism as it developed in the Rhineland was a direct response to the Crusades and the concomitant martyrdom that befell entire Jewish communities. Their plight is narrated in the *kinot* or elegies that Ashkenazic Jewry recite to this day on the fast of the Ninth of Av. Who has not been touched to the core by the account of the decimation of the once proud communities of Speyers, Worms and Mayence? And in the spiritual laboratory of Ashkenazic Jewry's limitless suffering was spawned the bacillus of—Kabbalah. (I use the term "bacillus" borrowed from the field of Biology to convey the tenor of Bodoff's perception of Jewish Mysticism, which is remarkably similar to that of the Jewish historian Heinrich Graetz. Had Bodoff written in German rather than English, I am convinced that we would have been treated to Graetz's vintage term of *"Schwärmerei"* as a depiction of Kabbalah.)

The problem with this original thesis is the same problem that critics point out in Scholem's much-vaunted thesis that Lurianic Kabbalah was a response to the Spanish Expulsion of 1492. While at first blush there might be something attractive about imagining Luria's "shattering of the vessels" and the cosmic exile of the sparks that ensued, as a trope for the catastrophe that befell Iberian Jewry—the facts do not support this notion. For starters, Isaac Luria was an Ashkenazic Jew born and bred in Egypt.[5] Though Safed, where he spent the last two years of his short life,

---

> Piskei HaRosh to Cologne, could have brought the Hiddushei HaRashba, had people in Germany been interested in them. Apparently, they weren't.

("Interview with Professor Haym Soloveitchik by Rabbi Yair Hoffman," *Five Towns Jewish Times*, Wednesday, January 8th, 2014 <http://www.theyeshivaworld.com/news/headlines-breaking-stories/209453/interview-with-professor-haym-soloveitchik-by-rabbi-yair-hoffman.html>)

Summing up, we see emerging a pattern whereby in both the exoteric and esoteric realms, for some yet unexplained reason, the *Ḥakhmei Sefarad* adopted what one might term a reverential attitude toward the *Ḥakhmei Ashkenaz*.

4 Daniel Abrams "argued for the Ashkenazi composition of the *Bahir* (outside of the German Pietist circles)" (Daniel Abrams, *The Book Bahir: An Edition Based on the Earliest Manuscripts*. Los Angeles: Cherub, 1994, p. *13).

5 Though it seems that Rabbi Moshe Schreiber erred when he wrote that Luria was a Sephardi, his point concerning the Lurianic *kavvanot* or mystical intentions

was populated by Sephardic Jews whose spoken language was Castilian, it does not strike one as convincing that Luria himself would be so moved by the traumatization of Spanish-Portuguese Jewry as to apotheosize their collective experience. He might be duly sympathetic to their ordeal, but that he would develop a cosmogony based on that historic event, beggars the imagination.[6]

Now Bodoff tells us that the mysticism of the Pietists of Ashkenaz (*Ḥasidei Ashkenaz*) was a response to the pillaging and rapine of the Rhenish Jewish communities during the Crusades. Though this thesis does not suffer from the same weakness as that of Scholem, whereby an Ashkenazic Jew takes up the litany of Sephardic Jewry, it does suffer from another major weakness (which in all fairness, Bodoff is sensitive to), namely that of dating. The major catastrophe of the Crusades is centered on the year 1096, while Ashkenazic mysticism reaches its crescendo in Rabbi El'azar of Worms (circa 1176–1238), a full century later. (Scholem's dates tend to be a tad tighter, with Luria [1534–1572] dying but eighty years after the Expulsion of 1492.)

Bodoff's rejoinder might have been that the historic consciousness of those tragic events of 1096 was a palpable reality for the likes of the author of the *Roke'ah*. On the night of 22 Kislev, 1196, Rabbi El'azar was busy composing his commentary on the Book of Genesis, when two men (possibly Crusaders) entered his home and killed his wife Dulce and daughters Belette and Hannah, and wounded his son Jacob. (The elegy *"Tsiyon, halo tish'ali li-shelom 'aluvayikh"* is attributed to Rabbi El'azar of Worms.)

Instead, Bodoff parries by positing something like the collective unconscious of Ashkenazic Jewry:

> I believe the evidence supports the powerful impact of external causes. From the facts developed by Chazan, Soloveitchik and

is well taken. The reason that Luria loaded his *kavvanot* onto the Sephardi rite (*Nusaḥ Sepharad*) was because that was the prayer book in use in Safed in his day. Had Luria transmitted his teachings in an Ashkenazic milieu, he undoubtedly would have adapted the *kavvanot* to the Ashkenazic rite (*Nusaḥ Ashkenaz*). See *She'elot u-Teshuvot Ḥatam Sofer, Oraḥ Ḥayyim,* No. 15(2).

According to Rabbi Ḥayyim Yosef David Azulai, the Ari would pray the entire year in the Sephardi rite with the exception of the Days of Awe, when he would pray in the Ashkenazi rite. See H.Y.D. Azulai, *Yosef Omets* (Livorno, 1798), 20:2; cited in Rabbi Israel of Shklov, *Pe'at ha-Shulhan* (Tsefat, 1836), *Hil. Eretz Yisrael* 3:14 (31). This explains Ari's positive recommendation of the *piyyutim* of Kalir, found in the Ashkenazic *mahzor.*

6 See Moshe Idel, *Kabbalah: New Perspectives.* New Haven: Yale University Press, 1988, p. 265.

> Kanarfogel, it appears that a milder form of asceticism and esotericism developed before the First Crusade in response to a milder Christian hostility at that earlier time, and a more radical Jewish response developed after it—and continued to do so in various forms in the face of new developments and an ever more pervasive, insistent and continuing Christian hostility to Jewry in its Diaspora environment. Therefore, any attempt to discount outside influences as a cause of Jewish mysticism simultaneously ignores not only the psychological mechanism of mystical responses, but that sense of continuing threat and vulnerability created by a triumphant, powerful, zealous, and hostile Christianity during virtually all of the last thousand years. Moreover, looking for *immediate* cause-and-effect manifestations reflects a too rigid and fragmented understanding and expectation regarding the nature of mystical responses, and—in particular—the pervasive and continuing nature of Christian threats and pressures on Jewry, and the Jewish responses to it. Sometimes the impetus to a mystical or messianic response may even be an event that provides hope that an apocalyptic end to history is imminent. But, that, too, is in no way inconsistent with the paradigm I have described. Psychoanalytic studies have shown that mysticism is a psychologically based response to a perceived threat to one's identity, presented by the abyss between the real and the ideal in the world, and can lie dormant for a prolonged period.

In endnote 31 we are told:

> A traumatic external cause may also induce a mystical effect that is not immediate, but survives, "underground" as it were, for a long period, emerging when circumstances are propitious.

All of this is but preparation for Bodoff's central argument and that is that mysticism in general, and Jewish mysticism in particular, poses an escape from reality. Rather than being life-affirming, it is life-negating. This is not the first time that we hear this complaint from a Jewish thinker. Rabbi J.B. Soloveitchik in his study *"Ish ha-Halakha"* (first published in *Talpiyot* in 1944) contrasted the mystic (specifically the adherent to Ḥabad Hasidism, to which Rabbi Soloveitchik was exposed in youth), with his otherworldly pining and his perception of the *Shekhinah* as being in exile in this world, to the halakhist, blessed with a robust, healthy this-worldly outlook. (So goes Rabbi Soloveitchik's typology.)

The complaint is certainly a valid one. Even a kabbalist such as Rav Kook observed that there are those who engage in Jewish mysticism as an escape from reality. But Kabbalah needn't be a rejection of everyday life and a retreat to the cave.

Bodoff is familiar with the writings of Martin Buber. (There is very little in the way of Judaic literature that Bodoff is not aware of.) He knows that Buber proposed a "Neo-Hasidism," which would be very much a celebration of life. In Buber's book *Ich und Du* (mistranslated into English as *I and Thou*, when *I and You* would have been the correct translation), the *Shekhinah* is precisely the Presence in every aspect of living. Rather than being a *"Shekhinta be-galuta,"* an exiled *Shekhinah*, it is the very here-and-now. Bodoff ends up (as do so many others before him, whether they be Hasidim of the old school, or academicians such as Scholem) trashing Buber's reading of Hasidism as wide of the mark, if not downright unlawful.[7]

The truth be told, Buber was a master at starting the conversation between the sacred and the secular. By effecting the interpenetration of the two, Jewish mysticism becomes pronouncedly this-worldly. I am not convinced that Buber got the immanentalism of the Ba'al Shem Tov so very wrong.

Another master at setting up the meeting of *kodesh ve-ḥol*, the holy and the profane, was Rabbi Abraham Isaac Hakohen Kook. (While not a disciple, Buber was certainly a great admirer of Rav Kook.)[8] Rav Kook's Kabbalah is a celebration of life, of the incarnate, of flesh and blood. There is nothing spectral or spooky about it. In Rav Kook's vision, not only would a deeper understanding of Kabbalah not undermine the Jews'

---

7 See Bodoff, note 65:

> While Buber sought to portray Hasidism as changing Lurianic kabbalah's anti-worldly approach, the better view of scholars is that he was incorrect; see Jerome Gellman, "Buber's Blunder," pp. 20–40 [= Jerome Gellman, "Buber's Blunder: Buber's Replies to Scholem and Schatz-Uffenheimer," *Modern Judaism*. Oxford: February 2000, pp. 20–40]. Buber's romanticized view, which has proved attractive to many, is discussed in Joseph Dan, "A Bow to Frumkinian Hasidism," *Modern Judaism*. Oxford: May 1991, pp. 175–194.

8 In Buber's book *Bein 'Am le-Artso*. Jerusalem: Schocken, 1944, which grew out of a series of lectures on the history of Zionism, a chapter is devoted to Rav Kook. The chapter is entitled aptly enough: "Ḥiddush ha-Kedushah" ("The Renewal of Holiness"). In the introduction, the author writes that the volume was inspired by meetings with two men: A.D. Gordon and Rav Kook. Buber met the latter in Jerusalem in 1927. For an analysis of the aforementioned chapter, see Paulina Sarah Sklarevski, "*Ḥiddush ha-Kedushah: Ha-Rayah Kook bi-re'i tefisat ha-tsiyonut shel Buber be-sefer 'Bein 'Am le-Artso'*," Term Paper, Jerusalem: Hebrew University, July 31, 2013). Available at <www.academia.edu>. Buber's book has been brought out in English translation under the title *On Zion: The History of an Idea*. Syracuse: Syracuse University Press, 1997.

return to a landed existence and to normalcy, but (drawing on the prediction of the *Ra'aya Mehemna*), "With this composition of yours, which is the *Book of Splendor* (*Sefer ha-Zohar*)...they shall emerge from exile with mercy."[9]

> A mass whose hearts have been touched by the Lord, of this divine camp, will be the power that establishes the foundation of the salvation, the power that gives grace, the light of life and the pride of greatness to the entire *élan vital* of the national renascence in the Land of Israel. The *Book of Splendor* (*Zohar*) that breaks new ways, making a way in the desert, a road in the wilderness, it and all its crop are ready to open doors of redemption. "Since Israel are destined to taste of the Tree of Life which is the *Book of Splendor* (*Zohar*), they shall emerge from exile with mercy" [*Zohar* III, 124b].[10]

While deploring delving into mysticism before one has paid one's dues to the revealed Torah, Rav Kook maintains that the exoteric and the esoteric are best conceived as two sides of the coin of reality. They complement and enhance one another.

> The schism between the esoteric and exoteric comes about always due to the lack of wholeness of both elements. The exoteric that is restricted to its borders, which does not long for its source and root, will feel a certain antipathy to the esoteric, which cares to know no restriction or limitation. Lack of preparation for the hidden, jumping into it only because of a weakness of inner appetite, coupled with sloppiness and impracticality, causes the form of the esoteric to be distorted. Only unrealism, weak vitality, and lack of ability to grasp the living world, its deeds, movements, events, and charming currents, full of majesty and strength, cause immersion in the depth of the esoteric despite lack of preparation. But neither can exist exclusive of the other; life cannot be established on only one side of the global and Torah coin.[11]

Drawing on Maimonides' prescription that one first fill one's belly with bread and meat before venturing into the speculative orchard (*Pardes*),[12] Rav Kook explains that "filling the belly" extends to all healthy aspects of life. These are the grounding necessary prior to ascent to the more rarefied levels of human existence:

---

9 Zohar III, 124b.

10 *Orot ha-Tehiyah* (Lights of Renascence), end chap. 57, in *Orot*, trans. Bezalel Naor. Jerusalem: Maggid, 2015, p. 395. Based on Kook, Rabbi Abraham Isaac. *Orot.* Jerusalem: Degel Yerushalayim, 1920.

11 Ibid., beginning chap. 60 (p. 401).

12 Maimonides, *Hilkhot Yesodei ha-Torah* 4:13.

> The germ of the esoteric is ready, but it will be successfully actualized only after the full preparation of the exoteric. Filling the belly with "bread, meat and wine" must precede the "stroll in paradise." "Filling the belly" in its full sense includes within it also knowledge of the world and life, ethical and character development, strength of will and recognition of human value, and all the good, aesthetic, and orderly in existence that comes from an education good and proper in all its facets, which joins together with all that is aroused to life and freshness, in all areas: man and nation, literature and life, secular and holy and holy-of-holies. The demand of the esoteric, which is filled when its time comes, is a firm demand, which brings the liberating word, which frees the great Israelite saying from the prison of its muteness. It renews firm life, it arouses the spirit of strength in the absolute holiness, which is much simpler and more natural than anything secular and mundane, and yet retains its loftiness and glory.[13]

Authentic Jewish mysticism comes not to escape but rather to enhance reality. Rav Kook is very clear about this, and indeed he revisits this theme on innumerable occasions in his vast literary *oeuvre.* I think that this point might best be illustrated by juxtaposing momentarily to the field of music.

Who of us has not felt at one significant moment or another the reality at hand enhanced by the accompaniment of music? Whether it was a life-cycle event such as a wedding or funeral, a picturesque scene, or a passage in a book, one felt a quickening, an enlargement, a maximizing, on account of the music playing in the background. Now for some, music might be attractive as an escape from reality, as a way of "tuning out" everyday life with its many challenges. And there is no denying that from an innocent attraction music might turn into a deadly addiction. (Youth in particular are susceptible to this siren call.) But would the thought arise in the mind of any sane human to therefore declare a "jihad" against music? Music, the invention of the Biblical figure Yuval, is one of the features that ennoble our being. How impoverished would our civilization be without fine music!

By the same token, I think it fair to say that Jewish mysticism in the hands of an ethical genius such as a Rav Kook or an Abraham Joshua Heschel, enriches rather than impoverishes, invigorates rather than vitiates our existence.

---

13 *Orot ha-Tehiyah*, end chap. 60 (pp. 401–403).

Bodoff's response to my summoning the spirit of Rav Kook (to whom he is sympathetic)[14] would be that the man was not a *homo mysticus*, but rather a poet![15] ☙

---

14 Bodoff's final sentence (Appendix 13) reads:

> Rav Kook offers the strongest and simplest argument for secular activities, dispensing with kabbalistic ideas of mystical exegesis, sefirotic emanations, and the intricate structure of mystical ritual activity. For him, spirituality is the *result* of using the tools of modern culture to guide the historical, earthly process of redemption; it is not achieved by casting off corporeality or by the negation of the self; see Eliezer Schweid, "Prophetic Mysticism in Twentieth-Century Jewish Thought," *Modern Judaism*. Oxford: 1994, pp. 166–169.

15 Bodoff writes in note 52:

> Marvin Fox applied a kind of hybrid analysis, similar to my own in some respects, in concluding that Rav Kook was—a poet! See his "Rav Kook: Neither Philosopher nor Kabbalist," *Rabbi Abraham Isaac Kook and Jewish Spirituality*. Ed. David Shatz and Lawrence Kaplan. New York: NYU Press, 1995, pp. 78–87.

Misinterpreting Rabbi Judah Ha-Levi

By: H. NORMAN STRICKMAN

Rabbi Judah Ha-Levi (ca. 1075–1141) was one of the greatest Jewish poets of the middle ages. He was acclaimed by his contemporaries as "the quintessence and embodiment of our country, our refuge and leader, an illustrious scholar of unique and perfect piety."[1] He was not only a great poet but also a great Jewish thinker. His philosophical work the *Kuzari*, which was written in Judeo-Arabic, is one of the great philosophical texts to come out of the Middle Ages. Many place it alongside Maimonides' *Guide for the Perplexed.*

Rabbi Samson Raphael Hirsch who was very critical of Maimonides' philosophy points to Rabbi Judah Ha-Levi as one of those "very few [who] stood with their intellectual efforts entirely within Judaism, and built it up of its inner concepts."[2] Rabbi Elijah, the Gaon of Vilna (1720–1797), taught, "The *Kuzari* is holy and pure, and the fundamentals of Israel's faith and the Torah are contained within it."[3]

One of the major points of the *Kuzari* is that God revealed himself to Israel and that no nation aside from Israel has the ability of receiving Divine revelation (*Inyan Ha-Elohi*).[4] *Inyan Ha-Elohi* is a potential power. Not

---

1 Lawrence J. Kaplan, "'The Starling's Caw': Judah Halevi as Philosopher, Poet, and Pilgrim," *Jewish Quarterly Review,* Volume 101, Number 1, Winter 2011.

2 R. Samson Raphael Hirsch, *The Nineteen Letters on Judaism,* (NY: Feldheim, 1969) pp. 121-122.

3 Yehuda Even Shmuel, *Sefer Ha-Kuzari Le-Rabbi Yehudah Ha-Le-vi*, Tel Aviv 1972, p. 12.

4 Josef Kafich renders *alamr elalahi* as *Ha-Davar Ha-Elohi.* However, Judah ibn Tibbon, the first translator of the *Kuzari* into Hebrew, renders *Alamr Elalahi* as

---

H. Norman Strickman is Rabbi emeritus of Marine Park Jewish Center, professor of Jewish Studies at Touro College, and past president of the Rabbinic Board of Flatbush. He received his M.H.L. from Yeshiva University, a PhD from Dropsie University and was ordained at Rabbi Isaac Elchanan Theological Seminary. He is the recipient of the *Histadrut Ha-Ivrit* prize in Hebrew Literature and his writings have appeared in *Jewish Quarterly Review, Midstream, Bitzaron* and *Ha-Darom.* He has also translated and annotated Ibn Ezra's commentary on the Pentateuch, the first two books of Psalms, and the *Yesod Mora.*

every Jew is a prophet, but every Israelite is a potential possessor of the *Inyan Ha-Elohi.*

Other nations can learn from Israel. They can convert to Judaism. The converts can be Torah scholars. They can be paragons of piety. They cannot, however, be prophets, for they have not inherited the potential to receive the Divine Element.

> Any Gentile who joins us unconditionally shares our good fortune without, however, being quite equal to us, because we are the treasure[5] of mankind.[6]

The *Inyan Ha-Elohi* was first possessed by Adam. Adam "was … perfect in body and mind. No flaw can be found in a work of a wise and Almighty Creator, wrought from a substance chosen by Him, and fashioned according to His own design… [7] Adam left many children, of whom the only one capable of taking his place was Abel, because he alone…" possessed the *Inyan Ha-Elohi.* After Abel was slain by Cain …the potential of receiving the *Inyan Ha-Elohi* passed to his brother Seth.[8]

The potential for receiving the *Inyan Ha-Elohi* was then passed on to select individuals from generation to generation. Noah inherited this potential as did Shem and Eber. The potential for receiving the *Inyan Ha-Elohi* was eventually passed on to Abraham. Abraham passed on this potential to Isaac, "to the exclusion of the other sons who were all removed from the land, the special inheritance of Isaac." From Isaac the potential of receiving the *Inyan Ha-Elohi* passed on to Jacob. Henceforth the potential of receiving the *Inyan Ha-Elohi* remained in the possession of the Jewish people.[9] This is the reason God chose them to be "His special treasure"[10] and a "kingdom of priests" and a "holy nation."[11]

While the greatest minds in Judaism have nothing but praise for the *Kuzari*, a number of modern writers have strongly attacked Rabbi Judah Ha-Levi. The Israeli journalists Yuval Elbashan and Sefi Rachelevsky; Rabbi Israel Drazin of Maryland and the late and noted Israeli thinker Dr.

Ha-Inyan Ha-Elohi (the Divine). Most of the translators of the *Kuzari* followed suit. This is the term we employ in this essay.

5 Arabic, *altzafu'ah*. Ibn Tibbon, Even Shemuel and Kapach render this as *segullah*. See Ex. 19:6: "Ye shall be Mine own treasure (*segullah*) from among all peoples."

6 *Judah Hallevi's Kitab al Khazari*. Translated by Hartwig Hirschfeld,1905, 1:27

7 Ibid. 1:95

8 Ibid.

9 Ibid.

10 Ex. 19:5.

11 Ibid. v. 6.

Yeshayau Leibowitz are representatives of those who are, to say the very least, uncomfortable with the *Kuzari*. Yuval Elbashan writes:

> I never liked the *Kuzari*. Since the first time I was exposed to the contents of this 12th-century Jewish apologia written by Golden Age philosopher, physician and poet Rabbi Yehuda Halevy, I viewed it as a racist book whose goal was to elevate the People of Israel above others. I sensed that the book's claims about the choosiness of Israel exempted us from basic moral constraints and caused us to close our eyes to unending acts of wrongdoing and abuse perpetrated against those who are under our control.[12]

According to Elbashin, not only is Rabbi Judah Ha-Levi a racist but he is responsible for the policies of today's Israeli government in Judea and Samaria, which Elbashan considers to be a series of "wrong doing and abuse perpetrated" against those who are under Israel's control. According to Elbashin,

> The Kuzari appears to say that the world is comprised of different strata. On the bottom there is the somnolent world, in the middle is the animal kingdom and above is the world of man. In the somnolent stratum there is nature; in the animal layer, there are matters spirit and emotion; and on the human level, there is rationality. In the stratum above man there is something the Kuzari calls "the divine matter;" in Halevy's breakdown of the world, this stratum avails itself only to Jews. Under this system, the reason for Jewish superiority is not that Gentiles are not human beings; it derives from the fact that non-Jews are only human beings. According to Halevy, the people of Israel exist on a more elevated level, and only Jews have the ability to connect to the divine stratum… It would be difficult to express a more blunt form of racism.[13]

Sefi Rachelevsky, an Israeli journalist, claims that the *Kuzari* teaches that non-Jews are nothing more than talking animals. He writes:

> Rabbi Yehuda Halevi maintained that there are four levels in nature: inanimate, vegetable, animal, speaker. The speaker is the talking animal, the Gentile. Above them is the fifth and highest level, the Jew,

---

12 Yuval Elbashan. "How I learned to love 'The Kuzari'," *Ha-Aretz*, Feb. 14:2013. This is a total distortion of R. Judah Ha-Levi's views.

13 Ibid.

> the only one defined as a human being and human rights exist for him alone.[14]

Dr. Yeshayahu Leibowitz claims that Rabbi Yehudah Ha-Levi believes that once one has achieved the status of belonging to a holy people it is no longer necessary for them to observe the commandments for one is already holy.[15]

Rabbi Israel Drazin similarly attacks Rabbi Judah Ha-Levi's thesis. He writes:

> Yehudah Halevi… holds the extreme view that Jews are inherently superior to non-Jews. He insists that Jews are the only people that God loves; God gives Jews special attention and even unearned assistance. Only Jews receive prophecy, which is an exclusive valuable gift from God, expressing his love for the Jews. Jews are smarter and more virtuous; they, and only they, with perhaps a few exceptions, are granted life after death.
> Thus, to illustrate Halevi's view of non-Jewish converts to Judaism: one cannot convert a camel into a sheep by a conversion process of immersion and circumcision because one is left with a clean and circumcised camel, but the camel is still not a sheep.[16]

Elbashan, Rachelevsky, Leibowitz and Drazin represent the opinion of many who are strongly opposed to Rabbi Judah Ha-Levi's concept of the Jews as being carriers of the *Inyan Ha-Elohi.*

Dr. Micah Goodman, of the Shalom Hartman Institute in Jerusalem and the Hebrew University, recently published a work on Rabbi Judah Ha-Levi.[17] He argues that the "*chaver*," the representative of Judaism in the *Kuzari*, does not necessarily represent the views of Rabbi Judah Ha-Levi. He argues that the Book is a dialogue and in a dialogue various sides are presented. In other words, according to Dr. Goodman, Rabbi Judah Ha-Levi does not really believe that Jews are the carriers of the *Inyan Ha-*

---

14 Sefi Rachlevsky, "The laws of education for violence," *Ha-aretz*, Sep. 8, 2010. See also Sefi Rachlevsky, *Chamoro shel Mashi'ach* (Israel 1998), p. 106.

15 Yeshayahu Leibowitz, "*Sheva Shanim Shel Sichot al parshat ha-shav'ah*," pp. 680-681. This is a totally wrong reading of R. Judah Ha-Levi. R. Judah Ha-Levi requires one to observe both the ritual and ethical laws before he is worthy and can activate the *Inyan Ha-Elohi.*

16 Israel Drazin, *The Mistaken Theology Of Yehudah Halevi.* <booksnthoughts.com /the-mistaken-theology-of-yehudah-halevi/>.

17 Micah Goodman, *The Dream of the Kuzari* (Or Yehudah: Dvir, 2012).

Elohi.[18] He mentions it because it was a view held by some Jews. However, he personally rejects it.

The *Kuzari* opens as follows:

> I was asked to state what arguments and replies I could bring to bear against the attacks of philosophers and followers of other religions, and also against [Jewish] sectarians who attacked the rest of Israel. This reminded me of something I had once heard concerning the arguments of a Rabbi who sojourned with the King of the Khazars. The latter, as we know from historical records, became a convert to Judaism about four hundred years ago. To him came a dream, and it appeared as if an angel addressed him, saying: 'Thy way of thinking is indeed pleasing to the Creator, but not thy way of acting.' Yet he was so zealous in the performance of the *Khazar* religion, that he devoted himself with a perfect heart to the service of the temple and sacrifices. Notwithstanding this devotion, the angel came again at night and repeated: 'Thy way of thinking is pleasing to God, but not thy way of acting.' This caused him to ponder over the different beliefs and religions, and finally become a convert to Judaism together with many other Khazars. As I found, among the arguments of the Rabbi, many which appealed to me, and were in harmony with my own opinions, I resolved to write them down exactly as they had been spoken.[19] The wise will understand.[20]

"The wise will understand" in Jewish Medieval writing usually indicates that there is a hidden meaning in the text. According to Goodman what Rabbi Judah Ha-Levi is hinting at is that he doesn't necessarily agree with everything the *Chaver* says, namely that the Jews and only the Jews are the carriers of the *Inyan Ha-Elohi.*

---

18 Elbashan changed his mind regarding R. Judah Ha-Levi after he read Goodman's book. Hence the title of Elbashan's article: "How I learned to love 'The Kuzari.'" It should be noted that Isaac Heinemann first put forth this idea that Rabbi Judah Ha-Levi did not seriously believe that Jews were biologically superior to non-Jews. See Introduction to "Yehudah Halevi: Kuzari," *Three Jewish Philosophers* (NY: Toby, 1981) p. 24. See also Lippman Bodoff, "Was Yehuda Halevi Racist?," *Judaism*, 38 (Spring 1989), p. 175.

19 *Book of Kuzari*: Translated by Hartwig Hirschfeld. New York, 1946, p. 31.

20 Hirschfeld omits the words "the wise will understand." I cannot fathom why he did so. The words are found in the Arabic original and in all the other translations of the *Kuzari* such as Ibn Tibbon, Even Shemu'al and Shilat. "The wise will understand" usually indicates that the writer does not want to be explicit about a sensitive issue and leaves it to the reader to ascertain his intention. For an example see Ibn Ezra to Gen. 12:6 and Lev, 12:6.

However, this is not necessarily true. According to the plain reading of the text, "The wise will understand" refers to what immediately precedes, namely, the account of the king's conversion. It means that the wise will understand that the Kuzari does not contain a verbatim record of the dialogue between the King and the *Chaver* but that the dialogue in the Kuzari was produced by Rabbi Judah Ha-Levi.

The truth of the matter is that the idea of the Jews being the carriers of the *Inyan Ha-Elohi* is not seriously challenged in the Kuzari. The King of the Khazars, early on in the book, questions the *Chaver's* assertion that Israel is a unique people. He asks, How can Israel be a superior nation when they made a golden calf after experiencing the revelation on Mount Sinai? [21]

The question is answered by maintaining that the golden calf was not worshipped as a god, but was an instrument used to focus the mind when worshiping God. The sin of Israel consisted in utilizing the golden calf as an object in religious ritual.[22] The worship of the calves in Dan and Bet El is explained away in the same manner.

In order to accept Dr. Goodman's thesis we must deconstruct the Kuzari. We must say that Rabbi Judah Ha-Levi did not really believe the argument put forward by the *Chaver,* that the worship of the golden calf and the worship of the calves in Bet El and Dan did not really entail idol worship, and that Rabbi Judah Ha-Levi identifies with the charge of the king of the Khazars that the supposed superiority of Jews is an exaggeration. This, however, is a stretch. It turns the Kuzari on its head. If Rabbi Judah Ha-Levi concealed his true belief as to Israel's potential possession of the *Inyan Ha-Elohi*, then he really succeeded, for no one from 1140 when the Kuzari was published until 2012, when Goodman published his work, unraveled its true meaning.

Dr. Goodman's thesis is not based on an objective study of Rabbi Judah Ha-Levi's thought. He put forth this interpretation to safeguard Rabbi Judah's Ha-Levi's reputation from the charge of racism.[23]

Rabbi Judah Ha-Levi claims, regarding Israel's place in God's plan, that it did not, as claimed by Elbashin, exempt Jews from basic moral constraints. Nor did it teach "that once one has achieved the status of belonging to a holy people it is no longer necessary for him or her to observe the commandments for one is already holy" as claimed by

---

21 *Kuzari* 1:7.

22 Ibid. 1:92.

23 Yitzchak Silat, "Segulat Yisrael enah gizanut," *Makor Rishon*, Jan. 4, 2013.

Leibowitz. In fact Rabbi Judah Ha-Levi was opposed to everything that Elbashin and Leibowitz ascribe to him.[24]

True, Rabbi Judah Ha-Levi argues that there are five levels of being: mineral, plant, animal, human, and prophet. He does not, however, say that there are five levels of being: mineral, plant, animal, human, and Jew.

Rabbi Judah Ha-Levi is not speaking politically. He is not preaching bigotry. He is not implying that people who have the potential to receive the *Inyan Ha-Elohi* are destined to rule over people who do not possess the *Inyan Ha-Elohi*. Rabbi Judah Ha-Levi does not propose that people who do not possess the potential to receive the *Inyan Ha-Elohi* should be enslaved. He is not saying that people who do not possess the potential for the *Inyan Ha-Elohi* should be denied human rights. He does not say that people who do not possess the *Inyan Ha-Elohi* be segregated. He says that the person who possesses the *Inyan Ha-Elohi* is in a unique category.[25] He asks:

> If we find a man who walks into the fire without hurt,[26] or abstains from food for some time without starving,[27] on whose face a light shines which the eye cannot bear,[28] who is never ill, nor ages, until having reached his life's natural end,[29] who dies spontaneously just as a man retires to his couch to sleep on an appointed day and hour,[30] equipped with the knowledge of what is hidden as to past and future:[31] is such a degree not visibly distinguished from the ordinary human degree?...

---

24 According to Rabbi Judah Ha-Levi, in order for a person to be a prophet he has to observe all the moral and ritual laws of the Torah.

25 See Ehud Krinis's letter to the Editor in *Ha-Aretz* 9/13/10:
ר' יהודה הלוי עצמו כתב את "ספר הכוזרי" כחיבור הגותי ולא כחיבור הלכתי. המסקנות שהוא גוזר מן ההבחנה בין הדרגה הרביעית של "המדבר" (היא דרגת "העניין השכלי") לדרגה החמישית של נבחרי האל (היא דרגת "העניין האלוהי") אינן מתייחסות ל"זכויות האדם" - מושג מודרני, שהוא זר למחבר שחי במאות ה-11-12 - אלא לטבע העל-אנושי של הנבחרים הנמצאים בדרגה העליונה, כפי שהוא משתקף בתופעות הייחודיות של הנבואה ושל שלטון הרצון האלוהי במהלך ההיסטוריה של עם ישראל.

26 Kafich (p. 13) believes that the reference is to Shadrach, Meshach, and Abednego (Dan. 3). However, what follows shows that the reference is to Moses who ascended Mt. Sinai which was ablaze with fire. See Ex. 19:18-19.

27 The reference is to Moses. See Ex. 34:28.

28 The reference is to Moses. See Ex. 34: 29–35.

29 Deut. 34:5–8.

30 *Sifrei, Ha'azinu.*

31 *Sifrei*, Deut 34:2. See also Rashi.

> Such an individual is in a special class by himself. He is of the divine and seraphic degree… [he] belongs to the province of the divine influence, but not to that of the intellectual, human, or natural world.

Rabbi Judah Ha-Levi says not that every Israelite is "of the divine and seraphic degree," but only that every Israelite has the potential of being a prophet under certain conditions.[32] Israel's place in God's plan did not, according to Rabbi Judah Ha-Levi, exempt Jews from basic moral constraints, as claimed by Elbashin. Nor did it teach "that once one has achieved the status of belonging to a holy people it is no longer necessary for him or her to observe the commandments for one is already holy" as claimed by Leibowitz.

Rabbi Judah Ha-Levi did not consider non-Jews as talking animals as claimed by Rachelevsky and Drazin. He considers Christians and Moslem as rational beings.

Those parts of the *Kuzari* that feature the points of view presented by Islam, Christianity and philosophy display a respect for those who hold these views. They are not pictured as irrational beasts. Rabbi Judah Ha-Levi was opposed to everything that Elbashin, Rachelevsky, Leibowitz and Drazin ascribe to him.[33]

Rabbi Judah Ha-Levi argues that there are five levels of being: mineral, plant, animal, human, and prophet. He then goes on to describe the prophet. Rabbi Judah Ha-Levi says not that every Israelite is a prophet, but only that every Israelite has the potential of being a prophet. Furthermore, while the convert himself cannot be a prophet his descendants can.[34]

A convert must undergo circumcision, for "circumcision is a divine symbol, ordained by God relating to the organs of overpowering desire. This sign was placed on these organs so that they be defeated and so that he use them in a fit manner, by placing his seed in a proper place, in a proper time and in a proper mode. If he does so then he has the possibility

---

32 Observing the commandments of the Torah and living in the Land of Israel at a time when the Temple in Jerusalem is in existence.

33 According to Rabbi Judah Ha-Levi, in order for a person to be a prophet he has to observe all the moral and ritual laws of the Torah.

34 Contrary to Drazin's claim regarding Halevi's view of non-Jewish converts to Judaism: [that is] "one cannot convert a camel into a sheep by a conversion process of immersion and circumcision because one is left with a clean and circumcised camel, but the camel is still not a sheep," see note 16.

of having praiseworthy seed that will succeed in receiving the Divine element."[35]

It should be noted that Rabbi Judah Ha-Levi's theory that non-Jews cannot be prophets is nuanced. The *Kuzari* opens with an angel of God appearing to the King of the Khazar with an oracle. The angel tells the King, Your intentions are good, but your deeds are not.

The opening of the *Kuzari* presents a problem. The appearance of an angel is a type of prophecy. In fact the Bible records many prophecies that come via an angel. The book thus opens with a prophetic revelation to a non-Jew and then goes on to say that non-Jews cannot be prophets, even if they convert to Judaism.[36]

The appearance of the angel to the king of the Khazars recalls the appearance of angels to non-Jews in Scripture.

Rabbi Judah Ha-Levi wrote for an audience that was well acquainted with Scripture. They could not fail to make the connection between the appearance of angels in Scripture and the appearance of the angel in the *Kuzari*.

The Bible records a number of encounters with angels who bring divine messages to non-Jews. When angels appear to non-Jews in Scripture, it is never for the revelations of Laws. It is to save them, to inform them of future events, or to prevent them from doing evil. Two angels appear to Lot to save him from being destroyed along with Sodom and Gomorrah. [37] The Lord appears to Abimelekh and tells him not to touch Sarah but to restore her to Abraham.[38] God appears to Laban and tells him not

---

35 *Kuzari*: 1:114. My translation of Kafich's and Shilat's Hebrew version of the *Kuzari*. See David Berger, "Jews, Gentiles, and the Modern Egalitarian Ethos: Some Tentative Thoughts," *Formulating Responses in an Egalitarian Age*, Rowman & Littlefield, 2005, "The divine element can somehow be attained [by descendants of a convert] within two generations through spiritual effort." Also see Dov Shyarts, "Central Problems of Medieval Jewish Philosophy," p. 87, "In the first generation… [converts] remain excluded from prophecy… [However,] the Divine Element can be attained within two generations." Lippman Bodoff quotes a contrary view in "Was Yehuda Halevi Racist?," *Judaism* 38 (Spring 1989), p. 175, fn. 10. One thing is certain. Rabbi Judah Ha-Levi never said that descendants of converts cannot be prophets. Had Rabbi Judah Ha-Levi believed it he would have said so. I believe that this segment indicates that the reason a convert cannot be a prophet is because he was not conceived in holiness.

36 This apparent anomaly in the *Kuzari* is one of the reasons that Dr. Goodman claims that the Chaver's assertion that only Jews can be prophets does not really represent the opinion of Rabbi Judah Ha-Levi.

37 Gen. 19:1–24.

38 Ibid. 20:1–7.

to harm Jacob.[39] Pharaoh has two dreams predicting a coming famine.[40] The Lord appears to Balaam and warns him not to curse Israel.[41] God reveals the future to Nebuchadnezzar, in a dream.[42]

The appearance of the angel of God to the king of the Khazars is similar to the above. The angel tells the king, "Your intentions are good, but your deeds are not." The angel does not tell the king what deeds are pleasing to God. Such a revelation is vouchsafed for those who possess the *Inyan Ha-Elohi.*

The angel keeps on reappearing to the king. This eventually leads the king on a quest to find the way that is satisfying to God. When the king finds the way pleasing to God he and many of his people convert to Judaism.

According to Rabbi Judah Ha-Levi, non-Jews are not cut off from connection to God. They are cut off from the revelation of mitzvoth, or a new religion.

What led Rabbi Judah Ha-Levi to believe that only Jews have the potential for the *Inyan Ha-Elohi*?[43] There are those who believe that Rabbi Judah Ha-Levi was trying to inspire a discouraged Jewry.[44]

In the twelfth century the Jews were under the heel of the Christians and Muslims. The first crusade had devastated the Jewish communities of the Rhineland. Islam was on the march. Rabbi Judah Ha-Levi asked, "Is there in the east or in the west a place where we can hope to be secure?"[45]

---

39 Ibid. 31:24.

40 See Gen. 41:25, "For what God is about to do He hath declared unto Pharaoh."

41 Num. 22:12.

42 Dan. 2:29.

43 Shlomo Pines and Ehud Krinis believe that Rabbi Judah Ha-Levi was influenced by Moslem thinking and took the idea of the *Inyan Ha-Elohi* from the Shi'ites. The Shi'ites believe that a divine light is passed down through the descendants of Ali the son-in-law of Mohamed. Only one from the line of Ali can be a Shi'ite imam and possess the Divine light. This is not exactly what Rabbi Judah Has-Levi teaches. Krinis, however, believes that Rabbi Judah Ha-Levi reshaped the Shi'ite idea for his own purposes. See Ehud Krinis, "God's Chosen People: Judah Halevi's Kuzari and the Shi'i Imam Doctrine," *Cultural Encounters in Late Antiquity and the Middle Ages* (N.V. Brepols Pub, February 28, 2014).

44 See Lippman Bodoff, "Was Yehuda Halevi Racist?," *Judaism* 38 (Spring 1989), p. 176. [Ha-Levi's] "primary reason for writing the *Kuzari* was to prevent Jews from weakening in their faith, faced as they were with the ascendancy of Islam and their own degradation." See also, Hillel Halkin, "Yehuda Halevi" (Schocken, 2010), and Micah Goodman, "The Dream of the Kuzari" (*Or Yehudah*, Dvir, 2012).

45 S.M. Urbach in *Amudei Ha-Machashavah Ha-Yisraelit*, Jerusalem 1971, p. 248.

The Jews were "of low station, few in number, and generally despised."[46] They were looked upon "as people of reduced condition… [whose] misery left them nothing commendable."[47]

Rabbi Judah Ha-Levi's response was that the Jews are far from being a God-forsaken people. They are, whether the world knows it or not, the "*segullah*" of mankind. They served as a link with God in the past, do so in the present and will continue to do the same in the future.

In reality, however, there is more than an attempt to uplift the Jewish ego in Rabbi Judah Ha-Levi's theory. Rabbi Judah Ha-Levi's assertion that the Jews are the carriers of the *Inyan Ha-Elohi* is based on his reading of Holy Scripture.

Rabbi Judah Ha-Levi lived in an age of faith. He, like all Jews, Christians and Moslems of his age believed that if the Holy Scripture says something, then it is so. Genesis states:

> Now the Lord said unto Abram: 'Get thee out of thy country, and from thy kindred, and from thy father's house, unto the land that I will show thee. And I will make of thee a great nation, and I will bless thee, and make thy name great; and be thou a blessing. And I will bless them that bless thee, and him that curseth thee will I curse; and in thee shall all the families of the earth be blessed' (Gen. 12:1-3).

Exodus reads:

> Now therefore, if ye will hearken unto My voice indeed, and keep My covenant, then ye shall be Mine own treasure from among all peoples; for all the earth is Mine; and ye shall be unto Me a kingdom of priests, and a holy nation (Ex.19:5-6).

Deuteronomy reads:

> For thou art a holy people unto the Lord thy God, and the Lord hath chosen thee to be His own treasure out of all peoples that are upon the face of the earth (Deut. 14:2).

Dr. Rachel Sabath Beit-Halachmi of the Shalom Hartman Institute in Jerusalem writes:

> I believe that the idea of choosiness must remain central to how we understand ourselves. That we are a chosen people is a core aspect of what it means to be Jewish. It is rooted in the origins of our people, in the biblical narratives of Abraham and in the redemption and revelation that made us who we are. Exodus 19 says it in three different ways. First, we are an *am segulah*, precious to God, as well

---

46 *Kuzari* 1:4.

47 *Kuzari* 1:12.

> as *mamlekhet kohanim*, God's nation of priests, and a holy nation or people, a *goy kadosh*. It is significant that this is how God names us at the moment we are given the Torah with its commandments to create an ethical society. I understand these three statements to mean that from ancient times to the present era, whether we were celebrated or decimated, we understood ourselves to be precious, priestly, and holy.[48]

Rabbi Shai Held of Mechon Hadar similarly notes:

> So central is election to the Bible that contemporary Jews who wish to have a theology rooted in scripture have no choice but to reckon with choosiness. To jettison the language of closeness, I fear, is to jettison the Bible itself.[49]

Rachel Sabath Beit-Halachmi and Shai Held are non-orthodox thinkers. Can we expect anything less from Rabbi Judah Ha-Levi? For Rabbi Judah Ha-Levi, to deny Israel's choosiness was tantamount to heresy.

The question that Rabbi Judah faced was: Why did God choose the Jews to be His own treasure (*segullah*)? According to Rabbi Judah Ha-Levi, God did not choose Israel because of political considerations. He chose Israel as the carrier of His word to mankind. Rabbi Judah Ha-Levi compared Israel to a seed planted in the soil which turns its environment into a plant identical to itself.

> God has a secret and wise design concerning us, which should be compared to the wisdom hidden in the seed which falls into the ground, where it undergoes an external transformation into earth, water and dirt, without leaving a trace for him who looks down upon it. It is, however, the seed itself which transforms earth and water into its own substance, carries it from one stage to another, until it refines the elements and transfers them into something like itself, casting off husks, leaves, etc., and allowing the pure core to appear, capable of bearing the Divine Influence. The original seed produced the tree bearing fruit resembling that from which it had been produced. In the same manner the law of Moses transforms each one who honestly follows it.

Christianity and Islam took many elements of their religions from Judaism "to pave the way for the expected Messiah, who is the fruition, and they will all become His fruit. Then, after they acknowledge Him, they

---

48 <http://shma.com/2015/02/are-jews-chosen>.

49 < http://shma.com/2015/02/a-bolt-from-the-blue>.

will become one tree. Then they will revere the origin which they formerly despised."[50]

If Rabbi Judah Ha-Levi was a bigot, if he believed that non-Jews are animals, would he say that Israel and the nations are destined to become one tree? If Rabbi Judah Ha-Levi was a bigot, would he believe that the descendants of converts could be prophets?[51]

Furthermore it must be emphasized that the defense of the Jewish people was not Rabbi Judah Ha-Levi's only concern in writing the *Kuzari.* The *Kuzari* is a defense of Judaism, God's revealed law.

The major part of the *Kuzari* is devoted to explaining Judaism. Rabbi Judah Ha-Levi deals with the attributes of God, the reasons for the Divine commandments, free will, the world to come, and the religious life.

Rabbi Judah Ha-Levi called his work "The Book of the Khazars: In Defense of the Despised Faith." He did not call his work "The Book of the Khazars: In Defense of a Despised People."

The *Kuzari* opens with a description of the King of the Khazars seeking a religion. It does not open with the king of the Khzars seeking a nation.

As noted above Rabbi Judah Ha-Levi believed that the world would ultimately accept Judaism. In other words Judaism was eternally valid. This was not, however, the position of Islam, Christianity, and philosophy. The Moslems and Christians argued that their religions replaced Judaism. The Moslems argued, "Our prophet is the Seal of the prophets,

---

50 *Kuzari* 4:23. Maimonides had a similar concept: "The thoughts of the Creator of the world are not within the power of man to reach them, 'for our ways are not His ways, nor are our thoughts His thoughts.' And all these matters of Jesus of Nazareth and that of the Ishmaelite who arose after him are only to straighten the way of the king Messiah and to fix the entire world, to serve God as one, as it is stated (Zephaniah 3:9), 'For then I will turn to the peoples (into) clear speech, to all call in the name of G-d and serve Him unanimously.' [12] How (will this come about)? The entire world has already become filled with the mention of the Messiah, with words of Torah and words of mitzvos, and these matters have spread to the furthermost isles, to many nations of uncircumcised hearts, and they discuss these matters and the mitzvot of the Torah. Some say: 'These mitzvoth are true, but were already nullified in the present age and are not applicable for all time.' Others say: 'Hidden matters are in them (mitzvos) and they are not to be taken literally, and the messiah has already come and revealed their hidden (meanings).' And when the true Messiah stands, and he is successful and is raised and exalted, immediately they all will retract and will know that fallacy they inherited from their fathers, and that their prophets and fathers caused them to err." (*Mishneh Torah, Laws of Kings,* 11:10–12.)

51 See note 33.

who abrogated every previous law, and invited all nations to embrace Islam."[52]

The Christians argued, "We belong to their number. Although we are not of Israelite descent, we are well deserving of being called Children of Israel (that is, we are the chosen people) because we follow the messiah."[53]

Medieval philosophy offered a major challenge to traditional Judaism. It taught that the way to God is through the intellect. The observance of commandments of the Torah is of no consequence.[54]

Philosophy teaches that he "who is equipped with the highest capacity, receives through it the advantages of disposition, intelligence and active power… wants nothing to make him perfect."[55] The philosopher tells the king, "seek purity of heart in which way thou are able, provided thou hast acquired the sum total of knowledge in its real essence; then thou wilt reach thy goal, viz. the union with this Spiritual, or rather Active Intellect. Maybe he will communicate with thee or teach thee the knowledge of what is hidden through true dreams and positive visions."[56]

The philosopher does not seek God in order to establish a relationship with God. The philosopher does not fear God for the sake of reward, nor does he refrain from committing crimes because of fear of Divine punishment. According to the philosopher, God does not know man and is not concerned with him.[57] The philosophers hold these beliefs because philosophy is not based on revelation.

The concept of the *Inyan Ha-Elohi* is vital to Judah Ha-Levi's defense of Judaism. Judah Ha-Levi is arguing that Judaism cannot be displaced by another religion, or by any philosophy, for their teachings are not based on Divine revelation.

Judah Ha-Levi's assertion that only the Jews are the bearers of the *Inyan Elhohi* is directed at the claim of the Christians and Muslims that Islam and Christianity have replaced Judaism. It is similarly directed at the philosopher who believes that religious rituals are meaningless and that philosophy is the only way to achieve perfection and gain immortality.

Judah Ha-Levi's thesis, that only Jews possess the potential for the *Inyan Ha-Elohi*, is thus an argument for the eternal validity of Judaism. If the way to religious truth is through the *Inyan Ha-Elohi* then Islam, Christianity and philosophy cannot supplant Judaism.

---

52 *Kuzari*: 1:5.

53 Ibid. 1:4.

54 Ibid. 1:1.

55 Ibid.

56 Ibid.

57 Ibid.

Islam cannot supplant Judaism for Mohammed was not Jewish and could therefore not be a prophet and have the *Inyan Ha-Elohi.*

Christianity cannot supplant Judaism because Christians do not possess the *Inyan Ha-Elohi.* How can they when they do not observe the mitzvoth of the Torah and the observance of the Commandments is a basic requirement for the *Inyan Elohi* to rest on a person? Judah Ha-Levi points out that Jesus knew this. He therefore said, "I came not to destroy one of the laws of Moses, but I came to confirm and support it."[58]

Rabbi Judah Ha-Levi's claim, that only very special Jews possess the *Inyan Ha-Elohi,* is the ultimate refutation of Moslem, Christian and philosopher arguments that they have replaced Judaism.[59]

Dr. Meir Soloveitchik argues that "It is not unreasonable to suggest that… the key to Jewish survival [is] the belief that the individual Jew must maintain his Jewishness because he is the beloved of God. This belief found expression not simply in creed but also in Jewish practice. The dedication of generations of Jews to Jewish law was not out of a blind sense of duty, but out of a firm belief that these laws were the expression of the Creator's special love for the Jewish people, and their betrayal would be a betrayal of that love. It is this belief, perhaps above all else, which sustained Jewish communities through the hardships of exile, persecution, and pogrom. And it may still."[60]

Rabbi Judah Ha-Levi's critics identify his theory of the *Inyan Elohi* with modern genetics. Hence they end up charging Rabbi Judah Ha-Levi with racism. *Inyan Elohi*, however, is not a gene. It is not subject to genetic engineering. You can't experiment with it, as you do with genes. It has no genetic markers. It cannot be injected. There is no *Inyan Elohi* gene.

The *Inyan Elohi* is a divine gift. It does not belong to the world of physics. It is in the realm of metaphysics. It pertains not to the natural but to the realm of the supernatural. It is in "the province of the divine" and not of the "human, or natural world."

---

58 *Kuzari* 1:4.

59 See Lippman Bodoff, "Was Yehuda Halevi Racist?" *Judaism* 38 (Spring 1989), p. 177. "For Halevi, therefore the inability of even converts to Judaism to achieve the level of prophecy is not a matter of Xenophobia but a matter of sound reasoning and experience. If individuals or groups could become spiritually equal to the Jewish people through an act of will and intellect, the true religion would have developed naturally, without the need for God's revelation."

60 Meir Soloveitchik, "God's Beloved: A Defense of Choosiness," *Azure* 2005.

One may disagree with Rabbi Judah Ha-Levi's interpretation of *am segullah*. In fact, according to some, Maimonides apparently did,[61] but one should not misrepresent what he taught. ☙

---

61 See David Hartman, "Maimonides: Torah and Philosophic Quest" (Jewish Publication Society, 2002) p. 267, note 73. Yitzhak *Shilat, Iggarot Ha-Rambam*, (Jerusalem, Maale Adumim, 1995), p. 234; James A. Diamond, "Maimonides and the Convert: A Juridical and Philosophical Embrace of the Outsider," *Medieval Philosophy and Theology*, Cambridge University Press, 2003, p. 125–146; Isador Twersky, "Introduction to the Mishneh Torah of Maimonides" (Hebrew), (Jerusalem, 1991), p. 34.

What Must a Jew Believe: Dogma and Inadvertent Heresy, Revisited

By: ELIYAHU KRAKOWSKI

The medieval debates over the fundamentals of faith continue to resonate in contemporary Judaism. In particular, one dispute among medieval authorities over the case of an "inadvertent heretic," i.e., a person who contradicts a tenet of the Jewish faith without intending to do so, is important for defining heresy, and by implication, for defining belief and what it means to be a Jew. Perhaps no one has written as much about this as Professor Menachem Kellner, who in a number of articles and books has argued that there is a basic dispute between medieval authorities on how to define heresy, and as a consequence, about how to define belief in Judaism.[1]

According to Kellner, one view maintains that "while we would certainly demand of the faithful Jew an attitude of trust, loyalty, and commitment to God and to His Torah, we could not be satisfied with that, but would also be forced to judge the faithfulness of every Jew in terms of the

---

1 See, e.g., Kellner, *Dogma in Medieval Jewish Thought: From Maimonides to Abravanel* (Oxford: Oxford University Press, 1986, published in Hebrew as תורת העיקרים בפילוסופיה היהודית בימי הביניים, 1991); "Heresy and the Nature of Faith in Medieval Jewish Philosophy," *Jewish Quarterly Review* 77:4, pp. 299–318; reprinted in *Science in the Bet Midrash: Studies in Maimonides* (Brighton, MA: Academic Studies Press, 2009), Ch. 5; כפירה בשוגג בהגות יהודית בימי-הביניים: הרמב"ם ואברבנאל מול רשב"ץ ורח"ק? in מחקרי ירושלים במחשבת ישראל ג,ג (תשמד); "What is Heresy?" in *Science in the Bet Midrash*, Ch. 6; and *Must a Jew Believe Anything?* (1st ed., London: Littman Library, 1999; 2nd ed., London: Littman Library, 2006). In each of these works, Kellner presents a version of the argument that I will critique here. In my opinion, Kellner expresses his view most clearly and succinctly in his *Jewish Quarterly Review* article, and I will therefore primarily refer to it. [This article has now been republished once again as part of a small selection of Kellner's articles in the recent volume of the Library of Contemporary Jewish Philosophers, *Menachem Kellner: Jewish Universalism* (Brill, 2015), suggesting that the editors (or the subject) of the volume agree with my assessment.]

Eliyahu Krakowski has a Master's degree in Jewish Philosophy from the Bernard Revel Graduate School. His last article in *Ḥakirah* appeared in Vol. 16.

specific doctrines which he or she affirms or denies." The other view, by contrast, defines belief only as an attitude of trust in God and the Torah but not as adherence to any specific set of doctrines—"the one has literally nothing to do with the other."[2] With these definitions of what it means to be a faithful Jew, it follows that an inadvertent heretic, inasmuch as he lacks affirmation of the proper doctrines, is a heretic only according to the former view. But according to the latter view, one who possesses the right attitude towards Judaism cannot be a heretic, despite maintaining doctrines that deviate from Jewish norms.[3]

The *locus classicus* for this discussion about the status of an "inadvertent heretic" is the dispute between Rambam and Ra'avad (in *Hilkhot Teshuvah* 3:7) about whether one who believes in a corporeal God is a heretic (*min*). Rambam classifies this person as a *min*, and Ra'avad objects, noting that there were great men who wrongly held this view because of their mistaken literal interpretation of *pesukim* and *aggadot*.[4] Here, then, we may have a dispute about the status of one who unwittingly contradicts one of the tenets of Judaism—Rambam seemingly does not make exception for the "innocent corporealist," whereas Ra'avad does.

If, in these words of Rambam and Ra'avad, the dispute about inadvertent heresy remains implicit and subject to alternative interpretations, it emerges explicitly among Jewish thinkers in the centuries that follow. The best-known proponents of the two opposing viewpoints are R. Joseph Albo and R. Isaac Abarbanel, with Albo taking the "lenient" view—an unintentional heretic is not a heretic—and Abarbanel taking the "strict" view, that espousing heresy, like ingesting poison, retains its effect

---

2 Kellner, "Heresy and the Nature of Faith," pp. 317-318.

3 Kellner bases this distinction on Martin Buber's "two types of faith": "faith in," which expresses a relationship of trust, and "faith that," which means accepting as true a given proposition. For another formulation of this distinction, see R. Aharon Lichtenstein's article "The Source of Faith is Faith Itself," in *The Jewish Action Reader I* (New York: Union of Orthodox Jewish Congregations in America, 1996) in which he recommends to those "struggling to develop faith…the counsel to focus persistently, in terms of Coleridge's familiar distinction, upon faith rather than belief, upon experiential trust, dependence and submission more than upon catechetical dogmatics."

4 Rambam writes: חמישה הן הנקראין מינים: האומר שאין שם אלוק, ואין לעולם מנהיג; והאומר שיש שם מנהיג, אבל הם שניים או יתר; והאומר **שיש שם ריבון אחד, אלא שהוא גוף ובעל תמונה...**. On this latter case, Ra'avad comments: א"א ולמה קרא לזה מין וכמה גדולים וטובים ממנו הלכו בזו המחשבה לפי מה שראו במקראות ויותר ממה שראו בדברי האגדות המשבשות את הדעות. For discussion of Ra'avad's position, see Isadore Twersky, *Rabad of Posquieres* (Cambridge: Harvard University Press, 1962), pp. 282–286.

regardless of one's intentions.[5] But as Kellner notes, in each case, these philosophers borrowed their arguments from lesser-known sources: from R. Shimon b. Tzemah Duran (Rashbetz) in the introduction to his commentary on Job, *Ohev Mishpat*, and R. Avraham Bibago in his philosophical work *Derekh Emunah*. These two thinkers, in turn, formulated their positions in a way that reveals the fundamental issues underlying their debate, and in fact anticipated much of the subsequent discussion about these topics.

In the course of his lengthy introduction to *Ohev Mishpat*, Rashbetz discusses the subject of the principles of Judaism, and says that Judaism can be reduced to one principle, or it contains as many principles as the number of letters or words in the Torah. As Rashbetz explains, the one principle of Judaism is to accept the entirety of what the Torah teaches; therefore, if one knowingly rejects *any* single word or letter of the Torah, that would qualify the individual as a heretic.[6] Following this, Rashbetz presents his view regarding inadvertent heresy:

> עוד יש לך לדעת כי מי שעלו בידו **שורשי התורה כראוי**, ועומק עיונו היטה אותו להאמין **בסעיף אחד מסעיפי האמונה** היפך ממה שהוסכם עליו שהוא הראוי להאמין... אע"פ שהוא טועה אינו כופר.

Rashbetz distinguishes between the "roots of the Torah" (*shorshei ha-Torah*) and the "branches of the faith" (*se'ifei ha-emunah*), and maintains that as long as one retains the "roots," an error concerning one of the "branches" does not qualify him as a heretic.[7]

---

5 See Albo, *Sefer ha-Ikkarim* 1:1-2; Abarbanel, *Rosh Amanah*, Ch. 12.

6 *Ohev Mishpat*, Ch. 9: דע אתה המעיין, כי העיקר הגדול בכל זה הוא להאמין מה שכללה אותו התורה בענינים אלו, ומי שכופר במה שכללה אותו התורה – עם היותו יודע שזהו דעת התורה – הוא כופר ואינו מכלל ישראל. ולזה יצדק לומר כי עיקרי התורה הם כמספר אותיות שבתורה או כמספר תיבות... כי מי שאינו מודה באחת מהן הוא משומד ואינו בכלל ישראל. ויצדק לומר גם כן שאין בתורה כי אם עיקר אחד והוא להאמין כי כל מה שכללה אותו התורה הוא האמת.

7 Kellner, in translating this passage ("Heresy and the Nature of Faith," p. 305), elides this distinction between "roots" and "branches":

> You also ought to know that one who has properly accepted **the roots of the Torah** but was moved to **deviate from them** by the depths of his speculation, and who thereby came to believe concerning one of the branches of the faith the opposite of what has been accepted as what one ought to believe… even though he errs, he is no denier. (Emphasis added.)

A more accurate translation would be: "One who has properly accepted the roots of the Torah, but the depths of his speculation swayed him to believe regarding **a single branch of the branches of the faith** the opposite of what

That the distinction between roots and branches is fundamental to Rashbetz's view is clear from the continuation of his discussion:

> וכן יש מחכמי ישראל מי שאמר שאין להם לישראל ימות המשיח שכבר אכלו אותו בימי חזקיה, ואע"פ שגינוהו חכמים על מאמרו וגילו טעותו אבל לא אמרו עליו שהוא כופר, אע"פ שמי שיאמין זה היום היה כופר לפי מה שהשרישוהו הרב [=הרמב"ם] ז"ל.[8] **והסיבה בזה הוא מה שקדמנו, שאחר שהם מודים בשורשים, אם בסעיף אחד מהשורשים הם בלתי מאמינים** מפני הכרח הפסוקים שעלו פירושהם בידם בטעות, אין להוציאם מפני זה מכלל ישראל. וענין אלישע בן אבויה הוא **סתירת העיקרים מכללם** והאמין בשתי רשויות הפך מצוות ה' אלקינו ה' אחד וכו', ומפני זה קראוהו מקצץ בנטיעות. **אבל המקיים הנטיעות בשורשיהם, ויקצץ פתילים בסעיפיהם, אף על פי שהוא טועה אינו כופר ומין.**

Here again, Rashbetz clearly distinguishes between "root" beliefs, such as divine unity, for which there can be no justification, and other beliefs, such as the advent of the messiah, which he maintains have the status of "branches," and which therefore can in certain cases be excused.[9]

To understand the significance of this distinction, let us turn to the opponent of Rashbetz's view, the aforementioned R. Avraham Bibago, a fifteenth-century Maimonidean philosopher. At the end of his work *Derekh Emunah*, R. Avraham Bibago responds to Ra'avad's attack on Rambam:

> אמנם מאמר הראב"ד הוא אצלי מבואר הפלא...והיה אפשר המצא איש מה בלתי מאמין בשום עיקר מהעיקרים ובשום אמונה מהאמונות התורה והיותו

---

has been accepted…" This example demonstrates the potential consequences of even a small error regarding the (translation of) roots of the Torah.

8 Here, Rashbetz seems to adopt a position similar to that of Hatam Sofer (*She'eilot u-Teshuvot*, *Yoreh De'ah*, no. 356) that although rejection of the belief in the messiah was not always heresy, the consensus of sages about this issue transformed its status as heresy: והאומר אין משיח וקים לי' כרבי הלל הרי הוא כופר בכלל התורה דכיילי אחרי רבים להטות כיון שרבו עליו חכמי ישראל ואמרו דלא כוותיה שוב אין אדם ראוי' להמשך אחריו כמו ע"ד משל במקומו של ר"א היו כורתים עצים לעשות פחמין לעשות ברזל לצורך מילה, ואחר דאיפסקא הלכתא ע"פ רבים מחכמי ישראל דלא כוותיה, העושה כן בשבת בעדים והתראה סקול יסקל ולא מצי למימר קים לי כר"א.
Perhaps, however, Rashbetz is arguing that following Rambam's explanation for this principle's inclusion as one of the thirteen principles of Judaism, it becomes nearly impossible for one to claim that his rejection of this principle was done without knowledge of the Torah's teaching on the subject, and therefore this is now considered to be a knowing rejection of the Torah's teaching.

9 For the distinction between "roots" and "branches," see *Ohev Mishpat*, Ch. 8, in which Rashbetz distinguishes between three "*avot*" and their "*toladot*."

בלתי מבין כוונת התורה ולא יקרא ולא יהיה מין וכופר. וזה כולו חוץ מן השכל ומן האמונה.[10]

In other words, according to Bibago, if one accepts Ra'avad's claim that beliefs arrived at by mistaken understanding do not constitute heresy, one can believe anything and still not be considered a heretic. This is a *reductio ad absurdum* argument—surely no Jewish thinker could arrive at the conclusion that all beliefs can be justified based on the ignorance of the one who holds them. Judaism, Bibago argues, is a religion defined by certain doctrines. Without adherence to these defining doctrines, one is not an adherent of the Jewish religion. Thus, inadvertence with regard to defining beliefs is not an excuse.

Kellner returns to this discussion in his *Must a Jew Believe Anything?* In this book, Kellner argues that Rambam distorted Judaism by defining it in terms of adherence to certain propositions. Kellner maintains that this Maimonidean innovation was rejected almost universally, and finds support for his own view from the case of inadvertent heresy: "The only two medieval thinkers who follow Maimonides [regarding inadvertent heresy] are R. Abraham Bibago and R. Isaac Abrabanel."[11]

However, the closer reading of Rashbetz presented above largely undermines Kellner's position. There is in fact *no* medieval thinker who endorses the notion that one can be a Jew in good standing lacking certain basic beliefs. In other words, Rashbetz accepts the *reductio ad absurdum* argument of Bibago: a Jew who innocently rejected every principle of Judaism, despite pure intentions, would not be a Jew in good standing, because Judaism is a religion defined by acceptance of certain doctrines. There is no such thing as a purely "attitudinal" faith in Judaism. Both Rashbetz and Bibago agree that Judaism has definitional beliefs. Their dispute is whether these definitional beliefs are identical with Rambam's thirteen principles (Bibago), or whether these *shorshei ha-emunah* are reducible to three principles (Rashbetz).

Kellner understood Rashbetz's reference to the "one principle" of Judaism—to accept everything taught in the Torah—as an articulation of "attitudinal faith," that all that matters is an *attitude* of acceptance of the

---

10 *Derekh Emunah*, p. 102c. Kellner (accurately) translates as follows:

> RABaD's statement is really amazing to me... It would be possible to find a man who does not believe in any one of the principles or beliefs of the Torah because of his failure to understand the meaning of the Torah. [On this position] such a one could be called neither a sectarian nor a heretic. All this opposes reason and faith. ("Heresy and the Nature of Faith," p. 302)

11 Kellner, *Must A Jew Believe Anything?* p. 68 n. 3.

Torah's teachings. Kellner therefore concludes his argument by claiming that Rashbetz was inconsistent, and that in fact Rashbetz did not understand the implications of his own position:

> All this is clear in retrospect. It was not so clear to the medieval figures whose texts we have been analyzing. This is indicated by the fact that strict consistency would demand that a thinker who defined "belief" in [attitudinal] terms ("belief in") should reject the notion of dogma or principles of faith altogether. This is emphatically not the case: Duran, Crescas, and Albo all put forward dogmatic systems of one form or another. They were willing to follow Maimonides' lead in laying down principles of faith for Judaism, even as they resisted adopting the conception of faith which underlay his system of dogmas.[12]

Rightly understood, however, Rashbetz's approach is entirely consistent. When Rashbetz refers to the (one) principle of accepting everything taught in the Torah, this means that one who knowingly rejects any teaching of the Torah is defined as a heretic. But this does not mean that there are no definitional beliefs that when lacking undermine one's standing as a Jew. Rashbetz's *shorshei ha-Torah* represent the (encapsulated) content of Judaism.[13]

Perhaps the best illustration of our argument comes from R. Yehuda Halevi's *Kuzari.* Kellner, in many of his works, presents Halevi's definition of being Jewish as the opposite of Rambam's—whereas for Rambam Judaism is defined as acceptance of a creed, for Halevi it is defined by means of biology, i.e., by descent from Abraham, Isaac, and Jacob.[14] For Kellner, the creedal definition of faith is a Maimonidean innovation that stands diametrically opposed to Halevi's notion of Jewish "essentialism."

Ironically, however, Halevi himself depicts the role of "propositional faith" in precisely the way that Rambam would subsequently. In his *Kuzari* (III:17), Halevi explains that the blessings of the *Shema* contain the principles of the Jewish faith, and that with acceptance of these principles, one can be called in truth part of Israel:

---

12 Kellner, "Heresy and the Nature of Faith," p. 318.

13 On the distinction between "two types of heresy," see also my article "ביאור שיטת מהרש"ל שחייב למסור נפשו שלא לשנות דברי תורה" in *Kovetz Hitzei Giborim*, vol. 8 (*Elul* 5775), pp. 829–833.

14 See, e.g., *Must a Jew Believe Anything*, pp. 2–5, 112-113; *Maimonides' Confrontation with Mysticism* (London: Littman Library, 2006), Ch. 7; *Maimonides on Judaism and the Jewish People*, p. 50: "Jewish identity is, contra Halevi, not a matter of genes, but of commitment."

ואחר כן יספר אותם עקרי האמונה אשר בהם תשלם האמונה היהודית, והם ההודאה באדנותו יתעלה, ובקדמותו, ובהשגחתו על אבותינו, ושהתורה מאתו, ובמופת על כל זה, והיא החתימה, והיא יציאת מצרים...**ומי שכלל את אלה בכוונה גמורה, הוא ישראלי באמת**, וראוי לו לייחל לדביקות בענין האלקי המתחבר בבני ישראל מבלעדי שאר האומות.[15]

Thus, even Halevi, who serves as Kellner's anti-Maimonidean foil in defining what it means to be a Jew, accepts the view that Jewish identity is defined by belief in certain key principles. In fact, not only staunch rationalists like Rambam (and the rest of the medieval Jewish philosophical tradition), but also "anti-rationalists" like Halevi, Nahmanides,[16] and Maharal[17] expounded what they saw to be the principles of Judaism.

In sum, Kellner has rightly identified two types of faith within Judaism, and this insight remains an important one. However, his application of this insight is flawed. Despite Kellner's best efforts, there is no support in the sources that he marshals for defining faith purely as an attitude of trust, which does not require acceptance of any specific doctrines. This seemingly minor point has significant ramifications for much of Kellner's discussion of dogma. Contra Kellner, all medieval authorities accept that Judaism requires belief in specific doctrines ("faith that"), because absent acceptance of the defining principles, the faith one "believes in" is not Judaism.[18] ☙

---

15 *Sefer ha-Kuzari*, trans. Y. Sheilat (Jerusalem, 2010), p. 76. This point about R. Yehuda Halevi maintaining that proper belief is a necessary criterion for entry into the Jewish people was drawn by Chaim Henoch, *Nachmanides: Philosopher and Mystic* (Jerusalem: The Harry Fischel Institute For Research In Jewish Law, 1982), p. 162 [Hebrew], as well as Isadore Twersky, *Halakhah ve-Hagut* (Tel Aviv: Open University, 1992), vol. 1, p. 74 n. 23.

16 See Henoch, *Nachmanides*, pp. 159–179.

17 Maharal, *Gevurot Hashem*, Ch. 47; R. David Cohen, *Ha-Emunah ha-Ne'emanah*, pp. 11–14.

18 Moshe Sokol, "Theoretical Grounds for Tolerance," in M. Sokol ed., *Tolerance, Dissent, and Democracy: Philosophical, Historical, and Halakhic Perspectives* (Oxford: Aronson, 2002), pp. 130–136, has already argued against Kellner's understanding of Rashbetz; however, I believe Sokol's interpretation remains imprecise. My own view is consistent with that of Julius Guttman, *Philosophies of Judaism*, pp. 279–280. After this paper was completed, I discovered another article by Menachem Kellner in which he addresses and disputes Guttman's position—see his "Rabbi Shimon ben Ẓemaḥ Duran on the Principles of Judaism: 'Ohev Mishpat,' Chapters VIII and IX," *PAAJR*, vol. 48 (1981), pp. 231–265; however, I found his arguments far from compelling. His "proofs" that Rashbetz does not distinguish between "roots" and "branches" require maintaining that there is no distinction between Rashbetz's "*avot*" and "*toladot*" in *Ohev Mishpat*, Ch. 8. Thus,

although belief in God's incorporeality and belief in the messiah are classified under the first and third of Rashbetz's principles, respectively, Rashbetz maintains that their denial is not equivalent to denial of an entire principle. On the other hand, denial of divine unity, i.e., belief in "two powers," undermines the entire principle of God's existence. Rashbetz himself makes this point explicitly, as quoted above. [See also above, note 7; Kellner repeats his mistaken translation in this article, p. 260.]

The Jewish Idea of Freedom

By: DAVID P. GOLDMAN

Never, perhaps in the history of human thought, has so much confusion surrounded the concept of freedom in the popular mind. Secular culture now asserts that all people are free to define themselves according to their whim, arbitrarily and without a nod to nature. This popular concept of freedom as expounded by the pop Existentialism of the 20th century now has been enshrined in American law, as in the first sentence of Justice Anthony Kennedy's majority decision in the Obergefell ruling on same-sex marriage: "The Constitution promises liberty to all within its reach, a liberty that includes certain specific rights that allow persons, within a lawful realm, to define and express their identity."

At the same time that secular culture asserts the absolute freedom of individual whim, it propounds an intellectual apparatus that altogether excludes the possibility of human freedom. It believes that scientists will make machines think the way that humans do, which means that human thought itself also must be mechanistic. It believes that analysis of brain waves somehow will account for human consciousness—even though physics cannot yet tell us what a wave might be. It believes that our consciousness is the product of random genetic mutation. It insists that endocrinologists and surgeons can take a person of one gender and make a person of the other gender. It believes that being determines consciousness, and that human nature can be transformed by an altered environment. Nonetheless, secular thought insists that we have the freedom to "define and express an identity," and that to assert natural constraints to human identity constitutes an offense to this freedom. The self-styled apostles of secular reason are as shameless as they are thoughtless in their inattention to the scandal of their own contradictions.

It is all the more urgent for religious Jews to make clear our concept of freedom, in contrast to this mishmash of crude determinism and pop-

---

David P. Goldman writes the Spengler column at *Asia Times Online* and blogs at PJ Media. He has written on Jewish topics for numerous publications including *First Things*, where he was a senior editor during 2009–2011, as well as *Tablet, The American Interest,* and *Commentary*. He is also a fellow at the Middle East Forum and at the London Center for Policy Studies. His book *How Civilizations Die (and Why Islam is Dying, Too)* was published in 2011 by Regnery. A book of essays, *It's Not the End of the World—It's Just the End of You* (Van Praag) also appeared in 2011.

existentialist bromides. This effort requires recourse to the tools and terminology of the Western philosophy founded on the thought of classical Greece, but it also exposes the failures of Western thought and sets in relief the alternative and in my view richer rabbinic account of man and the world.

The Jewish concept of freedom is the first such concept in human history and still the most radical. It asserts that the Covenant between God and man makes it possible for mortal man to rise to partnership with the Maker of Heaven in the continuing work of creation. It is different from the notions of freedom promulgated in the Christian West with its inheritance of Greek thought; indeed, the philosophical indifferentism of the secular West is the consequence of the failure of Greek philosophy and its successors.

Freedom is God's freedom, the freedom to create. Human freedom is *Imitatio Dei*, man's engagement in the divine work of creation. Freedom appeared first as a human possibility in the Hebrew Bible. It emerged in a rabbinic tradition that reaches from the Jewish sages of antiquity to the 20th-century writing of Rabbi Joseph Soloveitchik (known by his students as the "Rav") and other Jewish authorities. Our tradition teaches that man can become God's partner in creation, but to do so, he also must recreate himself. Man's mastery of nature in the cause of human majesty parallels man's self-mastery in covenantal community.

Man is dust and ashes, but he is also the master of nature. Freedom thus has a double meaning. Soloveitchik elaborated this view of humanity in his well-known homily on the two Adams in *The Lonely Man of Faith*. Adam the First is blessed with intelligence and creative drive *b-tzelem Elokim*, with the practical and functional intellect to gain control of nature. Adam the First establishes man's dignity by freeing humanity from hunger and disease: "Human existence is dignified because it is a glorious, majestic, powerful existence."

In the modern era, the Jewish idea of freedom is reborn in the political sphere through the 17th-century revolution in political thought that preceded the American Revolution. More subtle is the contribution of biblical and rabbinic thought to the contemporaneous scientific revolution.

We are not the passive victims of nature. We strive to establish human dignity by mastering nature. We do not need to worry whether there is an Intelligent Design, nor whether we might grasp such a design if it indeed exists: As creative beings, we are a wild card in the design. We cannot know the design, because we do not know what we have yet to accomplish. We do not agonize over natural disasters and what they might imply for divine justice: Nature itself is a challenge to humanity to rise to partnership with the Maker of Heaven.

Adam the Second, made from the dust of the earth, seeks the redemptive rather than the majestic. Cathartic redemption can be achieved not by control of one's environment, Soloveitchik wrote, but rather by control of one's self. Majestic man achieves a dignified existence by defying nature, a lower form of existence in Soloveitchik's words. Humble man achieves redemption by allowing himself to be defeated by a higher and truer Being. "Dignity is discovered at the summit of success, redemption in the depth of crisis and failure."

This parallel account of majestic and redemptive man involves more than homiletics: it is both an ontology and an anthropology that contends with the view of man and nature given to us by the Greeks. To say that Adam the First is creative implies that he is set in a natural world that is susceptible to further creation. And if God gave man the capacity for creation, then creative action must be not only possible but obligatory. God deliberately left the work of creation incomplete in order to provide room for man's creativity. This is perhaps the most original premise of Jewish philosophy. Any other ontological premise, though, reduces human creativity to a contingent and relative status, to the play of children amidst heavenly fixity.

Even the Greek gods were not free; they remained subject to the merciless rule of Fate, which decreed that Zeus would be overthrown just as he had overthrown his father Chronos. Humanity was the plaything of cruel and capricious gods, and where fate decreed a tragic outcome, the tragic hero could only proceed silently and helplessly to his doom. Oedipus had no choice in the killing of Laius, or Creon in the execution of Antigone, or Orestes in the murder of Clytemnestra. "The power of fate is a wonder, dark, terrible wonder—neither wealth nor armies nor towered walls nor ships' black hulls lashed by the salt can save us from that force," sang Sophocles' chorus in *Antigone.*

Greek ontology conforms to Greek anthropology. Neither Greek philosophy nor the Western philosophy that succeeded it can give an account of the most fundamental qualities of the real world as we perceive it, starting with the fact that we perceive different things in a world that changes. Parmenides postulated a world in which a static One was capable neither of individuation or change.[1] In Parmenides' theory, change and

---

1 The pre-Socratic philosopher Parmenides taught that the world was an unchanging, undifferentiated eternal One, and that change and differentiation belonged to the realm of illusion. The argument proceeded in the following steps. If we think or speak of something, it must exist (or "have Being"). The implications of Parmenides' assertion are elaborated In Plato's dialogue "Parmenides." If we cannot conceive of Non-Being, Parmenides tells the young Socrates, then we

multiplicity are illusions, and nothing really exists but the immutable One.[2] Socrates' theory of forms (*Ideon*) does not give us a remedy to Parmenides' paradox, for it dissipates into the infinite regress of the so-called

---

must think of Being as one big thing with no parts. It cannot change, for that would imply that some part of Being has become Non-Being, and we cannot conceive of Non-Being. Being cannot be differentiated into different kinds of Being, for that would imply that some part of Being contains Non-Being with respect to another part of Being, and so forth. Therefore the One exists, but not the Many.

Parmenides' theory is encapsulated in Fragments 6 and 8 of his surviving *Poem.*

6.1 That which is there to be spoken and thought of must be. For it is possible for it to be,
6.2 but not possible for nothing to be.
....

8.3 That being ungenerated it is also imperishable,
8.4 whole and of a single kind and unshaken and complete.
8.5 Nor was it ever nor will it be, since it is now, all together,
8.6 one, continuous. For what birth will you seek for it?
8.7 How and from where did it grow? I will not permit you to say
8.8 or to think from what is not; for it is not to be said or thought
8.9 that is not. What necessity would have stirred up
8.10 to grow later than earlier, beginning from nothing?
8.11 Thus it must either fully be or not.
8.12 Nor will the force of conviction ever permit anything to come to be from what is not,
8.13 besides it...
8.16 It is or it is not. But it has been decided, as is necessary,
8.17 to let go the one way as unthinkable and nameless (for it is not a true
8.18 way) and that the other is and is real.
8.19 How could what is be in the future? How could it come to be?
8.20 For if it came into being, it is not, not if it is ever going to be
8.21 In this way, coming to be has been extinguished and destruction is unheard of.
8.22 Nor is it divided, since it all is alike;
8.23 nor is it any more in any way, which would keep it from holding together,
8.24 or any less, but it is all full of what is.
8.25 Therefore, it is all continuous, for what is draws near to what is.
(Parmenides' Poem, trans. Richard D. McKirahan in *Philosophy before Socrates*, pp. 151–157).

2 Parmenides' argument seems valid only when we restrict the context to the perception of particular objects (obviously, we cannot perceive "no object"). It is exposed as a verbal trick to consider the *consciousness* in which perceptions arise. We cannot think of "nothing" as a particular object, but we can be bored by everything, and dread non-existence (in the form of our own death), as Martin

"third man problem."[3] Plato introduces intermediate states of being, or becoming, into the transient realm of perceived reality, while the Forms themselves remain eternal and unchanging. Human action can rearrange the ephemera but cannot affect the eternal realm. The heavens continue unperturbed in their perfection, set in motion by an indifferent Unmoved Mover. Humankind may have free will, but it is the freedom of children playing in the sandbox of the sublunar realm.

Plato's assertion that the perception of beauty leads us to the truth allows us only the freedom to appreciate a harmony that was complete before it drew our attention. Platonic beauty attracts us, leaving us only with the freedom that a moth has to approach the flame. In Jewish

---

Heidegger observed in "What is Metaphysics?" Sigmund Freud used a variant of Parmenides' paradox to make the opposite case: we cannot fear death because we cannot imagine our own death (if we try to imagine it we exist as a spectator). Therefore, Freud argued, religion's concern with mortality is merely a disguise for our real fears, for example, castration.

3 The Theory of Forms asserts that our sense perception is faulty, and that behind every object of perception there is an eternal and ideal form. This theory falls apart the moment we try to sort objects of perception according to specific forms. As Parmenides explains to the young Socrates in his eponymous dialogue, we can assert that there exists a form of "largeness" that governs our perception of size. The form of "largeness," though, also must itself be large, for it embodies the quality of largeness. The "largeness" of the form of largeness is a different, higher-order form of largeness than the largeness of ordinary measurement, and we require a new form of largeness that includes things that have both the quality of largeness and the form of largeness. But this new higher-order form of largeness must itself be large, so we require yet another higher-order form to include it as well as all the other manifestations of largeness, and so on ad infinitum.

The "Third Man" problem is an ancestor of Russell's Paradox in set theory, namely the attempt to define the set of all sets that are not members of themselves. If this set (by convention called "R") is not a member of itself then by definition it must contain itself; but if it contains itself, it cannot be the set of all sets that are not members of themselves. This is expressed informally in the example of a barber who shaves all men who don't shave themselves, and only men who don't shave themselves—which raises the question: Who shaves the barber?

There have been numerous attempts to resolve the "Third Man" problem, all of which involve an attempt to distinguish between different sorts of forms (the "largeness" of my grandmother's kneidlach is different from the "largeness" of the Form of "largeness"), none of them quite satisfactory. For a survey, see Pelletier and Zalta, "How to Say Goodbye to the Third Man Problem," in No^us, 34/2 (June 2000): 165–202.

thought, beauty is not a timeless Form that draws us to the Good, but a human perception, a temporal response to God's action in the world: God "made everything beautiful in its time; He also put an enigma [*Ha-Olam*] into their hearts so that man cannot comprehend what God has done from beginning to end," said Ecclesiastes (3:11).

If we reject Parmenides and declare instead with Heraclitus that Being is an illusion and that nothing exists but change, we come no closer to human freedom. I do not wish to enter into the debate about what Heraclitus actually meant, but in the understanding of the West, Heraclitus prefigures Nietzsche's embrace of non-Being as destruction.

Parmenides' problem of the One and the Many still haunts Western philosophy. Why do individual things exist, and not just one big thing? The problem of individuation remains a reproach to any philosophy that seeks to give an account of nature out of nature herself. Spinoza's *natura naturens* inherits the problem. God for Spinoza was merely nature, and the infinite substance he represents as God-in-nature is no more capable of generating many things than was the One of Parmenides.[4]

If we conceive of God as existing inside the natural world, then we can conceive of nothing else at all. Spinoza's God is a variant of Parmenides' One. Hegel quipped that the cause of Spinoza's death "was consumption, from which he had long been a sufferer; this was in harmony with his system of philosophy, according to which all particularity and individuality pass away in the one substance." That was nasty, but fair.

Gottfried Wilhelm Leibniz, the philosopher and mathematician who co-invented the Calculus, offered a cure for Spinoza's consumption. In place of a single "infinite substance," Leibniz proposed a "pre-established harmony" that governed an infinite number of independent "monads,"

---

4 Spinoza begins his Ethics with an ontological argument (Proposition XI): "God, or substance, consisting of infinite attributes, of which each expresses eternal and infinite essentiality, necessarily exists" because "if this be denied, conceive, if possible, that God does not exist: then his essence does not involve existence. But this is absurd. Therefore God necessarily exists." In Spinoza's words, "By God, I mean a being absolutely infinite" that is, a substance consisting in infinite attributes, of which each expresses eternal and infinite essentiality." God is reduced to the "substance" of nature. If God is inside nature, then there can be nothing in nature outside of God. Spinoza concludes: "As God is a being absolutely infinite . . . and he necessarily exists; if any substance besides God were granted it would have to be explained by some attribute of God, and thus two substances with the same attribute would exist, which is absurd; therefore, besides God no substance can be granted, or consequently, be conceived."

or atom-like entities each as unique as a snowflake. Leibniz added a theistic premise: By the law of sufficient reason, he argued, God does not do anything superfluous and therefore does not create anything twice. The systems of Spinoza and Leibniz seem to be mirror images: Spinoza's single substance cannot explain individuality, while Leibniz' individual monads cannot communicate with each other. We have a "pre-established harmony instead of infinite self-generating substance." But there is a fundamental difference: By turning Spinoza's system inside out, Leibniz makes room for God to return from his Babylonian captivity in *natura naturans*, to lordship over being.[5]

As Soloveitchik remarks (in a footnote to his doctoral dissertation), this was an ontological solution, one that no-one but the discoverer of the Calculus might have ventured.[6] The scientific revolution of the 17th century made it possible to conceive of the infinite within finitude, a concept that eluded the Greeks with their abhorrence of actual infinity. As Leibniz wrote to Foucher in 1692: "I am so in favor of the actual infinite that instead of admitting that Nature abhors it, as is commonly said, I hold that Nature makes frequent use of it everywhere, in order to show more effectively the perfections of its Author."[7] Ontology can rise above Parmenides' paradoxes only when it confronts the infinite. Inquiry about the infinite during the 20th century moved from philosophical abstraction to mathematical investigation. Soloveitchik was one of very few religious

---

5 Recent scholarship reports that Leibniz was deeply influenced by the Lurian Kabbalah; indeed, he criticized Spinoza for distorting the Kabbalah in his own system. In a 1706 letter to Foucher de Careil, Leibniz wrote:

> It is utterly true that Spinoza abused the Cabala of the Hebrews. And a certain person, who converted to Judaism and called himself Moses Germanus, followed his perverse opinions, as is shown in a refutation in German by Dr. Wachter, who knew him. But perhaps the Hebrews themselves and other ancient authors, especially in the East understand the proper meaning. Indeed, Spinoza formulated his monstrous doctrine from a combination of the Cabala and Cartesianism, corrupted to the extreme. He did not understand the true nature of monads...

Leibniz, comments author Allison Coudert, "was "interested in pointing out the ways in which Spinoza's philosophy distorted the Kabbalah and in relating both Spinoza's ideas and those of the Kabbalah to his own philosophy." See *Leibniz and the Kabbalah (Springer 2013)* by A.P. Coudert. There is an extensive literature on the influence of Kabbalah on 17th-century ontology. See for example *Leibniz et Spinoza*, by Georges Friedmann (Editions Gallimard, 1945).

6 Joseph Soloveitchik (Josef Solowiejczyk), *Das reine Denken und die Seinskonstituierung bei Hermann Cohen* (Berlin 1932), p. 82.

7 Quoted in *Leibniz's Metaphysics of Time and Space*, by Michael Futch (Springer 2008), p. 84.

thinkers to understand the theological importance of the mathematics of the infinite.[8]

---

8 Soloveitchik's essay *The Halakhic Mind* asserts that the collapse of the deterministic philosophy associated with Newtonian physics and Kantian philosophy made philosophy of religion possible in the first place, for if the deterministic model of the world holds true, religion is reduced to subjectivism and mysticism. The Rav was well aware that Kantian philosophy broke down in the face of the mathematical discoveries of the late 19th century.

Parmenides had asserted, "That which is there to be spoken and thought of must be," and Plato took this further to mean that all well-defined concepts must correspond to something that actually exists. Aristotelian realism countered that there are any number of things we can define in great detail (the mythical Phoenix, in St. Thomas Aquinas' example, or a hundred imaginary dollars in my pocket, according to Kant). Plato's Theory of Forms thus fails on two counts. First, we cannot satisfactorily define any Form (due to the "Third Man" problem of infinite regress), and second, we can define the Form of something imaginary as well as we can of something real. Aristotle countered that everything in the mind must come from the senses—the perception of something that actually exists"—and that we should restrict attention to "instantiated universals" (collections of things on which we have sense data). Aristotle's empiricism, in turn, failed on two counts. First, the 17th--century revolution in mathematical physics identified things in the mind (such as the infinitesimals of the Calculus and complex numbers) that do not exist in the senses yet correspond to real things in nature, such as planetary orbits and the trajectory of cannon balls. Second, as David Hume argued, cause and effect cannot be derived from sense data. Kant's synthetic a priori reason attempted to patch up the shattered Aristotelian system, by asserting an interaction between the mind's a priori capacity for synthetic judgments and sense data. Kant offered a model that united sense perception with transcendental thinking. As Rav Soloveitchik observed, this model collapsed when mathematicians discovered objects that cannot possibly be perceived by the senses but nonetheless are real. One example is the discovery of non-Euclidean geometries which can be understood but not 'seen' in the sense of conventional geometry. Another example is to be found in a set of functions first identified by Karl Weierstrass; these functions shift sign from positive to negative at infinitely small intervals. Weierstrass' curves have no tangents. Although they are continuous, they resist analysis by the Newton-Leibniz Calculus. The Rav writes on page 126:

> "That mathematics is not synonymous with receptive intuition, as Kant thought, was amply demonstrated by modern mathematics. It is sufficient to consider the Weierstrass curve in order to convince oneself of the incommensurability of mathematical knowledge with 'sensuous' intuition. The development of non-Euclidean geometry refuted Kant's 'Transcendental Aesthetics' completely." For more background on the theological implications of mathematical discoveries, see "The God of the Mathematicians: The Religious Beliefs That Guided Kurt Gödel's Revolutionary Ideas," in *First Things*, August 2010.

Leibniz' scheme had two defects. The first is that his assertion that a good God would make only the best of all possible worlds does not explain why nature can be so nasty. The second is that in this best of all possible worlds, all unpleasant things somehow must be for the best. (The Midrash conjectures that God had made and destroyed many worlds before this one, and that some might have been more beautiful than this one, Rav Soloveitchik observed).[9] Dr. Pangloss tells Candide at the end of the novel that if all those terrible things had not happened, he would not be eating preserved lemons and pistachio nuts. Voltaire was a scoundrel, but here he was correct.

The best of all possible worlds does not need us to improve it. All events must be a concatenation of one sort or another that works out for the best, even if it does not seem that way to us. Freedom remains as remote from Leibniz' system as from Spinoza's, or from those of Parmenides and Plato. Spinoza's infinite substance crowds out everything but the God of nature; Leibniz' best-of-all-possible worlds removes the need for change.

The Hebrew Bible and its rabbinic interpreters saw things otherwise. Psalm 102 declares (in the KJV translation):

> Of old didst thou lay the foundation of the earth; And the heavens are the work of thy hands.
> They shall perish, but thou shalt endure; Yea, all of them shall wax old like a garment; As a vesture shalt thou change them, and they shall be changed:
> But thou art the same, And thy years shall have no end.
> The children of thy servants shall continue,
> And their seed shall be established before thee.

It is not the sublunar realm that is ephemeral but the heavens themselves, and we servants of the Lord will endure forever while God changes the heavens like a suit of clothes. In the understanding of the rabbis, this is not hyperbole but ontology. The existence of the world in the presence of an infinite God—Spinoza's problem—requires an understanding radically different from that of Parmenides or Plotinus, and this we encounter in the concept divine self-contraction, or *tzimtzum*, as Soloveitchik notes.[10]

---

9 "The Midrash relates that God created and destroyed many worlds before He allowed this world to remain in existence. Some of the earlier worlds were even more beautiful than the present one, but the Creator eliminated them. He then went ahead and created this world, which has endured." Quoted in *The Rav*, by Aharon Rakeffet-Rothkof (Vol. 2), p. 15.

10 In *From There You Shall Seek*, Soloveitchik writes (p. 172):

It is not only that God by the principle sufficient reason does not make the same snowflake twice, as Leibniz argued; for the world to exist, God had to withdraw from the world in order to make room for it. Holiness for Soloveitchik "is the 'contraction' of infinity within a finitude bound by laws, measures and standards, the appearance of transcendence within empirical reality." Unlike the Greeks, Judaism embraces the actual infinite.

In this context Soloveitchik drew attention to a remarkable passage in the monthly Jewish prayer for the sanctification of the moon:

> May it be your will, O Lord, my God and God of my fathers to fill in the darkness of the moon that she not be diminished at all. And let the light of the moon be as the light of the sun, and as the light of the seven days of creation, just as she was before she was diminished, as it is said: "the two great lights." And may we be a fulfillment of the verse: "And they shall seek out the Lord their God and David their king."

We pray, in other words, for the restoration of the moon to its original status on par with the sun. This rests on the Sages' reading of Genesis 1:16, in which sun and moon first are called "two great lights," and immediately afterward the "greater light" and the "lesser light." God evidently diminished the moon. The Sages offered several homiletic explanations which are less important here than the remarkable assertion that God deliberately introduced an imperfection into the heavens, which we hope to see corrected in the Messianic era, and this in an epoch where all the peoples worshipped heavenly bodies as divine beings. It is clear how much the rabbinic differs from the idea of "fallen" nature; the diminution of the moon occurred before the creation of humans.[11]

This entire matter is explained in R. Isaac Luria's doctrine of *tzimtzum*. In this view, God "constricted" His glory in order to create the world, leaving an open, empty "space in the middle"—that is, the act of creation is composed of separation and advance. God separated himself from the world when He had the idea of creating it, and this separation is the beginning of the act of creation, since the world cannot exist in the bosom of the Holy One, Blessed Be He, as His infinite being precludes any other existence.

11 A stand of Christian theodicy attempts to explain human suffering at the hands of nature by reference to the "Fall of Man" in the Garden of Eden, before which nature supposedly was benign. The Orthodox Christian theologian David Bentley Hart writes of "Christian belief in an ancient alienation from God that has wounded creation in its uttermost depths, and reduced cosmic time to a shadowy remnant of the world God intends, and enslaved creation to spiritual and terrestrial powers hostile to God." See D.B. Hart, "Tsunami and Theodicy," in *First Things*, March 2005.

Brit milah according to Ḥazal was the supreme example of human intervention to improve on God's definitive work, the creation of *tzelem Elokim*, the human being itself. The work of man is greater than the work of God, Rabbi Akiva famously argued to the Roman Governor Turnus Rufus, because man transforms what God has created into something better:

> Once the evil [Roman governor] Turnus Rufus asked Rabbi Akiva, 'Whose deeds are greater—God's or man's?' He replied, 'Man's deeds are greater.' Turnus Rufus asked him, 'Is man then capable of creating heaven and earth, or anything like them?' Rabbi Akiva replied, 'I was not referring to the sphere beyond man's ability, over which he has no control. I refer to those creations of which man is capable.' He then asked, 'Why do you circumcise yourselves?' Rabbi Akiva replied, 'I knew that that was the point of your question, and therefore I answered in the first place that man's deeds are greater than God's.' Rabbi Akiva brought him grains of wheat and some bread, and said: 'These grains of wheat are God's handiwork, and the bread is the handiwork of man. Is the latter not greater than the former?'
>
> The Roman mocked Akiva, asking the sage, 'If God wanted you to perform circumcision, why did He not create the child already circumcised while still in the womb?' Rabbi Akiva answered, "Why do you not ask the same question concerning the umbilical cord, which remains attached to him and which his mother must cut? In response to your question—the reason why he does not emerge already circumcised is because God gave Israel the commandments in order that they would be purified by performing them. Therefore David wrote, 'Every word of God is pure' (or, purified).'[12]

There is no paradox of the one and the many in rabbinic thought: God made room for the world through self-contraction, and created it through acts of individuation, separating first light from darkness, and then sea from dry land. Nor is there a paradox of omniscience and omnipotence: God limited himself by making a covenant with man that made man a partner in the continuing work of creation.

---

12 *Midrash Tanhuma, Tazria* 5. See *Sefer Ha-Ḥinukh,* Mitzvah 2, "The eternal L-rd desired to perfect the [physical] character of the chosen people and he wished that this perfection be effected by man. He did not create him complete and perfect from the womb, in order to hint to him that just as the perfection of his physical form is by his own hand, so does it lie in his hand to complete his spiritual form by the worthiness of his actions."

The imperfection of the created world, we have seen, is explicit in Psalm 102, and implicit (as Jonathan Levenson observes[13]) in references to a primal chaos that threatens to reassert itself (as in Psalm 74:14 and Isaiah 27:1). Yet the rabbis first speak explicitly of man as co-creator in the sphere of Adam the Second, redemptive and covenantal man. We read in the Talmud: "The judge who judges his fellows fairly for just one hour, renders a just decision; it is as though he had collaborated with God in the work of Creation."[14] And again: "A person who recites [the blessing] *Vayekhelu* on eve of Shabbat is considered as if he were a partner with God in the work of creation."[15] To become God's partner in creation requires man to cleave to God's will, first of all in pursuing justice.

Teshuva—repentance, or "return"—is a creative act. Rav Soloveitchik wrote that "Man, through repentance, creates himself, his own I." Forgiveness of sin is possible because the penitent has recreated himself and become a new person. The classicist David Konstan (cited by Rabbi Lord Jonathan Sacks) observes that the first person to be forgiven in the annals of human experience is Judah, and the first person to forgive is Joseph. Forgiveness in this biblical sense did not exist for the ancient Greeks. One could appease the anger of the gods or of another person, but the offense cannot be erased.[16] Rabbi Sacks explains that Joseph can forgive Judah because Judah has become a different man: when Judah intercedes to save his brother Benjamin from slavery, he has become a different person than the envious older brother who sold Joseph into slavery twenty years earlier. Judah can be forgiven because he has become a new man.[17] In light of the sinner's self-transformation into a new person, the old sin is regarded as unintentional: the new person never would have intended to

---

13 In Creation and the Persistence of Evil (Princeton 1988), p. 15.

14 Shabbat 10a.

15 Shabbat 119b.

16 David Konstan, Before Forgiveness: the origins of a moral idea. Cambridge: Cambridge University Press, 2010

17 <http://www.rabbisacks.org/birth-forgiveness-vayigash-5775/>.
Rambam writes in Hilchos Teshuva (Section 2, Halacha 4) that the repentant sinner may take on a new name to declare that he is a new man:
Among the paths of repentance is for the penitent to
a) constantly call out before God, crying and entreating;
b) to perform charity according to his potential;
c) to separate himself far from the object of his sin;
d) to change his name, as if to say "I am a different person and not the same one who sinned";
e) to change his behavior in its entirety to the good and the path of righteousness; and f) to travel in exile from his home. Exile atones for sin because it causes a person to be submissive, humble, and meek of spirit.

commit such a sin. To the recreated penitent, the sin committed by his former self was an error that he would not commit now. If character is destiny, Judaism asserts that man can change destiny by changing his character. Greek literature is tragic; the subject of Jewish Scripture is tragedy averted or mitigated by *teshuva.*

Adam the Second is social man who seeks community and covenant. He enters freely into partnership with God. Soloveitchik states that "the giving of the Law on Mount Sinai was the result of free negotiation between Moses and the people who consented to submit themselves to divine will." In the biblical account God did not simply free Israel from Egyptian slavery, a unique event in human history, but he summoned them out of degradation and weakness to be a free people unlike the tribes and empires that surrounded them. According to Rabbi Lord Sacks, "The concept of the moral limits of power is more important to freedom than is democracy. For democracy contains within it a fatal danger. Tocqueville gave it a name: the 'tyranny of the majority.' A majority can oppress a minority. The only defense against this is to establish the moral limits of power… Biblical politics is limited politics—the political of liberal democracies, not of the Greek city state."

Modern democracy drew more from the Bible and rabbinic sources than it did from the Greek polis. As the historian Eric Nelson wrote in his book *The Hebrew Republic*, the English revolutionaries of the 17th century returned to the biblical concept of election in response to the catastrophic failure of the European political model. The Religious Wars of the 16th and 17th centuries contested the claims of kings by divine right and nations by divine election. In the standard account, the republican challenge to monarchy came from secular philosophers like Spinoza and Hobbes. This is misleading: As Nelson shows, the English republicans who sowed the seeds of the American founding drew their ideas from biblical and rabbinic sources. John Milton proposed an English Republic in 1649 on the strength of the Midrash Rabbah on Deuteronomy 17:14, which likens kings to idols and condemns as idolaters those who put their trust in princes. Milton, Algernon Sidney, James Harrington, and other English revolutionaries made a biblical case against monarchy that Thomas Paine later cribbed in his 1776 pamphlet "Common Sense." Israel's free choice to enter into the Covenant at Sinai became the founding principle of the American Constitution.

Adam the First and Adam the Second are the same man, and the ontological freedom of Adam the First must be of the same order as Adam the Second's ethical freedom. Adam the First's search for dignity and Adam the Second's search for redemption ultimately are the same quest by the same individual. "Halakhic man," the Jew whose religious impulse is channeled into Torah learning, acts more like a mathematician than a mystic. If the scientist seeks to penetrate infinite complexities of creation, the Torah scholar seeks access to the infinite mind of God. The Rav's grandnephew Rabbi Meir Soloveitchik writes, "The Torah draws the Jew into engagement with God's infinite mind… Although the Torah contains in potential all that God wants to teach us, all the generations of Israel labor together to make this manifest. Because the Torah is infinite and inexhaustible, learning Torah yields new insights—what the rabbis called *ḥiddushim*, or innovations."[18] The Rav's contention that the collapse of scientific determinism opened a new horizon for the philosophy of religion parallels the thinking of the great Austrian mathematician Kurt Gödel, whose proof of the incompleteness of mathematical systems destroyed the philosophical foundation of the deterministic model. Gödel, who was deeply religious, argued that mathematics entailed an infinite sequence of discoveries, where new axioms arose from intuition rather than formal logic.[19]

The parallel tracks of Torah learning and scientific investigation sometimes converge. The most striking example in my view is the influence upon mathematics of the biblical concept of time.

---

18 <http://www.firstthings.com/article/2010/10/torah-and-incarnation>.

19 Gödel wrote in a 1961 essay that the supposed "foundational crisis" in mathematics at the turn of the 20th century was not a problem for mathematics at all, but for philosophy: "Around the turn of the century…it was the antinomies of set theory, contradictions that allegedly appeared within mathematics, whose significance was exaggerated by skeptics and empiricists…I say "allegedly" and "exaggerated" because, in the first place, these contradictions did not appear within mathematics but near its outermost boundary towards philosophy, and secondly, they have been resolved in a manner that is completely satisfactory and, for everyone who understands the theory, nearly obvious." Gödel continued that "the certainty of mathematics is to be secured" not by looking for agreement with systems of philosophy, but "by seeking to gain insights into the solvability, and the actual methods for the solution, of all meaningful mathematical problems….it turns out that in the systemic establishment of the axioms of mathematics, new axioms, which do not follow by formal logic from those previously established by formal logic, again and again become evident…every clearly posed mathematical yes-or-no question is solvable in this way. For it is just this becoming evident of more and more new axioms on the basis of the meaning of the primitive notions that a machine cannot imitate." See Kurt Gödel, *Collected Works Volume III* (Oxford 1995) pp. 377–385. Unlike the determinists, who sought to reduce all mathematics to a single system of logic, Gödel demonstrated that mathematical discovery had to end, but rather involved the creative discovery of new axioms "which do not follow by formal logic by those previously established by formal logic."

Soloveitchik writes in his essay *The Halakhic Mind*:

> The reversibility of time and of the causal order is fundamental in religion, for otherwise the principle of conversion would be sheer nonsense. The act of reconstructing past psychical life, of changing the arrow of time from a forward to a retrospective direction, is the main premise of penitence...The homo religiosus, oscillating between sin and remorse, flight from and return to God, frequently explores not only the traces of a bygone past retained in memory, but a living "past" which is consummated in his emergent time-consciousness. It is irrelevant whether reversibility is a transcendental act bordering on the miraculous, as Kierkegaard wants us to believe, or a natural phenomenon that has its roots in the unique structure of the religious act. The paradox of a directed yet reversible time concept remains.

Repentance changes the future by redirecting the chain of the events set in motion by the original sin. *Teshuva* can change destiny. But the transformation of moral time has implications for the physical realm. The existential time of human existence is not the same as the clockwork of heavenly bodies. For the Greeks, time is the demarcation of events. But in Hebrew time, it is the moment itself that remains imperceptible. As Kohelet 3:15 states: "That which is, already has been; and that which is to be has already been; and only God can find the fleeting moment."[20]

A red thread connects the biblical notion of time to the 17th-century scientific revolution. After Ecclesiastes, we first hear of a point of time without duration in Book 11 of St. Augustine's Confessions. Aristotle's account of time as a sequence of moments, in Augustine's view, leads to absurdities. The moment itself is immeasurable as it passes with ineffable speed. Events that have passed no longer exist, which means that measuring past time is an attempt to measure something that does not exist. The future is not yet here. Our perception of past events thus depends on memory, and our thoughts about future events depend on expectation. Expectation and memory, Augustine adds, determine our perception of distant past and future: "It is not then future time that is long, for as yet it is not: But a long future, is 'a long expectation of the future,' nor is it time past, which now is not, that is long; but a long past is 'a long memory

---

20 The word *nirdaf* is usually translated as "the pursued." The19th-century Torah scholar and polymath Michael Friedländer (best known today as the first English translator of *The Guide for the Perplexed*) rendered it as "the fleeting moment" in his English version of the Tanakh, still in print as *The Jerusalem Bible* (Koren). Rabbi Friedländer may have been influenced by Goethe's Faust (verse 1700 et. Seq.).

of the past.'" Reflecting on Augustine, Franz Rosenzweig wrote in The Star of Redemption, "Revelation is the first thing to set its mark firmly into the middle of time; only after Revelation do we have an immovable Before and Afterward. Then there is a reckoning of time independent of the reckoner and the place of reckoning, valid for all the places of the world."

Augustine's meditation on the nature of time usually is portrayed as a psychology. But Augustine proposed this as an ontology of time as well. In Augustine's discussion of the moment in time without duration, we have the first intimation of the infinitesimal moment later embodied in the calculus of Newton and Leibniz. Applied to musical rhythm, Augustine's theory of time brings forth what he called "numeri iudiciales." These "'numbers of judgment'" bridge eternity and mortal time; they are eternal in character and lie outside of our ordinary concept of number, but act as an ordering principle for all other numbers.[21]

In Augustine's "numbers of judgment" we have the first intimation of the 17th-century mathematical revolution.[22] It portended the great leap from the world of Aristotle, for whom everything in the mind must first be in the senses, to the world of higher mathematics, where abstract thought created concepts that the senses could not fathom (infinitesimal magnitudes and multi-dimensional geometries, for example), but the intellect could apply to the mastery of nature. Kohelet's contemplation of human mortality before God's infinity as refracted through Augustine's meditation on time and mortality was the point of origin of modern mathematical physics.

Adam the First stands in fear and trembling before God, overwhelmed by his mortality. He perceives the infinite reach of eternity and the vanishing smallness of the moments of his life. In his search for redemption he reverses the arrow of time. He learns to "count his days and gain a heart of wisdom." With this wisdom Adam the Second reaches out to the infinite and joins God in the continuing work of creation. ☙

---

21 In the Sixth Book of *De Musica Libri Sei,* Augustine presents a hierarchy of rhythm that begins with "sounding numbers"—the rhythm we actually hear—followed by "memorized rhythms," that is, the mind's recognition and remembrance of a pattern. Rising above all such numbers is what Augustine calls "consideration," the numeri iudiciales. These "numbers of judgment" bridge eternity and mortal time; they are eternal in character and lie outside of rhythm itself but act as an ordering principle for all other rhythms. Only they are immortal, for the others pass away instantly as they sound, or fade gradually from our memory. They are, moreover, a gift from God, for "from where should we believe that the soul is given what is eternal and unchangeable, if not from the one, eternal, and unchangeable God?"

22 See David P. Goldman, "The Divine Music of Mathematics," *First Things*, April 2012.

God, Man, Chaos and Control: How God Might Control the Universe

By: ALAN KADISH

Introduction

In 1911 a Belgian Chemist by the name of Ernest Solvay hosted the world's leading scientists for a weekend of discussions and debates in Paris, now referred to as thc First Solvay Conference. The youngest invitee was none other than Albert Einstein, at the age of twenty-two. By the Fifth Solvay Conference in 1927, when Albert Einstein was an established member of the scientific community, the main topic on the discussion floor was the newly founded theory of quantum mechanics. A founding principle of quantum mechanics was that one cannot determine both the precise location and momentum of an electron with absolute certainty. This concept is known as the Heisenberg Uncertainty Principle.[1] Because the Uncertainty Principle, discussed at the conference, challenged a basic tenet of physics, claiming that the universe was inherently uncertain, it offended Albert Einstein's sensibilities. His reaction to this aspect of quantum mechanics was "God would not play dice with the universe."

---

1 Quantum mechanics was first proposed by Schrödinger and Heisenberg. One of its primary concepts states that at very microscopic sizes—those shorter than Planck's length, 1.616199(77) x 10^{-35M}—the location and momentum of an object cannot be determined simultaneously. One can state with a certain probability that an electron or other object would be present at a particular location, but not with certainty, except at the expense of knowing its velocity and motion.

Alan Kadish, M.D., is president of Touro College and University System, the largest Jewish-sponsored educational institution in the United States. He taught at the University of Michigan and enjoyed a 19-year tenure at Northwestern University, where he served as the Chester and Deborah Cooley Professor of Medicine, senior associate chief of the cardiology division, and director of the cardiovascular clinical trials unit, and served on the finance and investment committees of the Northwestern clinical practice plan. Dr. Kadish has published over 250 peer-reviewed papers and contributed to several textbooks. He graduated Albert Einstein College of Medicine at Yeshiva University and received postdoctoral training at the Brigham and Women's Hospital, an affiliate of Harvard Medical School, and at the Hospital of the University of Pennsylvania, where he was a fellow in cardiology.

Einstein believed that the physical principles that operate the universe must be precise and always quantifiable. His dismissal of quantum mechanics, a theory that has since been validated in a variety of experiments, is a widely cited example of an error made by a great genius. However, one could argue that Einstein's reservation about quantum mechanics reflects sensitivity for a deterministic nature of the universe that bridges the gap between science and theology. The acceptance of quantum mechanics as a factor in—and not a rejection of—God's method for affecting our reality opens a "backdoor" for divine intervention to affect physical events without the possibility of human detection.

The possibility that quantum mechanics represents a mechanism for God's control of the universe has been discussed by both physicists and theologians in the last few decades.[2] Most prominently Nicolas Saunders[3] and his critics have focused on whether advances in physics allow what Saunders calls SDA (Special Divine Action) to be part of the current universe as we understand it. Saunders concluded that SDA was not consistent with his understanding of modern physics. However, the discussion centered on an aspect of quantum mechanics that is still poorly understood, namely whether quantum mechanics is "deterministic," in its ability to provide ontological certainty even if there is no epistemological certainty. In other words, the aspect in question is whether the outcome of an immensely complex quantum interaction is predictable if all the variables are known in advance. In the years since Saunders first published, new theories have been developed to push this conversation further than ever before.

The purpose of this article is to review the problem of free will and divine intervention from the prism of Jewish sources, within the context of modern science. Among the many lenses the Jewish tradition provides for us to frame history is the division between times of open miracles and hidden miracles. The Bible is full of open miracles, divine revelation, and prophecies. Whereas there is controversy among rabbinic scholars and theologians about whether the miracles happened through natural or supernatural forces, either way, the miracles were still immediately recognizable as acts of God. However, since the destruction of the Jerusalem

---

2 For a few very recent examples: *The Divine Order, the Human Order, and the Order of Nature: Historical Perspectives,* Edited by Eric Watkins (Oxford University Press); Jeremy Brown, *New Heavens and a New Earth: The Jewish Reception of Copernican Thought* (Oxford University Press, 2013); Moshe Meiselman, *Torah, Chazal & Science* (New Jersey: Israel Bookshop Publications, 2013); Yoram Bogacz, *Genesis & Genes* (New York: Feldheim, 2012).

3 Nicholas Saunders, *Divine Action and Modern Science* (Cambridge: Cambridge University Press, 2002).

Temple in 70 CE, those aspects of the Jewish understanding of God's manifestation are absent from our modern world. Religious philosophers in the Jewish intellectual legacy, who will be discussed below, have offered many explanations for how God may intervene in our lives in a post-open-revelation era. Furthermore I will focus on more recent advances in the understanding of quantum mechanics as they have altered the discussion since a decade ago when Saunders concluded that SDA was not consistent with his understanding of modern theories of nonlinear dynamics (a theory that will be discussed in greater detail later) and quantum mechanics.

Free Will and God's Intervention: the Dilemma

One of the unresolved dilemmas that have troubled monotheistic religions over the past two millennia is the apparent contradiction between man's free will and providence, which is God's plan for the world and universe. On the one hand, the dilemma assumes that in order for accountability, human choice must be free. On the other hand, God has a specific plan for the future of the world. During times of miracles and revelation, God's immediate influence over world events and personal lives was unquestionable. However, in a time where God's immediacy is not inherently apparent, defining the nature of free will's relationship with divine providence is much more difficult.

At first approach, the Jewish tradition appears to be most comfortable with the view that man has unlimited free choice. This tradition begins with the text of the Bible, God telling the people of Israel: "See I have placed before you today two choices, those that will lead to a blessing and those that will lead to a curse" (Deuteronomy 11:26). In the most central of Jewish prayers, the Shema, the second of the three paragraphs deals extensively with the concept of reward and punishment, in response to good or bad. As Saadiah Gaon in the 10th century suggested, it would be inconceivable that God would reward or punish people based on their actions if they did not have free choice.[4]

However, one only need to look earlier in the Hebrew Bible for a contradicting source. God tells Abraham in a prophetic conversation: "Your descendants will be strangers in a land that is not theirs where they will be enslaved and worked for four hundred years. And the nation whom they will serve, I will judge them and afterward [your descendants] will leave with great wealth" (Genesis 15:13-14). This declaration by God would seem to imply that Abraham, his descendants, and the civilization

---

4 Rabbi Saadiah ben Yosef Gaon c. 882–942. *Emunot v-Deot,* Treatise 5, standard edition.

of Egypt will have no agency in preventing these events from unfolding in any other way than God decreed. This would seem to imply that God's divine providence, and not man's independent free choice, determines the course of history.

Furthermore, with regard to the exodus story, God seems to transcend the boundary of influencing global events to influencing the choices of an individual person. The verses in the exodus story where God hardens Pharaoh's heart can be interpreted as divine influence over free will.[5] This story demonstrates a biblical understanding that God does indeed have a mechanism to alter personal free will.

However, this unique story may be interpreted as the exception that proves the rule exemplifying God's reticence to manipulate free will. At no other point in the biblical stories does it recall this device again, even when it would have been advantageous. Moreover, the language of the verse can be read and interpreted differently. It is not clear that God forcibly changed Pharaoh's mind or independently hardened his heart. The verse could imply that God manipulated external events in such a way as to subtly influence Pharaoh to harden his own heart.

If the two precepts of free will and divine providence are true, God must influence the world and human action while not trampling on free choice, a balance that seems impossible. This paradox has troubled religious philosophers from a variety of religions for at least two millennia.[6] According to Josephus this dilemma was one of the major factors responsible for the development of different Jewish sects at the time of the second Temple.[7] The Sadducees,[8] Pharisees, and Essenes each had a widely disparate view on reconciling the unlimited free choice of individuals with the belief in a specific divine plan that guides events in the world. The Essenes[9] believed in predestination and vastly limited the scope of man's apparent free will. In contrast, the Sadducees believed that God's involvement in the world did not extend to controlling events. Finally, the Pharisees, who formed the basic tradition of rabbinical Judaism throughout the past two millennia, took a balanced approach and attempted to reconcile the inherent contradiction of faith in an activist deity who planned

5 See Exodus 9:12 and biblical commentaries.

6 See R.C. Sproul, *Willing to Believe: The Controversy over Free Will* (Grand Rapids: Baker Books, 1997).

7 *Antiquities*, 13:5:9.

8 For a brief description of this sect see the insert Sadducees in the Jewish Encyclopedia.

9 For a brief description of this sect see the insert Essenes in the Jewish Encyclopedia.

and controlled events in the world, and faith in the primacy of free choice for individuals. This dichotomy fueled many discussions in rabbinic Judaism.[10]

Returning to the dilemma of reconciling free will with divine intervention in a modern context, it is clear that in order to be considered free will, free-willed choice has to be unconstrained by the laws of nature and not determined by physical phenomena. Therefore, if the universe contains free will, then an exercise in free will must transcend both the determinism of classical physics and the randomness of quantum mechanics. This definition of free will demands the existence of each person's persistent consciousness free from a pure causal influence from outside physical sources.[11] However, the classical understanding of divine providence assumes that while individuals may influence the events around them, it is only with Divine approbation that the world is changed.[12] At the extreme, the two claims that free will exists and that God's providence influences the future are undeniably at odds with one another. Even if we suggest that the paradox of unfettered free will and divine providence is easier to reconcile as the degree of control one assumes that God chooses to exerts over day-to-day events diminishes, the very existence of God's power of providence, whether it is used or not, maintains the paradox.

In addition, to further clarify the relationship between an omniscient deity and the freedom of man, a parallel issue must be considered: the issue of free choice and divine foreknowledge. Some Jewish philosophers and theologians who believed that God accurately knows what choices

---

10 In the rabbinic literature, the most famous avowal of both God's providence and man's free will is made by Rabbi Akiva, who is recorded as saying, "everything is seen and freedom of choice is given" (Mishnah *Avot* 3:19). Though commonly understood to mean that everything is *foreseen*, there have been those who interpreted the term in the sense of *not able to be hidden*. For example, Ephraim Urbach writes, "The content of the Mishna likewise shows that R. Akiba's intention was not to resolve the contradiction between [God's] foreknowledge and [man's] freewill, but to make man realize his responsibility for his actions. This responsibility is grounded in two factors: in the permission given to man to choose his own way and in the realization that man is destined to account for his actions before Him who sees and examines his ways" (Ephraim Elimelech Urbach, *The Sages*, Volume 1 pp: 257-8 (Jerusalem: Magner Press, 1975). Yet Urbach was not the first to interpret Rabbi Akiva's words as such. See Dr. Michael Shmidman, "Radical Theology in Defense of Faith: A Fourteenth-Century Example," *Tradition* (41:2), for medieval exponents of this interpretation.

11 A. J. Ayer, "Freedom and Necessity," *Philosophical Essays* (London: Macmillan, 1954).

12 Mordechai's speech to Esther, *Megilat Esther,* 4:13-14.

man will make in the future considered that this knowledge could preclude free choice. This presents a fundamental question in theology: How can one's choices be free if the end result is already known? Other thinkers, such as Saadiah Gaon, who suggested that knowledge is not necessarily causative or determinative, are therefore not troubled by this paradox.[13] However, some modern Jewish philosophers, primarily leaders of the Mussar movement, continue to insist that man's free will is often limited (Rabbi Dessler[14]).[15] For those who do not think like Saadiah Goan, resolving the contradiction between unfettered free choice and unrestricted divine foreknowledge of events would seem to require the limiting of one or the other.

Other modern Jewish philosophers have attempted to gloss over this thorny issue and in an attempt to resolve the contradiction focus their efforts on better defining man's relationship with morality (Kant)[16] or with God (Buber).[17] It is fair to say that despite more than 2,000 years of inquiry, an accepted rational solution that reconciles the essential contradiction between providence and man's free will has not been widely recognized.

Religious philosophy and scientific advances

There is a long history of using scientific advances to illuminate theological and philosophical dilemmas. For example, there were attempts to synthesize theology and science by the medieval Jewish philosopher and rabbinical authority Gersonides, who suggested that divine influence on the world was mediated through the contemporary science of astrological theory[18]—a system of divination based on the premise that there is a relationship between astrological bodies and human events.[19]

---

13 *Emunot v-Deot,* Treatise IV.

14 Rabbi Eliezer Dressler c. 1892–1953.

15 *Mikhtav M-Eliyahu, Kuntres Ha-Bechirah.*

16 Emil Fackenheim, "The Revealed Morality of Judaism and Modern Thought: A Confrontation with Kant," *Contemporary Jewish Ethics*, Edited by Menachem Keller (New Jersey: Hebrew Publishing Company, 1978).

17 Martin Buber, *I and Thou*, translated by Walter Kaufmann (New York: Charles Scribner's Sons, 1970).

18 This should not be confused with astrology in the idolatrous sense. Gad Freudenthal, "Gersonides on the Disorder of the Sublunar World and on Providence," *Aleph* 12, 2 (2012) pp. 299–328.

19 *Milḥamot Ha-Shem*, Book 6, Chapter 10, standard edition.

One reason scientific discovery advanced in lockstep with theological innovation was that until the twentieth century, leading scientists and religious philosophers were often one and the same. For example, Sir Isaac Newton, one of the greatest physicists of all time, wrote extensively on Christian religion.[20] Maimonides,[21] in addition to being a leading Talmudist and rabbinic scholar, was also an honored court physician. These luminary figures often applied the same methods of explaining both physical and metaphysical realities.[22] In light of these examples, contemporary religious thinkers would have great precedent in using the scientific advances during the 1900s in response to the tension between the continuity of laws of science and the possibility of Divine intervention. However, Nicolas Saunders notwithstanding, there have been few attempts to do so to date.

20th Century Scientific Advances

Before we delve into contemporary science, we need to appreciate that in many ways, the first half of the twentieth century was the golden age of physics. Our contemporary understanding of the physical world bears almost no resemblance to our conception of it before the first Solvay Conference in 1911. In light of these advances, it is imperative to reexamine the issues of providence and free choice in a new context, i.e. that of quantum mechanics.

In order to relate this theory to our discussion of divine providence, two popular understandings of quantum mechanics must be explained. While it is clear that quantum mechanics makes predictions about microscopic events, an intuitive understanding of uncertainty in quantum mechanics has remained controversial. Indeed almost a century after quantum mechanics was developed there remains a fundamental disagreement about how to interpret quantum events. The Heisenberg Uncertainty Principle indicates that one cannot determine with certainty the location and momentum of a particle simultaneously, begging the question of where the particle actually is. Possible explanations include the Copenhagen Interpretation that all states of the particle exist simultaneously prior to measurement. In a variation of this interpretation, quantum particles are described by a waveform and thus the particle is not located in any single point until measurements are made, only after which the particle can be said to be located at a single point. A second theory to explain quantum mechanics involves a multiverse explanation in which each

20 See Newton's *Observations upon the Prophecies of Daniel and the Apocalypse of St. John.*

21 Rabbi Moses ben Maimon c. 1135–1204. Public Domain Books, London, 1723.

22 See Maimonides' Prefatory Remarks of *Moreh Nevukhim.*

quantum possibility exists in a separate universe (i.e. a theory that stipulates there are an unimaginable large number of universes in which every possible course of events that can occur does occur).

How are these variations in interpretation related to the fundamental issue of divine intervention at a time without God's active revelation? In its most basic form, the uncertainty principle of quantum mechanics could potentially allow for divine intervention in the world. For example, through this interpretation of the principle, one could posit that God *undetactably* alters the state of matter. Since according to one interpretation of the Heisenberg Uncertainty principle in which the state of matter is not complete, the precise location and momentum of a particle cannot be determined no matter how advanced the measuring equipment, and no intervention within the envelope predicted by quantum theory can be discovered, God could alter events in the world in a way completely consistent with the principles of physics. Saunders[23] raises two fundamental objections to the possibility of divine intervention through quantum mechanics: 1) quantum mechanics using one variation of the Copenhagen Interpretation can be deterministic, because a waveform equation would describe events precisely, therefore there is no room for undetectable interference. 2) Proponents of divine intervention have not defined precisely how God's intervention on the quantum (microscopic) level could exert meaningful control over the world at distances greater than Planck's length.

Both of these objections depend in part on our ability to interpret the quantum state prior to intervention. In response to Saunders' two objections, it may be fair to say that only a waveform can describe the actual location of a particle but the collapse of the waveform is not predictable and it is precisely that collapse that determines future events. Thus, God could cause a waveform to collapse in a way that alters events. The second objection requires a careful analysis of the relationship between microscopic and macroscopic principles of physics.

Attempts over the past 80 years to reconcile quantum mechanics with the equations of general relativity dealing with the motion of objects larger than Planck's length have been unsuccessful, primarily because any changes that take place at the quantum level fail to manifest in measurements of systems larger than Planck's length. Most recently, for example, Witten and others have developed a hypothesis called string theory,[24]

---

23 Nicholas Saunders, *Divine Action and Modern Science* (Cambridge: Cambridge University Press, 2002).

24 Edward Witten, "String Theory Dynamics in Various Dimensions," *Nuclear Physics* B 443 (1): 85–126 (1995).

which they believe intuitively will eventually resolve the contradictions between quantum mechanics and general relativity. Nonetheless, even this construct will leave intact some of the "weirdness" of quantum mechanics, including the notion that the location and momentum of an object cannot be simultaneously determined because the process of measuring these quantities will alter the results.

There is another branch of physics and mathematics that is subject to some of the same strange predictions that quantum mechanics provides, developed in the last half-century and fueled by the development of the computer. While fully deterministic, non-linear dynamics, or chaos theory, was developed in the latter half of the twentieth century. It states that in non-quantitative terms, the end result of its system state is highly dependent on initial conditions.

Take the following example to illustrate the complexity of non-linear dynamics and chaos theory: we look at a group of runners involved in a 10-kilometer race. In a linear system, one runner may run more quickly or more slowly than the other, but their relationship to each other is predictable. If two start running, with one runner five feet in front of the other, it will make only a five-foot difference in the outcome of the race. In contrast, in a non-linear system, the result will be quite different. A small difference in the starting point of the race may interact with an incalculable number of other variables to make a large difference in the outcome. For example, one runner starting five feet away from his original starting position may lead to his breaking an ankle and being unable to finish the race. There is ample evidence that a number of physical systems, such as the earth's weather and the electrical beat of the heart, are governed by non-linear systems. Indeed, many of the more complex phenomena throughout the world appear to be subject to non-linear dynamics.

Just as with quantum mechanics, the predications of non-linear dynamics seem counterintuitive. One can't help but wonder why the world that otherwise appears intuitive and ordered contains strange situations where physical laws do not apply to particles of all sizes, where the location of objects cannot be determined with certainty, and where a minute change in starting location can have a dramatic effect on where particles (or runners) end up.

To illustrate the counterintuitive implications of quantum mechanics, Schrödinger developed a thought experiment now famously called "Schrödinger's Cat," in which he attempted to show the strange predictions of quantum mechanics. In the hypothetical experiment, a cat is placed in a sealed box and exposed to radiation. Based on one state of a subatomic particle the radiation would be lethal, based on another state of that subatomic particle it would be benign. Since the final states of the subatomic particle could not be defined with precision, one would not know until the box was open whether the cat was alive or dead. Indeed, rather than measuring the location of the subatomic particle, a box would be opened to confirm whether the cat was alive or dead, and this would seem to determine the result. A number of divergent explanations have intuitively defined the time at which Schrödinger's cat might be alive or dead. For example, according to the explanation of a waveform mentioned earlier, that all possible states exist simultaneously until measurement, the cat would be both alive and dead until the box was opened. While this famous thought experiment supports the hypothesis that macro-level reality can be influenced by quantum events, in this case the life or death of a cat, the nature of this specific case does not describe a medium for divine intervention that is scalable or useful.

Attempts at Reconciliation

Attempts to reconcile providence and free will in the Jewish intellectual tradition essentially fall into four categories. A first approach is to suggest that the paradox remains and is inexplicable to man. Although he attempts more complex and other explanations in the Guide for the Perplexed, Maimonides espouses this approach in his laws of repentance, where he addresses one of the problems of personal choice and divine foreknowledge. He essentially states that we cannot understand the nature of Divine knowledge and that we must simply take unfettered free choice on faith.[25] This approach has not stopped philosophers and theologians from probing the question further.

The second approach involves placing extensive limitations on free will, so that free will can be controlled through divine intervention. The Jewish tradition that conceives of an active creator who manages the world on a day-to-day basis ought to allow for this to occur. Some sources beginning with the Talmud support the notion that all events in the world are carefully controlled by God. The Talmud in Tractate *Ḥullin* suggests that a person does not bruise his thumb unless it is ordained from above.[26] However, several sources, which we will discuss below, have a problem with the system of reward and punishment in which the dice are loaded. While it is possible that somewhat of a limitation on free will exists,[27] this

25 *Hilkhot Teshuva* 5:5.

26 BT *Ḥullin* 7b.

27 Baḥya ibn Pakuda, *Ḥovot ha-Levavot*, ch. 3.

does not eliminate the problem of how to adjust for the influence of disruptive, freely made choices with an activist plan for the world.

Modern Hasidic tradition is more explicit in its support for unlimited divine providence.[28] The Ba'al Shem Tov[29] believed that every blade of grass in the world was directly controlled by God's intervention through His emanations.[30] Nothing was left to chance. Nothing could be felt that was not under direct control. Regardless of the extent to which God exerts direct daily control over each of the objects in the world, we conclude that all traditional Jewish sources believe that a plan is in place for both the world as a whole and the people of Israel, and that plan is under direct or indirect control. Placing limitations on Providence also directly contradicts this interventionist theory.

A third approach is to limit the extent of providence. That is to say, whether God has a specific plan for the world or not, his ability and/or will to influence the world ends at the sovereignty of free will.[31] However, the issue arises when we ask the question whether the limit of God's influence is self-imposed. In this case, one can make a free choice only if God declines to intervene. While the implications of this question would question the nature of free will, it assumes that from the human perspective as well as from a scientific perspective, free will must be absolute.

During the century following Maimonides' time, Gersonides,[32] a rabbinic authority mentioned earlier, presents a view that creates a complex system of rules for the world involving a number of physical phenomena that include the motion of the planets to define events and outcomes. Yet this system, which proscribes an observable schematic for divine action, disallows a particularized Divine providence.[33] This contention has not

---

28 This position is predated by Rabbi Ḥasdai Crescas, who argues for a complicated reconciliation between free will and providence. Rabbi Crescas argues that free will exists because humans are ignorant of the causes by which they are affected. See *Ohr Hashem*. See also Meyer Waxman, "The Philosophy of Don Ḥasdai Crescas: Chapter V," *The Jewish Quarterly Review*, New Series, Vol. 10, No. 1 (Jul., 1919), pp. 25–47.

29 Rabbi Yisroel ben Eliezer 1698–1760. Gad Freudenthal, "Providence, Astrology, and Celestial Influences on the Sublunar World," in Shem-Tov ibn Falaquera's "De'ot ha-Filosofim," *The Medieval Hebrew Encyclopedias of Science and Philosophy* (2000) 335–370.

30 An oft-quoted saying by Ba'al Shem Tov, based on *Bereshit Rabba* 10:7. For example, see Joseph Isaac Schneersohn, *Sefer Ha-Ma'amarim Kuntresim*, Vol. II, p. 740 (New York: Kehot, 1977).

31 *Milḥamot Hashem*, Book 6, Chapter 10.

32 Rabbi Levi ben Gershon also known as RaLbaG 1288–1344.

33 *Milḥamot Hashem*, Book 6.

been widely accepted, primarily because Jewish tradition seems far more comfortable with the concept that God cares and intervenes in events on a day-to-day basis. Although the Gersonides approach helps to explain the relationship between the righteousness of one's actions, God's influence through astrological forces, and their outcomes, it places God too far from the daily events we experience to be widely accepted by mainstream Jewish thinkers.[34]

The fourth and final approach is to search for ways to reconcile unfettered free will with divine providence without limiting either. There have been extensive attempts to do this by Jewish philosophers starting in the Babylonian Talmud, where it refers to accidents and events resulting in death that illustrate this point. One such instance is based on the verse in Deuteronomy 21:8—"If you build a new house, you shall make a fence for your roof, so that you will not place blood in your house if a fallen one falls from it." The Talmud on Shabbat comments: "When the fallen one falls"—this man was destined to fall since the time of creation, for he had not yet fallen, yet the Torah designates him as a "fallen one." Here is an example of the legal intersection of personal responsibility and divine providence being discussed in classic Jewish sources. The fall had been decreed upon the falling man by Providence, but it was the homeowner's negligence that caused the faller to fall on the owner's property.

Similarly, on the verse in Exodus 21:13: "And if a man lie not in wait, but God caused it to come to hand," the Talmud on Makkot explains that: "If one man killed a person accidentally, and another slew a person intentionally, the willful murderer ... falls by the hand of the innocent." This approach allows free choice to be integrated with a divine plan. If the man closes his roof thereby avoiding accidentally killing a person, God will cause the faller to die in another way. These excerpts from the Talmud demonstrate a complex relationship between free will and divine providence; however, they do not clearly define a mechanism for their interaction.[35]

---

34 See Gersonides' commentary on *Iyov*. Amos Funkenstein, "Gersonides' Biblical Commentary: Science, History and Providence" (or: The importance of being boring), *Studies on Gersonides* (1992) 305–315.

35 The tension between free will and Divine providence is manifest in a number of examples that demonstrate the general disagreement between Rabbi Akiva and Rabbi Ishmael. Rabbi Ishmael has an idea of intergenerational cause and effect, which does not contradict his school's distinction between living by virtue of a forefather's merit versus one's own; rather, reconciliation must be understood through his understanding of providence. Contrary to the view of Rabbi Akiva, which primarily focuses on man's understanding the power of his own actions

In the Guide for the Perplexed, Maimonides suggests a sliding scale mechanism in which the degree to which divine providence influences a person's life depends upon the state of intellectual perfection and unity with God that an individual achieves. However, at other points, he suggests that all individuals, and perhaps objects regardless of their state of intellectual perfection, may be subject to divine providence.

The 11th century prayer *Unesanoh Tokef*[36] from the text of the High Holiday services seems to balance the outcomes of divine judgement based on our individual efforts. This language implies a philosophy of reward and punishment in which human choice has a clear relationship with divine action.

Gersonides suggests a different apparatus for this relationship. He believed that God created a series of natural forces that rule the world and determine events on both the large and small scale. In some cases, God may choose not to pay attention to the details on a day-to-day basis. This radical approach is not shared by many others, but it has its adherents. For example, *Sefer ha-Ḥinuch* reads that a fence must be put around a roof, because there are some individuals who may not merit such providence

---

to affect the world around him, Rabbi Ishmael broadens the discussion to acknowledge God's foreknowledge of events. For example, regarding the verse "When the faller falls from it" (Deuteronomy 22:8), the school of Rabbi Ishmael comments that this man was predestined to fall since the six days of Creation, for, behold, he has not yet fallen, and Scripture already calls him a faller. (BT *Shabbat* 32a) If the man was destined to fall anyway, one would think that the commandment to build a parapet is irrelevant. The existence of the commandment reinforces the idea of free will, albeit without negating God's foreknowledge, as exemplified by the following statement of Rabbi Ishmael: "'When I shall see the blood…' Rabbi Ishmael says: Is not all revealed before Him, as it states, 'He knows what is in the darkness, and light dwells with Him' (Daniel 2:22), and also, 'Even darkness obscures not from You.' (Psalms 139:12) What is 'When I shall see the blood…' coming to explain? Rather, that as the reward of the commandment that you do, I will be revealed and have pity upon you." (*Mekhilta d-Rabbi Ishmael, Bo, Masekhta Pisha* 6).

36 "Let us now relate the power of this day's holiness, for it is awesome and frightening. On it Your Kingship will be exalted; Your throne will be firmed with kindness and You will sit upon it in truth. It is true that You alone are the One Who judges, proves, knows, and bears witness; Who writes and seals, Who counts and Who calculates. You will remember all that was forgotten. You will open the Book of Remembrances—it will read itself—and each person's signature is there. And the great shofar will be sounded and a still, thin voice will be heard. Angels will hasten, a trembling and terror will seize them—and they will say, 'Behold, it is the Day of Judgment, to muster the heavenly host for judgment!'—for even they are not guiltless in Your eyes in judgment."

and who may fall off and die if a fence is not present. This would imply, as Gersonides suggests, that God does not necessarily control the day-to-day events of a person's life. In the context of this discussion, some peoples' lives are governed by providence while others are left to the vicissitudes of chance and free will. However, the Rabad,[37] who wrote a commentary that debated Maimonides and who lived prior to Gersonides, suggested that while astrological theory has power over the world, free will has the power to overcome the force of that influence. I would like to suggest an alternative approach to address this paradox by applying Jewish sources to modern science.

Physics and the Paradox

The recent advances in physics noted above provide a potential mechanism for resolving the paradox between divine providence and free choice. As theories have improved, and as the accuracy of physical measurement has dramatically increased, the number of macroscopic events that occur by chance has become more limited. Therefore, it is hard to reconcile direct divine providence with modern scientific practical observation. However, the combination of theories of quantum mechanics and non-linear dynamics provides a model through which direct divine intervention can act unobserved. One could even argue that physical principles were designed by God to allow direct divine intervention to occur in an apparently deterministic and scientifically advanced world.

Both the theories of quantum mechanics and non-linear dynamics are necessary to maintain this potential model of divine providence, which does not necessarily interfere with free choice. It is reasonable to suggest that the Heisenberg Uncertainty Principle exists precisely because it allows divine providence to be undetected. Therefore, no level of scientific advancement will allow us to know both the position and momentum of a particle. This concept is almost a century old, though it has significant limitations when applied to our problem.

It is difficult to understand how God's undetectable control of an electron's position can affect macroscopic events in a way that would alter observable events in our world, let alone reconcile that intervention with an alteration and free choice. This has indeed been one of the major objections to suggesting that by manipulating quantum events God might affect events in the universe, and was Saunders' second objection.[38] Two advances in physics, one going back decades and one more recent, may

---

37 Rabad, commentary on the *Mishneh Torah*, *Laws of Repentance* 5:5, standard edition.

38 Op. cit.

have altered the principles on which this prior skepticism was based. They are non-linear dynamics and recent advances in a phenomenon called quantum entanglement.

As previously noted, the popularization of non-linear dynamics in the last 25 years, as well as advances in its understanding, creates a new paradigm in which microscopic events could be amplified, and affect observable occurrences in a way that they might modify the apparent outcome in daily life. The classic scientific example that is used to represent this point is that a butterfly might flap its wings over the Pacific Ocean and through the amplification of non-linear dynamics cause a hurricane in the Atlantic Ocean. A similar cascade of events could be postulated to occur when the location of individual subatomic particles is altered in an undetectable way, similar to Schrödinger's cat. Small perturbations in the location or movement of subatomic particles could result in larger macroscopic perturbations, such as alterations in weather conditions, the creation of seismic activity or other natural phenomena that could affect events in the world. This theory could, for example, explain the occurrence of a catastrophic event, such as Hurricane Sandy, based on undetectable intervention on a microscopic level.

However, until recently evidence of subatomic events manifesting beyond Plank's length to macroscopic events was lacking. That is, although one could postulate that quantum events could appear on a microscopic scale and be amplified through non-linear dynamics up to Planck's length, there was no direct experimental evidence that this could function at larger distances. Indeed a property called quantum decoherence suggests that when quantum particles exist on a macroscopic scale, they lose their quantum-like properties in a very short time period. However, work in the past 3 years has begun to demonstrate that quantum properties can be maintained in macroscopic systems.[39] Barthel et al (2014) demonstrated the ability of particles to maintain their quantum properties on a macroscopic scale by showing that multi-particle systems "shield" quantum effects from the decoherence or breakdown that occurs with single particles.

---

39 Anthony J. Leggett, "Macroscopic quantum systems and the quantum theory of measurement" *Progress of Theoretical Physics Supplement* 69 (1980): 80-100. Université of Genève. "What if quantum physics worked on a macroscopic level? Researchers have successfully entangled optic fibers populated by 500 photons," *Science Daily*, 25 July 2013. <www.sciencedaily.com/releases/2013/07/130725104851.htm>.

Yong-Chun Liu and Yun-Feng Xiao, "Macroscopic mechanical systems are entering the quantum world," *National Science Review* first published online August 19, 2014, Doi:10.1093/nsr/nwu050

Quantum Entanglement is an area of scientific advancement that would allow for the projection of microscopic events over large distances. One of the objections raised to quantum mechanics by Einstein and others (ERP 1935) was that the predictions of quantum theory led to the possibility that "information" would be passed faster than light. Suppose two coin flips were linked on a quantum level, the link being that if one was heads the other must be tails. Now suppose that these two coins were separated by a light-year. Determining whether one of the coins was heads or tails would simultaneously determine the state of the other coin (heads or tails). In that scenario the instantaneous revelation of information about the distant coin would travel faster than light. Einstein believed this impossible. However, quantum entanglement as this phenomenon is called has been shown experimentally to be valid on the macroscopic level. Two studies from the University of Geneva have demonstrated that quantum entanglement can occur in small and in fiber optic cable transmission (Gisin et al 2011, 2013).

Quantum entanglement adds a dimension to the potency of nonlinear dynamics in amplifying quantum events past Plank's length. Not only can localized quantum events contribute to shielding a quantum system from decoherence, because of entanglement, quantum events at significant distance can also contribute to this phenomenon without being constrained by locality. Both non-linear dynamics and quantum mechanics make the tools of divine intervention more powerful in separate ways.

If we apply these findings to our paradox and our discussion of free will, I would argue that the universe was intentionally designed with quantum mechanics to allow divine providence to be undetected. I propose that God's undetected intervention might alter a particle's location by moving it to one of several positions that fall within the location probability distribution, which I would term "Quantum Manipulation." This quantum disturbance would set off a pre-calculated chain reaction, magnified through the mechanism provided by non-linear dynamics and preserved beyond Planck's length, to affect observable phenomena and alter reality in an intended and specific way.

While this postulated mechanism combining quantum manipulation with non-linear dynamics in a particle state "shielded" from decoherence explains how divine intervention could be undetectable in the physical world, despite substantial advances in measurement techniques, it does little to enhance understanding of how free choice could be preserved in such a circumstance. It does avoid the need for direct divine intervention in human choice or in the thought process in order for God to affect our reality, but does not easily explain how free choice can be preserved in the presence of divine intervention.

This problem can be further analyzed using similar physical principles. To a large extent, the choices we make as human beings are based on the situations and problems we are forced to solve. If our circumstances were altered by undetectable divine intervention, that would manipulate the choices available to us and alter our future while maintaining our freedom of choice. For example, most of us will never have to face the choice of whether to resort to cannibalism after having crashed in the Andes Mountains. However, if those survivors were immediately rescued, that could represent divine intervention removing the need to choose cannibalism. Thus, the existence of a mechanism for undetected divine intervention does not exclude our free choice, however it means that we are not guaranteed that the intended results of our choices will be realized if God intends otherwise.

There is a theory that stipulates free choice is only a perception. It goes on to explain that our so-called choices are defined by a combination of our inborn genetic dispositions reacting with the stimuli of our environment and then modified through our learned behaviors. However, regardless of the philosophical underpinnings of such a theory, for the purpose of this discussion, we are dealing with the practical implications of free choice.[40]

Furthermore, the extent to which divine providence is universally exerted on every event in the world, depending on size of the event, affects how easy it is for us to understand that these physical mechanisms are operational. If only the broad strokes of large events are defined by God and defined so roughly as to disregard the details, it is relatively easy to see how those large events could be controlled using the combination of quantum mechanics and non-linear dynamics. However, it is more difficult to understand how these seemingly complex and indelicate mechanisms could control events on a minute and detailed scale. Because of the inherent complexity in the system, we must conclude that within all the uncountable possible locations for each and every particle in the universe, there must be one arrangement of all matter and energy that will change the universe in a specific and intentional way. But the complexity of achieving small changes to reality would not be immediately obvious and require "divine" intelligence to fully actuate.

---

40 David Shatz, "Is Matter All that Matters? Judaism, Free Will, and the Genetic and Neuroscientific Revolution," *Judaism, Science, and Moral Responsibility* (Lanham: Rowman and Littlefield, 2006) 54–103.

Conclusion

If one wanted to construct the universe in which events, large or small, were controlled through divine providence, yet preserved free choice, there would be two requirements. First, divine intervention would have to be undetectable so that there is no interference with free choice. This can potentially be explained through divine intervention in the state of matter. Secondly, microscopic events in which intervention could not be identified would require amplification to the point where they would alter our observable world and lives.

While the combination of quantum mechanics and non-linear dynamics in systems shielded from decoherence does not prove the existence of God, it would indeed be a very intelligent way for Him to have designed the universe to allow a measure of control through nature, while preserving the concept of a human being's freedom of choice. When Einstein said, "God does not play dice with the universe," Niels Bohr responded, "Einstein, stop telling God what to do." As our scientific knowledge grows, we have faced criticism and concern from some religious thinkers who believe that science is an affront to religion. However, an educated approach to these big questions reveals that not only is there a history of using scientific lenses to better understand religion, an advanced knowledge of the complexities of our world magnifies the awesomeness of God. Galileo famously said that when he looked through his telescope, at the magnificence of the universe, he saw God. ☙

A Short History of the Jewish Fixed Calendar: The Origin of the Molad

By: J. JEAN AJDLER

I. Introduction.

It was always believed that the transition from the observation to the fixed calendar was clear-cut, with the fixed calendar immediately adopting its definitive form in 358/359, at the date of the inception. Indeed according to a tradition[1] quoted in the name of R' Hai Gaon,[2] the present Jewish calendar was introduced by the patriarch Hillel II in the Jewish Year 4119 AM (*anno mundi*, from creation), 358/359 CE.

The only discordant element with regard to this theory that the calendar adopted immediately its definitive form, was the fact that we find already in the Talmud that the postponement of Rosh Hashanah from Sunday was a later enactment.[3] Only some rare rabbinic authorities already recognized the later character of this postponement.

Indeed a passage of the epistle of R' Sherira Gaon implying that Rosh Hashanah of the year 505 C.E. was still on Sunday was generally considered as the result of a copyist mistake.[4]

It is only in the first decade of the twentieth century that new evidence appeared after the discovery of new documents in the Cairo Geniza.

---

1 *Sefer ha-Ibbur* by R' Abraham bar Ḥiyya edited by Filipowski, London 1851, p. 97 quotes a responsum of R. Hai Gaon dated from 4752 AM = 992 C.E. reporting this tradition.

2 R. Hai Gaon (939-1038) was the last and the most prolific Gaon. He belonged to the Yeshiva of Pumbedita.

3 See B. Niddah 67b. It appears that in the time of R' Yemar (427-432) Rosh Hashanah could fall on Sunday. See Ajdler (1966): *Hilkhot Kiddush ha-Ḥodesh al-pi ha-Rambam*, Sifriati 1996, p. 670 and 684.

4 See *Iggeret Rav Sherira Gaon* part III, chap.4, p. 85 in the edition of R' Aaron Heyman, London 1910.

J. Jean Ajdler has an MS in engineering and works as a civil and structural engineer. He writes about medieval Jewish astronomy, the history of the Jewish calendar, and Talmudic metrology. He is the author of *Hilkhot Kiddush ha-Hodesh al-pi ha-Rambam,* Sifriati 1996, and has published in *Ḥakirah*, *Tradition* and *BDD.*

The former conviction that the Jewish calendar immediately assumed its definitive shape at the moment of its inception was shaken by two major discoveries:

- The discovery of letters attesting the existence of an important dispute between the Babylonian community led by R' Sa'adia Gaon and the Palestinian community lead by (Aaron?) ben Meir about the *keviyah*[5] of the years 4682, 4683 and 4684.[6]
- The discovery and the publication in 1922 of a document from the Cairo Geniza: a letter from a Babylonian *Resh Galutah*[7] showing that the *keviyah* of the year 4596 (835/836 C.E.) was different than in our present-day calendar and that the Babylonian community received its calendric information from Palestine.

This last discovery was especially important; it proved beyond any doubt that almost five hundred years after the inception of the fixed calendar of Hillel, the fixed calendar in its present-day form had still not yet been instituted.

These two important discoveries were at the origin of much speculation about the history of the Jewish calendar. This history remains mostly conjectural because of the weak number of available pieces of evidence. But one thing is certain: our modern calendar in its final form was definitively not instituted before 922-924, after the end of the R. Sa'adia/Ben Meir controversy.

Ḥayyim Jeḥiel Bornstein[8] (1845-1928) played a major role in the analysis of these documents and in their correct interpretation. Tzvi Hirsh

---

5 The *keviyah* refers to the length of the year and the weekday on which the month of Tishrei starts. These two pieces of information determine the exact layout of the entire year. This will be discussed in greater detail later in the paper.

6 See Bornstein, H. J: *Maḥaloket Rav Sa'adia Gaon u Ben Meir*, Warsaw 1904.

7 For the text of the letter of the *Resh Galuta* see note 98.

8 He is the author of the following papers, in connection with the problems of the Jewish calendar:

מחלקת רב סעדיה גאון ובן מאיר בקביעת שנות ד"א תרפ"ב-תרפ"ד, ספר היובל לכבוד מו"ה נחום סוקאלאוו, ורשא תרס"ד

משפט הסמיכה וקורותיה, התקופה, ספר רביעי, תרע"ט

סדרי זמנים והתפתחותם בישראל, התקופה, ספר שישי, תר"ף

תאריכי ישראל, התקופה, ספר שמיני, תרפ"א

תאריכי ישראל, התקופה, ספר תשיעי, תרפ"א

חשבון שמיטין ויובלות, התקופה, ספר האחד-עשר, תרפ"א

דברי ימי העיבור האחרונים, התקופה, ספר ארבע עשר וחמישה עשר, תרפ"ב

דברי ימי העיבור האחרונים, התקופה, ספר ששה עשר, תרפ"ג

עיבורים ומחזורים, התקופה, ספר עשרים, תרפ"ד

Jaffe [9] (1853-1927) also made important contributions in this field. In general he appears more as the associate of Bornstein but some of his conclusions are more elaborate and more definitive than those of Bornstein. Akavya (Avraham Aryeh Leib Yakobovits) (1882-1964) devoted many years of research on the Hebrew calendar. He edited *Korot Ḥeshbon ha-Ibbur*, the book of Jaffe and studied the tombstones of Zoar, which were discovered from about 1940 onwards and revealed the great diversity of the Jewish calendar even after the institution of the rabbinic calendar and even in Palestine in places not remote from the rabbinic centers. Stern, a historian, surveyed again all the available historical elements and put them in perspective in his book "Calendar and Community."[10] He put special emphasis on the lack of unity of the Jewish calendar and its great diversity through all the Jewish communities of the Diaspora. Furthermore, when later, after the sixth century, the rabbinic calendar asserted itself, all the distant communities, except the Babylonian and other neighboring communities, certainly remained unaware of the *keviyah* adopted by the Palestinian academy and had to live according to parallel approximate calendars of their own. It is only after the end of the R. Sa'adia Gaon-Ben Meir dispute that the rules of the calendar and the Four Gates Table[11] became known to the entire Diaspora.

In the present paper we try to outline the history of the Jewish calendar from the time of its inception until the tenth century, when it reached its definitive form.

At this stage, when mentioning influential scholars who made significant contributions to the field of the Jewish calendar, we must also mention the role of pioneer of Ḥayyim Selig Slonimski[12] (1810-1904). Before

---

9 Tzvi Hirsh Jaffe was born in Russia on 11 Sivan 5613. He had a thorough Talmudic education. He was an autodidact mathematician and talented engineer and inventor of a calculating machine. He was the editor of Azaria de Rossi's book מאור עיניים Warsaw 1899. He wrote explanatory notes to the Hebrew translation by Shaeffer of the History of the Jews of Graetz. He wrote the article Ben Meir in the *American Encyclopedia Otzar Israel.* But his opus magnum is his book קורות חשבון העיבור that was edited by Akavia in Tel Aviv 1931.

10 Sacha Stern, *Calendar and Community, History of the Jewish Calendar, Second Century B.C.E.-Tenth Century C.E.* (Oxford University Press, 2001).

11 Table discovered by the Babylonian *meabrim* (mathematicians and specialists of the Jewish calendar). It allows finding the *keviyah* of a given year in function of its rank in the cycle of 19 years and the Molad of that year, i.e. the Molad of the month of Tishrei, at the beginning of that year. See Appendix C.

12 Hebrew popular science writer, popularizer and inventor (he was awarded a prize by the Russian academy of Science in 1844 for a calculating machine).

the discovery of the documents of the Cairo Geniza, he had already discovered that the Jewish Molad is derived from the table of mean conjunctions of Ptolemy's Almagest.[13] Similarly he was the first to state the late character of the *tekufah* of R' Adda bar Ahava. This concept seems to be a Spanish invention of the tenth century.[14]

In order to describe the evolution of the Jewish fixed calendar we will examine thoroughly the tables constructed by Jaffe in order to reconstruct the Jewish calendar in its different stages of development and make the critical analysis of the assumptions on which they are built.

Jaffe was probably overconfident in his mathematical achievements. The aim of this paper is to show how Jaffe constructed his tables for the different stages of development of the Jewish calendar and to distinguish between established and more questionable facts.

In this manner, the main achievements of Jaffe in his book *Korot Ḥeshbon ha-Ibbur* will be made available to the modern reader who has no access to both the papers of Bornstein and the more systematic but difficult book of Jaffe. Even if some of their conclusions may be contested, these works remain authoritative in many respects. This paper aims at paying them homage, especially to Jaffe, Talmudist, mathematician and historian of great value, closely bound to all the research and discoveries of Bornstein but forgotten and neglected. He was even forgotten by the editors of the *Encyclopedia Judaica.*

II. The calendar of Hillel[15] from 359 until the beginning of the seventh century (about 648).

According to a tradition quoted in the name of R' Hai Gaon, the present Jewish calendar was introduced by the patriarch Hillel II in 4119 (358/359).

13 *Yessodei ha-Ibbur*, Zitomir 1865, pp. 49-51.

14 *Yessodei ha-Ibbur*, Zitomir 1865, pp. 43-45.

15 The name of Hillel II the Patriarch is associated with the calendar instituted in 358/359 C.E. according to the tradition reported in the responsum of R' Hai Gaon. However the name of Hillel II is not mentioned in the Talmud and it is not certain at all that he had a direct part in this calendar. Maimonides does not mention him and is probably not aware of the tradition reported by R' Hai Gaon. It is clear that Rabbi Yose or Yousa, always mentioned in the Jerusalem Talmud in connection with the rules of the calendar, must have had a preponderant part in the foundation of this calendar.

We already demonstrated[16] that a pre-calculated calendar was established by the Court of Tiberias and sent to Babylonia from about 325 onwards. This calendar, however, was still a semi-empirical calendar replicating a calendar based on the first visibility of the new moon. By contrast the calendar instituted in 359 seems to be a completely calculated calendar based on a mean conjunction called Molad. The basic assumptions of this calendar, according to Jaffe, were probably the following:

- The Molad of Nissan 4119 was chosen near to the moment of the maximum of the solar eclipse,[17] which occurred on Monday afternoon 15 March 359 C.E. exactly the day of the inception of the new calendar.[18]
- The lunation adopted in the new calendar was 29 days – 12 hours – 792 *ḥalakim*[19] (written 29-12-792).[20] At this epoch they did not use the

16 See Ajdler (1996): "Hilkhot Kiddush ha-Ḥodesh al-pi ha-Rambam," *Sifriati* 1966, p. 693-697 and Ajdler (2004), "Rav Safra and the Second Festival day," *Tradition*, vol 38, no. 4, pp. 3 – 28.

17 Solar eclipses always occur at the true lunar conjunction. The Molad used in the calculation of the Jewish calendar is a mean conjunction and an approximation of the true conjunction. If the sun and the moon were moving in the same plane (apparent movement seen from the earth) we would have a solar eclipse at each lunar conjunction. In fact these planes are distinct and the solar eclipses occur rarely. Anyhow the solar eclipses always occur at a true lunar conjunction, near to a mean conjunction and a Molad.

18 It is noteworthy that the day of inception of the calendar, the Molad of the calendar coincided with the true conjunction.

19 792 *ḥalakim* is 44 minutes. The lunation currently used, 29 – 12 – 793, was probably adopted at the end of the eighth century. Indeed Rabbi Pinḥas, a Palestinian liturgical poet mentioned the division of the hour in 1080 parts. This division of the hour was specifically designated for the lunation of 29 days 12 hours and 793 parts. It is not known to have been used in any other context. Similarly the same Rabbi Pinḥas mentions in his composition *Kiddush Yeraḥim* the cycle of 19 years. This cycle is also mentioned at the end of chapter 8 of *Pirquei de R. Eliezer.* The lunation of 29 – 12 – 793 and the leap years in each 19 year cycle, 3-6-8-11-14-17-19, could thus have been adopted at about the end of the eighth century. See Stern (2001) p. 197 and p. 204.

20 According to the statement of Ravina in B. *Arakhim* 9b: מתקיף לה רבינא, והאיכא יומא דשעי ויומא דתלתין שני.

יומא דשעי the day of hours. It corresponds to a day resulting of the accumulation during 3 years of the excess of the length of the Jewish month of 29 days 12h 40m with regard to 29 days 12h: 36 * (2/3) = 24 hours = 1 day.

ḥelek and did not divide the hour into 1080 *ḥalakim*. They satisfied themselves with the division of the hour in 15 *ḥayil*,[21] a *ḥayil* representing 4 minutes or 72 *ḥalakim*. The length of the month was thus noted 29 – 12 – 11 (i.e., 29 days 12 hours and 11 *ḥayil*). The length of a month is thus 4 weeks and 1 – 12 – 11. We say that the remainder[22] of a month is 1 – 12 – 11. Similarly the remainder of 6 months is 2 – 4 – 6, the remainder of 12 months is 4 – 8 – 12 and the remainder of 13 months is 5 – 21 – 8.

- The rules of the calendar were about the same as today except that the first day of Rosh Hashanah may fall on Sunday. The rules were thus the following:
- The postponements were DU (Wednesday and Friday) and יח or 18 hours (noon).[23]

יומא דתלתין שני is an additional day resulting from the accumulation during 30 years of the difference between 29d 12h 44m and 29d 12h 40m: 12 * 30 * 4m = 1440m = 1 day.
The length of the Jewish lunation was thus 29d 12h 44m = 29 – 12 – 792.

21 See *Baraïta de Shemuel* chap 2 and 3. 1 *Ḥayil* = 1° of the equator and therefore also 4 minutes. We also have 1 *ḥayil* = 72 *ḥalakim* and 1 minute = 18 *ḥalakim*. 11 *ḥayil* = 792 *ḥalakim*.

22 With regard to the greatest multiple of 7 days included.

23 I.e., Rosh Hashanah is declared on the day of the Molad except when the Molad is on Wednesday (D for *dalet* the 4th day of the week) or Friday (U for *vav* the 6th day of the week), or when the Molad is at noon or later on any of the other days. In these cases Rosh Hashanah is postponed to the next day, unless that day is Wednesday or Friday in which case it is postponed to the next day, thus in all two days). The noon cut-off point is called Molad *Zaken*. Our current calendar has ADU postponements, i.e., besides not allowing RH to be on Wednesday or Friday we also do not allow it to be on Sunday (A for aleph). The DU postponements have deep roots in the Talmud. Until the second half of the third century, Rosh Hashanah could fall on any day of the week and Yom Kippur could be on Friday and Sunday (this is possible only if Rosh Hashanah is on Wednesday or Friday); see references in the Mishnah: Shabbat XV; 3, Shabbat XV; 19, Menaḥot XI; 7 (see also Maimonides' commentary ad locum), Menaḥot XI; 9. The ancient tradition reported in Rabbi Eliezer's name in *Vayikra Rabbah* XXIX; 1, according to which the seven days of the creation began on Sunday, Elul 25 of the year 1 AMI (the first year of *Beharad*), belongs to this period. Indeed it implies that Tishrei 1 of the year 2 AMI (the second year of *Beharad* or the first year of *Weyad*) was on Friday. According to the rules of our present calendar, this is impossible, Tishrei 1 cannot be a Friday and Elul 25 cannot be a Sunday. According to our modern calendar Elul 25 was a Monday and Tishrei 1 was a Saturday. The postponement DU was introduced during the second half of the third century by Rabbi Joḥanan in the time of Ulla ben Ishmael, see B. Rosh

- The length of the year was:

For an **ordinary** year: 353, 354, or 355 days with the following designations:

353: A **defective** year, in Hebrew ח for חסרה. Shift of successive RH, 3 days.
354: A **regular** year, in Hebrew כ for כסדרן. Shift of successive RH, 4 days.
355: A **full** year, in Hebrew ש for שלמה. Shift of successive RH, 5 days.

For a **leap** year: 383 days, 384, or 385 days with similar designations:

383: A **defective** year, in Hebrew ח for חסרה. Shift of successive R.H: 5 days.
384: A **regular** year, כ for כסדרן. Shift of successive RH, 6 days.
385: A **full** year, ש for שלמה. Shift of successive RH, 7 = 0 days. (When the length of the year is a multiple of 7, successive RH are on the same day.

- The derivative postponements (resulting from the former rules) were then[24]:

  1–9–3 (א ט ג) in an ordinary year (בפשוטה), i.e., if the Molad is at or later than Sunday 3:12 am Rosh Hashanah is postponed to Monday.

  2–15–8 (ב טו ח) in a year following a leap year (עיבור), i.e., if the Molad is at or later than Monday 9:32 am, Rosh Hashanah is postponed to Tuesday.

- There are 18 different types of years. Years that have the same starting day for Rosh Ḥodesh Tishrei and Nissan are said to have the same

Hashanah 20a and Y. Megilah I; 2. Our current calendar also does not allow Rosh Hashannah to be on Sunday (A for 1st day of the week) This postponement is also discussed in the Talmud; see B. Succah 43b, Y. Succah IV; 1. We can deduce from B. Niddah 67b that in the time of Rav Yemar, head of the academy of Sura (427-432) Rosh Hashanah could still fall on Sunday.

24 At times the application of the standard postponements can lead to years, which do not conform to the 3 possible year lengths for regular and leap years. These anomalies are rectified by the introduction of *derivative* postponements. See Appendix B for a discussion of these derivative postponements in the early calendar and in our current calendar.

keviyot. This *keviyah* was often designated by a triplet of letters,[25] e.g., זשג where the first letter (ז) designates the starting day of Tishrei (Shabbat), the second letter (ש) designates the length of the year (full) and the third letter (ג) designates the starting day of Nissan (Tuesday). The 6 possible year lengths and 5 possible weekdays of RH led to 18 types of years: 9 types of ordinary years and 9 types of leap years.
Ordinary years: אכג, בשה, גכה, גשו, החו, הכז, השא, זחא, זשג
Leap years: אכה, בחה, בכו, בשז, גכז, החה, השג, זחג, זשה[26]

- The cycle of intercalation of 19 years did not yet exist. The rule of intercalation or the rule of the equinox is that Pesaḥ cannot fall before March 19.[27] However the years were classified in table א of Jaffe,[28] in groups of 19 years, according to the principle of a fictitious cycle of intercalation of 19 years allowing an easy examination of the leap years with regard to our cycle of intercalation today.

The table א of Jaffe for the years 4119 (358/359) until 4408 (647/648) was constructed on the preceding assumptions. It gives for each year the *keviyah* and the date of the first day of Passover. The leap years were chosen in such a way that Nissan 15 is never before March 19.

Let us come back to these different assumptions. The solar eclipse of Monday, March 15, 359 was at 15h 54m [29]Jerusalem mean time (ancient

---

25 The 3rd letter in the triplet while convenient is not necessary. It is automatic based on the first 2 letters. Note: Tur gives 2 day *Keviyot* while *Prei Ḥadash* gives the triplet. Note: In this system Pesaḥ can start on Friday, in ours it cannot (because Rosh Hashanah would then be on Sunday).

26 Instead of 14 types of *keviyot* in our present-day calendar. i.e.
Regular : זשג, השא, בחג, גכה, זחא, בשה, הכז
Leap: גכז, זחג, בחה, בשז, השג, החא, זשה,
Indeed when we consider the six possible lengths of the year and the four possible weekdays of Rosh Hashanah, we find 14 different types of years.
For a complete table of these 14 calendars, including the distribution of the Shabbat's readings and *haftarot* see Akavya (1953) pp. 50 – 53, *Otzar Yisrael*, vol. 7, p. 310, Friedman (1971) pp. 218 – 219, Sar Shalom (1984) pp. 55 – 69, Slonimski (1852) pp. 50- , Slonimski (1865) pp. 59 -.

27 This questionable assumption of Jaffe will be discussed beneath.

28 See *Korot Ḥeshbon ha-Ibbur*, Zevi Hirsh Jaffe, edited by Akavia, ha-Darom. Jerusalem 1931. The book is available at the New York public library *ZP 735 Microfilm. See also the detailed appendices at <www.Hakirah.org/vol20Ajdler Appendices.pdf>.

29 This is 3:54 pm conventional time where the day begins at midnight.

style),[30] slightly less than the time calculated by Jaffe of about 6 p.m. Jaffe assumed that the Court fixed the epoch of the Molad at 18h. The epoch of the Molad was thus 3 – 0 – 0.[31] Jaffe believed that the true conjunction was near to 6 pm, the conventional beginning of the night and therefore his assumption was genuine. This assumption is thus acceptable although 2 – 22 – 0 would have been more precise. We will see that Jaffe's assumption allows explaining and justifying different pieces of evidence, which could not be explained otherwise.

1. As the conjunction and the beginning of Nissan was on March 15, 359 Pesaḥ was certainly after the spring equinox and therefore the rule of the equinox according to which, Pesaḥ must be in the month of the spring, was respected for an ordinary year. The year 4119, corresponding to the fifteenth year of a fictitious cycle of 19 years was thus an ordinary year. It is thus easy to calculate the modern Molad of this month; we find 3 – 3 – 671 instead of 3 – 0 – 0 thus a difference of 3 hours 671 *ḥalakim*.[32]

2. The most problematic aspect of the table א is Jaffe's assumption about the adopted rule of the equinox that Pesaḥ cannot fall before March 19. Jaffe assumed that the rule of intercalation of the Jewish calendar was the rule of the equinox that Rabbi Huna bar Abin sent to Rava (Rosh Hashanah 21a):

    שלח ליה רב הונא בר אבין לרבא: כד חזית דמשכא תקופת טבת עד שיתסר בניסן, עברה לההיא שתא ולא תחוש לה.

    When you see that the winter lasts until Nissan 16, intercalate that year and don't pay attention to any other sign of intercalation.

---

30 The eclipse of March 15, 359 on 1582256.14547 JD at 15h 29h 29s ET (See Mucke, H. and Meeus, J. Canon of Solar eclipses – 2003 to + 2526. Astronomisches Büro, Wien. 1983). The difference ΔT = ET – UT ~ 1h 40 m. Therefore the time of the eclipse was 15m 29m 29s – 1h 40m + 2h 21m = 16h 10m 29s Jerusalem modern mean time, and 15h 54m al-Battani Jerusalem mean time (ancient style of calibration of the mean time) (See Ajdler (2005): The Equation of Time in Ancient Jewish Astronomy, BDD 16, p. 14.) slightly before the time calculated by Jaffe of about 18h, probably using the tables of the Canon of Oppolzer, (Theodor Ritter von Oppolzer (Prague 1841 – Vienna 1886) : Canon Der Finsternisse, Vienna 1887).

31 3 – 0 – 0 means the beginning of the third day, hence Monday at 6 p.m.

32 See Appendix D, I for the detail of the calculation.

According to modern scientific data, during the fourth century the true equinox was on March 20[33] and the mean equinox was on March 22.

According to the rule of the equinox of Rabbi Huna bar Abin Nissan 16 may fall on the day of the mean equinox, according to the understanding of R' Ḥananel[34] and R' Abraham bar Ḥiyya.[35] It may fall on the day following the mean equinox according to Rashi[36] and Rambam.[37] Thus according to the rule of the equinox, with the understanding of R' Abraham bar Ḥiyya, Nissan 16 could fall on March 22 and the first day of Passover could be on March 21. We know of effective cases of Pesaḥ beginning on March 21.[38] Thus Pesaḥ could begin on March 21 and the limit of March 19 adopted by Jaffe seems difficult to justify.

However the Christians considered that the true equinox is on March 21 and therefore, according to the rules adopted at the Council of Nicaea, Easter could fall the earliest on Sunday March 22. Indeed the rule of intercalation adopted by the council of Nicaea said: Easter is on Sunday following the fourteenth day of the moon, which reaches this stage on March 21 or slightly later.[39]

---

33 See J Meeus, *Astronomical Tables of Sun, Moon and Planets*, Willmann-Bell, 2nd edition 1995, pp. 109-110.

34 Commentary on B. Rosh Hashanah 21a.

35 *Sefer ha-Ibbur, Ma'amar* III, chap. 5; edition Filipowski 1846, p. 92.

36 Rashi on B. Sanhedrin 13b: and B. Rosh Hashanah 21a: In fact Rashi understands that R' Huna bar Abin requires that the *tekufat* Nissan falls the latest on Nissan 14. But if it were on Nissan 15 he would make the month of Adar full and the year would remain an ordinary year. If we transpose this in the modern fixed calendar, in which Adar of an ordinary year has always 29 days, this could be understood as the possibility of having the *tekufah* on Nissan 15. The reasoning of Tossafot is similar to that of Rashi but they require that the *tekufah* falls the latest on Nissan 15. If the *tekufah* were to fall on Nissan 16 they would make Adar full and they would behold an ordinary year. Therefore I consider that the position of Rashi can be compared to that of Rambam while the position of Tossafot could be compared to that of R. Abraham bar Ḥiyya and R. Ḥananel despite the formal differences.

37 *Hilkhot Kiddush ha-Ḥodesh* IV: 2.

38 From a piece of evidence mentioned beneath it appears that effectively Passover i.e. Nissan 15 could begin as early as March 21 and the eve of Passover, which the Christians called the "Pascha" could fall as soon as March 20. This was considered too early by the Christians, for whom Easter could not occur before March 22, the day following March 21 which they considered as the day of the true equinox.

39 Thus according to the rule of Nicaea, Nissan 14 was the earliest on March 21 and Easter is the earliest on Sunday March 22. By contrast, if the Jews considered the rule of the equinox according to the understanding of R' Abraham bar

At many occasions the Christians complained during the period of the second –fourth century and even later that the Jews did not respect the rule of the equinox and celebrated their festival of Passover too early. One must however be very cautious in the appreciation of these accusations. As noted by Stern, there was a great diversity among the Jewish communities, some following the rabbinic calendar, others not. Furthermore remote communities far from Palestine and Jewish rabbinic centers were not aware of the rabbinic calendar and could not follow it. It is important to note that when the Christians reproached the Jews about their early celebration of Passover they didn't take into account that the beginning of the festival, the night of the Seder, belongs to the next day. For them, in the Julian calendar, it belongs to the day before. Furthermore, the Christian writers confuse the ostentatious preparations of the feast on Nissan 14 and the public burning of the leaven, with the actual festival, which is more intimate and less spectacular. In all Christian sources the Jewish "Pascha" referred to Nissan 14, the day when the Passover sacrifice, if applicable, would have been prepared.[40] They may have considered that this day is the beginning of the festival. Jaffe mentioned two pieces of evidence about the alleged early celebration of Pesaḥ by the Jews.

The first piece of evidence[41] is related to the year 387; it states that the Church of Alexandria, which considered that Easter cannot fall before Sunday 22 March because of the rule of the equinox adopted at the Council of Nicaea, reproached the Church of Rome, that they celebrated Easter on March 21, together with the Jews, before the limit accepted by the ecclesiastical rules.

A second piece of evidence[42] mentions that the Christian Church had adopted a cycle of intercalation of 84 years in 298 C.E. This cycle departed from the incorrect assumption that the true vernal equinox falls on March 18. Jaffe assumes that the rabbinical Court in Palestine accepted this true equinox and considered that March 20 is the mean equinox and accepted

Ḥiyya and consider the *tekufah* on March 22, Nissan 16 is the earliest on March 22 and Pesaḥ which begins on Nissan 15, begins the earliest on March 21. In fact the Seder evening was even on March 20. The Christians considered that the Jews began Pesaḥ too early and did not respect the rule of the equinox. We have a piece of evidence relating that the Jews began Pesaḥ in 387 C.E. on March 21.

40 See Leviticus XXIII; 5.

41 L Ideler, *Handbuch der mathem. Und technischen Chronologie*, 2 vol. (Berlin 1825). Vol II, p. 255.

42 L Ideler. Vol II p. 232.

therefore that the first day of Passover falls on March 19.[43] Only if the first day of Passover falls on March 18 would they intercalate the year. Apparently this is the justification of the date of March 19 adopted by Jaffe in his tables, as the limit of Passover and this is the basis of the calculation of the leap years in his reconstructed calendar. It leads to empirical fictitious cycles of intercalation 3-6-8-11-14-16-19[44] or 3-6-8-11-14-17-19.[45] We will see that this assumption is unlikely; it is very problematic and must be considered with much reservation. The most probable empirical order of intercalation was the fictitious cycle of 19 years, 3 – 5 – 8 – 11 – 14 – 16 – 19.[46]

3. The first piece of evidence mentioned by Jaffe concerned the year 387 C.E. Stern (2001) mentions other sources from which it appears that the year 387 C.E. was a very special year; it was the subject of many intense polemical debates. In the West it set the Alexandrians against the Romans, in the East it set the Alexandrians against the early Easter observers who followed the Eastern tradition of observing Easter "with the Jews". Besides the piece of evidence mentioned by Jaffe we know the third homily of John Chrysostom "against the Jews" which was delivered in Antioch early in 387 C.E. against the Jews observing Passover before the equinox and against the Christians following them. Similarly, the letter of Ambrose, bishop of Milan, from 387 C.E. was a pro-Alexandrian document and an attack against the Roman Church.

We examine in Appendix D, 2 the year 4147 AMI corresponding to 386/387. We prove that this year was not a leap year. Its Molad, according to Jaffe's assumptions, was 5 – 9 – 360. It corresponds perfectly to the Molad of Jaffe: 5 – 9 – 5 in his table א.

The *keviyah* of the year 4147 was thus in the calendar of Hillel as it is also the case in our modern calendar: השא. Thus 1st day of Nissan was on Sunday, March, 7; the 15th of Nissan was on Sunday, the 21st of March 387, and the preparations of the festival and the public burning of the

---

43 According to the rule of the equinox of Rabbi Ḥuna bar Abin as understood by R' Abraham bar Ḥiyya.

44 This is the order ascribed to *Ḥakhamim* in the Baraita of the order of intercalation.

45 This is the present order of intercalation; it is ascribed to Rabban Gamliel in the Baraita of the order of intercalation.

46 This is the order ascribed to Rabbi Eliezer in the Baraita of the order of intercalation.

leaven was exceptionally early, on Friday the 13th of Nissan[47] or March 19.

Our assumption that the year 4147, the fifth year of the fictitious cycle of 19 years was an ordinary year is thus perfectly justified as we see that Nissan 15 of this ordinary year fell on Sunday 21 March and satisfied the rule of the equinox.[48]

This historical piece of evidence gives us precious indications about the practical rule of the equinox used by the Court of Tiberias at the end of the fourth century, during the first decades of the Jewish calendar.

However, according to the Christian rules adopted at the Council of Nicaea, Easter must be on the Sunday following the 14th day of the moon which reaches this stage on March 21 or immediately after.

In 387, Nissan 14 was on Saturday, March 20, and for the Church, this lunation was not paschal because it fell before March 21. The year 387 was thus a limit case for the Christians. In fact it appears that even according to the Christian lunar tables the 14th day of the moon was even a day before on March 19.[49] Therefore this year must be intercalated in the Ecclesiastic calendar. The full moon of March 387 was not paschal and Easter must be delayed to the next lunation. Now the 14th day of the next lunation, according to the Christian tables, was on Sunday April 18 and Easter must then be celebrated on the following Sunday, on April 25.[50] The Roman Church could not accept such a late celebration of Easter. We see now that the year 387 was really exceptional. It is because of the exceptional lateness of the Alexandrian Easter that the date of Easter became in that year the object of such intense polemical debates.

Regardless, we see that the Jews celebrated Passover on March 21 in accordance with the Jewish rule of the Equinox, according to the understanding of R' Abraham bar Ḥiyya and R' Ḥananel of the rule of *Shitsar* given by Rabbi Ḥuna bar Abin. Indeed Nissan16 was on March 22, the day of the *tekufah* or mean equinox.

4. The second piece of evidence given by Jaffe is related to the fact that the Church of Rome considered in its intercalation cycle that the true equinox is on March 18. It is likely that this data could have influenced the local Jewish community and its calculation of the intercalated

---

47 Because of the Shabbat.

48 The *tekufah* or mean equinox was on March 22 and the rule of the equinox of rabbi Huna bar Abin must be understood according to the understanding of R' Abraham bar Ḥiyya and R' Ḥananel.

49 Stern (2001) p. 144.

50 Thus 35 days later!

years but there is no reason that the Palestinian Court would have been influenced by the data used by the remote Church of Rome. The only undisputable data is that the Jews in the East celebrated Passover in 387 C.E. on March 21. If they celebrated Passover even on March 19, we would certainly have more polemical material extant. Apparently their early celebration of Passover on March 21[51] was enough to create intense disputes because it was a sufficient reason for the Christians to intercalate their ecclesiastic year. Now if the Court of Tiberias accepted an early Passover on March 19, in contradiction with the rule of the equinox of Rabbi Ḥuna bar Abin and the other rules of the equinox defined in the Talmud,[52] the number of disputes would certainly have been much greater and the year 387 would not have been the most exemplary case of Jewish deviation. In summary, this second piece of evidence could apply to the Jews of Rome, distant from Palestine and the Court, but not to the Court of Tiberias.

5. In conclusion, table א corresponding to the calendar of Hillel during the period 4119- 4408 with the *moladot* and the *keviyot* of the different years is a tremendous work. However, it was built on the basis of a problematic[53] assumption that the limit of Passover was March 19. Therefore the sequence of the leap years is problematic and in consequence also the *moladot* and the *keviyot* of the years following the problematic and critical years. At the inception of the calendar of Hillel the limit of March 21 for Passover seems the most likely. It would be generally associated with the orders of intercalation 3-5-8-11-14-16-19[54] and 3-6-8-11-14-16-19.[55] However we know that the Julian calendar has an excess of 1 day in 128 years with regard to the length of the tropical year and it is therefore likely that the accepted limit of Passover of March 21 moved back with the time to March 20, March 19 and probably March 18 at the end of the eighth century. It appears therefore that it is impossible to establish a fixed table reconstituting the Jewish calendar because there remain too many unknowns. These considerations are also valid for all the tables of Jaffe whose purpose

51 Preceded by the burning of the leaven on March 19.

52 See B. Sanhedrin 13b-14a.

53 And probably erroneous.

54 This is the order of intercalation of Rabbi Eliezer in the Baraita of the order of the leap years in the cycle of 19 years quoted in *Sefer Yessod Olam*, book IV chap 2. It would correspond to the oldest order of intercalation.

55 This is the order of intercalation of *Ḥakhamim* in the same Baraita.

is the reconstitution of the Jewish calendar between 359 C.E. and 838 C.E.

6. Another factor of uncertainty in the tables of Jaffe is a problem raised by Bornstein[56] and Jaffe:[57] did the ancient masters of the calendar take into account, at a moment of history, the *Molad Zaken*[58] in months other than Tishrei?[59]

7. The origin of this problem is the discovery, by these scholars, in *Sefer ha-Pardes*[60] of the school of Rashi and in the tractate Soferim, of elements about an unknown *keviyah* גשא, for a leap year. It could only be the reminiscence of an ancient *keviyah* no longer in use.
Jaffe noted in his tables the years which would have been affected by this problem. The problem of *Molad Zaken* in Shevat and possibly in Kislev is an intricate problem which will be examined in <www.Hakirah.org/vol20AjdlerAppendices.pdf>.

In order to examine the merits of the Table of Jaffe, despite the weak point mentioned above, let us examine other pieces of evidence mentioned by Jaffe.

- The date of the death of R. Aḥai bar R. Huna on Sunday 4 Adar 4266 AMI.[61] It implies that the next year 4267 began on Sunday. This was the eleventh year of the fictitious cycle 224 of 19 years. It is likely that it was a leap year. In our modern calendar the Molad of 4267 is

56 *Ha-Tekufah* vol 16, 1923, pp. 270-273.

57 *Korot Heshbon ha-Ibbur*, Tel Aviv 1931, pp. 168-172.

58 The Molad is *Zaken*, when it falls, on a permissible day for Rosh Hashanah, at noon or after. Then 1 Tishrei is delayed to the next permissible day.

59 In the months of Tishrei and Nissan, days and nights are approximately 12 hours long and Jewish civil days begin at sunset, close to 6 p.m. This cannot be said for the other months. When days are > 12 h then nights are < 12 hours. This, however, is of no practical consequence because according to the rules of the Jewish calendar, we consider the situation as if we were at the equator. Thus we consider them as standard days with day = nights = 12 hours. The Jewish civil days begin at 6 p.m. and the molad is *Zaken* if it is at noon of a permissible day for Rosh Hashanah or later. Tishrei 1 is then delayed to the next permissible day.

60 *Sefer ha-Pardes*, edited by R' H.L. Ehrenreich, Budapest 1924, p. 340 lines 33-34: אם יבוא סוכות יום שלישי ויהיו מרחשון וכסליו שלימין, יהיו כ"ט שבתות ולא נצטרך לכפול. See Appendix E, 3.

61 AMI refers to *Beharad*, as we do today and AMII refers to *Weyad*.

1 – 22 – 983. The Molad of Hillel was 1 – 17 – 648 corresponding exactly to the Molad given by Jaffe 1 – 17 – 9.[62]
We see that the modern Molad could not have fitted because it introduces a *Molad Zaken* and Rosh Hashanah would have been postponed to Tuesday. The Molad calculated according to the assumptions of Jaffe explains that we just avoided the postponement of *Molad Zaken*,[63] and that Rosh Hashanah and Adar 4 were on Sunday.

- Jaffe mentioned a reference[64] from the Christian writer Victorius according to which in 590 C.E. Passover, Nissan 15, fell on Sunday March 26 together with the Christian Easter and indeed some churches celebrated Easter on that day.[65] However, the Alexandrian Church, to which the writer belonged, decided to celebrate Easter on the 22nd day of the lunar month, on the next Sunday,[66]in order not to celebrate Easter together with the Jews. Let us check this situation and check if it was indeed an exceptional case. We saw already in other examples how the calculations must be performed, allowing the checking of Jaffe's tables.[67] We can calculate the following table for the year 4350 AMI and for following years, which seem to also have Pesaḥ beginning on Sunday. We note that in our modern calendar Pesaḥ falls on the Sunday of Easter in 4350, 4354 and 4374. However when we check the situation according to the Calendar of Hillel, there is a coincidence only in 4350, with Pesaḥ occurring on Saturday in the two other years. Similarly if we examine the calendar of Hillel, we note that Pesaḥ falls on Sunday in the years 4350, 4353, 4357 and 4377.

---

62 See Appendix D, 3.

63 Stern (2001) p. 182 note 113 wants to prove that the Molad was already the modern Molad but *Molad Zaken* was not yet observed. He ascertains even that in 836 C.E. (see the letter of the *Resh Galuta*) the *Molad Zaken* was not yet applied. This position seems indefensible. It seems unconceivable that the rules of the calendar would still have changed in 836 C.E. and that a new postponement, would have been introduced. I have always championed the principle that the rules of the calendar were introduced at its inception; only the postponement A was introduced later but it was already debated at the origin. Only technical elements subject to new observation or measurement could be adapted: the Molad, the length of the Jewish lunation or the date of the *tekufah*.

64 Ideler II, p. 264.

65 Together with the Jews.

66 Sunday 2 April 590.

67 The *keviyah* is deduced from the Molad, using the Four Gates Table (see appendix C). The date of Easter was calculated using the algorithm of the Julian Easter by Spencer Jones p. 69 in Astronomical Algorithms Jean Meeus; Willmann-Bell 1991.

However Pesaḥ coincided with Easter only in 4350. The piece of evidence of the Christian writer Victorius, seems to indicate that the year 590 was an exceptional year with the coincidence of Passover and Easter. Our modern calendar cannot explain this exceptional character because the same coincidence should have occurred also in 4354 and 4374. The calendar of Hillel, based on the assumptions of Jaffe, gives a satisfactory explanation:

Table 1: Pesah and Easter on Sunday in 590 CE and the following years. An asterisk (*) indicates a leap year, and a *keviyah* in bold character indicates that Pesaḥ was the same day as Easter.

Years	Modern Calendar			Calendar of Hillel			Easter
	Molad	Keviyah	Pessah	Molad	Keviyah	Pessah	Sunday
4350	5-20-1074	**זחא**	26/3/590	5-14-11	**השא**	26/3/590	26/3/590
4353	6-12-175	זשג	24/3/593	6-5-13	זחא	22/3/593	29/3/593
4354*	3-20-1051	**החא**	11/4/594	3-14-10	גכז	10/4/594	11/4/594
4357*	4-12-152	השג	9/4/597	4-5-12	החא	7/4/597	14/4/597
4374	5-11-75	**השא**	31/3/614	5-4-8	הכז	30/3/614	31/3/614
4377	6-2-256	זחא	27/3/617	5-19-10	זחא	27/3/617	3/4/617

Pesaḥ and Easter coincided only in 4530. In 4353, 4357 and 4377 Nissan 14 was on a Saturday later than March 21 and Easter could have been on the next Sunday, together with the Jews. However it seems that the Ecclesiastic lunar calendar was slightly different than the Jewish lunar calendar and, in these three cases, the fourteenth day of the moon was a day later, on the Sunday, delaying automatically Easter to the next Sunday.[68] It is of interest to note that the Christians created scandals when the Jews celebrated their festival "too early" before them but yet they felt obliged to delay Easter when both festivals coincided.

We see again that the modern calendar and the modern Molad cannot explain why the coincidence of Passover and Easter in 590 C.E. was such a particular event. By contrast the assumptions of Jaffe explain that this coincidence was unique.

Conclusion

The table א of Jaffe is related to the period 359 – 648 C.E. The amount of evidence related to this period is not large but, nevertheless it is not negligible and greater than for any other period. The assumptions of Jaffe,

68 The algorithm of Spencer Jones takes these situations into account.

about the limit of Passover, are questionable and, even untenable and the order of the leap years is at times questionable.

Therefore, in the present paper we always try to verify any data and we do not rely on Jaffe's table. The examination of different pieces of evidence shows that the assumptions of Jaffe about the epoch of the molad and the length of the Jewish month give interesting results and explain many historical facts that would otherwise not be understandable. It is, however, necessary to be cautious and question the order of intercalation. We can finally say that his table is reliable except for years with Pesaḥ (Nissan 15) before March 21, which raise a problem. For such a year we must delay Pesaḥ a month and make it a leap year ending a month later. The next year then begins a month later and becomes an ordinary year. The *keviyah* of both years must be adapted using the Four Gates Table.[69] This makes it necessary to adopt a likely date for the limit of Passover and then adapt the table of Jaffe for the problematic years.

As a result of the date of the true equinox, the theoretical acceptable limit date for the beginning of Passover should be:

> From about 300 until about 430, the limit of Passover[70] should be March 21.
> From about 430 until about 560, the limit of Passover should be March 20.
> From about 560 until about 690, the limit of Passover should be March 19.
> From about 690 until about 820, the limit of Passover should be March 18.

This table is of course purely theoretical. However the ancients did not know the length of the tropical year and the date of the equinox with precision and we don't know at which rate they moved back the limit of Passover.

The Tables of Jaffe inform the reader about the civil date of Passover and allows changing the order of intercalation without too much difficulty.

---

69 See Appendix C.

70 Nissan 15.

III The Jewish Calendar from about 648 until 776. The Introduction of the postponement "lo ADU Rosh" in the seventh Century.

We have seen that Rosh Hashanah could fall on Sunday in the calendar of Hillel. We found evidence in the Talmud that in the beginning of the fifth century under the reign of Rav Yeimar, Rosh Hashanah could still fall on Sunday.[71]

In the epistle of Rav Sherira Gaon it mentions that R' Aḥai bar R' Huna died on Sunday 4 Adar 817 of the era of the contracts[72] or 4266 AMI of *Beharad*.[73] This implies that 14 Adar (Purim) would have been on Wednesday, the following Passover on Friday and the following Rosh Hashanah on Sunday.

In the *Sheiltot*[74] of R' Aḥai Gaon[75] the postponement A seems already old history and is presented at the same level as the two former postponements **DU**. For this reason Jaffe and Bornstein considered that the postponement **A** must have been introduced during the first half of the seventh century. Stern (2001) also refers to an additional reference, the *Sefer ha-Ma'asim*.[76] In this work reference is also made to Rosh Hashanah occurring on Sunday.

Jaffe constructed the table א until 4408 and the table ב, related to the second period with the postponement A from 4390 onwards. This places the introduction of this postponement between 629 and 648 C.E. This last date seems to fit all the extant pieces of evidence.

The rules of the calendar were thus the same as before except the additional postponement A. There was probably not yet a regular cycle of intercalation; the intercalations were probably calculated on the basis of

---

71 See note 3 above.

72 Also the Seleucid era.

73 The relation between these two eras is: 1 SE = 3450 AMI

74 *Sheiltot of Rav Aḥai*, chapter 79. This work was completed after R' Aḥai Gaon settled in Palestine, in about 750 C.E.

75 R' Aḥai of Shabha (680-752) is generally called R' Aḥai Gaon although he never was Gaon. When a vacancy occurred in the geonate of Pumbedita in 748, the exilarch named a pupil of R' Ahai as Gaon. Incensed at this slight R' Ahai left Babylonia and settled in Palestine where he ended his masterpiece the *Sheiltot*.

76 The *Sefer ha-Ma'asim li-benei Yisrael*, Hillel Newman, Yad Ben Tsvi, is a book of *halakhot* of Palestinian composition; the date of composition is uncertain but the first half of the seventh century is likely. See Stern (2001) p. 184.

an adopted limit for Passover which was adapted according to the acquired knowledge about the length of the solar year and the date of the equinox.

The basic assumptions of Jaffe for the calendar in that period were thus the following:

- The Molad had been chosen near the moment of the maximum solar eclipse, which occurred on March 15, 359 C.E. exactly the day of the inception of the calendar. This Molad was still valid.
- The lunation was still 29 d – 12 h – 792 *ḥal* or 29d 12h 44m. At this epoch they did not yet use the *ḥelek*[77] and did not divide the hour into 1080 *ḥalakim*. They could suffice themselves with the division of the hour in 15 *ḥayil*[78] a *ḥayil* representing 4 minutes or 72 *ḥal*. The length of the month was thus noted 29 – 12 – 11. The remainder of a month was 1 – 12 – 11, the remainder of 6 months was 2 – 4 – 6, the remainder of 12 months was 4 – 8 – 12 and the remainder of 13 months was 5 – 21 – 8.
- The rules of the calendar were about the same as today and the postponements were now the same as today. The rules were thus the following:
- The postponements were ADU (Sunday, Wednesday and Friday) and יח or 18 hours (noon).
- The length of the year for an **ordinary** year:
  353 days for a **defective** year. Shift of RH, 3 days.
  354 days for a **regular** year. Shift of RH, 4 days.
  355 days for an **abundant** year. Shift of RH, 5 days.
  The length of the year for a **leap** year:
  383 days for a **defective** year. Shift of RH, 5 days.
  384 days for a **regular** year. Shift of RH, 6 days.
  385 days for an **abundant** year. Shift of RH, 7 = 0 days.

  Indeed when the number of days of the year is a multiple of 7, the day of RH has no shift and remains unchanged.
- The derivate postponements (resulting from the former rules) are then:[79]
  3 – 9 – 3 in an ordinary year or ג ט ג בפשוטה.
  2 – 15 – 8 in a year following a leap year or נ טו ח אחר עיבור.

---

77 1 minute = 18 *ḥalakim*.

78 1 *ḥelek* = 4 minutes and 1 *Ḥayil* = 72 *ḥalakim*.

79 See Appendix B.

- Because of the introduction of the postponement A, the number of possible *keviyot* was reduced to 14 as today and the possible *keviyot* were the same as today:
For ordinary years בחג, בשה, גכה, הכז, השא, זחא, זשג;
and for leap years בחה, בשז, גכז, החא, השג, זחג זשה.

The weak point of the table ב of Jaffe is again the list of the intercalated years. However the limit of Passover of March 19 seems suitable during the period 560 – 690. It appears that from about 690 onwards the limit of Passover should have been March 18. By contrast with the first period, no piece of evidence could be produced.

IV The Observation of September 776 C.E and the adaptation of the Molad.

Chapter V of the *Baraita of Samuel*, in our printed version,[80] begins as follows:

> בשנת ארבעת אלפים וחמש מאות ושלשים ושש שוו חמה ולבנה שמטות ותקופות ולא נשתיר לחמה אלא שעה אחת בלבד[81]. מן ארבעת אלפים ותקל"ו שנה[82] ואילך שנה ראשונה מולד לבנה בתשרי בתחילת ליל ד', בניסן בליל ו' בשתי שעות גדולות. הרוצה לידע מולד לבנה יחשוב משוו חמה ולבנה כמה שנים ויתן ד' ימים וארבע שעות גדולות לכל שנה ושנה.

80 As it appears in *Sefer Poel ha-Shem* with a commentary of R. Arieh Leib Lipkin based on the edition by R' Nathan Amram, Salonika 1861.

81 It speaks of a "great hour" equal to two hours.

82 The year 4536 mentioned in the *Baraita* of Samuel is counted according to the style AMII (*Weyad*) and it corresponds to 4537 AMI (*Beharad*). This year is the first year of *shemitah* and the first year of the great cycle of 28 years. This is certainly an important piece of evidence in favor of the thesis of the Gaonim against Maimonides and against Rashi and Rosh: the *shemitah* is always on years multiple of 7 when counted in the style AMI from *Beharad*. We can assume that the members of the council of intercalation had made an observation of the equinox on Thursday September 19, 776 and deduced from it the mean equinox or *tekufah* on Tuesday, September 17, 776 at 16h Jerusalem time. This was a fairly good observation with a precision of about 7 hours with regard of modern calculations. We see that the ancient original text which assumes a primitive lunation of 29 – 12 – 720 (see below) was adapted in the manuscript used by R' Nathan Amram, in order to perpetuate this observation and the decisions of the Council of intercalation.

This text did not exist in the version of the Baraita of Samuel quoted by R' Abraham ibn Ezra[83] and R' Abraham bar Ḥiyya;[84] their chapter V began with:

הרוצה לידע בכמה בשבת מולד לבנה נופלת יחשוב משנברא העולם עד עכשיו כמה שנים ויתן ארבעה ימים וארבע שעות גדולות לכל שנה ושנה.[85]

It appears that the Molad Tishrei 4537 was fixed on Tuesday, September 17, 776 at 6 p.m. or 4 – 0 – 0 and the *tekufah* of Tishrei which occurred at 3 – 22 – 0 was apparently delayed to 4 – 0 – 0 in order to create an epoch when *tekufah* and Molad coincided.[86] This coincidence fitted perfectly the biblical narrative of the creation of the luminaries on the fourth day.

The year 4537 is the 15th year of a fictitious cycle of 19 years; it is assumed to be an ordinary year.

The Molad of Hillel of Tishrei 4537 was 3 – 18 – 1008. It was corrected after the observation of September 776 to 4 – 0 – 0 by the addition of 5 – 72, thus 5 hours and 1/15. The modern value of the corresponding Molad is 4 – 3 – 363.[87]

We ascertain that the consequence of the use of a lunation of 29 – 12 – 792 from the inception of the calendar brought an accumulated difference of 5108 *ḥal* = 4h 788 *ḥal*. It is not far from the correction of 5h 1/15 that was made by adopting the Molad of 4 – 0 – 0. We don't know how they found the new value of their mean conjunction, the Molad. Did they find it from a number of eclipses like Ptolemy or did they simply consider that the lunation of 29 – 12 – 793 is more correct and they simply added the accumulated difference and rounded the result off? Anyhow it seems that they adopted a new epoch for the Molad on Tishrei 4537, 4 – 0 – 0.

---

83 Commentary on Shemot XII: 2.

84 *Sefer ha-Ibbur*, p. 36 edition Filipowski, London 1851.

85 The remainder of 12 months is 4 – 8 – 876 in the modern calendar, the remainder 4 – 8 – 0 corresponds to a month of 29 – 12 – 720. The text of the Braita of Samuel seems to consider the more primitive value of the Jewish month of 29 – 12 – 720. See the dictum of Ravina in B. Arakhin 9b. See also Ajdler (2004): "Rav Safra and the Second Festival Day: Lesson about the evolution of the Jewish calendar," p.17, *Tradition* Vol 38, N° 4, Winter 2004.

86 This is reminiscent of a situation in our modern calendar during the year 1 AMI. The Molad Nissan 1 AMI was on 4 – 9 – 642 and the *tekufah* of Nissan was on 4 – 0 – 0, both *tekufah* of Samuel and of Rabbi Adda (exactly a week before). Rosh Hashanah 4537 was on Thursday September 19, 776. The mean conjunction (based on experimental observation) and the Molad were placed at 4 – 0 – 0 or Tuesday, September 17, 776 at 6 p.m.

87 See Appendix D, 4.

By contrast it is certain that the moment of the autumnal equinox must have been determined experimentally. They apparently found a true equinox on Thursday 19 September 776 at about 4 p.m. and deduced from it the mean equinox on Tuesday 17 September 776 at about 4 p.m. in Jerusalem.[88] The date of the equinox given in the *Baraita of Samuel* is the mean equinox. This is a proof that the equinox generally considered in the study of the Jewish calendar and in the rule of the equinox is always the mean equinox. This confirmed that Nissan 16 could fall on March 19 and Pesaḥ could then be on March 18 at the end of the eighth century.

We observe also, from the text of the Baraita, that their counting of the Sabbatical years was the same as today, according to the counting of the Geonim mentioned by Rambam in his *Ḥibbur, Hilkhot Shemitah ve-Yovel* X; 6 the year 4536 AMI was a sabbatical year.

Jaffe has constructed table ח of Moladot[89] from 4542 onwards, based on the results of the observation of September 776. He adopted the following assumptions:

- The cycle of intercalation is now fixed; it is the cycle 3 – 6 – 8 – 11 – 14 – 17 – 19

This assumption makes sense.[90] The earliest mentions of the19-year cycle is in the end of chapter 8 of *Pirquei de-Rabbi Eliezer*, a work generally dated to the eighth or the ninth century. It is also mentioned in the liturgical poem *Kiddush Yeraḥim* of R' Pinḥas which was written not earlier than the mid eighth century.[91]

The adoption of a fixed order of intercalation represents a considerable evolution in the solar regulation of the Jewish calendar. Instead of being obliged to be dependent on the *keviyot*, and compare Nissan 16 with a date of the *tekufah*, the rule of the equinox of Rabbi Huna bar Abin

---

88 The spring equinox occurs about 2 days before the mean equinox. This difference is practically exactly 2 days in Ptolemy's Almagest.

89 See Appendix H at <www.Hakirah. org/vol20AjdlerAppendices.pdf>.

90 But it could also have been introduced a little later. This new procedure represents an improvement and a simplification of the Jewish calendar. It is also the origin of the problems of the Jewish calendar. The adopted cycle fitted during the period 838 – 1160. Afterwards it will become the origin of an increasing discordance between the Jewish calendar and the solar year. The rule of intercalation or the rule of the equinox will not more correctly work because Pesaḥ will begin later and later with regard to the spring equinox and Pesaḥ will dwell outside the month of spring towards the summer.

91 Because there is mention in this liturgical poem of a fast commemorating the earthquake of January 748 C.E.

would depend now, after the introduction of a fixed order of intercalation, on the distance of the *tekufah* to the Molad of Nissan.[92] The rule of the equinox would simply imply that the vernal *tekufah* may not fall later than 16 days or 384 hours after the Molad of Nissan in the sixteenth year of the cycle, in which Pesaḥ is the earliest.

This new procedure would be perfect if the length of the tropical year was exactly equal to the length of the mean Jewish year. In reality the Jewish year is longer than the tropical year and the Jewish year will shift toward the summer. In fact it appears that this cycle of intercalation was probably introduced several tens of years too early. Indeed the adopted *tekufah* on September 17, 776 at 18h corresponds to a true vernal equinox on 19 March 18 p.m. and a first day of Pesaḥ or Nissan 15 on 18 March. We observe in table ה that the introduction of the cycle of intercalation 3 – 6 – 8 – 11 – 14 – 17 – 19 leads to a limit of Passover of 17 and 18 March. The date of March 17 is still too early for the first day of Passover.[93] Although there is no clear-cut limit it seems that this order of intercalation would have fit better during the period 838 – 1160. It was introduced a little too early.

The *tekufah* used at this stage is not yet the formal *tekufah* of Rabbi Adda bar Ahava but the mean equinox deduced from the observed astronomical true equinox.

- The Council adopted a cycle of 13 * 19 = 247 years corresponding to a synodical lunation of 29 – 12 – 793 + 905 / (13 * 235) = 29 – 12 – 793.2962.

This assumption rests on a minor clue, an allusion of Ibn Ezra about the relinquishment of the cycle of 247 years[94] also called עיגול דרב נחשון גאון, which convinced Jaffe that this cycle was once in use. Indeed the *Iggul* of Rav Naḥshon of 247 years =13 * 235 months corresponds to a remainder of 6 – 23 – 175 = 7 days – 905 *ḥal.*

---

92 This principle was already proposed by R' Isaac Yisraeli in *Yessod Olam*, Ma'amar IV, chap 2, p. 4a and chap 4, p. 6a. Jaffe, in *Korot* (1931) p.112 adopted the same principle to explain the evolution of the understanding of the rule of the equinox. Loewinger in *Al ha-Sheminit*, Tel Aviv 1986, pp. 25-26 proposed to understand Rambam H.K.H. IV, 2 on the basis of this principle but the argument is questionable.

93 In other words the cycle 3 – 6 – 8 – 11 – 14 – 17 – 19 was introduced too early.

94 רמז לעגולת רמ"ז, הלוחות הראשונים אשר שברת, יישר כחך ששברת.
Ibn Ezra in *Sefer ha-Meorot*, Leiden 1496 and 1550; Rome 1544; Frankfort on the Main 1624. This reference was mentioned by Jaffe p. 159 and Bornstein *Makhaloket* p. 142. See also Jaffe p. 158 two references to *seder de rav Nahshon* and *iggul de rav Nahshon.*

The cycle of 247 years contains 3055 months. If a month had a length of 29 – 12 – 793 then 3055 months = 121,201,015 ḥal = [M(181440)] – 905 ḥal.

Thus introducing a regular cycle of 247 years gives a supplement of 905 *ḥal* for 3,055 months.

Jaffe built the table ה with the following assumptions. The Jewish month is still considered as (29 – 12 – 11) = (29 – 12 – 792), but after the first year and then after successively all the 4 and 5 years, he adds 1 *ḥayil*. With this procedure he adds the complete cycle of 55 *ḥayil* or 3960 *ḥal* corresponding to 3055 months * 1 *ḥal* + 905 *ḥal*.

The procedure proposed by Jaffe is thus rigorously correct, but it the fruit of his inventive spirit and his ingenuity. There is not the least piece of evidence that this cycle was **really in use** and, if this was the case, it is not sure at all that it was implanted this way.

It is also possible that this cycle was only a working hypothesis, which was abandoned and never used. The length of the lunation would have been fixed from 4542 onwards to 29 – 12 – 793.[95] The difference has no practical consequences for us.

V The Letter of the *Resh Galuta* of 836 C.E

J. Mann discovered an exceptional document from the Cairo Geniza and published it in 1922.[96] This document was called the letter of the *Resh Galuta*,[97]because its author appeared to be a very important and authoritative personality.

This letter reveals that Passover (15 Nissan 4596) of the year 836 C.E. was due to occur on a Tuesday, March 21, 836 while according to the

95 It is generally accepted that only at the introduction of the Jewish month of 29 – 12 – 793 the necessity to introduce the *ḥelek* (1/1080 of the hour) was felt. The first mention of the division of the hour in 1080 parts is made in a liturgical poem of Rabbi Pinḥas. Similarly the earliest mention of the 19- year cycle of intercalation is made at the end of chap VIII of *Pirquei de-Rabbi Eliezer* (generally dated to the eighth or ninth century) and in the *Kiddush Yeraḥim* of Rabbi Pinḥas. R' Pinḥas is supposed to have lived in the late eighth or early ninth century. See Stern (2001) p. 197 and 204. R' Pinḥas mentions in his *Kiddush Yeraḥim* the fast commemorating the earthquake of January 748 C.E. and wrote certainly after this date.

96 J. Mann, (1920-1922) "The Jews in Egypt and Palestine under the Fatimid Caliphs" 2 vols. London. See vol. 2. pp. 41-42.

97 The Babylonian Exilarch. There is indeed at the end of the letter an allusion on the authority of the letter's author.

present-day calendar, it should have occurred on Thursday, March 23, 836. According to the Exilarch the year must be defective in order to prevent the visibility of the new moon of Nissan before the first day of the month.

Today, however, we are not concerned about this problem and the Talmud accepted the case of a first visibility one day before the first day of the month or a day later.[98]

Table 2: The situation according to our modern calendar. Rosh Hashanah is on Saturday in both 4596 and 4597. 4596 is the 17th year of a cycle; it is a leap year זשה of 385 days and 1 Nissan is on Thursday.

4596 AM1	835 C.E.	Tishrei 1	Nissan 1
385 days		Saturday, August 28 Molad (6)-22-660	
	836 C.E.		Thursday, March 23 Molad (3)-15-811 *Molad Zaken* if Molad >=(3)-13-642
4597 AM1		Saturday, Sept. 16 Molad (5)-20-169 *Molad Zaken*	

Table 3: The data According to the Letter of the Resh Galuta

4596 AM1	835 C.E.	Tishrei 1	Nissan 1
383 days		Saturday August 28	
	836 C.E.		Tuesday, March 21
4597 AM1		Thursday, Sept. 14	

The year 4596, the seventeenth year of a cycle of 19 years, was a leap year. According to the modern calendar it was a full year of 385 days of the type זשה with Passover on Thursday, April 6. It appears from the letter of the *Resh Galuta* that in reality the year was defective of the type זחג and Passover was on Tuesday, April 4. The calendar was different than the present-day calendar. In order to go further we must examine the following passage of the letter:[99]

---

98 See B. Erakhim 9b. See J. Ajdler, *Hilkhot Kiddush ha-Hodesh al-pi ha-Rambam*, Jerusalem 1996, p. 221.

99 For a complete transcription of the letter of the Resh Galuta see:
1. J. Mann, note 96.

משום סיהרא דניסן דקא מתיליד **בימּמא** דתלתא בשבא בארבע שעות

- Bornstein followed the reading of Mann and understood that the Molad of Nissan was on Tuesday at 4 Jewish hours: 3 – 4 – 0 in our notations, Monday at 10 p.m. about 12 hours before our modern Molad.[100] This explains that there was no *Molad Zaken* in Tishrei 4597 and therefore the year was defective.
- Jaffe did not read ארבע שעות but assumed ארבע ידות or ארבע דנקות. He understood that the Molad was 40 minutes in the **morning** thus a Molad 3 – 12 – 720, very near to the Molad used at that time after the adaptation of the Baraita of Samuel in 776. We understand now why Jaffe championed the *Iggul* of Rav Naḥshon; it allowed the assumed Molad used by the Palestinians to coincide with the Molad mentioned by the *Resh Galuta*. This also explains why there was no *Molad Zaken* in Tishrei 4597 and the year was defective and had 383 days. Now according to this understanding of Jaffe, the *Resh Galuta* was aware of the effective Molad of 3 – 12 – 720 and the *keviah* sent from Palestine was correct and incontestable. Why was he then justifying the decision sent from Palestine and championing the unity of the communities of Israel as if he was facing opposition and objection against the *keviyah* sent from Palestine? In order to answer this question Jaffe must invoke the problem of *Molad Zaken* in Shevat.[101] The Molad of Shevat 4597 would indeed be (3 – 12 – 720)[102]+(2 – 4 – 438)[103] + (6 – 2 – 1012)[104] = 4 – 20 – 10: The problem of *Molad Zaken* in Shevat was in the news and the Palestinians decided not to pay attention to it and not delay Rosh Hashanah 4597 to Saturday because of it.
- Stern (2001) proved irrefutably that the reading is ארבע שעות. He understands that the Molad was at four hours in the **morning** thus the Molad was 3 – 16 – 0. This Molad was very near the modern Molad

---

2. H. J.Bornstein, *Ha-Tekufah* Vol 14-15, Warsaw 1922, p. 346.
3. M. Kasher, 1949, *Torah Shelema* XIII, p. 170.
4. R Sar Shalom, 1985, *Shearim le-Luah ha-Ivri* p. 27.
5. S Stern, 2001, *Calendar and Community* pp. 277-283 (with Xerox copy of the original).

100 Such a difference seems difficult to justify.

101 See Jaffe (1931) pp. 98-102. See also Appendix E at <www.Hakirah.org/vol20AjdlerAppendices.pdf>.

102 The assumed Molad of Nissan 4596.

103 The remaining of 6 months in order to get the Molad Tishrei 4597.

104 The remaining of 4 months in order to get the Molad of Shevat 4597.

3 – 15 – 811 and perhaps it was exactly the same but the *Resh Galuta* rounded it off. Thus the Molad was already the same as the modern Molad and the *Resh Galuta* knew this Molad. The question is then: why was this year defective? Stern answers that the postponement of *Molad Zaken* was not yet in observance.[105]

It must be noted that all these positions are untenable:

- Bornstein does not explain the aim of the letter of the *Resh Galuta.* Indeed this letter is certainly not a letter of announcement of the *keviyah* of the year 4596. It does not even mention that the year 4596 is a leap year. On the other hand he doesn't explain and justify the discrepancy of 12 hours with regard to the modern Molad.
- Jaffe founded his explanation and his elaborate theory on an incorrect reading.
- Stern understands that the Molad is the same as today but the rule of *Molad Zaken* did not yet exist. It would be introduced only in about 838 C.E. The position of Stern seems unacceptable for many reasons.
    1. It seems difficult to imagine that a rule like *Molad Zaken*, of which the origin is "as obscure as is its rational",[106] would have been introduced so late at a moment when it seems that the Babylonians could already have been associated with the calendar committee and without their objection. Furthermore we do not see a plausible motivation for such an innovation.
    2. It is certainly less problematic to keep the rules of the calendar and adapt the Molad according to the latest understanding of astronomy than to change the rules, which are sanctified by their age.
    3. If we consider[107] that the work of al-Kwarismi about the Jewish calendar was genuine, it would mean that in about 825, the rules of the calendar, including *Molad Zaken* were known, the only unknown elements were the epoch of the Molad and of the cycle of 19 years.[108]

---

105 Stern (2001) p. 196. Stern had already used the same argument in order to explain the *keviyah* of the year 4266, the year of the death of R. Aḥai bar Rav Huna (see above). Again he assumed that the Molad in Tishrei 4266 was the same as today or very near to it and he explains that at this time the postponement of *Molad Zaken* was not yet in observance. See Stern (2001) p. 195.

106 Stern (2001) p. 195.

107 This is an assumption but there is no certitude. See Langermann (1987) and Sar Shalom (1988) in *Sinai* no. 106, pp.26-51.

108 See Stern (2001) p. 185.

4. The assumption of Stern that the present-day Molad was already the same in 836 and in 506 C.E. and even earlier is in contradiction with the theory that the Molad was derived from Ptolemy's Almagest in about 838 C.E. after the completion of an Arabic translation.[109]
5. Stern does not provide a plausible explanation of the purpose of the letter of the *Resh Galuta*. He does not explain the reason an objections was raised against the *keviyah* sent from Palestine.

Because of all these arguments I propose another explanation. It rests on the general theory of the evolution of the Molad of Jaffe but it deviates from his interpretation of the letter of the *Resh Galuta* and its purpose.

We assume that in Tishrei 776 C.E. the Molad was fixed at 4 – 0 – 0 according to the observation of the Baraita of Samuel and in March 836 the Molad was still based on the Molad of Tishrei 776 and was 3 – 12 – 448 (for a lunation of 29 – 12 – 793) or 3 – 12 – 680 (for a lunation of 29 – 12 – 793.2962, following the *iggul de Rav Naḥshon* according to Jaffe's assumption. This value is very near to that calculated by Jaffe).[110]

This Molad of Nissan was thus certainly before the limit of 3 – 13 – 642 and therefore there was no *Molad Zaken* in the following month of Tishrei;[111] the leap year 4596 was a defective year of 383 days and Pesaḥ was on Tuesday and not on Thursday.

Under the caliph al-Mamun (786-833) the son of the celebrated Harun al-Rashid (766-809) there was a cultural renaissance and the translation of Ptolemy's Almagest appeared in two versions; an older one by al-Hassan ibn Quraysh and another dated 827/828 by al-Hajjaj. This letter would be a piece of evidence of the first critics against the Palestinian authority. Some influential scholars had studied the new translation of the Almagest and had probably deduced from the table of mean conjunctions of the Almagest that the mean conjunction of Ptolemy of March 836 was 3 – 14 – 1041[112] in Alexandria and after transformation to Bagdad time it was indeed close to 3 – 16, corresponding to 10 a.m. or 4 hours in the morning as indicated in the letter of the *Resh Galuta*. They argued that the molad being about 3-16, there must be a *Molad Zaken* in Tishrei 4597 and

---

109 See Stern (2001) p. 209 about the death of R. Aḥai bar R. Ḥuna on Sunday 4 Adar 4266.

110 Thus the *Resh Galuta* knew already the Molad used by the Palestinian *meabrim*. For the justification of the calculations see Appendix D, 5.

111 (3 – 13 – 642) + (2 – 4 – 438) = 5 – 18 and we reach the limit of *Molad Zaken*.

112 The mean conjunction of Ptolemy in Alexandria is always the modern Molad – 850 *ḥal*. The modern Molad of Nissan 4596 was 3 – 15 – 811, therefore the conjunction of Ptolemy in Alexandria of Nissan 4596 was 3 –14 – 1041.

therefore the year 4596 should be an abundant year of 385 days and Passover should be on Thursday. These scholars contested thus the *keviyah* sent from Palestine on the basis of the data found in the Almagest, which had just been translated into Arabic. The scenario could have been the following: the Exilarch was not aware of the true Molad used by the calendric calculators or *meabrim* and accepted the Molad 3 – 16 proposed by his contradictors, the readers of the Almagest. He must advocate in favor of the Palestinian's *keviyah* and against those contradictors who contested the fixing of the year on the basis of the Ptolemaic conjunction. This allows an understanding as to why this letter advocated in favor of the Palestinian's decision and the primacy and the unity of the communities. This letter was thus not a letter announcing the *keviyah* to the communities; it was a letter advocating for the unity of the communities around the *keviyah* sent from Palestine. It is probable that concurrently the Exilarch expressed the view of his contradictors and his doubts to the Palestinians. It is likely that the Exilarch's intervention led to a common meeting in around 838 in the course of which the new Molad was adopted, in order to solve the contradiction between the Palestinian Molad and the Molad deduced from the Almagest.

In my opinion the rules of the calendar were already fixed long ago but the Molad was still the object of changes and adjusting. The postponement of *Molad Zaken* was, like the other postponements, old history. Except for postponement A, all the postponements already belonged to the calendar of Hillel at the inception of the fixed calendar.

VI Our Present Molad is derived from the Almagest.

At a period when the evolution of the Jewish calendar was not yet imagined, Ḥayyim Selig Slonimski[113] had already remarked on the dependence of our Molad on the table of mean conjunctions of the Almagest. Slonimski had remarked that the first conjunction of the table of Ptolemy corresponds to the conjunction of Nissan 3014.

The epoch of the Almagest is 1 Toth, year 1 of the Era of Nabonassar corresponding to Wednesday, February 26, 746 C.E. at noon.

---

113 See the bibliography at the end of the paper.

The first conjunction of the table of mean conjunctions[114] in Ptolemy's Almagest is 24 Toth; 44'17"[115] corresponding to Toth 24, 17h 42m 48s after noon[116] or Saturday, March 22 – 746 at 5h 42m 48s a.m. (after midnight) or 11h 770.40 *hal* in Jewish hours corresponding after rounding off to 7 – 11 – 770. Ptolemy's table gives also the distance of the common position of mean sun and mean moon, at the moment of the mean conjunction, from the sun's apogee. For this first mean conjunction this distance was: 288°; 38' 50". After addition of the sun's apogee of 65°; 30' we get the common mean longitude of 354°; 08' 50". This conjunction preceded thus slightly the equinox; it was thus certainly the mean conjunction of Nissan 3014.

Now if we calculate the modern Molad of Nissan 3014[117] we find that it was on 7 – 12 – 540,[118] thus Saturday at 6h 30m a.m. in round figures. Slonimski considered that this coincidence could not be a mere chance. He considered that our modern Molad was deduced from the Almagest by the addition of 850 *halakim*. It is a noticeable point that the number of lunations between the Molad *Weyad*[119] and the Molad of Nissan 3014 is

---

114 Ptolemy's Almagest, G.J. Toomer, London 1984, p.278. On page 275, in the text it calculated that the conjunction was 23; 44, 17 days after the epoch, which was noon of Toth 1 of the era of Nabonassar. The astronomical day began at noon. By contrast Ptolemy tabulated 24; 44, 17 with the meaning: the 24th day of Toth, 44, 17 after noon (the whole day being 60 parts, 44'17" represents 0.738055555 of a day of 24 hours, i.e. 17h 42m 48s). Apparently the convenience of this notation to the user became so obvious that he adopted it also in the Handy Tables. This is probably also the origin of the inclusive notation for dates adopted in the Jewish calendar. For example 6 – 12 – 540, the Molad of Nissan 3014 means Friday at 12h 540 *hal.* In many calculations it would be more convenient to use the exclusive and homogenous notation 5 – 12 – 540 giving the time elapsed since the beginning of the week at Sunday 0h but the custom of the *meabrim* is to use the inclusive notation and designate the beginning of the week by 1 – 0 – 0 instead of 0 – 0 – 0 (after the beginning of the week).

115 44' 17" represents a fraction of the day; the whole day is 60'. Thus 44' 17" represents 44/60 + 17/3600 = 0.73333 + 0.00472 = 0.738055 of a day= 17h 42m 48s after noon.

116 The day of the ancient astronomers began at noon. This practice was in use until the beginning of the nineteenth century.

117 In the Jewish proleptic calendar meaning the fictitious calendar extrapolated before its inception.

118 We note that (7 – 12 – 540) – (7 – 11 – 770) = 850 *halakim.*

119 The Molad of Tishrei 2 AMI (Tishrei of the second year of the era of *Beharad*). It is also called *Molad Adam* by contrast with *Beharad* called *Molad Tohu.* Originally the Aera Mundi was counted from the second year; it was the Era of *Weyad*, 2

37260.[120] It gives a shift of the Molad of 24300 *hal* = 22.5 hours and therefore the epoch or Molad of *Weyad*[121] was (7 – 12 – 540) – (0 – 22 – 540) = 6 – 14.

VII The meeting ועד המאוחר between Palestinians and Babylonians in ca. 838[122] C.E.

Bornstein and Jaffe assumed that a meeting was held in Palestine with the participation of the Babylonian specialists.[123] Their participation could have been motivated by the fact that the Babylonians had provoked this meeting in order to debate about the discrepancies observed between the *keviyah* sent from Palestine on the basis of their Molad, and the *keviyah* deduced from the mean conjunction found in the Almagest. This was the beginning of the active participation of the Babylonians to the fixing of the calendar.

We have seen that the Council of intercalation adopted in 776 C.E. a new Molad; its epoch was 4 – 0 – 0, Tuesday, September 17, 776 at 6 p.m. The modern Molad of this month of Tishrei 4537 is 4 – 3 – 363; thus a difference of 3 – 363 = 3.3361 hours.

AMI or 1 AMII. AMI is the new style of *Beharad* and AMII is the ancient style of *Weyad.*

120 The number of lunations between *Beharad* and Nissan 3014 is 235 * 158 + 12 * 7 + 13*4 + 6 = 37272.
The number of lunations between *Weyad* and Nissan 3014 is then 37272 – 12 = 37260.

121 During a long period this Molad was the epoch of the Molad (Adam). Ibn Ezra, in his *Sefer ha-Ibbur* related this Molad to the Biblical passage in Deut XXIII, 13.

122 In fact the date of 838 is a pure assumption; it is shortly after the letter of the Resh Galuta and about 80 years before the dispute, which began in 921.

123 We have no real evidence of such a meeting. Bornstein and Jaffe based themselves on the contents of a letter addressed by the Babylonians to the Palestinians at the occasion of the R' Sa'adia-Ben Meir dispute, mentioning the existence of such a meeting which would have given to the Babylonian scholars all the elements allowing them to perform by themselves all the calendar calculations. See Jaffe *Korot* (1931) p.187 and Bornstein, *Makhaloket*, 1904, pp. 88-89.
However such a meeting makes sense. We have seen that the letter of the *Resh Galuta* was probably a piece of evidence of the contestation against the *keviyah* sent from Palestine because it was in contradiction with the table of conjunctions of the Almagest. This problem justified a meeting with the Babylonians, the authors of the contestation. Besides, only such a meeting could explain how the Babylonians acquired the knowledge allowing them to make independent calculations of the *keviyah* and contradict the Palestinians at the occasion of the dispute between Ben Meir and Sa'adia Gaon in 922.

It is likely that the purpose of the meeting was to reform the molad to bring it in accordance with the Almagest, which was the authoritative reference. In fact we have no real piece of evidence proving the reality of this meeting and therefore no information about its decisions. However, from the elements of the dispute between R' Sa'adia Gaon and Ben Meir and from the different exchanges of letters between both parties which were found in the Cairo Geniza, Bornstein and Jaffe found an allusion to a common meeting some eighty years before and they deduced that the object of the dispute between both parties was a difference of 642 *ḥalakim* between their Moladot. The Molad of the Palestinians was 642 *ḥalakim* less than that of the Babylonians. It thus seems that they adapted at this meeting the Molad according to the table of the Almagest. However it seems that without paying too much attention to this point, they made the adaptation differently. They did not realize that this difference would bring in the future such a dispute. The Molad of the Almagest for Nissan 3014 was after rounding off, 7 – 11 – 770 in Alexandria. According to Ptolemy's Geography the difference of longitude between Alexandria and Jerusalem is 5°; 30' corresponding to 22m or 396 *ḥalakim*. The Molad in Jerusalem was thus 7 – 12 – 86. The Babylonians added another 454 *ḥalakim* in order to get a rounded off number, 7 – 12 – 540, for the Molad of Nissan 3014, from which they deduced the epoch of the era of the creation, (7 – 12 – 540) – (0 – 22 – 540) = 6 – 14.[124] By contrast the Palestinians subtracted the remainder of six months i.e. 2 – 4 – 438 from the

---

124 Nowadays we consider exclusively the era of *Beharad*. But before the eleventh century the era of the creation was counted from the second year, it was the era of *Weyad*. This era is already mentioned in the Talmud, Avoda Zara 9b. All the dates in the Talmud are expressed in AMII. In B. Avoda Zara 9b it writes:
403 years of the era of the Destruction = 4231 AMII.
Thus 1 Era of the destruction= 4231 – 402 = 3829 AMII = 3830 AMI = 70 C.E. It seems interesting at his point to give the chronology of the first year of *Beharad*. This era was probably introduced because it placed the epoch of this era at the beginning of a cycle of 19 years.
The *tekufah* of Samuel of Tishrei: the *tekufah* of Samuel was on 24 September at 3 a.m. The Molad *Beharad* 2 – 5 – 204 was on Sunday, October 6 – 3760 at 23h 11m 20s.
1 Tishrei AMI was Monday, October 7 – 3760.
30 Marheshvan 1 AMI was Thursday, December 5 – 3760.
30 Kislev 1AMI was Saturday, January 4 – 3759.
The *tekufah* of Samuel of Nissan was on Wednesday 22 Adar at 0h i.e. 4 – 0 – 0 or Tuesday, March 25 – 3759 at 6 p.m.
26 Adar 1 AMI was Sunday, March 30 – 3759.
29 Adar 1 AMI was Wednesday, April 2 – 3759.

Molad of Nissan 3014: 7 – 12 – 86 and found 5 – 7 – 728 for the Molad of Tishrei 3014. They rounded off this Molad to 5 – 7 – 540 by subtracting 188 *ḥalakim*. This led them to a rounded off Molad for Nissan of *Tohu*: (5 – 7 – 540) – (0 – 22 – 540) = 4 – 9 – 0.

Apparently the participants did not find an agreement for a common decision. Thus Palestinians and Babylonians left each other with different Moladot, the Babylonians added 454 *ḥalakim* to the conjunction of Ptolemy while the Palestinians subtracted 188 *ḥalakim*. The Palestinians, who considered themselves as the principal concerned, probably left the problem open in the hope that new observations would help solve it definitively.

Jaffe supposed that at the end of the ninth century the members of the Palestinian council of intercalation were made aware of the observations of al-Battani: the determination of the equinox of 19 September 882 and the observation of the lunar eclipse of 21 July 882.[125]

The observation of the equinox[126] confirmed to them that the observation of 776 was acceptable and it informed them that the limit of Passover of March 17 connected to the new system of a regular cycle of intercalation 3 – 6 – 8 – 11 – 14 – 17 – 19 was now acceptable and justified.[127]

---

24 Elul 1 AMI was Sunday, September 12 – 3759.
Molad *Weyad* or 6 – 14 was on Friday, September 26 – 3759 at 8 a.m.
1 Tishrei 2 AMI was Saturday, September 27 – 3759.
In *Vayikra Rabbah* XXIX, 1 it states that the creation began on Sunday 25 Elul; this seems in contradiction with our table giving Sunday 24 Elul. Apparently this passage is anterior to the rule **lo DU Rosh.** The 1 Tishrei 2 AMI was on Friday and therefore the preceding Sunday was the 25 Elul. Similarly the Sunday 26 Adar 1 AMI was in this ancient calendar Sunday 27 Adar, the year 1 AMI being an abundant year of 355 days. This day would be Sunday 25 Adar 1 AMI if this year of Tohu was a defective year of 353 days. But this is contrary to our calendar. In other words the ancient traditions placing the beginning of the creation of the world on Sunday 25 Elul or on Sunday 25 Adar are anterior to our calendar and don't agree with it.

125 Jaffe had apparently no access to the original treatise of al-Battani and knew these observations through secondary sources like the information provided by *Yessod Olam* of R' Isaac Israeli. See *Yessod Olam*, *ma'amar* IV, chap. 7, p. 12a for the lunar eclipse.

126 See al-Battani Vol 1 pp. 42 and 210. The equinox occurred on 19 September 1h 15m a.m. ar-Raquah or 18 September 22h 39m UT. The modern value is 23h 05m. This observation is considered as one, if not the most, exceptional astronomical observation of history.
This observation justifies already Passover on March 17.

127 The equinox "observed" by al-Battani was on September 19, at 1h 15m a.m. ar-Raquah or at about 0h 48m corresponding to a mean equinox on 17 September

The observation of the lunar eclipse[128] would have persuaded the members of the council of intercalation that the mean conjunctions preceded the mean conjunctions of Ptolemy and therefore the rounding off adopted by the Palestinians seemed justified to them by contrast to the rounding off adopted by the Babylonians. Apparently Palestinians did not inform Babylonians of these last developments.

The problem is that there is no proof that the members of the council of intercalation already knew the treatise of al-Battani. Furthermore the details of the observation of the lunar eclipse are insufficient to know the mean conjunction[129] and al-Battani is unlikely to have published his works before the beginning of the tenth century. It is, however, correct that the comparison of the table of conjunctions of the Almagest and that of al-Battani allows us to conclude that the mean conjunctions of al-Battani preceded those of Ptolemy by 31 minutes if we take into consideration the longitudes of ar-Raquah of 73°; 15' and Alexandria of 60°; 30'.[130]

Thus the astronomical treatise of al-Battani would arbiter in favor of the Palestinian position. But it is not sure that the Treatise of Astronomy of al-Battani was known by the Palestinian council of intercalation before the outbreak of the dispute. In any case it seems likely that the entire discussion between Palestinians and Babylonians about the Molad was forgotten and two concurrent and contradictory methods of calculation of the *keviyah* coexisted until the outbreak of the dispute in 922 C.E, without the protagonists remembering the origin of the discrepancy.

---

at about the same hour. The following vernal mean equinox was then on 18 March at about 4 p.m. Thus Nissan 16 may fall on March 18 and Passover may fall on March 17. The observation of al-Battani supported the cycle of intercalation adopted, 3 – 6 – 8 – 11 – 14 – 17 – 19. This is the meaning of the statement of R' Juda ha-Levi in *Sefer ha-Kuzari*, book IV, chap 29 that the *tekufah* of Adda is in agreement with the observation of al-Battani.

128 See al-Battani, Vol 1, pp. 57 and 230. The lunar eclipse was on Tuesday 23 July 883 at 8h 06m p.m. or Wednesday 15 Av 4643 in the beginning of the evening.

129 We know that the relative position of the two bodies, the sun and the moon, may vary 1.9° + 5.4° = 7.3° from their mean value near the conjunction. As the hourly motion of D, the elongation moon-sun is 0.51°, the maximum interval between the mean new moon and the true new moon is 14.3 hours. At the moment of the full moon the situation is similar between the true and the mean full moon.

130 The time difference between ar-Raquah and Alexandria is thus 51 minutes. However in the book of al-Battani, *Opus Astronomicum*, Vol 1, p.42, it writes in the main text that this difference is 40 minutes; this would reduce the difference to 20 minutes.

VIII The Dispute of R' Sa'adia Gaon and Ben Meir

On *Hoshana Rabbah* 921 C.E. The Palestinian Gaon Ben Meir or his son proclaimed on the Mount of Olives that the months of Marheshvan and Kislev of 4682 would be defective. As a result Passover 922 would fall on Sunday instead of the following Tuesday if the year had been made full. And in fact, in 922 the Jews of Palestine and probably the communities in Egypt celebrated Passover on Sunday, two days before the Jews of Babylonia. This split between the communities of Palestine and Babylonia caused considerable agitation throughout world Jewry. References to this event can be found in non-Jewish documents. The Syrian Elias of Nissibis[131] wrote that in the year 1232 of the Seleucid era[132] dissension broke out between the Jews of the West (Palestine) and those of the East (Babylonia) with regard to the calculation of their holiday. The Jews of the West celebrated Rosh Hashanah 4683 on a Tuesday and those of the East celebrated it on the next Thursday.[133] Similarly the Karaite Sahal ben Mazliah[134] also referred this event and sought to prove from this controversy that the rabbinic calendar calculations were groundless. According to the Babylonian Molad, in Tishrei 4683 there was the postponement *Gatrad* and in Tishrei 4684 there was the postponement *Yah*, therefore the *keviyah* of the three years 4682, 4683 and 4684 were then: בחג, הכז, השג. By contrast, the Molad of the Palestinians was 642 *ḥal* less and there was no postponement in Tishrei 4683 and 4684 and the *keviyah* of the three years 4682, 4683 and 4684 were: זשג, גכה, החא.. Furthermore the astronomical situation was exceptional on Rosh Hashanah 4683: the true conjunction occurred about 1.5 hours after sunset on Monday evening. The lunar latitude was about 5°, an exceptional fact, the moon was seen on Tuesday evening in Egypt, in Palestine and even in Babylonia.

---

131 See Bornstein, *Divrei Yemei ha-Ibbur ha-Aharonim*, ha-Tekufah, Vol 16, Warsaw 1923 pp. 237-238.

132 According to the Jewish *Minian Shtarot*: 1 SE = 3450 AMI and 1232 SE = 4681 AMI. See Rambam, *Hilkhot Kiddush ha-Ḥodesh* 11, 16 and *Hilkhot Shemitah ve-Yovel* 10, 4. However there were other methods of calculation of the Seleucid era differing by a year or differing by the epoch adopted in March instead of September. Here it seems that the date corresponds to 4682 AMI.

133 *Otzar Israel*, entry "Ben Meir," written by Jaffe.

134 See Bornstein, "Divrei Yemei ha-Ibbur ha-Aharonim," *ha-Tekufah*, Vol. 16, Warsaw 1923, p. 237.

Table 4: The years 4682, 4683 and 4684 according to the Palestinians and the Babylonians

Year	Year	Babylonian Molad	Keviyah	Palestinian Molad	Keviyah
921-922	4682*	4 – 11 – 932	השג	4 – 11 – 290	החא
922-923	4683	3 – 9 – 441	הכז	3 – 8 – 879	גכה
923-924	4684	7 – 18 - 237	בחג	7 – 17 – 675	זשג

The vision of the new lunar crescent was thus one day before the first day of Rosh Hashanah adopted by the Babylonians. The Karaites, who sanctified the first day of Tishrei at the moment of the vision of the new moon, celebrated their Rosh Hashanah on Wednesday. This was also an exceptional event: never before had the Karaites celebrated Rosh Hashanah before the Babylonian Rabbis. This event made a great stir and agitation in Egypt and the pupils of Rabbi Sa'adia Gaon were distraught. The letters exchanged between them and Sa'adia Gaon were preserved in the Cairo Geniza.

The Palestinian community saw with this vision the proof of the correctness of the calculation of Ben Meir and his *keviyah*. The truth is that the Talmud accepts such an inevitable situation: it is possible that the new crescent is seen one day before the *Keviyah*.[135]

Maimonides wrote about this problematic first visibility of the lunar crescent one day before the *yom ha-keviyah*,[136]

ודבר זה הלכה למשה מסיני הוא, שבזמן שיש סנהדרין קובעין על פי הראייה ובזמן שאין שם סנהדרין קובעין על פי החשבון הזה שאנו מחשבין בו היום ואין נזקקים לראייה, אלא פעמים שיהיה יום שקובעין בו בחשבון זה הוא יום הראייה או קודם לו ביום או אחריו ביום, וזה שיהיה אחר הראייה ביום פלא הוא, ובארצות שהן למערב ארץ ישראל.

It is thus a Mosaic tradition from Sinai that in times when there was a (Palestinian) Sanhedrin, declaration of New Moon Days was based on visual observation, while in times when no Synedrium existed, this declaration was based on calculations such as we are using today and no attention was paid to observation of the new crescent. Rather the day established by calculation might well coincide with the day

135 B. Erakhim 9b. See J. Ajdler (1996): "Hilkhot Kiddush ha-Hodesh al-pi ha-Rambam," *Sifriati* 1996, pp. 225-226. This passage has raised many difficulties.

136 *Hilkhot Kiddush ha-Ḥodesh* V; 2.

in which the new moon became visible, but it might sometimes be the day before it or the day after[137] it. The latter case, however, when the calculated New Moon Day happened to be the day after the new moon became visible, occurred only rarely,[138] and then in the countries west of Palestine.[139]

It would be better to understand that, according to Maimonides' statement, the first vision of the lunar crescent before the *yom ha-keviyah*, the first day of the month, is a very rare event. However in areas situated west to Israel, the possibility of an early vision of the lunar crescent before the *yom ha-keviyah*, the first day of the month, is less exceptional.[140]

---

137 It can in fact last until two and even three days later. This passage is contradicted by another difficult passage in HKH VII: 7-8; see J. Ajdler "Hilkhot Kiddush ha-Hodesh al-pi ha-Rambam," *Sifriati* 1996, pp. 226-227. Jaffe in *Korot* (1931) p. 197 at the note on bottom already proposed to correct the text and wrote, « או ביום או ביומים ». Ibn Ezra in his commentary on *Vayikra* XXIII, 3 writes also that it happens sometimes that in Tishrei the *keviyah* is on Thursday and the new moon is seen only on Friday evening.

138 We must probably understand that the visibility of the new moon before the *yom ha-keviyah* is exceptional, but in the countries west to Palestine it is less exceptional.

139 Translation of Solomon Gandz in *Sanctification of the New Moon*, Yale Judaica Series, Volume XI, pp. 22-23.

140 R' Raphael ha-Levi from Hanover writes in his book "כללי סוד העיבור" still in manuscript in Jews College library in London:

ובמדינות שהן למערב ארץ ישראל, פירוש במדינות שהן למערב ארץ ישראל יהיה עת הראייה מאוחר לעת הראייה שבארץ ישראל, ואז אפשר אם היה המולד ג יח, או ה יח, או ז יח, לראות הירח באותן המדינות בליל ד' והקביעה יהיה ביום ה', כי בהקביעה הן שווין, ולפי זה במדינות ההן אין הפלא כל כך גדול כמו שהוא בארץ ישראל, אף על פי שהראייה בחוץ לארץ אינה מועלת כי אם בארץ ישראל והוא לא כתב זה אלא לדמיונו.

About the exceptional character of this early vision one day before the *yom ha-keviyah*, he adds :

והוא פלא כי צריך להיות מולד אמצעי בתשרי ב" גטרד" וצריך שנה פשוטה וגם צריך להיות הקיבוץ מוקדם לאמצעי כדי שיהיה ריוח בין רגע קיבוץ עד עת הראייה יתר מן כ"ד שעות, וצריך שיהיה רוחב הירח צפונית חמש מעלות, ודבר זה שיהיו כל התנאים הממהרים הראייה ביחד הוא פלא גדול ואפשר שלא המצא תמצא בחמש מאות שנים. וכבר יגעתי ומצאתי תאמין שחקרתי וחפשתי בחיפוש אחר חיפוש משנת ד' אלפים עד שנת ה' אלפים ליצירה ולא מצאתי רק במשל אחד בשנת ד"א תרפ"ג שהיה המולד אמצעי בתשרי ג ט תמא ונדחה לחמישי ונראה הירח בליל ד' והיה יום הראייה ביום ד' יום אחד מוקדם ליום הקביעה.

This passage, which is a quotation from an unpublished manuscript from R' Raphael ha-Levi from Hanover is an exceptional piece of evidence of his calculation abilities (and patience) and of the reliability of Maimonides' visibility criterion. Imagine that Raphael Hanover, who had not the least idea of the R' Saadia-Ben Meir dispute, discovered the critical year 4683, among thousand years,

The conclusion of the R' Saadia-Ben Meir controversy at the advantage of the Babylonians had a tremendous consequence at the level of the unity of the Jewish people. Before 922 C.E, the Jewish calendar was communicated by the Palestinian *Gaon* on an annual or multi-annual basis.

It appears that from about 838 onwards, the Babylonians were able to make their own calculations and during the period of about eighty years preceding 922 C.E. they always agreed with the *keviyah* sent from Palestine. However the remote communities in Europe and Africa were certainly not informed in time of the calendar data and were not able to keep the festivals at the same time as the two great centers of Palestine and Babylonia.

However, Spain and Kairouan, two centers having narrow bonds with Babylonia, were probably informed in time. Only after the end of the dispute, did the rules of the calendar and the Four Gates Table became universally known and only then was the complete unity of the Jewish communities of the Diaspora achieved in the celebration of their festivals.

A second consequence, not less important, of the supremacy of the Babylonian community, was that, parallel to the fact that the Jewish calendar became universally known, it became also definitively stiff and rigid. As long as the Babylonian community accepted the Palestinian *keviyah*,[141] the council of intercalation, acting with much secrecy, had the possibility to adapt and improve the calendar. From this time onwards, the Jewish communities could participate in the development and the study of the Jewish calendar. It seems that the custom to count the Jewish calendar according to the era of Tohu (*Beharad*), beginning the era with a year L+1,[142] following a leap year, at the beginning of a cycle of 19 years of the proleptic[143] Jewish calendar, instead of the era of the creation (*Weyad*) beginning the era with a year L – 1,[144] preceding a leap year, was introduced

in which exceptionally the new crescent was visible one day before the Babylonian *keviyah*.

Ibn Ezra noted in his commentary on *Vayikra* XXIII; 3 that this early visibility of the moon can happen in Nissan or in the three former months. However, he considered incorrectly this early vision of the moon one day before the *keviyah*, to be a commonplace and he wrote that it happens rather frequently.

141 As we still see in the letter of the *Resh Galuta*.

142 A year following a leap year. The first year of a cycle of 19 years is a year L+1.

143 Extrapolated in the past before its inception in 358 / 359 C.E.

144 The second year AMI is also the first year AMII, it is a year L-1, preceding a leap year.

by the Jews of Spain and Italy.[145] Similarly the *tekufah* of Adda, a system of mean equinox and solstices fixed rigidly to the cycle of 19 Jewish years and having a good coincidence with the mean equinox and solstices during the 10th and 11th century, was probably introduced in Spain and it was thoroughly studied by the Spanish *meabrim*. Finally the Four Gates Table,[146] a Babylonian discovery, was generalized by the French Tossafist Ritsva,[147] of the 12th century and gave birth to the table of the 61 lines, a table giving the *keviyah* of all the 19 years of a cycle by the simple knowledge of the Molad Tishrei of its first year.

It is interesting to note that this important event of 922-924 remained unknown until the beginning of the twentieth century, until the discovery and the study of the documents of the Cairo Geniza. It is a fact that R' Sherira Gaon and R' Hai Gaon did not mention the event at all. At first glance we could think that the leaders of the Babylonian community did not want to leave a remembrance of this schism for posterity; it could have thrown a shadow on the authority of the Jewish calendar and on the doctrine of its *Sinaïtic* origin taught by R' Sa'adia Gaon. This, however, is not the case. We know that R' Sa'adia Gaon wrote two books: ספר הזיכרון and ספר המועדים. The first book was intended to be read publicly in order to recall the event. The second book was probably a treatise on the festivals and the Jewish calendar and it probably also mentioned the events of the famous dispute of 922- 924[148] in order to prevent the possibility of a new schism in the future. It was the fear of *maḥaloquet* that prompted him to write the first and probably the second book. R' Sa'adia's works on the calendar are lost, although they appear to have been well known in the middle ages (Rashi, R' Tam and R' Jacob ben Shimshon[149] refer to it). It is a mystery why these two books did not survive.

---

145 The principle of beginning the counting of the Jewish years one year before the era of *Weyad* (AMII) was already discussed by R' Sa'adia Gaon and R' Hai Gaon but it was rejected by them (see Bornstein, *Maḥaloket* 1904, p. 127). It must be remembered that the counting from the year of *Weyad* corresponds to the counting of the Talmud (B. Avoda Zara 9b) according to the era of the creation.

146 See details in Appendix C.

147 R' Isaac ben Abraham, elder brother of R' Samson ben Abraham of Sens. This attribution was demonstrated by Bornstein.

148 Encyclopedia Judaica Vol. 14, entry Sa'adiah, p.544 bottom, affirms, without evidence or reference, that the *Sefer ha-Moadim* gave a complete account of the dispute.

149 For details about R' Jacob ben Shimshon, the "secretary" of Rashi after R' Shemaya, see Abraham Grossman, *Hakhmei Sarfat ha-Rishonim*, (Jerusalem: Magnes, 1996) pp. 411-426.

By contrast, it is evident that the Palestinian side was not interested to speak about this event and indeed they never did mention this dispute again. It is worth mentioning that in Tishrei 4686, the Molad was 5 – 18 – 214 and a new schism should have appeared about the *keviyah* of 4686. Indeed according to the Babylonians Rosh Hashanah 4686 was on Saturday and the year had the *keviyah* זחא. But for the Palestinians the Molad must occur 642 *ḥal* before, at: 5 – 17 – 652 and Rosh Hashanah should have been on Thursday, with the *keviyah* השא. They were confronted with exactly the same problem as four years earlier.

In fact there is no information left about a new dispute about the *keviyah* of that year. It seems that the Palestinian Gaon adopted the Babylonian Molad and proclaimed the *keviyah* as usual, as if nothing occurred. Later in the *Megilat Abiathar*,[150] the Palestinian Gaon did not mention anything about the incident but he still claimed the Palestinian authority on the calendar.[151]

The present day calendar was the calendar of the Babylonians since about 838 C.E. that emerged after the dispute of 922-924. This calendar did not change any more.

In the following two tables we show the weak point of the present calendar, i.e., that the Jewish year is shifting with regard to the Gregorian calendar, in the direction of the summer. This brings us to contemplate

---

150 See "Megilat Abiathar," Schechter *JQR* Vol XIV (1901-1902) pp. 449-474.

151 It is also likely that the Palestinians went on calculating the Molad according to their more ancient methods referring to Nissan. Indeed Bornstein discovered that R' Jacob ben Shimshon used methods of calculation similar to that of the Palestinians in the time of Ben Meir. Similarly the Four Gates Table in *Maḥzor Vitry* (Vol. 2 end) is constructed according to Nissan. It appears clearly that the French Rabbis were under the influence of the Babylonian but also the Palestinian Gaonim. We know that the German Jewish establishment was of Palestinian origin and had ties with Palestine. We are aware of the responsum of the Palestinian Gaon Elijah ben Solomon ha-Cohen, R' Abiathar's father, to R' Meshulam ben Moses of Mainz in 1070. It was also signed by R' *Abiathar ha-revi'i*, then the fourth in rank in the *yeshivah*. Grossman has discovered in the Library of the JTS the following passage: דוד בן אברהם קיבל אילו המסורת של חשבון מר' שבתי בר כרמי שקיבל מר' אליהו הכהן זצ"ל הרביעי שבחבורה בן אדונינו אביתר הכהן ראש ישיבת גאון יעקב תתמ"ח ליצירה.

See Grossman, *Ḥakhmei Tsarfat ha-Rishonim*, Magnes 1996, p. 423. This document, dated 1088, makes sense: In 1081, while his father was still alive, R' Abiathar was appointed gaon and his son Elijah (named as his still alive grand-father) was appointed the fourth in rank in the yeshiva.

again a slight adaptation of the Jewish calendar in order to remain in agreement with the solar year. This subject is beyond the scope of the present paper. It was already thoroughly examined in two other papers.[152]

IX The Present-day Jewish Calendar and the rule of intercalation.

Table 5: The dates of Nissan 16 and the following Tishrei 21 during the 243rd cycle: Pessah was perfectly calibrated in the *ḥodesh ha-aviv*

N	Year	Jewish Year	Nissan 16 Gregorian	Tishrei 21 Gregorian
1	2036	5796-5797	April 13	October 12
2	2037	5797-5798	April 1	September 30
3	2038	5798-5799	April 21	October 20
4	2039	5799-5800	April 10	October 9
5	2040	5800-5801	March 30	September 28
6	2041	5801-5802	April 17	October 16
7	2042	5802-5803	April 6	October 5
8	2043	5803-5804	April 26	October 25
9	2044	5804-5805	April 13	October 12
10	2045	5805-5806	April 3	October 2
11	2046	5806-5807	April 22	October 21
12	2047	5807-5808	April 12	October 11
13	2048	5808-5809	March 30	September 28
14	2049	5809-5810	April 18	October 17
15	2050	5810-5811	April 8	October 7
16	2051	5811-5812	March 29	September 27
17	2052	5812-5813	April 15	October 14
18	2053	5813-5814	April 4	October 3
19	2054	5814-5815	April 24	October 23

[152] Ajdler (2011), "The Future of the Jewish Calendar." *BDD* 25.
Ajdler (2013/1), "The Gregorian Revolution of the Jewish Calendar," *BDD* 27.

Table 6: The dates of Nissan 16 and Tishrei 21 in the 304th cycle. We note a shift of a few days. Pesaḥ is no more completely in the *ḥodesh ha-aviv*

N	Year	Jewish Year	Nissan 16 Julian	Nissan 16 Gregorian	Tishrei 21 Julian	Tishrei 21 Gregorian
1	839	4599-4600	April 4	April 8	October 3	October 7
2	840	4600-4601	March 24	March 28	Sept. 22	Sept. 26
3	841	4601-4602	April 11	April 15	Oct. 10	Oct. 14
4	842	4602-4603	March 31	April 4	Sept. 29	Oct. 3
5	843	4603-4604	March 21	March 25	Sept. 19	Sept. 23
6	844	4604-4605	April 7	April 11	Oct. 6	Oct. 10
7	845	4605-4606	March 27	March 31	Sept. 25	Sept. 29
8	846	4606-4607	April 16	April 20	Oct. 15	Oct. 19
9	847	4607-4608	April 6	April 10	Oct. 5	Oct. 9
10	848	4608-4609	March 25	March 29	Sept. 23	Sept. 27
11	849	4609-4610	April 12	April 16	Oct. 10	Oct. 14
12	850	4610-4611	April 2	April 6	Oct. 1	Oct. 5
13	851	4611-4612	March 22	March 26	Sept. 20	Sept. 24
14	852	4612-4613	April 10	April 14	Oct. 9	Oct. 13
15	853	4613-4614	March 29	April 2	Sept. 27	Oct. 1
16	854	4614-4615	March 18	March 22	Sept. 16	Sept. 20
17	855	4615-4616	April 7	April 11	Oct. 6	Oct. 10
18	856	4616-4617	March 27	March 31	Sept. 25	Sept. 29
19	857	4617-4618	April 14	April 18	Oct.13	Oct. 17

Appendices[153]

Appendix A
The Modern Jewish Calendar

I **References:** See <www.Hakirah.org/vol20AjdlerAppendices.pdf>.

II **The fundamental formula of the Jewish calendar.**

A. The number of months preceding the *molad* of the Jewish year N + 1, counted from *Beharad*, is given by

$\mathbf{F_t = INT\ [(235N + 1)/19]}$.[154]

The following table gives the practical demonstration of this formula.

Table 7: Number of months at the beginning of the year N + 1 in a cycle of 19 years.

N	F_t	N	F_t	N	F_t	N	F_t
1	12	6	74	11	136	16	197
2	24	7	86	12	148	17	210
3	37	8	99	13	160	18	222
4	49	9	111	14	173	19	235
5	61	10	123	15	185	20	247

The numbers of columns F are indeed the number of the months preceding the beginning of the different years of the cycle of 19 years. It is based on a cycle of intercalation of the years 3 – 6 – 8 – 11 – 14 – 17 – 19.

This formula is general. It allows calculating the *molad* of any year.

B. The Molad expressed as a part of the week is:

---

153 Due to space constraints the appendices to this article were shortened. The full version can be found at <www.Hakirah.org/vol20AjdlerAppendices.pdf>.

154 This formula was given for the first time in *Al ha-Sheminit*, Y Loewinger, Tel Aviv 1986. The formula $\mathbf{F_t = INT\ [(235N)/19]}$ fits except for N = 8. Indeed for N = 8, INT [(235*8)/19]= 98 instead of 99. This is the justification of the formula $\mathbf{F_t = INT\ [(235N + 1)/19]}$.

$$Mol = [31524 + F_t * 765443]_{181440}{}^{155} = [31.524 + F_t * 39673]_{181440}$$

31524 is the span of time between the beginning of the week, Saturday afternoon at 6 p.m. noted 1 – 0 – 0 and the moment *Beharad* or 2 – 5 – 204; 765443 is the length of the Jewish lunation 29 – 12 – 793 in *ḥalakim* and 39673 is the rest of the division of 765443 by 181440.

III Converting a Jewish date into a civil date by using the Julian day.

The classical methods for converting a Jewish date into a civil date are long and dull. The principle rests on the calculation of the *tekufah* of Samuel of September with regard to Tishrei 1 and on the fact that the *tekufah* of Tishrei always falls on September 24 in the Julian calendar. Louis A, Resnikoff[156] described an algorithm based on the same principle applicable to pocket calculators. Another method of computation makes use of the formula of Gauss[157] giving the date of Nisan 15 in the Julian calendar.[158]

We propose here a simple method in which we calculate the molad as a moment of the week and as a precise moment in history thanks to the Julian day. The method is conceptually very simple but it must, however, be applied with care and precision.

---

155 $[A]_B$ is the remainder of the division of A by B.

156 *Scripta Mathematica* Vol. IX, pp. 191-196 and 274-277.

157 Gauss, Werke VI Bd. 1874, pp. 80-81. *Berechnung des Judischen Osterfestes.* Zach's *Monatliche Correspondenz zur beforderung der Erd und Himmelskunde*, Mai 1802, p. 435.
Different authors tried to demonstrate this formula:

- "Ableitung der gausschen formel zur bestimmung des Judischen Osterfestes, M. Hamburger," *Crelles Journal fur die reine und angewandte Mathematik*, Band 116 (1896).
- *Computation of the dates of the Hebrew New Year and Passover*, Ida Rhodes, Comp. & Maths with Appls. Vol 3, pp. 183-190, Pergamon Press 1977.
- A short and elegant demonstration has been proposed by the author of this paper in J. Ajdler (2013/1).

158 Other formulas were proposed, for example:

- *Eine algemeine Formel fur die gesamte judischen Kalenderberechnung, Slonimsky aus Bialystock, Crelles Journal fur die reine und angewandte Mathematik*, Band 26 (1844).
- "Beitrage zur Chronologie, Nesselman in Königsberg," *Crelles Journal fur die reine und angewandte Mathematik*, Band 28 (1844).

Let us consider a concrete example: Nisan 15, 5751.

1. The characteristics of the Jewish year A = N + 1 = 5751.
    a. The rank of the year 5751 in the cycle of 19 years.

$[5751]_{19} = 13$; the year 5751 is the 13th year of the cycle 303 of 19 years; it is a regular year preceding a leap year.

    b. The Molad of the year 5751.

The number of Jewish months preceding the Molad of year 5751 is given by the fundamental formula of the Jewish calendar:[159]

F_t = INT [(235N+1)/19] = INT [(235 * 5750+1)/19] = 71118.

The Molad expressed as a part of the week is:

Mol = $[31524 + 71118 * 765443]_{181440}$ [160]= $[31.524 + 71118 * 39673]_{181440}$ = 103938 hal.= 4 – 0 – 258 = (5) – 0 – 258.

This Molad is thus after 4 days and 258 *ḥalakim* or at the beginning of the fifth day at 0h 258 *halakim* i.e. Wednesday at 18h 258 ḥal. Tishrei 1 falls on Thursday.

The Four Gates Table gives then the *keviyah* of the year, הכז. Rosh Hashanah is Thursday and Pesaḥ is on Saturday.

This result can also be reached directly by calculating the Molad of the years 5751 and 5752 and the days of Tishrei 1 of these two years by the application of the four rules of postponement.

F_t = INT [(235 * 5751 + 1)/19] = 71130.

Mol = $[31524 + 71130 * 765443]_{181440}$ = 35694 ḥal = 1 – 9 – 54 = (2) – 9 – 54. Tishrei 1 falls on Monday. The shift of Tishrei 1 between 5751 and 5752 is thus four days and the number of days lying between these two days, exclusive of the two days of Tishrei 1, is 3.[161] Therefore the year

---

159 See: Mathematical appendix in "The Gregorian Revolution of the Jewish Calendar", J. Ajdler (2013/1), pp. 17 - 76. See also J. Loewinger (1986).

160 $[A]_B$ is the remainder of the division of A by B.

161 This is the algorithm described by Maimonides in *Hilkhot Kiddush ha-Ḥodesh VIII*, 7 and 8. He counts the number of days between the two days of Tishrei 1, exclusive of the two days of Tishrei 1. The length of the year is thus 353, 354 or 355 days according whether this difference is 2, 3 or 4 for a common year, 383, 384 and 385 according whether this difference is 4, 5 or 6 for a leap year. By contrast R. Abraham bar Ḥiyya counts the shift of Rosh Hashanah between the two years, i.e. he counts the day of Rosh Hashanah of one year + the number

5751 is a regular year and its length is 354 days. Thus Rosh Hashanah falls on Thursday because of the rules of the *dehiyot* (postponements) and the length of the year is 354 days.

c. The year 5751 is thus an ordinary[162] year; it is a regular[163] year of 354 days beginning on a Thursday.

Nisan 15 is the 192nd day of this year and it falls on a Saturday.[164]

2. The Jewish calendar and the Julian day.

The Julian period's epoch is Monday, January 1, – 4712 at noon. At this moment the number of elapsed day of the Julian period was 0 days. The Julian day n° 1 began on Monday at noon and ended on Tuesday at noon. Similarly, until the twentieth century, the astronomical days began at noon of the civil days of the same name.

The Molad of *Beharad*, beginning in the Jewish era AMI, was on Sunday October 6, - 3760 at 23h 204*ḥal*; Jerusalem mean time. This moment already belonged to the second Jewish day of the week, which began at 18h, hence (2) – 5 – 204. It means the second day at 5 h and 204 *ḥalakim*. It could be written as 1 – 2 – 204, meaning 1 day 5 h and 204 *hal* after the beginning of the week or 31524 *hal* after the beginning of the week.[165]

Expressed in Julian days, the molad of Beharad was 347997. 466203703703. On Sunday, October 6, - 3760 at noon, 347 997 days of the JP[166] had elapsed and on Monday, October 7, - 3760 = Tishrei 1, 1 AMI, at noon, 347 998 days of the JP had elapsed. Tishrei 1, 1 AMI began thus at 347997.25 JD and ended at 347998.25 JD. Tishrei 1 corresponded in its majority to the day 347998 of the JP.[167]

---

of days between. Therefore the length of the year is 353, 354 or 355 days according whether the difference is 3, 4 or 5 for a common year and 383, 384 or 385 according whether the shift is 5, 6 or 7 for a leap year.

162 An ordinary year has 12 months and a leap year has 13 months.

163 A regular year has 354 or 384 days, a defective year has 353 or 384 days and a full year has 355 or 385 days according to whether the year is a regular or a leap year.

164 See the fourteen possible calendars of the Jewish calendar: *Yesodei ha-Ibbur*, Hayim Zelig Slonimski, Warsaw 1852, end of the book. *Shearim le-luah ha-Ivri*, Rahamim Sar Shalom, Natania 5744, p. 35.
Ha-Luah ve-Shimusho ba-Kronologia, A. A. Akabia, (Jerusalem: Magnes, 1953), pp. 50-53 and E. Mahler, *Handbuch Der Jüdischen Chronologie*, 1915 and 1967 Hildesheim, pp. 614 – 627.

165 See note 114.

166 Julian Day.

167 Julian Period.

There is a second style of the Jewish calendar AMII, beginning on Tishrei 1, 2 AMI.

The molad of this year was *Weyad*: 6- 14.

The first day of this year was Tishrei 1, 1 AMII = Tishrei 1, 2 AMI; it corresponds to Saturday, September 27, - 3759 or 348353 JD, beginning at 348352.25 JD and ending at 348353.25 JD.

We note also that Elul 25, 1 AMI = Monday, September 22, - 3759 = 348348 JD.

3. The year 5751 and the civil year.

Expressed in Julian days, the molad of 5751 is given by the formula:[168]

Mol = 347997.466203703 + 29.530594135804 * 71118 = 2448154.25995370370 JD

This molad is thus on a civil Wednesday 18h 258 hal or on a Jewish Thursday at 0 h 258 ḥal.

Rosh Hashanah is thus Thursday, from 2448154.25 JD until 2448155.25 JD.

Tishrei 1, 5751 corresponds thus to 2448155 JD and Nisan 15 = 2448155 + 191 = 2448346 JD. This day corresponds to Saturday, March 30, 1991.[169]

---

168 This formula gives the same result as the formula of Shram.

169 For the conversion of a Julian day into a civil date see Astronomical Algorithms, Jean Meeus, Willman-Bell, 1991, p. 59. Idem for the determination of the week-day.

Appendix B
The Derivate Postponements

I The Derivate Postponements in the Modern Calendar

1. The postponement 3 – 9 – 204 or **ג ט רד בפשוטה** .

If the Molad of Tishrei of an ordinary year is 3 – 9 – 204 or greater, then the Molad of the following Tishrei is 7 – 18 or greater. If we apply the general rules we will begin Tishrei of the present year on Tuesday and Tishrei of next year on Monday. The shift of Rosh Hashanah from one year to the other will be 6 days and therefore the ordinary year must be a multiple of 7 plus 6, thus necessarily 356 days. This is impossible; the Jewish ordinary year must have 353, 354 or 355 days. In order to solve this difficulty we must impose to postpone the first day of Rosh Hashanah to Thursday as soon as the molad is 3 – 9 – 204 in an ordinary year.

2. The Postponement 2 – 15 – 589 or **ב טו תקפט אחר עיבור.**

If the Molad of Tishrei following a leap year 2 – 15 – 589 or more the Molad Tishrei of the preceding year is 3 – 18 or more. If we apply the general rules the 1 Tishrei of the leap year is Thursday and the 1 Tishrei of the following year is Monday. The shift from one year to the other is 4 days. The number of days of the leap year must be a multiple of 7 plus 4. It is necessarily 382 days. This is impossible; the number of days of a leap year is 383, 384 or 385 days. In order to solve this difficulty we must postpone the first day of Rosh Hashanah of a year following a leap year from Monday to Tuesday as soon as the Molad reaches 2 – 15 – 589 and this will bring the number of days of the leap year to 383 days.

II The Calendar of Hillel, from about 648 C.E. till 776 C.E.

The reasoning is the same. The limit 3 – 9 – 204 in an ordinary year becomes 3 – 9 – 3 or ג ט ג בפשוטה.

Similarly the limit 2 – 15 – 589 after a leap year becomes 2 – 15 – 8 after a leap year or ב טו ח אחר עיבור.

III The Calendar of Hillel from 359 until about 648.

1 Tishrei could be on Sunday. By similar reasoning it is easy to demonstrate that the two derivate postponements are:

1 – 9 – 3 in an ordinary year or א ט ג בפשוטה.

2 – 15 – 8 after a leap year or ב טו ח אחר עיבור.

Appendix C
The Four Gates Table

The Four Gates Table is a Babylonian invention from the 9th century. It represents a higher degree of sophistication and knowledge of the rules of the calendar. It allows knowing the *keviyah* of a year by the knowledge of its Molad and its rank in the cycle of 19 years.

Maimonides did not describe this method in *Hilkhot Kiddush ha-Hodesh*. He must find the day of 1 Tishrei of two consecutive years in order to find the characteristics of the first year. R' Abraham ibn Ezra worked the same way in his *Sefer ha-Ibbur*.

The Four Gates Table is mentioned in a letter of R' Sa'adia Gaon related to the dispute.[170] He also gave the detailed rules of the Four Gates Table. We also have a description of the Four Gates Table in a poem of R' Yose ben al-Naharwani.[171] The Four Gates was thus well-established knowledge in Babylonia. The Four Gates Table was thoroughly examined by R' Abraham bar Ḥiyya in *Sefer ha-Ibbur*[172] and in R' Isaac Israeli's *Yessod Olam*. In the supplement at the end of the second volume of *Maḥzor Vitry*[173] we find the table of the Four Gates according to the molad of the preceding Nissan.

---

170 See Bornstein, "Divrei Yemei ha-Ibbur ha-Aharonim," *ha-Tekufah* 16, p. 247. He accuses Ben Meir of copying the Babylonian Four Gates Table and adapting the different limits by the addition of 642 *ḥal*.

171 Epstein, A. (1901) : La querelle au sujet du Calendrier entre Ben Meir et les académies Babyloniennes, REJ 42, pp. 173-210.

172 Pp. 63-69.

173 This supplement begins after page 798. It is likely that this chapter was greatly influenced, if not copied from the *Sefer ha Ibbur* by R' Jacob ben Samson, which was part of his great composition: the *Sefer Elkoshi*. In *Maḥzor Vitry* we find also the commentary on *Avot* by R' Jacob ben Samson. Abraham Berliner, on pp. 15-16 of the calendar supplement to *Mahzor Vitry* seems to ignore that the book of R' Jacob ben Samson has the general name of *Sefer Elkoshi* and he assumes that the author of the manuscript was called Nahum according to Nahum I; 1. In any case, it seems that R' Jacob ben Samson exerted an important influence on different parts of the *Maḥzor Vitry*.

I. The Four Gates table for the modern calendar according to the Molad of Tishrei.[174]

Table 10: The Four Gates Table for the modern calendar. For the explanation of the precise meaning of this table, let us consider the left column devoted to the years L – 1.
If 7 – 18 – 0 <= Molad <=1 – 9 – 203 the year is בחג.
If 1 – 9 – 204 <= Molad <=2 – 17 – 1079 the year is בשה, etc.

The Four Gates Table — לוח ארבע שערים							
Ordinary Years						Leap Years	
L – 1		L + 1		L+ – 1		L	
ערבי עיבור		מוצאי עיבור		ביני עיבור		שנות עיבור	
2 – 5 – 10 – 13 – 16		1 – 4 – 9 – 12 – 15		7 – 18		3 – 6 – 8 – 11 – 14 17 – 19	
Molad	Kev	Molad	Kev	Molad	Kev	Molad	Kev
7 – 18 – 0 1 – 9 – 203	2d בחג	7 – 18 – 0 1 – 9 – 203	2d בחג	7 – 18 – 0 1 – 9 – 203	2d בחג	7 – 18 – 0 1 – 20 – 490	2D בחה
1 – 9 – 204 2 – 17 - 1079	2f השב	1 – 9 – 204 2 –15 – 588	2f בשה	1 – 9 – 204 2 –15 – 588	2f בשה	1 – 20 – 491 2 –17- 1079	2F בשז
2 – 18 – 0 3 – 9 – 203	3r הכג	2 – 15 – 589 3 – 9 – 203	3r גכה	2 – 15 – 589 3 – 9 – 203	3r גכה	2 – 18 – 0 3 – 17–1079	3R גכז
3 – 9 – 204 5 – 9 – 203	5r הכז	3 – 9 – 204 5 – 9 – 203	5r הכז	3 – 9 – 204 5 – 9 – 203	5r הכז	3 – 18 – 0 4 – 11 – 694	5D החא
5 – 9 – 204 5 – 17 – 1079	5f השא	5 – 9 – 204 5 –17– 1079	5f השא	5 – 9 – 204 5 –17 – 1079	5f השא	4 – 11 – 695 5 – 17–1079	5F השג
5 – 18 – 0 6 – 9 – 203	7d זחא	5 – 18 – 0 6 – 0 – 407	7d זחא	5 – 18 – 0 6 – 9 – 203	7d זכא	5 – 18 – 0 6 – 20 – 490	7D זחג
6 – 9 – 204 7 – 17 – 1079	7f זשג	6 – 0 – 408 7 –17– 1079	7f זשג	6 – 9 – 204 7 –17– 1079	7f זשג	6 – 20 – 491 7 –17– 1079	7F זשה

174 See <www.Hakirah.org/vol20AjdlerAppendices.pdf> for more details.

Appendix D
Calculations of Moladot of the Jewish Calendar in the period 359 C.E. – 921 C.E. considered in the present paper

1. The year 4119 AMI, at the inception of the calculated Jewish calendar.

Calculation of the modern Molad of Nissan 4119.

The fundamental formula of the modern calendar allows calculating the number of lunations elapsed from *Beharad* until the molad of the year 4119. 4119 is the 15th year of the fictitious cycle of 19 years; the preceding year was probably a leap year.
Ft = Int [(235 * 4118 + 1) / 19] = 50933.
The number of lunations before the Molad of Nissan 4119 is then 50939.
The molad of Nissan 4119 is thus:
Mol = $[31524 + 50939 * 39673]_{181440}$ = 55751 *ḥal* = 2d + 3h + 671 *ḥal* =3 – 3 – 671 thus 3h 671 *ḥal* later than the epoch adopted by Hillel: 3 – 0 – 0.
In order to make later calculations easier, we will calculate the modern Molad for the year 4124 representing the first year of the fictitious 218th cycle of intercalation (of 19 years).
The number of lunations between *Beharad* and Tishrei 4124 is:
Ft = Int [(235 * 4123 + 1) / 19] = 50995.
Mol = $[31524 + 50995 * 39673]_{181440}$ = 100159 = 3d+20 h+799 hal = 4 – 20 – 799. (Modern Molad).
The Molad of Hillel is 4 – 17 – 1 (*ḥayil*) = 4 – 17 – 72 *ḥal*
The difference is 3h 727 *ḥal* = 3h 671*ḥal* + 50995 – 50939 = 3h 727 *ḥal*. between our modern molad and the assumed molad of Hillel.
The Molad of Hillel is thus 4 – 17 – 1 (*ḥayil*) = 4 – 17 – 72 *ḥal*

2. *Keviyah* of the year 4147 AMI (386/387 C.E.).

Calculation of the modern Molad.
The number of lunations preceding Tishrei 4147 is:
Ft = Int[(235*4146 + 1) / 19] = 51279.
The Molad in the modern calendar is:
Mol = $[31524 + 51279 * 39673]_{181440}$ =118011= 4d+13h+291*ḥal* = 5 – 13 – 291
Calculation of the Molad of Hillel.
In the calendar of Hillel the Molad was thus:
5 – 13 – 291
– 3 – 727 difference in 4124

– 284 = (51279 – 50995)

\-\-\-\-\-\-\-\-\-\-\-\-\-\-

5 – 9 – 360

It corresponds perfectly to the Molad of Jaffe: 5 – 9 – 5 in his table א.

The *keviyah* of the year 4147 was thus in the calendar of Hillel as it is also the case in our modern calendar: השא.

Molad Nissan 4147.

The year 4147 is assumed to be an ordinary year. The number of lunations preceding Nissan is thus 51279 + 6 = 51285.

The molad in the modern calendar is:

Mol = $[31524 + 51285 * 39673]_{181440}$ =174609=6d+17h+729 *hal* = 7 – 17 – 729

In the calendar of Hillel the Molad was thus:

7 – 17 – 729

– 3 – 727

– 290 = (51285 – 50995)

\-\-\-\-\-\-\-\-\-\-\-\-\-\-\-

Molad in the calendar of Hillel 7 – 13 – 792

Now if we write the modern Molad in terms of the Julian Period, we get: Mol = 347997.466203703 + 29.530594135804 * 51285 = 1862473.98645 JD. Thus our modern Molad falls slightly before the beginning of the day 1862474. It corresponds to Saturday 6 March 387. But Nissan 1 was a Sunday; the Molad Nissan 387 was thus on Saturday 6 March 387, 1 Nissan was Sunday 7 March and 15 Nissan, the first day of Passover was on Sunday 21 March 387. The rule of the equinox was satisfied and therefore our assumption that it was an ordinary year is validated.

3. The year 4267AMI.

Year 4267 began on Sunday. This year was the eleventh year of the fictitious cycle 224 of 19 years. It is likely that it was a leap year.

In our modern calendar the Molad of 4267 is 1 – 22 – 983

We can deduce the Molad of Hillel: – 3 – 727

1768 = (52763–50995)

\-\-\-\-\-\-\-\-\-\-\-\-\-\-\-\-

Molad of Hillel of year 4267: 1 – 17 – 648

It corresponds to the Molad of Jaffe 1 – 17 – 9.

If we adopt the Molad of the modern calendar, we have a *Molad Zaken* and 1 Tishrei could not be on Sunday but it should have been delayed to Monday. By contrast, with the Molad of Hillel, 1 – 17 – 9, there was no *Molad Zaken* and 1 Tishrei was indeed on Sunday.

4. The year 4537 AMI (776 /777 C.E.).

The year 4537 is the 15th year of a fictitious cycle of 19 years; it is assumed to be an ordinary year. The number of lunations preceding Tishrei 4537 is given by the formula:

Ft = Int [(235 * 4536+1) / 19] = 56103.

The modern Molad is given by:

Mol = $[31524 + 56103 * 39673]_{181440}$ =81363=3d+3h+363*hal*

= 4 – 3 – 363

Modern Molad	4 – 3 – 363.
	– (3 – 727)
In the calendar of Hillel the Molad was thus	– 5108 = (56103 – 50995)

	3– 18 –1008= 3 – 18 - 14

Thus the Molad of Hillel of Tishrei 4537 was 3 – 18 – 1008. It corresponds exactly to the Molad of Jaffe 3 – 18 -14. It was corrected after the observation of September 776 to 4 – 0 – 0 by the addition of 5 – 72, thus 5 hours and 1/15. The modern value of the corresponding Molad is 4 – 3 – 363. Thus in 776 the difference after introduction of the new epoch 4 – 0 – 0, there still was a difference of 3 – 363 with regard to the modern Molad.

5. The year 4596 AMI (835 / 836 C.E.).

First assumption: The Jewish lunation is 29 – 12 – 793. The Molad Nissan 4596 is deduced from the modern Molad by subtracting 3 – 363.
Thus 3 – 15 – 811 – (3 – 363) = 3 – 12 – 448.

Second assumption: The Jewish lunation is 29 -12 – 793.2962 (*Iggul de Rav Naḥshon*).

The difference between the modern Molad and the ancient Molad is reduced by 0,2946 * (56890 – 56103) = 232 hal. The Molad Nissan 4596 would then be 3 – 12 – 680 very near to the value calculated by Jaffe in his table. Similarly the Molad Tishrei 4596 was 6 – 19 – 297 or 6 – 19 – 529.[175]

---

[175] There was a Molad *Zaken* in Shevat, see Appendix H at <www.Hakirah .org/vol20AjdlerAppendices.pdf>.

Appendix E

See <www.Hakirah.org/vol20AjdlerAppendices.pdf>.

Appendix F

Historical evidence of the existence of the *keviyah* גשא.

1. R' Abraham bar Ḥiyya.

In his *Sefer ha-Ibbur*,[176] he mentions twice the *keviyah* גשא. He first mentions the *keviyah* as a possible *keviyah*[177] but later he writes that this possible theoretical *keviyah* did not find a practical application because this was not necessary.[178]

2. *Massekhet Sofrim*.[179]

In *Massekhet Soferim* XX, 12 it deals with the reading of the Torah on both days of *Rosh Ḥodesh* Tevet when *Rosh Ḥodesh* falls on Sunday and Monday.[180]

There are two days of *Rosh Ḥodesh* if the year is regular or full. In the first assumption the first day of *Rosh Ḥodesh* is Tishrei 89. But if the year is full then the first day of *Rosh Ḥodesh* is Tishrei 90. The first assumption implies that 1 Tishrei was four weekdays before the first day of *Rosh Ḥodesh*. Thus if the first day of *Rosh Ḥodesh* is Sunday, 1 Tishrei is on Wednesday. This is impossible. The only possibility is then that we are in a full year גש. If it is an ordinary year it has 355 = M7 + 5 days and Rosh Hashanah of next year is on Friday. This is impossible. It must then be a leap year of 385 = M7 days and next year will also begin on Tuesday.

---

176 Ed. Filipowski, London 1851.

177 P. 63.

178 P. 65.

179 The reference to *Massekhet Sofrim* was mentioned for the first time by Ḥayyim Jeḥiel Bornstein in "Divrei Yemei ha-Ibbur ha Aharonim," *Ha-Tekufah* 16, Warsaw, 1923, p. 283.

180 In the text of *Massekhet Sofrim* published in the Vina Romm edition and in the *Massekhet Soferim* edited in *Maḥzor Vitry*, ed. Simon Horowitz, Nuremberg 1923, Vol. 2, p. 716 there is an additional interpolation, שאין חשבון ראש חדש מיום שני אלא בזמן שהשנים כסדרן. The signification of this interpolation is that *Rosh Ḥodesh* Tevet has two days only if the year is regular (Marḥeshvan defective and Kislev full) or full (Marḥeshvan and Kislev full). This interpolation is not necessary at all and Gra suppressed it.

Pesaḥ of this year will be two days before, on Sunday and the *keviyah* is then **גשא**.This *keviyah* does not exist today but we can assume that it once existed or, at least, that it was once taken into consideration.

3. *Sefer ha-Pardes.*[181]

Sefer ha-Pardes is one of the books issued by the "school of Rashi"; Berliner assumed that it was composed by R' Shemaya.

In *Sefer ha Pardes*, about the Shabbat and festivals readings,[182] it writes that if Sukkot is on Tuesday and Marḥeshvan and Kislev are full there will be 29 Sabbaths and we won't be obliged to read two sections together. The year considered is a full leap year beginning on Tuesday. It has 385 days and the next year also begins on Tuesday. Pesaḥ will be two days before the day of Rosh Hashanah of next year, on Sunday. It is a year **גשא**.Apparently, these two quotations are remnants of ancient calendar rules which were not adapted or corrected and which fortunately could reach us.[183] They attest to the depth of their knowledge of the Jewish calendar.

---

181 The reference to *Sefer ha-Pardes* was mentioned for the first time by Ḥayyim Bornstein in "Divrei Yemei ha-Ibbur ha Aharonim," *Ha-Tekufah* 16, Warsaw, 1923, p. 273.

182 *Sefer ha-Pardes*, ed. R' H.L. Ehrenreich, Budapest 1924 and Bnei Berak 1990, p. 340 five lines from bottom.

183 We note that the Gra corrected the reading in Soferim XX, 12 but he did not react and note the impossibility of this configuration. It is thus normal, because of the difficulty of the subject, that the copyists copied without amending the text and let survive these interesting passages.

Bibliography

Abraham bar Hiyya, (1852). *Sefer ha Ibbur*, ed Filipowski, London.

—— (1969). *Sefer Heshbon Mahalekhot ha-Kohavim*, Poel ha-Shem.

Abraham ibn Ezra, (1874). *Sefer ha-Ibbur*, ed. Halberstam, Mekitsei Nirdamim, Lyck, 1874.

—— *Sefer ha-Me'orot*, Leiden 1496 and 1550, Rome 1544 and Frankfort on the Main 1624.

Ahai Gaon of Shabha, *She'iltot*, ed. Daniel Bomberg, Venice, 1546; Vilna 1861 and 1908, Cracow 1908.

Ajdler, J.J. (1996). *Hilkhot Kidush ha-Hodesh al pi ha-Rambam*. Jerusalem.

—— (2004). "Rav Safra and the Second Festival Day: Lessons about the Evolution of the Jewish Calendar." *Tradition*, vol. 38, n°4, Winter 2004.

—— (2005). "The Equation of Time in Ancient Jewish Astronomy," *BDD* 16.

—— (2011). "The Future of the Jewish Calendar," *BDD* 25.

—— (2013/1). "The Gregorian Revolution of the Jewish Calendar," *BDD* 27.

—— (2013/2). "The Period of 689,472 Years in the Jewish Calendar and its Applications in Frequency and Probability Problems," *BDD* 28.

Akabia, A.A. (1953). *Ha-Luah ve-Shimusho ba-Kronologia*, Magnes. Jerusalem.

al-Battānī (1903 – 1905), *Albatanei Opus Astronomicum*, ed Nallino, C.A. Milano.

Bornstein,H.J (1904). *Mahaloket.Sefer ha-Yovel likhevod Nahum Sokolow*, Warsaw.

—— (1919). *Mishpat ha-Semikha, ha-Tekufah* vol 4, Warsaw.

—— (1920). *Sidrei Zemanim, ha-Tekufah* vol 6, Warsaw.

—— (1921). *Ta'arikhei Yisra'el, ha-Tekufah* vol 8 and 9, Warsaw.

—— (1921). "Heshbon Shemittin ve-Yovelot," *ha- Tekufah* vol 11, Warsaw.

—— (1922). "Divrei Yemei ha-Ibbur ha-Aharonim," *ha-Tekufah* vol 14 and 15, Warsaw

—— (1923). "Divrei Yemei ha-Ibbur ha-Aharonim," *ha-Tekufah* vol 16, Warsaw.

—— (1924). "Ibburim u-Mahzorim," *ha-Tekufah* vol 20, Warsaw.

Braita de Samuel, (1861) ed. Nathan Amram, Salonika.

Casher, M. (1949). *Torah Shelema*, vol XIII.

Epstein, A. (1901). *Revue des Etudes Juives*, n° 42, pp. 173 – 210.

Grossman, A. (1996). *Hakhmei Tsarfat ha-Rishonim*, Magnes, Jerusalem.

Halma, l'abbé, (1813-1816). *La Composition Mathématique de Claude Ptolémée, (traduction française) + commentaire de Delambre*. Paris.

Hanover, R. Levi. (1756). *Tekhunat ha-Shamayim*, Amsterdam.

—— (1756-1757). *Luhot ha Ibbur*. Hanover and Leiden.

Ideler, L. (1825). *Handbuch der Mathem. Und Technischen Chronologie*, 2 vol, Berlin.
Jaffe, T. H. (1931). *Korot Heshbon ha-Ibbur*, Jerusalem.
Ha-Levi, Judah (1075 – 1141). *Sefer ha-Kuzari*, Warsaw, 1867.
Langermann, Ts. (1987). "Eimatay nossad ha-Luah ha-Ivri?" *Assufot*, 1 pp. 159 – 168.
Loewinger, J. (1986). *Al ha-Sheminit*, Tel-Aviv.
Mahzor Vitry, ed. Horowitz, Nuremberg, 1923.
Mann, J. (1920 – 1922). *The Jews in Egypt and in Palestine under the Fatimid Caliphs.* 2nd edition with introduction By S.D. Goitein. 1970.
"Megilat Aviathar", *Jewish Quarterly Review*, vol XIV, 1901 -1902, pp. 449 – 474.
Meeus, J. (1991). *Astronomical Algorithms.* Willman Bell, Richmond, Virginia.
—— (1995). *Astronomical Tables of Sun, Moon and Planets*, Willman Bell.
Mucke, H and Meeus, J. (1983). *Canon of Solar Eclipses.* Wien.
Nallino, C.A. (1903-1905). *al-Battānī sive Albatenii Opus Astronomicum*, Milano.
Neugebauer, O. (1975). *History of Ancient Mathematical Astronomy*, Springer.
Oppolzer, Th. (1887). *Canon Der Finsternisse*, Vienna.
Pedersen, O. (1974). *A Survey of the Almagest.* Odense.
Resnikoff, L. A. *Scripta Mathematica*, vol. IX pp, 191 – 196 and 274 – 277.
Sar Shalom, R. (1984). *Shearim le-Luah ha-Ivri*, Natania.
—— (1988). „=Matay Nossad ha-Luah ha-Ivri? *Sinai*, n° 102, pp. 26 – 51.
—— (1992/93). Mahaloket R. Sa'adia Gaon and Ben Meir, Sinai, n° 111, pp. 97 – 124.
Sefer ha-Pardes, ed. Ehrenreich, H.L. Budapest, 1924.
Sefer ha-Ma'assim li-Benei Yisra'el, Hillel Newman, Yad Ben Tsvi, 2011.
Slonimski, H.S. *Yessodei ha-Ibbur*, Warsaw, 1852 and expanded ed. Zitomir, 1865.
Smart, W.H. (1931). *Textbook on Spherical Astronomy.* Cambridge University Press.
Sherira Gaon, *Iggeret Rav Sherira Gaon*, ed. Aaron Heyman, London 1910.
Stern, S. (2001). *Calendar and Community*, Oxford.
Toomer, G.J. (1984). *Ptolemy's Almagest.* Duckworth.
Yisraeli, Isaac ben Yossef. (1848). *Yessod Olam*, ed. Baer Goldberg, Berlin.

ᏩᏒ

Redacting Tosafot on the Talmud
Part II—Editing Methods

By: ARYEH LEIBOWITZ

Introduction

This article is the second in a series of articles on R. Eliezer of Tukh's redaction of *Tosafot*.[1] R. Eliezer of Tukh was a German Tosafist who flourished in the second half of the thirteenth century.[2] His most lasting contribution to Torah study is *Tosafot Tukh* (תוספות טוך), an edited version of the great French Tosafist tradition of Talmud study. *Tosafot Tukh* is the "printed" *Tosafot* that appears on the outer margin of the Talmud page in many of the major tractates, including: Tractates *Shabbat*, *Eruvin*, and *Pesahim* in *Seder Moed*, tractates *Yevamot*, *Ketubot*, and *Gittin* in *Seder Nashim*, tractates *Bava Kamma*, *Bava Mezia*, *Bava Batra*, and *Shevuot* in *Seder Nezikin*, tractate *Hullin* in *Seder Kodashim*, and tractate *Niddah* in *Seder Taharot*. Indeed, when people make reference to "*Tosafot*" they are, more often than not, unknowingly referring to *Tosafot Tukh*.

The first article in this series addressed R. Eliezer's sources. It demonstrated that R. Eliezer's primary sources were the Tosafist commentaries that emerged from Ri's academy in Dampierre, France. The primary examples we discussed were the *Tosafot Shanz* of R. Shimshon of Shanz, and the *Tosafot* commentaries of R. Yehudah of Paris, R. Barukh, R. Elhanan of Dampierre, and R. Yehiel of Paris. These highly integrated commentaries generally contained a record of Ri's lectures, with the additions of

---

1 The first article in this series is "Redacting Tosafot on the Talmud: Part I – Sources," *Hakirah* 18 (2014) 235–249. For the development of the Tosafist enterprise as a whole, from its origin through the editing stage undertaken by R. Eliezer, see A. Leibowitz, "The Emergence and Development of Tosafot on the Talmud," *Ḥakirah* 15 (2013): 143–163.

2 For biographical information regarding R. Eliezer, see E. Urbach, *Ba'alei ha-Tosafot* (Jerusalem, 1986), 581–585, and A. Leibowitz, "R. Eliezer of Tukh: A German Tosafist," *Yerushaseinu* 7 (2013): 5–18.

Aryeh Leibowitz is a *Ra"m* at Yeshivat Sha'alvim and serves as the Assistant Dean of the Moty Hornstein Institute for Overseas Students. He is a *musmakh* of RIETS and earned his Ph.D. from Yeshiva University's Bernard Revel Graduate School.

his most celebrated and accomplished students.

This article will explore the editing methods utilized by R. Eliezer when redacting his *Tosafot.* It will discuss the extent that R. Eliezer made changes to the text, and the role that R. Eliezer's own original teachings played in the editing process. The overarching goal will be to determine R. Eliezer's primary objectives in editing his sources.

Syntactical Editing

R. Eliezer's sources were highly developed works that cast the early Tosafist tradition in a sophisticated framework. For this reason, it was often unnecessary for R. Eliezer to edit the passages in his sources. A large number of the inherited passages were already complete and well presented. In such instances, R. Eliezer merely copied the text and included it, as is, in his *Tosafot.*

For this reason, many passages in *Tosafot Tukh* are strikingly similar to passages in R. Eliezer's source texts, oftentimes bearing little or no signs of editing by R. Eliezer. The most extreme form of this phenomenon is when passages in *Tosafot Tukh* are exact verbatim copies of an earlier Tosafist source. In these cases, R. Eliezer did not merely *consult*, but rather *copied* from the earlier sources.[3]

Yet in most cases, passages in *Tosafot Tukh* are not completely identical to the corresponding passages in R. Eliezer's source text. Nonetheless, the differences are generally slight and non-substantive in terms of content. That is, in many instances we find that the *content* in *Tosafot Tukh* is practically identical to the content in the source text. This indicates that in many passages R. Eliezer only engaged in syntactic editing.[4]

---

3 Compare *Tosafot Tukh* to *Tosafot Shanz* in tractate *Bava Batra* 6b *s.v.* עד, *Ketubot* 61b *s.v.* והני, and *s.v.* הלכה. Even when passages in *Tosafot Tukh* bear definite editing, there are often sections in the passage, even multiple sections that were unaltered. Examples: tractate *Ketubot* 3b *s.v.* ולידרש and *Ketubot* 42a *s.v.* או. R. Eliezer's tendency to leave his source unchanged sometimes resulted in his not even altering statements made in the first person, if the veracity of their intent remained. Hence when R. Shimshon wrote (*Ketubot* 80a *s.v.* ישבע), "As **I** will explain later, with God's help (כמו שאפרש לקמן בעזרת השם)," R. Eliezer has no problem leaving the personal reference untouched, for in his *Tosafot* too he will "explain later, with God's help."

4 This suggestion is verifiable in tractates *Ketubot* and *Bava Batra. Tosafot Shanz* on these two tractates are extant and a comparison of *Tosafot Tukh* with *Tosafot Shanz* shows that many passages in *Tosafot Tukh* closely parallel the *Tosafot Shanz* passages. Note that in some cases it is hard to determine if the slight syntactical differences are due to actual editing undertaken by R. Eliezer, or if they stem

Non-Substantive Editing

Beyond mere syntactical changes, R. Eliezer did engage in actual editing of his source material. Often, though, it was limited and had little bearing on the intent of the original source. For instance, R. Eliezer sometimes rearranged the order of presentation in a specific passage, seemingly in an attempt to convey the material in a clearer fashion.[5]

R. Eliezer also added attributions into the text. This occurs most often with regard to the teachings of Ri. Since R. Eliezer's sources emerged from Ri's academy, many of the sources did not state Ri's name explicitly. Instead, they simply referred to Ri with the title "my teacher" (רבי), or omitted a reference to him completely and appended a signature of "מ"ר," meaning "מפי רבי," to the end of the passage. As editor, R. Eliezer changed "my teacher" to "Ri," or deleted the "מ"ר" signature from the end of the passage, replacing it with phrases like "Ri answered," or "Ri explained" at the beginning of the passage.[6]

---

from textual variations, a common occurrence when material is transmitted by hand from generation to generation. See the following example from *Bava Batra* 6a *s.v.* מהו (the differences are underlined).

תוספות שאנץ ו ע"א ד"ה מהו	**תוספות טוך ו ע"א ד"ה מהו**
וא"ת והיכי ס"ד דהוה מצי למימר	וא"ת והיכי הוי ס"ד דמצי למימר ליה
הכי דאטו מיירי משו'ם דקדם זה	הכי דאטו משום דקדם זה
ועבד הורע כחו	ועשה הורע כחו
ויכול זה לדוחקו לעשות כל הכותל	ויכול לדוחקו זה לעשות כל הכותל
ויש לומר דסד"א כיון דאם לא	ויש לומר דס"ד כיון דאם לא
קדם ועשה חצי הכותל...	קדם זה ועשה זה...

5 Compare *Tosafot Tukh Bava Batra* 7a *s.v.* אספלידא to *Tosafot Shanz*.

6 Scores and scores of examples of this are readily verifiable in tractates in which *Tosafot Shanz* is extant, such as tractates *Ketubot* and *Pesahim*. There are also examples of R. Eliezer deleting a signature of "ת"ם," which refers to R. Tam, from the end of a passage and inserting "R. Tam explained" to the beginning of the passage, see *Pesahim* 2a *s.v.* וכאור. At times, it appears that R. Eliezer had conflicting reports as to the proper attribution, and he had to make a decision regarding which source to follow. Such is the case in *Bava Batra* 6a *s.v.* ומודה that provides a definition of two words mentioned in the Talmud. Whereas *Tosafot Shanz*'s only attribution of the definitions is the מ"ר signature appended to the end of the passage, indicating that R. Shimshon heard the definitions from Ri, other sources attribute the material to R. Tam (see *Tosafot Yeshanim al Massekhet Bava Batra*). R. Eliezer apparently conjectured that Ri himself had heard the definitions from R. Tam and subsequently taught it to R. Shimshon, and hence R. Eliezer attributed it to the earlier R. Tam.

Besides Ri, R. Eliezer also introduced attributions to R. Shimshon. As discussed in the previous article, *Tosafot Shanz* not only was a conduit for the teachings of R. Tam and Ri, but also contained many of R. Shimshon's own original insights. R. Shimshon indicated his own contributions by introducing them with relevant terms, such as "It appears to me (ונראה לי)." When R. Eliezer included this material in *Tosafot Tukh* he removed these phrases, replacing them with explicit attributions to R. Shimshon. In such situations, R. Eliezer generally used the acronym "רשב"א," which stands for "רבינו שמשון בן אברהם." Attributions to R. Shimshon appear frequently in *Tosafot Tukh* on certain tractates and reflect the many original insights of R. Shimshon that R. Eliezer chose to include in *Tosafot Tukh*.[7]

Condensing and Abridging

R. Eliezer also engaged in more significant forms of editing, such as condensing and abridging of his source texts. Research reveals that many passages in *Tosafot Tukh* are shortened versions of parallel passages in R. Eliezer's source texts. It appears that this form of editing was engaged in often by R. Eliezer, and various traditions suggest that it earned R. Eliezer his fame. The 15th-century German Talmudist R. Yisrael Isserlin (Terumat ha-Deshen, תרומת הדשן) writes regarding *Tosafot Tukh*, "We drink from the waters of *Tosafot Shanz* that were shortened by R. Eliezer of Tukh," and his younger Italian contemporary R. Yosef Colon (Maharik, מהרי"ק) remarks, "*Tosafot Tukh* in many places is merely a shortened version of *Tosafot Shanz*."[8]

In this study we utilize two distinct verbs—"condensing" and "abridging"—to differentiate between two distinct undertakings of R. Eliezer in shortening passages from his sources. "Condensing" describes R. Eliezer's method of shortening the text *without removing any substantive material*. This form of shortening is generally syntactical and stylistic in

---

7 Examples abound; see for instance *Ketubot* 3a *s.v*, *Pesahim* 5a *s.v.* לא and 27b *s.v.* מה. Besides attributions to Ri and R. Shimshon, R. Eliezer also made other attributions based on the various sources that were available to him. Hence, we find in tractate *Ketubot* 2a *s.v.* שאם and 2b *s.v.* פשיט that although *Tosafot Shanz* recorded the material anonymously, the same material appears in *Tosafot Tukh* with attribution to R. Tam.

8 *Terumat ha-Deshen* #19 and *She'elot u-Teshuvot Maharik* #160 and #211. Note R. Avraham Shoshana's introduction to *Tosafot ha-Rosh al Massekhet Pesahim* (Jerusalem, 2006), 31, where he states that unlike Rosh who often quotes *Tosafot Shanz* verbatim, R. Eliezer often paraphrased the *Tosafot Shanz* in order to present the material in a more condensed fashion.

nature. "Abridging" describes R. Eliezer's method of shortening the text by *removing substantive material*, such as questions, proof texts, or additional answers for the sake of brevity. This form of shortening is much more significant as it affects the actual content of the source passage.

When R. Eliezer *condensed* material his goal was to rewrite the Tosafist teachings in a more terse fashion. Condensed passages in *Tosafot Tukh* contain little alterations of the passage's content. R. Eliezer deleted superfluous material and shortened language, while maintaining the overall content and intent of the passage.[9]

In a more aggressive form of condensing, R. Eliezer sometimes removed the question from his source, but recorded the answer in a way that the original question could still be inferred. In such cases, the attuned reader is still able to determine the question based on context, even though the question is not stated explicitly. Indeed, the "unstated yet implied question" is one of the hallmarks of the printed *Tosafot*.[10] Similar to

---

9 An illustration: In tractate *Bava Batra* 6b *s.v.* שתי *Tosafot Tukh* condenses the question asked by *Tosafot Shanz*, recording it in a much more succinct fashion. In this specific example, the question remains the same, yet half as many words are utilized.

תוספות שאנץ בב"ב ו ע"ב ד"ה שתי
וא"ת ותחתון אמאי יסייע לעליון [כל כך לא יסיי לעליון] אלא כדי שיהא גבוה ד' אמות מקרקעי'ת חצר התחתון דמהשת'א לא יוכל לראות עוד בחצר העליון והעליון יבנה לבדו עד שיהא גבוה מקרקעי'ת חצירו כדי שלא יראה בחצר התחתון

תוספות טוך בב"ב ו ע"ב ד"ה שתי
וא"ת ותחתון למה יסייע לעליון דמכי מטי לארבע אמות ולא יוכל התחתון לראות בחצר העליון יבנה העליו

10 An example is found in tractate *Bava Batra* 6b *s.v.* האי. *Tosafot Shanz* records an inquiry and solution proposed by R. Tam. *Tosafot Shanz* reads as follows:

תימ'ה אמאי קא מייתי הכא מילת'א דרבינא דבשלמ'א מילתי'ה דרב נחמ'ן דכווי מייתי איידי דפליג רב הונא ורב נחמ'ן דאסמיך לפלגא ואמרי'נן ומוד'ה רב נחמ'ן באפריזא ובקביעת'א דכשורי והכשורי מעמידי'ן בתוך הטי אלא מילתי'ה דרבינא לקמ'ן בחזקת הבתי'ם הוה ליה לאתויי. וא'מר לי ר"ת דאמתני'תן קאי וה"פ האי כשור'א דמטללתא שהניחן על הכותל עד תלתין יומין לא הוי חזק'ה דהוי בחזק'ת שלא נתן עד שיביא ראייה מכאן ואילך הוי בחזקת שנתן.

In *Tosafot Tukh* the inquiry has been removed and the solution is rewritten in a way that the original inquiry can be inferred, although it is not stated explicitly. The abridged text in *Tosafot Tukh* reads:

אומר ר"ת דאמתני' קאי דעד שלשים יום לא הוי חזקה והוי בחזקת שלא נתן מכאן ואילך הוי בחזקת שנתן ואתי שפיר דנקטיה הכא ולא בחזקת הבתים

Another good illustration of this phenomenon can be found in tractate *Pesahim* 6b *s.v.* אבל.

what R. Eliezer did with questions, we also find many cases where he rewrote answers and proofs in a way that they could be inferred, but are not stated explicitly.[11]

A much more significant form of shortening undertaken by R. Eliezer was when he *abridged* the material in his source text. Many early Tosafist compositions were quite verbose and contained long-winded dialectics. This style provided a broad perspective on the dialectic discussion, but also confounded the issues and served as a weighty impediment for even the most accomplished scholars.

R. Eliezer's abridgments generally deleted proofs, digressions, and other non-vital steps from a discussion. But in some cases, R. Eliezer even removed entire discussions—such as, a question and its answer—from a passage.[12] In most of these instances it appears that R. Eliezer abridged the material simply because the discussion was too long. For the sake of brevity, he apparently felt justified in deleting any material that could be removed without sacrificing the major points of the passage.[13]

In most cases of abridgment R. Eliezer deleted material completely, leaving no trace. This placed R. Eliezer's indelible mark on the tradition he was transmitting. Yet, there are some exception cases where R. Eliezer explicitly noted that he was omitting material or not giving the topic full treatment, by writing, "And this is not the place to elaborate (אין להאריך כאן),"[14] or by directing the reader to another location where he elaborated

---

11 For example, in *Tosafot Shanz Bava Batra* 5b *s.v.* ואפילו a proof is recorded in the name of Rivam but then rejected by R. Samson's teacher (Ri). However in *Tosafot Tukh* the proof of Rivam and the rejection of Ri have been condensed, with R. Eliezer writing in place of the proof and rejection: "And don't bring a proof from…"

12 Abridgment, both in its lesser and more extreme form, is demonstrable throughout many tractates of *Tosafot Tukh*. For a number of examples, compare *Tosafot Tukh* with *Tosafot Shanz* at the beginning of tractate *Pesahim*. Note especially *Tosafot Tukh* 2a *s.v.* אור and compare it with the much longer and richer parallel passage in *Tosafot Shanz*. See also *Pesahim* 40b *s.v.* האלפס.

13 One such justification is cases where later Tosafists rejected a suggestion made by an earlier master, or when a Tosafist recanted his own suggestion. An example is *Ketubot* 19b *s.v.* אמר. The *Tosafot Tukh* passage is identical to the corresponding passage in *Tosafot Shanz* except that an additional answer ascribed to Ri, plus Ri's own recanting of this additional answer, is omitted from *Tosafot Tukh*.

14 Such is the case in tractate *Ketubot* 57a where *Tosafot Shanz s.v.* שתים elaborates on a particular issue and in *Tosafot Tukh* the issue only appears briefly followed by "and this is not the place to elaborate (אין להאריך כאן)."

more on the topic.[15]

R. Eliezer's abridging of his source texts demonstrates that he was not merely a passive editor, but an active and creative participant in the Tosafist enterprise. The removal of content took editorial confidence and reflects R. Eliezer's important role in the transmission of the Tosafist tradition.[16] Although the Talmud (*Pesahim* 3b) instructs a teacher to teach his student in a terse fashion, it is still a testament to R. Eliezer's scholarship and greatness that he was successful in producing an accepted work that deleted material of the earlier generations.

R. Eliezer's abridging of the Tosafist tradition made it more approachable, and likely contributed to the long-term popularity of the Tosafist teachings.[17] In fact, there were those who saw the abridgement as a sign of generational decline, and as an attempt by R. Eliezer to make the study of the Tosafist teachings easier.[18] However, not everyone saw the terseness of R. Eliezer's *Tosafot* in this way. Quite the contrary, there were those who saw its terseness as an impediment to clearly understanding the

---

15 See *Shabbat* 78b *s.v.* ת"ק where R. Eliezer refers the reader to the parallel passages and writes, "However, I have explained in *Bava Kamma*, *Bava Mezia*, and *Gittin*… and there I elaborated more." See *Gittin* 2a *s.v.* ואם, *Bava Kamma* 8b *s.v.* דינא and *Bava Mezia* 13b *s.v.* הא.
Another example, this one more extreme, appears in tractate *Ketubot* 3a *s.v.* ואפקיהו. Instead of recording the long discussion found in *Tosafot Shanz*, R. Eliezer simply directs the reader to *Tosafot Tukh* on tractate *Gittin* 33a *s.v.* ואפקינהו where the same issue is addressed at length. In this case, the passage in *Tosafot Shanz* on *Ketubot* is a couple of hundred words long, while the passage in *Tosafot Tukh* on *Ketubot* consists of only three words: "בריש השולח פירשתי."

16 It should be noted that there are no indications that R. Eliezer sought to *replace* the earlier Tosafist commentaries with his *Tosafot*. He did not necessarily think that his commentary would be so dominant in subsequent generations that it would eradicate the memory of the earlier commentaries. It is likely that in R. Eliezer's mind the earlier texts would always be available, and one who wished to consult the long-winded primary sources would always have the opportunity to do so.

17 R. Eliezer's goal of abridging the early Tosafist material was not unique. The verbose nature of the early works was bemoaned by other Tosafists as well. They too sought to abridge the long-winded dialectics. With a similar stated goal, the French Tosafist R. Moshe of Coucy introduced his popular work *Sefer Mizvot Gedolot* (Semag, סמ"ג), stating that he wished to record the "foundations of the commandments according to tradition *without* all of their long-winded dialectics (חילוקיהם באורך)." Although R. Moshe's halakhic work was of a different nature than R. Eliezer's *Tosafot*, the identification of the long-windedness of the earlier Tosafist works is the same.

18 *Orhot Zadikim*, Chapter Twenty-Seven.

Tosafist teachings. In fact, R. David Messer Leon, a sixteenth-century Italian Talmudist, saw the terseness of *Tosafot Tukh* as a testimony to its complexity and sophistication. He notes the great challenge facing a person who wishes to master R. Eliezer's work, and hence he states proudly that his culture's custom is to study the "deep and terse [*Tosafot*] of Tukh."[19]

The above attitudes, however, are not contradictory. While R. Eliezer's intent was likely to simplify the Tosafist corpus, it was only his contemporaries and immediate successors that benefitted from his shortening of the text. The level of scholarship in R. Eliezer's day, which included a familiarity with the Tosafist tradition, coupled with access to the earlier source texts, allowed his contemporaries and immediate successors to appreciate his shortening of the Tosafist teachings. However, by the time of R. David, and even more so in contemporary times, the terseness of *Tosafot Tukh* often makes it more challenging to study.[20]

Integration

Another significant form of editing undertaken by R. Eliezer was "integration." In our context, integration means the splicing together of material from two or more source texts to create one new unified passage. The necessity for integration was directly reflective of the success and growth of the Tosafist movement. The increase of Tosafist teachers, academies, and students in the generations following R. Tam led to a proliferation of Tosafist commentaries.[21] As the Tosafist corpus burgeoned, constant integration was necessary to avoid inundation. When new commentaries emerged, Tosafists studied them and integrated their teachings with those from other works. This produced further integrated works. Within a short time these further integrated works had to again be integrated with the new commentaries that continually appeared. The result of this multi-level

---

19 *Kavod Hakhamim* (Berlin, 1899), 129.

20 We should also note that R. Eliezer's tendency to condense and abridge the earlier material is not absolute. There are a few times that instead of condensing or abridging, R. Eliezer's *Tosafot Tukh* are actually wordier and contain more content. For example, in tractate *Ketubot* 3a *s.v.* שבתי R. Eliezer's redaction is both more verbose than *Tosafot Shanz* and includes material not found in *Tosafot Shanz*, i.e. it is not condensed or abridged. However, these instances are the exception and not the rule.

21 According to R. Hayyim Yosef David Azulai (Hida, *Shem ha-Gedolim Ha-Shalem*, *Sefarim*, section ת, #56) each of the major Tosafists wrote a commentary on the entire Talmud.

integration was that the later generations received highly integrated works that reflected the best of the Tosafist tradition.

Critical integration of the early teachings of R. Tam and his colleagues had already been done by Ri and his students. They surveyed the earliest Tosafist writings—the teachings of R. Tam, Riba, Raban, Rashbam and R. Meshulam, among others—in order to collect and collate the best questions, most cogent answers, and sharpest insights. This early integration established the landscape of the future Tosafist commentaries, highlighting the focal issues in each tractate that would be addressed by future generations. The result of this early integration was the highly developed commentaries that emerged from Ri's academy and served as the source texts for R. Eliezer.[22]

Like Ri, R. Eliezer engaged in integration. R. Eliezer's integration of material was done in two distinct forms. In some cases, R. Eliezer took an entire passage from one source and included it alongside a passage from another source. In such cases, the actual passages remain the same. They are simply placed alongside one another. But in other cases, R. Eliezer integrated material from a passage in one source directly into a passage from another source. The result in these cases was a new creation—a single passage that consisted of material from both the primary passage and the augmenting source.[23]

It is important to stress that R. Eliezer's integration was different from the early integration done by Ri and his students. They integrated using the original teachings of the early Tosafists, but R. Eliezer integrated using their already integrated commentaries. That is, R. Eliezer was integrating material that had already gone through a process of integration. Using the works of Ri's academy, R. Eliezer spliced together material to produce *further* integrated passages.

It is our contention that because R. Eliezer inherited works that were themselves already integrated, he did not utilize the original commentaries of R. Tam, Riba, or other early Tosafist masters when producing *Tosafot Tukh*. The teachings of the early Tosafists were already integrated into the Tosafist corpus well before R. Eliezer flourished, and they were already part and parcel of the Tosafist tradition that he inherited. For this reason,

22 For more on integration and Ri's role in integrating early Tosafist material, see A. Leibowitz, "The Emergence and Development of Tosafot on the Talmud," *Ḥakirah* 15 (2013): 153–155.

23 In many tractates it appears that R. Eliezer chose one commentary to be the primary source. For example, in tractate *Ketubot*, R. Eliezer generally used *Tosafot Shanz* as his primary source, but he integrated into the *Tosafot Shanz* passages material from the commentaries of Ri's other students.

R. Eliezer is not to be credited as the one that introduced the teachings of the early Tosafists into the discussions found in *Tosafot Tukh*.

The veracity of this contention is validated by Tosafist commentaries that predate R. Eliezer and clearly demonstrate that the teachings of the early Tosafists were integrated into the Tosafist corpus generations before R. Eliezer flourished. Take for example *Tosafot Shanz* on tractate *Ketubot*. Practically every reference to early Tosafists that appears in *Tosafot Tukh* is already integrated into the Tosafist discussion in *Tosafot Shanz*.

Let us look in-depth at one additional example. Analysis provides clear evidence that R. Eliezer is not to be credited with the integration of early Tosafist teachings that appear in *Tosafot Tukh* on tractate *Shabbat*. Besides R. Tam, whose name is quoted close to two hundred times throughout *Tosafot Tukh* on tractate *Shabbat*, many other early Tosafists occupy a prominent position in the work. Riba appears over fifty times in *Tosafot Tukh* on tractate *Shabbat*, including two passages (20a *s.v.* איבעיא and 23a *s.v.* מכבה) that conclude with a signature of Riba, indicating that the entire passage reflects Riba's opinion, and likely his actual wording. R. Yosef b. Moshe Porat (רב פורת) was a younger French contemporary of R. Tam from Troyes who studied with R. Tam's older brother, Rashbam. R. Porat's name appears close to fifty times in *Tosafot Tukh* on tractate *Shabbat*, including passages that contain a signature of R. Porat's name. Rashbam appears over thirty times, most often with the deferential title "Rabbenu Shmuel." Included in Rashbam's appearances are dialectic debates between Rashbam and an early German Tosafist, R. Eliezer b. Nathan (Raban, ראב"ן). Other early Tosafists that appear in R. Eliezer's redaction, albeit to a lesser degree than the above-mentioned Tosafists, are R. Isaac b. Meir, R. Yaakov of Corbeil, and R. Eliyahu of Paris, who each appear a handful of times.

Recently, a manuscript of a *Tosafot* commentary on tractate *Shabbat* composed by an early student of Ri who flourished before R. Shimshon of Shanz, was printed as *Tosafot Ri ha-Zaken ve-Talmido ve-Rishonei Ba'alei ha-Tosafot al Massekhet Shabbat*, ed. A. Shoshana (Jerusalem, 2007). In this manuscript the teachings of basically all the aforementioned early Tosafists already appear, fully integrated into the text. The fact that these teachings were already integrated generations before R. Eliezer began producing his *Tosafot Tukh* indicates that R. Eliezer inherited the integration of these early Tosafist teachings and did not integrate these teachings himself. [24]

---

[24] Another example is a manuscript of a Tosafist commentary on tractate *Bava Kamma* redacted by an anonymous student of R. Tam, printed as "Tosafot

In truth, it is hard to identify integration in *Tosafot Tukh*. This is because R. Eliezer generally made no indication of his sources when he engaged in integration. Since the sources from which R. Eliezer drew were primarily only *reporting* material from earlier generations, he seemingly felt no need to indicate which particular student of Ri provided him with the early material. Only when a source contributed original material did R. Eliezer provide attribution to his source.[25]

For this reason, many passages in *Tosafot Tukh* do not contain direct references to R. Eliezer's immediate sources nor do they provide specific indications of which source text they were drawn from. For instance, let us assume a particular discussion appeared in both *Tosafot Shanz* and *Tosafot R. Yehudah*. Both sources recorded a question and an answer in the

---

Talmid Rabbenu Tam ve-Rabbenu Eliezer," ed. M. Blau, *Shitat ha-Kadmonim al Massekhet Bava Kamma* (New York, 1977), 1–282. The manuscript contains teachings from at least seven early Tosafist works, including *Tosafot ha-Ri*, *Tosafot Ri ha-Lavan*, *Tosafot Rivam*, and *Tosafot Rashbam*. The teachings of various early Tosafists contained in this anonymous commentary appear throughout R. Eliezer's *Tosafot*, and demonstrate that the integration of these teachings was completed a number of generations before R. Eliezer flourished.

Another source is a manuscript fragment of *Tosafot Shanz* on *Bava Batra* 5b – 9a, printed as "Tosafot Shanz al Massekhet Bava Batra," ed. Y. Lifshitz, *Hiddushei ha-Rishonim Massekhet Bava Batra* (Jerusalem, 1991). Every single teaching of an early Tosafist master that appears in *Tosafot Tukh* on *Bava Batra* 5a-9a is already present in this manuscript fragment of *Tosafot Shanz*. Additionally, there is a more complete *Tosafot* commentary on tractate *Bava Batra* printed under the title *Tosafot Yeshanim al Massekhet Bava Batra*, ed. Y. Amrani (Jerusalem, 1997) that predates *Tosafot Tukh*, according to Y. Lifshitz, "Tosafot Ketav Yad le-Massekhet Bava Batra," *Sefer ha-Zikaron leha-Rav Yizhak Nisim*, Vol. 3, ed. M. Benayahu (Jerusalem, 1985), 27–68. There is no direct indication that R. Eliezer had access to this specific text, but it is still significant that a large number of the early Tosafist teachings that appear in *Tosafot Tukh Bava Batra*, such as those of R. Abraham (5a *s.v.* ארבע), R. Hayyim Cohen (58b *s.v.* אנבג, 74a *s.v.* פסקי, 82a *s.v.* בצרן, 86b *s.v.* כדאמר, 88b *s.v.* התם, 92b *s.v.* אי, 111a *s.v.* קל, 134b *s.v.* פלומי), R. Eliezer of Palira (79b *s.v.* אימר), and R. Jacob of Orleans (128b *s.v.* ואפילו) are already present in *Tosafot Yeshanim*.

25 The best examples of this are the many original contribution of R. Shimshon that R. Eliezer included in his *Tosafot*. We noted earlier that R. Shimshon included many original contributions in his *Tosafot Shanz*. When R. Eliezer recorded these original contributions he included the appropriate attribution to R. Shimshon. Hence, when Tosafot Shanz contained an original question of R. Shimshon—indicated by "וקשה לי" in *Tosafot Shanz*—R. Eliezer recorded it in his Tosafot as "וקשה לרשב"א," and when R. Shimshon provided an original perspective, "ונראה לי," R. Eliezer wrote, "ונראה לרשב"א."

name of R. Tam, but *Tosafot R. Yehudah* also contained an additional answer suggested by Ri. R. Eliezer would record in *Tosafot Tukh* the question and answer of R. Tam followed by the answer of Ri. R. Eliezer would not note that he received the question and first answer from *Tosafot Shanz* and *Tosafot R. Yehudah*, nor would he report that it was the *Tosafot R. Yehudah* that provided the second answer. This is because both *Tosafot Shanz* and *Tosafot R. Yehudah* were merely relaying material.[26] However, had R. Yehudah of Paris, the author of *Tosafot R. Yehudah*, recorded his own answer then R. Eliezer would have referenced R. Yehudah's name as the source for that answer.

For the above reason it is also difficult to measure with any certainty the extent of R. Eliezer's use of integration. Moreover, even relatively late material found in *Tosafot Tukh* was often integrated before R. Eliezer. For example, *Tosafot Tukh* on tractate *Bava Batra* includes references to R. Menahem, R. Ezra, and Rizba.[27] However, practically all of the material from these later Tosafists is also found in earlier Tosafist works, demonstrating that this material was already incorporated into the Tosafist corpus before R. Eliezer.[28] We see that even some of the later material in *Tosafot Tukh* was not necessarily integrated by R. Eliezer himself, but may have been inherited by R. Eliezer from his sources.

---

26 *Tosafot R. Yehudah* contain many teachings from R. Elhanan. When R. Eliezer included the teaching of R. Elhanan he would quote it in the name of R Elhanan and make no reference to *Tosafot R. Yehudah*, the conduit through which R. Eliezer received the teaching of R. Elhanan.

27 R. Menahem: 26a *s.v.* עד, 84a *s.v.* האי, 96b *s.v.* כל, 135a *s.v.* חזיא, R. Ezra: 28a *s.v.* אי, and Rizba: 8b *s.v.* אכפיה, 12b *s.v.* כגון, 13a *s.v.* אית, 13b *s.v.* ומסיים, 18a *s.v.* היו, 22b *s.v.* זאת, 23a *s.v.* והתניא, 23b *s.v.* רוב, 24a *s.v.* ושמע, 25a *s.v.* מקום, 25b *s.v.* אפומא.

28 The earlier work is *Tosafot Yeshanim al Massekhet Bava Batra*, ed. Y. Amrani (Jerusalem, 1997). That it predates *Tosafot Tukh* is shown by Y. Lifshitz, "Tosafot Ketav Yad le-Massekhet Bava Batra," *Sefer ha-Zikaron leha-Rav Yizhak Nisim*, Vol. 3, ed. M. Benayahu (Jerusalem, 1985), 27–68. I write "practically" because the reference to Rizba on 12b is not found in the *Tosafot Yeshanim*.
Another example is in tractate *Shabbat*. *Tosafot Tukh* in tractate *Shabbat* contains material from later Tosafist generations, such as teachings of Rizba (58b *s.v.* אלא) and R. Shimshon of Coucy (28b *s.v.* ור"י). However, their teachings also appear in *Tosafot ha-Rosh* and suggest that R. Eliezer did not integrate these teachings himself. Yet this is not the case with all the material from Ri's students. There are many examples in *Tosafot Tukh* on tractate *Shabbat* where material might have been integrated by R. Eliezer. In these cases, the material does not appear in extant earlier works, nor in *Tosafot ha-Rosh*. These examples include R. Eliezer's direct references to R. Elhanan (2a *s.v.* שתים and 54b *s.v.* מעשר), R. Yonah (39b *s.v.* ממעשה), and R. Shmuel of Verdun (112b *s.v.* אבל).

Conclusion

This article has focused on R. Eliezer's editing methods in producing *Tosafot Tukh*. It has identified a number of different forms of editing undertaken by R. Eliezer. In some cases, R. Eliezer included passages from his sources with few alterations. In these instances, he was seemingly satisfied with the content and presentation of the material in his source text. Indeed, there are even passages that he copied verbatim from his sources and included untouched in *Tosafot Tukh*. Other passages were included in *Tosafot Tukh* with only minimal editing. Much of this minimal editing was in the realm of attribution, style, and presentation.

There were also many passages in which R. Eliezer altered the actual content of his source material. When he did alter the content, it was generally in the form of condensing the text or abridging the material. R. Eliezer also integrated material from the different sources available to him. In this realm, this article suggested that R. Eliezer generally did not utilize the actual writings of the early Tosafists, but integrated using the already integrated commentaries that emerged from Ri's academy. Hence, much of the material included by R. Eliezer in *Tosafot Tukh* had already undergone integration and editing by earlier generations.

Our presentation differs from that of Prof. Ephraim E. Urbach in his well-known work *Ba'alei ha-Tosafot* (Jerusalem, 1986). Although Urbach explicitly acknowledges that *Tosafot Tukh* was largely based on the commentaries of Ri's students, he understates the extent of R. Eliezer's dependence on these sources. For example, in his treatment of the *Tosafot Tukh* on tractate *Bava Batra*, Urbach claims that "a significant source that was utilized by [R. Eliezer] was the *Tosafot* commentary of R. Isaac b. Mordekhai [Rivam]."[29] It appears, however, that Rivam's commentary was not actually utilized by R. Eliezer, for the teachings of Rivam were *already integrated* into the Tosafist corpus years prior to R. Eliezer's *Tosafot Tukh*. We know this from the above-quoted manuscript fragment of *Tosafot Shanz* on *Bava Batra* 5b – 9a. In this manuscript the teachings of Rivam already appear fully integrated into the *Tosafot Shanz*.[30] This manuscript fragment indicates that R. Eliezer did not utilize the *Tosafot* of Rivam in redacting *Tosafot Tukh* on tractate *Bava Batra*, but rather, R. Eliezer drew the teachings of Rivam from *Tosafot Shanz*.

---

29 *Ba'alei ha-Tosafot*, 639

30 Rivam's opinion in *Tosafot Tukh* 5b *s.v.* מי appears in *Tosafot Shanz* 5b *s.v.* ואפילו, and was therefore integrated into the discussion by R. Shimson, or possibly by Ri. Similarly, Rivam's question that appears in *Tosafot Tukh* 6a *s.v.* כל also appears already in the parallel passage in *Tosafot Shanz*.

Similarly, in Urbach's treatment of tractate *Shabbat*, he maintains that it was R. Eliezer himself who integrated the *Tosafot Shanz* with the *Tosafot* of R. Porat. Urbach writes, "[R. Eliezer] integrated the *Tosafot* of R. Yosef b. R. Moshe—R. Yosef Porat, the student of Rashbam—with the *Tosafot* of *Rash mi-Shanz*."[31] Here too, manuscript research indicates that this is not correct. The earlier-referenced Tosafist commentary on tractate *Shabbat*, authored by an early student of Ri, contains the teachings of R. Tam, Riba, and R. Porat *already integrated* with one another, indicating that the integration of the teachings of R. Porat and Riba not only predated R. Eliezer, but even predated R. Shimshon himself.

Final Thoughts

Based on the conclusions of this article regarding R. Eliezer's editing methods and the conclusions of the first article in this series regarding R. Eliezer' s sources, we are now able to assess the nature of *Tosafot Tukh*. The research from these two articles has shown that R. Eliezer's work relied heavily on his source texts from Ri's academy. He drew his material consistently from these texts, and he left much of the content unchanged, as he utilized material that was already integrated and edited. The findings of our research point to an extreme faithfulness by R. Eliezer to his sources, and demonstrate that more than an "originator," R. Eliezer was a faithful "transmitter" of the rich Tosafist tradition.

In the next article in this series we will discuss the various types of passages found in *Tosafot Tukh*, and consider the place of R. Eliezer's own original teachings and those of his teachers and contemporaries in the production of *Tosafot Tukh*. The result will hopefully be a clear understanding of the nature of *Tosafot Tukh* and an outline of its salient characteristics. ☙

---

31 *Ba'alei ha-Tosafot*, 603

The Mysterious Origin of Lag Ba-Omer[1]

By: MITCHELL FIRST

It is typically assumed that there is a well-grounded tradition that R. Akiva's students stopped dying around the time of *Lag Ba-Omer*[2] and that this cessation is the basis for the *Lag Ba-Omer* holiday. This article will analyze the earliest sources that refer to the holiday and will show that neither of these assumptions is correct. The article will further analyze the interesting evolution of the holiday in its earliest stages, the time of the *rishonim*.[3] It will be concluded that the origin of the holiday still remains a mystery.

---

1 I would like to thank Rabbi Avrohom Lieberman, Rabbi Alan Zelenetz, and my son Rabbi Shaya First for commenting on and improving the draft.
I would like to dedicate this article to the memory of Rabbi David Feldman who passed away in 2014. He was a world-renowned rabbi, bioethicist and scholar. He authored several books including the classic *Marital Relations, Birth Control, and Abortion in Jewish Law* (1968). He was fascinated by the origin of the holiday of *Lag Ba-Omer* and devoted much research to this topic. (See below, n. 4.)

2 For simplicity, I will refer to the holiday as *Lag Ba-Omer*, which is how the earliest known source refers to it. The term used by R. Abraham b. Nathan ha-Yarḥi, a few decades later, is unclear. In some manuscripts of his work, the holiday is referred to as *Lag La-Omer*. In others, it is referred to as *Lag Ba-Omer*.

3 For the evolution of *Lag Ba-Omer* in the period of the *aḥaronim*, see the fascinating article of May 19, 2011 at seforim.blogspot.com by Eliezer Brodt, "A Printing Mistake and the Mysterious Origins of Rashbi's Yahrzeit." Brodt points out that the notion that R. Shimon b. Yoḥai died on *Lag Ba-Omer* is not found prior

---

Mitchell First resides in Teaneck and practices personal injury law in NYC. He has an M.A. in Jewish History from Bernard Revel Graduate School and is the author of "Jewish History in Conflict: A Study of the Major Discrepancy Between Rabbinic and Conventional Chronology" (Jason Aronson 1997); "The Origin of Ta'anit Esther" (AJS Review 34:2, November 2010); and other articles on history and liturgy in Biblical Archaeology Review (July-August 2012), <seforim. blogspot.com> and *Ḥakirah* (vols. 11, 13, 16 and 18). His most recent book (collecting eleven of his articles) is *Esther Unmasked: Solving Eleven Mysteries of the Jewish Holidays and Liturgy* (Kodesh Press, 2015).

The earliest references to *Lag Ba-Omer* are found in brief anonymous annotations in the London manuscript of *Maḥzor Vitry*.[4] Most likely, the author of these annotations was R. Isaac b. Durbal,[5] who died circa 1175. He seems to have been from northern France, as he was a student of R. Tam.[6] R. Isaac references *Lag Ba-Omer* in an annotation on a section of *Maḥzor Vitry* on the Jewish calendar. He points out that Purim and *Lag Ba-Omer* fall on the same day of the week every year:

---

to the 18th century and seems to have originated based on an erroneous printing of the word שמח as שמת.

4 See the edition of A. Goldschmidt (Jerusalem: Mekhon Otzar Ha-Poskim, 2004), vol. 2, p. 581 and the earlier edition of S. Hurwitz (Nurnberg, 1923), pp. 222-223. The London manuscript of *Maḥzor Vitry* is not the earliest manuscript of this work. The earliest is MS ex-Sassoon 535. It dates to the second quarter of the 12th century. See S. Stern and J. Isserles, "The Astrological and Calendar Section of the Earliest *Maḥzor Vitry* Manuscript (MS ex-Sassoon 535)," *Aleph* 15.2 (2015), pp. 199-318.
The best discussions of the origin of *Lag Ba-Omer* that I have come across are: 1) D. Feldman, "A Dvar Torah Suggested by Lag Ba-Omer," *Proceedings of the Rabbinical Assembly* 26 (1962), pp. 201–224, 2) D. Feldman, "Omer," in *EJ* 12:1382–89 (1972), 3) D. Sperber, *Minhagei Yisrael*, vol. 1 (Jerusalem: Mossad Harav Kook, 1990), pp. 101–11, 4) Z. Goren, "*Al Mekoro Shel Lag Ba-Omer ve-Gilgulav*," *Meyḥkerei Ḥag* 3 (1992), pp. 36–43, and 5) E. Reiner, *Yehoshua Hu RShB"Y, Ḥatzor Hiy Meiron*, *Tarbitz* 80 (2012), pp. 179–218 (at pp. 200–207). Also important is L. Silberman, "The Sefirah Season: A Study in Folklore," *HUCA* 22 (1949), pp. 221–237. All of these extensively researched articles overlooked this passage in *Maḥzor Vitry*.

5 These comments are followed by the letter ת in the London manuscript, indicating that they were additions (תוספת) to the basic text of *Maḥzor Vitry*. According to Justine Isserles (private correspondence), most likely all of these sections with a ת reflect additions by R. Isaac b. Durbal. (Compare the slightly different formulation at *EJ* 11:737.) Dr. Isserles is an authority on *Maḥzor Vitry* manuscripts and I am grateful to her for her assistance.
The London manuscript of *Maḥzor Vitry* dates to 1242, so the annotations are not those of R. Isaac b. Durbal. Rather, according to Isserles, the author of the London manuscript had before him three manuscripts of *Maḥzor Vitry*, and probably one of these was the manuscript with the annotations of R. Isaac himself. (Another seems to have been a manuscript of *Maḥzor Vitry* with the annotations of R. Abraham b. Nathan ha-Yarḥi; these annotations are usually signaled in the London manuscript with the acrostic אב"ן.)

6 He is also known to have traveled to places such as Bohemia and Russia.

וביום פורים הוא ל״ג בעומר. וזכר לדבר "שם האחד פל"ג"[7] - פורים ל"ג בעומר...

But these remarks shed no light on the origin of the holiday.[8]

The second earliest reference to *Lag Ba-Omer* is found in the *Sefer Ha-Manhig* of R. Abraham b. Nathan ha-Yarḥi, composed in Toledo in 1204. Prior to composing this work, R. Abraham had traveled widely and one of the main purposes of this work was to explain the various Jewish customs he had encountered.[9] The background to R. Abraham's statement is that, according to the Talmud (*Yevamot* 62b), R. Akiva had 24,000 students and they all died in one period, מפסח ועד עצרת.[10] In the context of his discussion of marriage rituals, R. Abraham writes (emphasis added): [11]

ואך מנהג בצרפת[12] ופרובינצ' לכנוס מל"ג לעומר ואילך.[13] ושמעתי בשם רבי' ר' זרחיה מגירונדא שמצא כתו' בספר ישן הבא מספרד,[14] שמתו

---

7 His citation is to Gen. 10:25. His claim is that the *pe* preceding the *lamed* and *gimmel* is an allusion to Purim.

8 He uses the phrase ביום פורים ל״ג a few words later as well.

9 See *EJ* 2:154 and R. Abraham's introduction to his *Sefer Ha-Manhig* (ed. I. Raphael, Jerusalem: Mossad Harav Kook, 1978), p. 8.

10 See similarly *Kohelet Rabbah* 11:6. Compare *Bereshit Rabbah* 61:3, where the death of R. Akiva's students *be-perek eḥad* is mentioned without a specification of the particular time period. See also *Tanḥuma Ḥayyei Sarah* 6 and *Tanḥuma Buber, Ḥayyei Sarah* 7. It has been suggested that originally there was no tradition of the time period that the students died and that the specification of the time period is a later invention. See, e.g., Reiner, pp. 200-201. It has also been argued that the entire story of the death of a large number of the students of R. Akiva in one period is a literary fiction. See A. Amit, "The Death of Rabbi Akiva's Disciples: A Literary History," *JJS* 56 (2005), pp. 265–84. But a mainstream approach is to believe that there is a historical kernel to the tradition (i.e., that a large number of students of R. Akiva did die in one period, perhaps in connection with the Bar Kokhba rebellion). See, e.g., the scholars cited by Amit on p. 268.
On the term תנא at *Yevamot* 62b, see Amit, p. 268, n. 10 and Reiner, p. 201, n. 58.

11 *Sefer Ha-Manhig*, vol. 2, p. 538 (*Hilkhot Erusin ve-Nissuin*).

12 He probably does not mean all of France here, as there is no mention of any such leniency in *Sefer Ha-Orah*. There we find, in section 92, a prohibition of *kiddushin* and *nissuin* for the entire 49-day period.

13 The manuscript that Raphael printed (the earliest one) reads מל"ב לעומר here. But Raphael points out that מל"ב is obviously an erroneous reading. The four other manuscripts read מל"ג. Regarding the next word, both לעומר and בעומר are found in the manuscripts. One cannot tell what the original reading was.

14 The implication of the phrase ספר ישן הבא מספרד is that it was a reliable source. See Reiner, p. 205, n. 68, citing Y. Zusman.

מפסח ועד **פרוס העצרת**, ומאי פורסא? פלגא כדתנן שואלין בהלכו' הפסח קודם לפסח ל' יום ופלגא **חמשה עשר** יום קודם העצרת וזהו ל"ג לעומר.

His citation כדתנן is to an explanation of פרוס as fifteen made in another context, at *Bekhorot* 58a.[15]

It is unclear whether the "49-15" explanation offered for *pros ha-atzeret* in the context of the death of the students of R. Akiva originated with R. Zeraḥiah (author of *Ha-Maor*, d. 1186[16]) or with R. Abraham.[17] But the explanation is merely an attempt at a rationale for a **pre-existing** custom to marry from the 33rd day onwards.[18] There is no tradition elsewhere that R. Akiva's students stopped dying around the 33rd day of the *omer*. Whether R. Akiva's students stopped dying around the 33rd day of the *omer* depends on the merits of the interpretation of *pros ha-atzeret* offered here. On close analysis, the interpretation is almost certainly wrong. Saul Lieberman has surveyed the use of the word פרוס in early rabbinic literature.[19] These four letters can reflect a Hebrew word that means "broken" or "half," or a Greek word (πϱὀς) that means "before."[20] Lieberman's survey reveals that when the word is used in connection with a holiday, it is almost always the Greek word that is being used, and the meaning is

---

It would be interesting to check manuscripts of *Yevamot* and *Kohelet Rabbah* to see if there is other support for this reading. But I have not done so. In light of S. Lieberman's conclusion as to the meaning of the word פרוס in our passage, the variant is now of little significance.

15 His citation merely paraphrases the passage. See also *J. Shekalim* 3:1. In both of these sources, the Sage quoted is R. Abahu. See also a similar passage in *Tosefta Shekalim* 2:1 and *Tosefta Bekhorot* 7:6, both in the name of R Yose b. Yehudah.

16 R. Zeraḥiah left Gerona, Spain in his youth and settled in the region of Provence. There he lived for many years in the city of Lunel. This accounts for the name of his commentary on the Talmud, *Ha-Maor*.

17 I lean towards the view that the explanation originated with R. Abraham.

18 It would be extremely farfetched to view the leniency as having arisen as a consequence of the finding of this variant. First, that is not what the passage says. Second, to start acting in accordance with such a leniency would have been going against the contemporary tradition and acting against the previously accepted reading in the Talmud. Third, and most important, a new practice created as a consequence of this reading would have generated a leniency commencing only, at the earliest, at some point on the **34th** day. (After some mourning on the 34th day, the principle of *miktzat ha-yom ke-khulo* on the last day could have been invoked.)

19 Quoted in Sperber, *Minhagei Yisrael*, vol. 4, pp. 237–39.

20 The prefix in English "pre-" derives from the Greek word πϱὀς.

"**just before** the holiday."[21] Moreover, in our case, the argument for interpreting the word as Greek is even stronger. We already have a source that records that the students of R. Akiva died *mi-pesaḥ ve-ad atzeret.* When we find another source that records that they died *mi-pesaḥ ve'ad pros ha-atzeret*, our presumption should be that the sources can be reconciled. Therefore, we should interpret the second source in a manner consistent with the first source, and not in a manner that creates a contradiction between them.

Moreover, even if פרוס was used as a Hebrew word in this passage, and it meant "half of thirty," the explanation suggested would only explain a custom to marry starting on the 35th or 34th day of the *omer.*[22] It would not explain a custom to marry starting on the 33rd day.[23]

***

Meiri (d. 1316) writes that there is a *kabbalah be-yad ha-geonim* that R. Akiva's students stopped dying on the 33rd day of the *omer.*

But there is no other source documenting such a tradition in the Geonic period. Moreover, as I will point out in the next section, there are many sources from the Geonic period in Palestine documenting that the 18th of *Iyyar* (*Lag Ba-Omer*) was observed there as a fast day commemorat-

---

21 Lieberman suggests that the precise *hiddush* of the statements of R. Yose b. Yehudah and R. Abahu (see above, n. 15), who both interpreted פרוס in their contexts to mean "half of a month," was that these were the exceptional cases. They both made their statements precisely because elsewhere in early rabbinic literature פרוס meant "just before the holiday."

22 From the beginning of the 35th day until the end of the 49th day, it is 15 days. If one makes the further (unnecessary) assumption that the dying stopped at some point during the 34th day, or one alternatively invokes the principle of *miktzat ha-yom ke-khulo* on the last day, this would explain a leniency commencing at some point on the 34th day. This point is noted by authorities such as R. Yehoshua Ibn Shuiv (Spain, early 14th century, cited in *Beit Yosef* to *OḤ* 493) and R. Shimon Duran (Spain and North Africa, d. 1444, also cited in *Beit Yosef* there). Based on this reasoning, the alternative custom arose among Sefardic Jewry of continuing the mourning until the morning of the 34th day. See the codification of R. Yosef Caro in *Shulḥan Arukh*, *OḤ* 493 (2).

23 Why do R. Zeraḥiah or R. Abraham not mention this mathematical difficulty? I can only suggest that the leniency of marrying from the 33rd day onwards was viewed as very puzzling. When either R. Zeraḥiah or R. Abraham came up with this explanation, he probably viewed it as a major accomplishment, even though it was off by one day.

ing the death of Joshua. When Meiri used the term *geonim* here, it is possible that he was misinformed, as it is likely that he did not have access to *Sefer Ha-Manhig*.[24] Alternatively and more likely, when Meiri used the term *geonim* here, he was not referring to the rabbinic authorities in Babylonia from the late 6th to early 11th centuries. Rather, he was referring to the rabbinic authorities in Europe in the generations just before him.[25] There are many other examples of Rishonim using the term *geonim* in a similar manner.[26] Unfortunately, Meiri's statement connecting *Lag Ba-Omer* with the *geonim* is usually taken too literally and has been widely quoted.[27]

It is also interesting that what originated as a weak suggestion by R. Zeraḥiah or R. Abraham is now referred to by Meiri as a *kabbalah* (tradition)!

Something similar occurred in the *Tur* (*OH* 493) of R. Jacob b. Asher (early 14th cent.). R. Jacob first discusses the customs of not marrying and not taking a haircut for the entire 49 days. He then adds: "*ve-yesh mistaprin me-Lag Ba-Omer va-eylekh she-omrim she-az pasku la-mut*." From the brief and conclusory manner in which the explanation is presented here, readers would never know that it was only a speculative suggestion. While Meiri likely did not have access to the *Sefer Ha-Manhig*, R. Jacob b. Asher certainly did.[28]

***

---

24 In his introduction to *Sefer Ha-Manhig*, Raphael lists the *Rishonim* who cited the *Sefer Ha-Manhig*. Meiri is not one of them. As Raphael points out, *Sefer Ha-Manhig* was not a well-circulated work.

25 This view is expressed by Dr. Shnayer Leiman in his May 2003 lecture on the origin of *Lag Ba-Omer* ("The Strange History of Lag Ba-Omer"), available on YU Torah.

26 See, e.g., E. Urbach, *Ba'alei Ha-Tosafot* (Jerusalem: Mossad Bialik, 1957), vol. 1, p. 446, giving the example of R. Isaac of Vienna (d. mid-13th cent.; author of *Or Zarua*), and S. Elitzur, *Lammah Tzammnu?* (Jerusalem: Ha-Iggud ha-Olami le-Maddaei ha-Yahadut, 2007), p. 115, giving the example of R. Tzidkiyah ha-Rofei (d. c. 1300, Italy; author of *Shibbolei Ha-Leket*). At least one time, Rambam used the term to indicate all post-Talmudic rabbis, including *Rishonim* in Spain and France. See Isadore Twersky, *Introduction to the Code of Maimonides* (*Mishneh Torah*) (New Haven: Yale Univ. Press, 1980), p. 66 (citing a passage from the introduction to the *Mishneh Torah*). See also Haym Soloveitchik, *Collected Essays, Volume II* (Oxford and Portland: Littman Library of Jewish Civilization, 2014), p. 40.

27 See, e.g., B. M. Lewin, *Otzar Ha-Geonim* (Haifa and Jerusalem: 1928–44), *Yevamot*, p. 140, *EJ* 10:1356 and 12:1387, and Rabbi S.Y. Zevin, *The Festivals in Halahah* (*Pesach, Omer, Shavuos*) (Brooklyn: Mesorah Publications, 1982), p. 218 (ArtScroll English edition). Meiri's work was not widely read until modern times.

28 See *Sefer Ha-Manhig*, intro., pp. 67-68.

There are many sources from the Geonic period in Palestine documenting that the 18th of *Iyyar* (*Lag Ba-Omer*) was observed there as a fast day commemorating the death of Joshua. These sources are collected by Shulamit Elitzur.[29] For example, this fast day is mentioned by the *paytannim* R. Eleazar Kallir (c. 600) and R. Phinehas (8th century).[30] It is mentioned in other sources from Palestine and Egypt in the subsequent centuries as well.[31] The existence of this fast day is strong evidence that the concept of *Lag Ba-Omer* as a festive day was not yet in existence in the Tannaitic, Amoraic or Geonic periods.[32]

In a recent article,[33] Elchanan Reiner made the suggestion that when the Jews in 13th century Europe[34] realized that the prohibition to marry for seven weeks was too hard, they chose the 18th of *Iyyar* as the day for the relaxation of the prohibition because it already was a special day, the day commemorating the death of Joshua. But it is very hard to accept this suggestion. The transformation of the day in the manner that Reiner has suggested seems extremely unlikely. Moreover, Reiner's explanation does not adequately explain why the permission to marry would continue after the 18th of *Iyyar*. It is probably merely a coincidence that *Lag Ba-Omer* falls out on the same date as the prior fast day.

***

---

29 See her *Lammah Tzammnu?*

30 See Elitzur, pp. 18-19 and 26.

31 See Elitzur, pp. 172 and 276–77. (Some of the later sources list the 26th of *Nissan* as the date, and not the 18th.)

32 Many speculative suggestions for an origin of *Lag Ba-Omer* in the Tannaitic or Amoraic periods have been offered. Some of these are summarized by Feldman at *EJ* 12:1388-89. See also Y. Tabory, *Moadei Yisrael be-Tekufat ha-Mishnah ve-ha-Talmud* (Jerusalem: Magnes Press, 1995), p. 145. (Regarding the latter, and a possible link between the 18th of *Iyyar* and the attempt to rebuild the Temple in the reign of the Roman emperor Julian in 363 C.E., see S. P. Brock, "A Letter Attributed to Cyril of Jerusalem on the Rebuilding of the Temple," *Bulletin of the School of Oriental and African Studies* 40 (1977), pp. 267–86.)

33 See above, n. 3.

34 Reiner erroneously focuses his analysis on the mindset of the Jews in the 13th century because he was not aware of the 12th-century reference to *Lag Ba-Omer* by R. Isaac b. Durbal. But Reiner does correctly point out that the explanation offered in *Sefer Ha-Manhig* was not based on any tradition, and was only an attempt to justify an already existing practice.

The work *Maaseh Ha-Geonim* records the custom of not marrying between *Pesaḥ* and *Shavuot* due to the death of the students of R. Akiva. It then continues:

> אבל ראיתי שנושאין לאחר הפסח עד ראש חדש אבל לאחר ראש חדש מתחילין שלא לישא.[35]

Maaseh Ha-Geonim is a work that derives almost entirely from *Maaseh Ha-Mekhiri*, a work of *halakhah* compiled by four brothers (sons of a R. Makhir) that is no longer extant and that reflects mainly the practices of Mainz, Worms and Speyer at the end of the 11th and beginning of the 12th centuries.[36] It seems from the above passage that the holiday of *Lag Ba-Omer* was not known to the authors of *Maaseh Ha-Mekhiri*.

Moreover, one wonders if those following this leniency initially followed the practice of not marrying for the entire 49 days. If they did, their leniency would seem to be a historically earlier relaxation of the 49-day prohibition than the one reflected by *Lag Ba-Omer*. But alternatively perhaps this community never adopted the prohibition of marrying for the entire seven weeks,[37] and at the outset adopted a prohibition starting only

---

35 *Ma'aseh Ha-Geonim*, ed. A. Epstein (Berlin, 1909), p. 51.

36 See A. Grossman, *Ḥakhmei Ashkenaz ha-Rishonim* (Jerusalem: Magnes, 1988), pp. 361–386. *Ma'aseh Ha-Mekhiri* was not the original name of this work. It was called this by one early source and it is how Grossman and other scholars typically refer to the work today.

37 Perhaps the earliest source for the tradition of mourning during the Omer, a Geonic responsum attributed to R. Natronai Gaon (included in *Otzar Ha-Geonim*, *Yevamot*, p. 141), claims that the mourning for the students of R. Akiva originated shortly after their deaths in the 2nd century C.E. (ומאותה שעה ואילך). But since there is no actual evidence for this mourning custom in the Tannaitic or Amoraic periods, the antiquity of the custom can be questioned. See, e.g., Silberman, p. 222, n. 5. The R. Natronai Gaon referred to could be the earlier R. Natronai (8th century) or the later (9th century). The latter is much more likely. Robert Brody believes that the attribution to R. Natronai is erroneous and that most likely the responsum was authored by R. Hai (d. 1038). See Brody, *Teshuvot R. Natronai bar Hilai Ga'on* (Jerusalem: Mekhon Ofek, 1994), p. 48, n. 90. See also Reiner, p. 204, n. 64.

A recently discovered manuscript records a similar responsum in the name of R. Sherira, the father of R. Hai. See E. Kupfer, *Teshuvot u-Pesakim* (Jerusalem: Mekitzei Nirdamim, 1973), p. 114. This responsum also seems to imply that the custom originated in the 2nd century C.E. (But the precise term ומאותה שעה ואילך is not found here.)

The absence among Yemenite Jewry of a custom of mourning in the Omer is some evidence that the custom is not ancient. But that absence may merely be the result of the custom not being mentioned in Rambam.

from *rosh ḥodesh Iyyar.* Moreover, their prohibition may have had nothing to do with the death of the students of R. Akiva.[38]

***

An interesting statement is found in *Sefer Minhag Tov,* an anonymous work composed in Italy sometime after the year 1273. The author writes that from *pesaḥ* to *atẓeret* it is a *minhag tov* to refrain from the following activities: getting a haircut, wearing new clothes, acquiring anything new, going to a bathhouse, and doing one's nails, all in honor of *he-ḥasidim ha-temimim ve-ha-yesharim* who gave up their lives in *kiddush Hashem* (the martyrs of the Crusades).[39] He then continues:

> אבל ביום ל"ג בעומר מותר בכל אילו **מפני הנס שהיה** ומל"ג ועד עצרת במקומו עומד לחומר.

It can be argued that his reference to a *nes* is a reference not to the cessation of the deaths of the students of R. Akiva, but to some other

---

Since Rambam does not mention the practice of mourning in the Omer, he also does not mention *Lag Ba-Omer.* More significantly, in *Hilkhot Ishut* 10:14, after listing the days on which marriages may not be solemnized (such as Sabbaths and festivals), Rambam explicitly codifies that one can marry any other day. This is pointed out by Feldman, p. 210. Rambam composed his *Mishneh Torah* in Egypt.

Scholars have also theorized that the original reason for the mourning in the Omer may not have had anything to do with the students of R. Akiva. See, e.g., the discussion at Silberman, pp. 221–32 and Feldman, pp. 201-02.

38 Sperber (*Minhagei Yisrael,* vol, 1, pp. 105–11) theorized that the practice of mourning in *Iyyar* arose because some of the most severe losses of Jewish communities at the time of the Crusades occurred in the five-week period commencing with *Iyyar.* But Sperber did not realize how early the practice of mourning in *Iyyar* can be documented, as he did not cite *Ma'aseh Ha-Geonim.* Nor did he cite *Sefer Ha-Pardes,* where the practice is also mentioned. See the edition of. H.L. Ehrenreich (Budapest: ha-Aḥim Katzburg, 1924), p. 264. I would like to thank Dr. Pinchas Roth for pointing out to me that the passage in *Sefer Ha-Pardes* was taken from *Ma'aseh Ha-Geonim.*

39 It seems that the observance of mourning in the Omer became more stringent, and probably more widespread, after the Crusades. See also the statement in *Asufot* below. In all but one of the Geonic sources, only two prohibitions are referred to: the prohibition of marriage, and a prohibition of working from evening until morning. (The Geonic source published by Kupfer specifies an additional prohibition, that of making new clothing. But it has been suggested that this prohibition was not found in the original responsum. See Sperber, vol. 1, p. 107, n. 26).

positive event that occurred on the 33rd day, perhaps related to the Crusades, that generated only a one-day leniency.[40] But more likely, the author is referring to the death of the students of R. Akiva. I suspect that once the leniency from the 33rd day onwards came to be understood as reflecting that the students of R. Akiva stopped dying on the 33rd day, a stringency that would have developed next in some communities was the limitation of the leniency to the 33rd day. I adopt this interpretation of *nes* in *Sefer Minhag Tov* because there is another source, from a student of R. Eleazar b. Judah of Worms,[41] that also seems to adopt only a one-day leniency and that explicitly takes the position that the 33rd day reflects the cessation of the death of the students of R. Akiva.[42]

Conclusions

In 1202, there is a clear reference by R. Abraham b. Nathan ha-Yarḥi to a custom in France and Provence of allowing marriages from the 33rd day onwards. The existence of the custom cannot be denied, even though the explanation for the custom suggested by R. Abraham or R. Zeraḥiah cannot be accepted. The custom is also referred to in annotations to *Maḥzor Vitry* that are most likely those of R. Isaac b. Durbal. He was writing a few decades earlier. Most probably, he was writing in France. Since it seems that the holiday of *Lag Ba-Omer* was not known to the authors of *Maaseh Ha-Mekhiri* in late 11th – early 12th century Germany, the origin of *Lag Ba-Omer* probably lies in 11th or 12th century France or Provence.[43]

---

40 The author's context is the martyrs of the Crusades. It can be argued that we would expect more of an explanation if he were switching to a different context. Also, *nes* is perhaps not the right word to describe a cessation of deaths. Silberman (p. 234) is one scholar who takes the approach that the cessation of the death of the students of R. Akiva is not what is being referred to here.

41 R. Eleazar died circa 1230.

42 See the manuscript *Asufot*, sec. 382, p. 66b (quoted in Z. Cohen, *Bein Pesaḥ la-Shavuot*, Jerusalem: Hal-Or, 2d. ed., 1985, p. 219):
מנהג הוא בזה המלכות שאין נושאין נשים בין פסח לעצרת ואין מקיזין דם עד ל"ג בעומר, לפי שהימים הן עלולין, שנפלה מגפה בתלמידי חכמים רבי עקיבא, כמה אלפים שמתו מן פסח עד ל"ג בעומר, וכולם מתו עבור שנאת חנם, ואותו היום נעצרה המגפה **ועשו אותו היום יום טוב**, ולפיכך נהגו להקיז **בל"ג בעומר**. ועוד נראה לי, מה שאין נושאין נשים **בין פסח לעצרת**, מפני צער הגזרות שנהרגו הקהילות בכל זה המלכות...

43 In the past two centuries, many scholars have made speculative suggestions for the origin of *Lag Ba-Omer*. Typically these suggestions are made without adequate consideration of the evidence as to when and where the holiday first arose. They do not even merit being discussed. Many of them are collected in Feldman,

Although we still do not know the origin of the leniency, we can make interesting observations about its evolution.

At some point in the Geonic period or prior,[44] a large segment of Jewry accepted upon itself a custom of not marrying for 49 days. Eventually, the need for a leniency must have been felt, and a leniency from the 33rd day onwards arose in a limited area, based on a justification that still remains unknown. An erroneous belief about the cessation of the death of the students of R. Akiva[45] then became attached to this leniency and this helped the leniency spread. The fact that the leniency made its way into the *Tur* and the manner of its presentation there also helped the leniency spread. From the brief and conclusory manner in which the explanation for the leniency is presented in the *Tur*, readers would never know that it was only a speculative suggestion. Its precariousness is evident in the language of R. Abraham b. Nathan ha-Yarḥi, but the *Tur* does not quote this language.[46] The need for the leniency also surely helped the leniency spread.

After the leniency erroneously became associated with the cessation of the death of the students of R. Akiva, the leniency was further re-defined. In some areas, the leniency was limited to one day, the day of the cessation.[47] In other areas, the areas subject to Sefardic decisors, the mathematical anomaly of 49-15 not equaling 33 was corrected. It was decided that the cessation of the death of the students of R. Akiva must have occurred on the 34th day and that only from this day onwards would the leniency be applied.[48]

EJ 12:1389 and Silberman, p. 236. As I have tried to show, the origin of *Lag Ba-Omer* seems to lie in 11th or 12th century France or Provence.

44 See above, n. 37.

45 The cessation of the death of the students of R. Akiva symbolizes, on some level, the continuation of Torah study.
In this context, it is interesting to observe (as pointed out to me by my friend Ariel Zell) that many Jewish holidays eventually develop Torah-related themes that were not part of the holiday originally. For example, Shavuot was perhaps originally only an agricultural holiday. Purim was expounded hermeneutically to represent a second acceptance of the Torah (see Shabbat 88a). *Yom Teruah* (Rosh Hashanah) was interpreted in the writings of Philo as the day commemorating the giving of the Torah, and a similar interpretation is found in the writings of R. Saadiah Gaon. Shemini Atzeret has taken on the additional theme of the completion of the yearly Torah-reading cycle.

46 Also, as mentioned earlier, Meiri referred to the weak suggestion by R. Zeraḥiah or R. Abraham as a *kabbalah* (tradition). But Meiri was not widely read.

47 See, e.g., *Asufot* and *Sefer Minhag Tov.*

48 See above, n. 22.

Finally, an accepted view had been that there was a widely embraced Jewish practice of not getting married for 49 days and that the leniency of *Lag Ba-Omer* was the earliest break with it. But it seems from *Maaseh Ha-Geonim* that this is not the case. The leniency recorded in *Maaseh Ha-Geonim*, assuming that it derives from *Maaseh Ha-Mekhiri*, would seem to date earlier than the original *Lag Ba-Omer* leniency. Also, the leniency recorded in *Maaseh Ha-Mekhiri* may have been one adopted in communities that followed a different paradigm and never accepted the full 49 days of mourning.

Endnote: A Proposal

In a famous passage in his commentary to *parashat Ḥukkat*, Samuel David Luzzatto remarked that Moses committed only one sin in this *parashah*, but the commentators heaped upon him at least 13 possible sins; each commentator invented a new sin. After this criticism, Luzzatto then went on to suggest his own new sin! In this spirit, I offer my own proposal to explain the origin of the period of leniency that begins with *Lag Ba-Omer*.[49]

The prohibition of marriage for the full 49 days must have been very difficult. Perhaps the following leniency developed in some parts of France or Provence: once a **majority** of the 49 days was observed, that would suffice. After the eight days of Passover, if a community would not conduct marriages from the 23rd of *Nissan* through the 17th of *Iyyar*, the community would have refrained from conducting marriages for 25 days. This would reflect observance of the majority of the original 49-day prohibition (assuming credit is given for refraining from conducting marriages on *Shabbat*). Perhaps this was the original leniency that was later given new meaning with the erroneous connection to the students of R Akiva.[50] In the most explicit early source, *Sefer Ha-Manhig*, the prohibition on marriages ceased on the 33rd day and was not just temporarily suspended for a day. This supports the idea that the solution is not tied to a

---

49 I am also inspired by Dr. Haym Soloveitchik, who, in a recent essay "The 'Third Yeshivah of Bavel' " suggested a creative and groundbreaking solution to a historical problem, without any hard evidence for his solution. Aware of the speculative nature of his solution, he decided to characterize it as only a "proposal." See his *Collected Essays, Volume II*, pp.150–201. I do the same here.

50 A somewhat similar suggestion was made by J. Derenbourg at *REJ* 29 (1894), p. 149. Derenbourg observed that *Lag Ba-Omer* was approximately the midpoint of the *Omer* mourning period and suggested that for this reason the prohibition was relaxed for this day. But since it is more likely that *Lag Ba-Omer* originally reflected the complete cessation of the marriage prohibition (as evidenced by *Sefer Ha-Manhig*), Derenbourg's explanation does not fit.

particular historical event that occurred around the 33rd day. Also, the name of the holiday is not tied to a particular historical event. This also supports the idea that what we are looking for is some type of mathematical/calendrical basis for a leniency, and not a historical event.

ꙮ

Christian-Hebraism in England: William Wotten and the First Translation of the Mishnah into English[1]

By: MARVIN J. HELLER

> *And if we consider that the Observations of this Fourth Commandment in the Decalogue, was guarded in the Pentateuch by more secondary Laws, than any other single Command, (if you will except the Prohibition of worshipping strange Gods,) it will not be unpleasant in so curious a Man as your self, to observe what Contrivances these Wise Men had to make it in very many Instances of none Effect, by their Traditions. For if these Constitutions be nicely examin'd, there are none of them but what have something which may be plausibly alledged in their Justification.*
>
> (William Wotton, Preface *Shabbat and Eruvin*)

Christian-Hebraism, the serious gentile scholarship of Jewish sources, is an unusual flower, with both sweet and bitter buds. Its primary flowering was not of long duration, flourishing for only a few centuries. The lengthier Christian study of Jewish texts has a convoluted history, ranging from the reading of Hebrew books for the purpose of refuting the tenets of Judaism, to investigation of those same works by Christian-Hebraists to better understand their religion's roots. At times, Christian review of Jewish books, and perhaps it is unfair to attribute this to Hebraists, resulted in attacks, vicious and at times often physical, that is, the burning of Jewish books. In contrast, many Christian scholars produced bilingual Latin and Hebrew works of merit. Christian-Hebraism has been well studied

---

1 I would like to thank Eli Genauer for reading this paper and for his suggestions and my son-in-law R. Moshe Tepfer for his assistance and research in the National Library of Israel. Illustrations for *Shabbat and Eruvin* are Courtesy of the National Library of Israel.

Marvin J. Heller writes books and articles on Hebrew printing and bibliography. His *Printing the Talmud: A History of the Individual Treatises Printed from 1700 to 1750* (Brill, Leiden, 1999) and *The Sixteenth Century Hebrew Book: An Abridged Thesaurus* (Brill, Leiden, 2004) were, respectively, recipients of the 1999 and 2004 Research and Special Libraries Division Award of the Association of Jewish Libraries for Bibliography.

and is outside the scope of this work.[2] What has generally received less attention are the studies of early Hebraists in England, particularly as they relate to non-biblical Hebrew works.

This article will begin with a brief overview of Christian-Hebraism and translations of the Mishnah, primarily into Latin, in the seventeenth and early eighteenth centuries, followed by a brief discussion of such works in England; then the life and background of William Wotton, whose translation of two tractates of the Mishnah is our subject; next his translation of those tractates; concluding with a brief summary.

---

2 To note a brief number of the works addressing the activities of Christian Hebraism see Allison P. Coudert and Jeffrey S. Shoulson, Editors, *Hebraica Veritas?: Christian Hebraists and the Study of Judaism in Early Modern Europe* (Philadelphia, 2004); Jerome Friedman, *The Most Ancient Testimony: Sixteenth-Century Christian-Hebraica in the Age of Renaissance Nostalgia* (Athens, Ohio, 1983); Aaron L. Katchen, "Christian Hebraism from the Renaissance to the Enlightenment," *Christian Hebraism: The Study of Jewish Culture by Christian Scholars in Medieval and Modern Times.* Proceedings of a colloquium and catalogue of an exhibition arranged by the Judaica Department of the Harvard College Library on the occasion of Harvard's 350th anniversary celebration. May 5, 1986. Arranged and Prepared by Charles Berlin and Aaron L. Katchen (Cambridge, Mass., 1986); and Frank E. Manuel, *The Broken Staff: Judaism Through Christian Eyes* (Cambridge, Mass., 1992). In addition, there are several studies about particular Christian-Hebraists. Concerning the persecution of Hebrew books, particularly the Talmud in the medieval period, see Robert Chazan, "Christian Condemnation, Censorship, and Exploitation of the Talmud," in *Printing the Talmud: From Bomberg to Schottenstein*, eds. Sharon Lieberman Mintz and Gabriel M. Goldstein (New York: Yeshiva Univ. Museum, 2005), pp. 53–59; *idem.*, *Medieval Jewry In Northern France* (Baltimore, 1973); Solomon Grayzel, *The Church and the Jews in the XIIIth Century* (New York, 1966); *idem.*, "Popes, Jews, and Inquisition," In *Essays on the Occasion of the Seventieth Anniversary of Dropsie University* (Philadelphia, 1979), pp. 151–85; Marvin J. Heller, *Printing the Talmud: A History of the Earliest Printed Editions of the Talmud* (Brooklyn, 1992), pp. 201–15; and Judah M. Rosenthal, "The Talmud on Trial," *Jewish Quarterly Review*, XLVII (1956), pp. 58–76, 145–69. Concerning the burning and censorship of the Talmud in the sixteenth century see Heller, *Printing the Talmud*, pp. 217-28; Kenneth R. Stow, "The Burning of the Talmud in 1553," *Bibliotheque d'Humanisme et Renaissance*, XXXIV (1972), pp. 435–59; Avraham Yaari, "Burning the Talmud in Italy" in *Studies in Hebrew Booklore* (Jerusalem, 1958), pp. 198–234 [Hebrew] and for censorship of the Talmud see William Popper, *The Censorship of Hebrew Books* (reprint New York, 1968) and Amnon Raz-Krakotzkin, *The Censor, the Editor, and the Text: The Catholic Church and the Shaping of the Jewish Canon in the Sixteenth Century* (Philadelphia, 2007).

I

Protestants evinced considerable interest in the study of the Hebrew Bible (Old Testament). As a result, books were written, grammars, lexicographic works, and translations of Hebrew texts, among them translations of Mishnaic tractates, were printed with commentaries. Hebrew was considered to be of significance to students of theology and related texts were therefore of importance.[3] Fuks and Fuks-Mansfeld note that when Hebrew texts were published, however, it was done with the explicit understanding that the university faculty members who prepared these works did so to "repudiate the fallacies of Jewish law." Examples of prominent professors of Hebrew unambiguously so informed by the theological faculties of their universities are Constantin L'Empereur (1619–48) at Leiden and Johannes Leusden (1653–99) at Leusden.[4] A somewhat more sanguine view is expressed by Aaron L. Katchen who writes that the basic works of rabbinic Judaism, Mishnah and Talmud, got a new hearing. Despite still being the subject of abuse, new editions of the Mishnah, with extracts of the Talmud, "often served to dispel illusions. Most often, to be sure, these works were produced for the greater glory of the Christian Republic of Letters.... However there was also a blunting of prejudice that sometimes came to the fore in such studies. For these studies reflect a mixture of Christian Purposes and a new vision of either rationalism or Enlightenment."[5]

Elisheva Carlebach too observes that "Some of the Christian Talmudists were animated by polemical anti-Jewish motives." She cites Johannes Leusden as an example for whom "Jewish adherence to the Talmud

---

3 Christian-Hebraism was not only a seventeenth- and eighteenth-century phenomenon, but had considerable earlier antecedents. Those scholars who expressed an interest in rabbinic subjects, for whatever reason, did not prepare translations of the Talmud. Concerning Christian-Hebraism in the sixteenth century, see Friedman; and Cecil Roth, *The Jews in the Renaissance* (New York, 1959), pp. 137–64. Friedman, pp. 1-2, notes the controversial nature of Hebrew studies, for example, the Reuchlin-Dominican controversy, the Luther-Sabbatarian conflict, as well as the battles between the Hebraists of Basle and those of Wittenberg as to the proper use of Jewish sources and the optimum approach to rabbinic material. Apart from Hebraists with an interest in Hebrew texts were Christian scholars and clergymen who studied biblical Hebrew, for example, those who translated the Bible into English, most notably the King James Bible (1611) and its predecessors.

4 L. Fuks and R. G. Fuks-Mansfeld, *Hebrew Typography in the Northern Netherlands 1585–1815* I (Leiden, 1984–87), p. 14.

5 Katchen, p. 11.

proved that Jews were in a perpetual state of disobedience to God, having abandoned the Bible for the Talmud." Carlebach, however, also observes that Aramaic lexicons and grammars, particularly from the Buxtorfs, "provided welcome tools for serious students of Talmud."[6] Christian interests in the Talmud were varied; their interest in the developing new relationship of states and their legal systems is exemplified by L'Empereur's translation of *Bava Kamma* (Leiden, 1637), dealing with civil law, whereas others, such as John Lightfoot, searched the Talmud for insight into the Christian Bible, and Hugo Grotius cited the Talmud as proof that God had bestowed laws applicable to mankind in addition to those specifically applicable to Jews, viewing the Talmud as a natural evolution of biblical law for contemporary society.

The study of Jewish sources centered primarily on Bible and grammar. Nevertheless, a number of Hebraists addressed rabbinic texts, translating several tractates of the Mishnah into Latin. We have already noted Constantin L'Empereur and Johannes Leusden. Among the many others are such scholars as Johannes Cocceius Coccejus (1603–69), *Sanhedrin et Maccoth* (Amsterdam, 1629); Johann Christof Wagenseil (1633–1705), *Sota: Hoc est: liber mischnicus de uxore adulterii suspecta* (Altdorf, 1674); Gustavo Peringero (Gustav von Lilienbad Peringer, 1651–1705), *Duo Codices Talmudici Avoda Sara et Tamid…* (Altdorf, 1690); and Wilhelm Surenhuis (Surenhuys, Surenhuysen, Gulielmus Surenhusius, 1698–1703), *Sive Legum Mischnicarum, Liber qui inscribitur* (Amsterdam, 1698–1703), to name but a few.

That there were Christian-Hebraists at this time in England is not in dispute. What is little known is that there were such Hebraists in the medieval period. Judith Olszowy-Schlanger informs of a unique Hebrew-Latin–Old French dictionary written in 13th-century England by Christian scholars. She describes it as an exceptional work, one that did not follow the patristic tradition of Christian Hebraism but instead utilized Jewish rabbinic and medieval sources to understand the text of the Hebrew Bible. She notes that 26 bilingual Hebrew-Latin manuscripts are known today, produced in England from the mid-12th through the late 13th centuries, explicitly for the use of Christian-Hebraists. There is substantial evidence that these English Christian scholars possessed and studied Hebrew books, that is, the Bible, Rashi, and grammars. This is in contrast to the low opinion of modern historiography as to the knowledge of the Hebrew language and grammar of medieval Christian scholars, exemplified by the remark by Roger Bacon (c. 1214–1294) in his *Opus Tertium* that, among his contemporaries, "fewer than four of which knew Hebrew grammar

---

6 Elisheva Carlebach, "The Status of the Talmud in Early Modern Europe" in *Printing the Talmud: From Bomberg to Schottenstein*, pp. 85-86.

well enough to teach it." Olszowy-Schlanger writes that it is something of an irony that most of the Christian scholars who did master the Hebrew language and were able to study Hebrew texts are not known to us by name, while Roger Bacon "... and his Franciscan milieu came to be acclaimed 'the Christian Hebraists of the Middle Ages' *par excellence*, despite the lack of evidence that they achieved any proficiency in Hebrew."[7]

That there were a fair number of Hebraists in England in the seventeenth century is also well known.[8] Of interest is Hugh Broughton (1549–1612), who not only mastered Hebrew but also studied Jewish classical works, including *Seder Olam*, adopting that title for one of his own chronological works; among his titles is *The Familie of David* (*Familia Davidis*, Amsterdam, 1605), a treatise on the lineage of King David printed in bilingual Hebrew-English and Hebrew-Latin editions.

The first published translation of a Mishnah in London, this of *Yoma* into Latin, *Joma. Codex Talmudicus, in quo agitur de sacrificiis . . .* (London, 1648) with annotations, was by Robert Sheringham (1602–78). It is one of only a few books with Hebrew letters to be printed in that period in London, then devoid of Jews. Sheringham was a proctor of Cambridge

---

7 Judith Olszowy-Schlanger, "A School of Christian Hebraists in Thirteenth Century England: a Unique Hebrew-Latin-French and English Dictionary and its Sources," *European Journal of Jewish Studies* 1:2 (Leiden, 2008) pp. 249–51. Also see Raphael Loewe, "The Mediaeval Christian Hebraists of England: Herbert of Bosham and Earlier Scholars" *Transactions of The Jewish Historical Society of England* 17 (1951-52), pp. 225–49; *idem.*, "the Mediaeval Christian Hebraists of England: The *Superscriptio Lincolniensis*" *Hebrew Union College Annual*, 28 (1957), pp. 205–252; and C. Phillip E. Northaft, "Robert of Leicester's treatise on the Hebrew *computus* and the study of Jewish knowledge in medieval England," *Jewish Historical Studies* 45, pp. 63–78.

8 The interest in Jewish studies can be appreciated from a list of Christian-Hebraists of note in London and Cambridge in the *Jewish Encyclopedia* in the seventeenth and eighteenth centuries, with the caveat that there were certainly many more not worthy of mention, this despite the absence of a formal Jewish community. Those worthy of mention are: London: William Bedwell (1561–1632), John Dove (c. 1746), John Gill (1697–1771), Hilaric Prache (b. 1614– 1679), Thomas Smith (b. 1638–1710), William Wotton, (1666–1720), Elisabeth Tanfeld (d. 1639), Paulus Fagius (Buchlin) (1504–49), W. H. Lowe, Henry More, (1614–1687), Rob. Sheringham (1602–1678, Cambridge), and Franc Taylord. 1660). Not really germane to our subject but of interest is that inserted into unsold copies of the famed London Polyglot Bible (1653–57) in 1660 were two dedications, one to Oliver Cromwell, the other to Charles II, inserted by Royalist scholars "marooned in Cromwell's London or revolutionary Oxford" (Peter N. Miller, "The 'Antiquarianization' of Biblical Scholarship and the London Polyglot Bible (1653–57)," *Journal of the History of Ideas* (2001), pp. 469-70.

University, but, due to his adherence to the royalist cause, was ejected from his fellowship, at Caius, soon after. He retired to London, and then to Holland, where he instructed in Hebrew and Arabic at Rotterdam and in other towns. On the restoration of the monarchy in 1660, Sheringham was restored to his fellowship, thereafter leading a studious and retired life, being "esteemed 'a most excellent linguist, as also admirably well versed in the original antiquities of the English nation.'"[9] *Joma* was preceded by Robert Wakefeld's *Oratio de laudibus et utilitate trium linguarum Arabice Chaldaice et Hebraice* (1524), a woodblock book with a few Hebrew words, and, in 1643, the first book with a significant amount of Hebrew letters, a Psalms with Hebrew, Greek, Latin, and English.[10]

Two other translations of Mishnayot in England at this time, these by Jews, need to be noted. The first was prepared by R. Jacob ben Joseph Abendana (1630–85), *ḥakham* of the Spanish and Portuguese synagogue in London, who published, together with his brother Isaac, R. Solomon ibn Melekh's Bible commentary, *Mikhlol Yofi*, with a super-commentary, *Lekket Shikḥah* (1660-61) with approbations from Christian-Hebraists, among them Johannes Buxtorf. Abendana, under commission from Christian-Hebraists, translated the Mishnah into Spanish (c. 1660). It was later used by several Christian-Hebraists, among them William Surenhusius. Never published, it is no longer extant. R. Isaac Abendana translated the Mishnah into Latin for the Cambridge scholars between 1662 and 1675. Also never published, the manuscript is now in the University Library of Cambridge.[11]

---

9 Thompson Cooper, "Sheringham, Robert" *Dictionary of National Biography*, (London: Smith, Elder, & co., 1885–1900), <http://en.wikisource.org/wiki /Sheringham,_Robert_%28DNB00%29>.

10 Freimann, Gazetteer, p. 46; Cecil Roth, *Magna Bibliotheca Anglo-Judaica; a Bibliographical Guide to Anglo-Jewish History* (London, 1937), p. 361 no. 2. Roth, in that work, in the section on Christian Hebrew Scholarship (B 14), representing works "in the Mocatta Library with a few others of outstanding importance," records 113 titles from 1558 through 1837 under that heading, 67 of them through 1749. Wotten is not represented in the listing; Isaac BenJacob, *Otzar ha-Sefarim* (Vilna, 1880), p. 574 no. 459, records a 1596 *Shir al ha-Otiyot* by R. Sa'adiah ben Joseph (Gaon?) [Hebrew]. Additional works of possible Jewish interest but without Hebrew were printed, such as an English translation of the *Travels of Benjamin of Tudela* (1625), but Hebrew printing in London by and for Jews begins only in the first decade of the eighteenth century.

11 Harm den Boer, "Abendana, Jacob ben Joseph," *Encyclopaedia Judaica* (*EJ*). Ed. Michael Berenbaum and Fred Skolnik, I (Detroit, 2007), 251; Cecil Roth, "Abendana, Isaac," *EJ* I, 250. Concerning this translation see J.W. Wesselius, "'I

II

William Wotten (1666–1727) and his *Shabbat and Eruvin*, addressed here, gives us insight into the background and perspective of a Christian-Hebraist, what kind of person he was, and, it being in English rather than in Latin as are almost all of the other contemporary translations of Mishnayot, is more accessible to most readers of this article. Wotton, an erudite person of considerable accomplishments, indeed a prodigy and a polymath, has been described by Alexander Chalmers as "an English divine of uncommon parts and learning . . . and well skilled in Oriental Languages." In a letter dated September 16, 1671, by Sir Philip Skippon to Mr. John Ray, we read about Wotten's background,

> I shall somewhat surprise you with what I have seen in a little boy, William Wotton, five years old the last month, the son of Mr. Wotton, minister of this parish, who hath instructed his child within the last three quarters of a year in the reading the Latin, Greek, and Hebrew languages, which he can read almost as well as English; and that tongue he could read at four years and three months old as well as most lads of twice his age.[12]

Chalmers continues, concerning Wotten's memory, that he is "never forgetting anything."[13] Wotton was admitted to Catherine Hall, Cambridge several months prior to his tenth birthday, where the masters of the college praised his learning and skill in languages. He received his B. A. when twelve and five months, his M. A. in 1683, and commenced his Bachelor of Divinity in 1691. In the same year, Wotton received the sinecure of Llandrillo in Denbigshire. He was appointed curate in Brimpton on September 20, 1686, nominated by Richard Worrell, Vicar of the same and afterwards as Vicar, *ad Vicariam perpetuamin*, in Lacock from October

---

don't know whether he will stay for long': Isaac Abendana's early years in England and his Latin translation of the Mishnah," *Studia Rosenthaliana*, 22:2 (1988) pp. 85–96. Also see David S. Katz, "The Abendana Brothers and the Christian Hebraists of Seventeenth-Century England," *Journal of Ecclesiastical Hebrew* 40:1 (1989), pp. 28–52.

12 Alexander Chalmers, *The General Biographical Dictionary*: Containing an Historical and Critical Account of the Lives and Writings of the Most Eminent Persons in Every Nation, Particularly the British and Irish, from the Earliest Accounts to the Present Time XXXII (London, 1817), p. 306. Wotton's skill as a linguist is also noted in George Godfrey Cunningham's *A History of England in the Lives of Englishmen* 4 (London, 1853), pp. 241, where it states, "he died in 1726, leaving behind him no competitor, perhaps, in variety of acquisitions as a linguist."

13 Chalmers, p. 310.

3, 1693.[14] Among Wotton's positions and achievements was that he was a scholar of St. John's College, Cambridge, a Fellow of the Royal Society, and a prebend of Salisbury.

In 1694, Wotton published *Reflections upon Ancient and Modern Learning*, addressing the branches of literature, arts, and sciences, as extended by both ancients and Moderns. It is a defense of the moderns, for which Jonathan Swift attacked and satirized Wotton in his *Tale of a Tub* and *Battle of the Books* (1704).[15] Wotton described *Tale of a Tub* as having "a good deal of wild wit" but on the whole being "the profanest piece of ribaldry" since Rabelais. Among Wotton's other titles is a *History of Rome* (1701), and he is also remembered for his collection and translation of Welsh works. In 1714, Wotton relocated to Carmarthen, Wales, where he learned to speak and write Welsh, writing *Legis Wallicae*, largely printed in 1727, the finished work published posthumously in 1730 by his son-in-law.[16]

Given the above, much was expected of Wotton. His personal life, however, and the circumstances that resulted in relocations and Wotton's not fully achieving the positions and successes anticipated of him, can be attributed to his personal failings, having feet of clay. The antiquary Abraham de la Pryme described Wotton in his diary as "a most excellent preacher, but a drunken whoring soul." Such comments were repeated over the years, William Cole, rector of a neighboring parish, writing that Wotton was "known in the learned World for his ingenious writings in the country where he inhabited for his Levities and Imprudencies." [17]

While all of this reflects poorly on his personal life it does not detract from his many intellectual and literary accomplishments, among them the translation of tractates *Shabbat* and *Eruvin*. Indeed, while living in Carmarthen, and having become reformed, now a model clergyman, visiting the sick and resuming his studies, Wotton undertook this work, in 1714, to give young divinity students a basic understanding of Jewish learning, in order to "show of what authority it was and what use it might be made of within Christian teaching."[18]

---

14 *CCEd, the Clergy of the Church of England database*, <http://db.theclergydatabase.org.uk/jsp/search/index.jsp>.

15 Berlin and Katchen, *Christian Hebraism*, p. 55 no. 108.

16 David Stoker, "William Wotton's exile and redemption: an account of the genesis and publication of *Leges Wallicae*" *Y Llyfr yng Nghymru/Welsh Book Studies,* 7 (2006), pp. 7–106, a detailed work on *Legis Wallicae*, as the book is known, with considerable detail on Wotton's life.

17 Quoted in Stoker, p. 12.

18 Stoker, p. 24.

III

We turn now to that second translation of Mishnayot with a London imprint, the very first in English, this the edition of *Shabbat and Eruvin:... Translated into English, with Annotations* by W. Wotton. *Shabbat and Eruvin* is part two of a two-volume work entitled *Miscellaneous Discourses relating to the traditions and usages of the Scribes and Pharisees...* (1718). Part one, *Texts relating to the religious observation of one day in seven, with annotations*, begins with a dedication to William, Lord Archbishop of Canterbury, followed by a lengthy preface ([i], ii-l) in which Wotton relates how he came to write this work. Four years previously a "very ingenious Gentleman, whose Curiosity had led him to make Enquiries into things not relating to his Profession (which is the Law of the *England*), had a long discourse with me concerning the Reasons of Christians not observing the Sabbath which is enjoined by the fourth Commandment." This gentleman remarked that whereas the Catholic Church "unanimously" denied the *Mosaic Sabbath*, in their Church, regularly, every Sunday, "the *Mosaic Sabbath* is expressly commanded to be remembered."

Wotton set about responding to his friend, resolving to do so as soon as he had leisure, reviewing all the pertinent texts, resulting in this work. The text of the first volume is, as the title informs, discourses on the nature, authority, and usefulness of the Mishnah; the contents of all the titles of the Mishnah; the recital of the Shema, phylacteries, schedules of gates and door-posts; and text relating to the religious observance of one day in seven.

It is the second volume ([16], [1] folded leaf, 279, [25] pp.), comprised of the Hebrew and the English translation of the Mishnah of two tractates, that is of interest to us. The text of the title page begins,

SHABBATH
AND
ERUVIN
Two Titles of the
MISNA or **CODE**
Of the
Traditional Laws,
Which were observed by the
Scribes and Pharisees...

...

Printed by *W. Bowyer*, for T. Goodwin at the Queens-Head against St. *Dunstan's Church* in Fleetstreet. 1718.[19]

The volume begins with a dedication, also the preface, to Thomas Kilpin of the Middle Temple, Esq., indicative of Wotton's positive view towards his subject matter and its rabbinic authors. There are critical remarks about Judaism, to be expected, consistent with Wotton's beliefs and position as a Protestant clergyman. He writes, "You will wonder possibly, Sir, that I should prefix your Name to two Hebrew Tracts, when your Studies have all along lain in so different a Road. But when you see that they are Decrees and Constitutions of eminent Lawyers, upon a Subject of no less Importance than one of the Ten Commandments, your Wonder, I hope, will cease. . . . They are part of the Text of the Talmud, which was the true authentic Law of the Pharisees . . ." He refers to the authors as those inspired Writers and notes that

> You will see there is an incredible Minuteness in Things seemingly the most trivial, which frequently appears very impertinent; and yet you will also observe that these Masters had constant Rules by which they proceeded, which were subservient still to one main End, which was to teach Men how to evade the Law, when they seemed most solicitous to observe it. . . . For if these Constitutions be nicely examin'd, there are none of them but what have something which may be plausibly alledged in their Justification.
>
> Whether the Jews, that live among us in these Western Parts of Europe, are pleased to see that these their Mysteries have been laid open to Christians, in this and the last Age, I know not. They will by this means, however, appear not to have been such a weak, stupid Nation, as learned Men have described them to be. Their Blindness has not been intellectual, but moral. Their Hearts have been harden'd, and not their Heads....[20]

---

19 William Bowyer the elder (1663–1737) was a leading printer in late seventeenth, early eighteenth century England. He was nominated as one of the twenty printers allowed by the Star Chamber. His son, also a William Bowyer (1699–1777), worked together with his father. The Bowyer press was considered among the most learned of contemporary presses. Their activities are recorded in a four-volume work, The Bowyer Ledgers, ed. Keith Maslen and John Lancaster (London, 1991), p. xxvi (*Encyclopedia Britannica*, 1911: <http://www.studylight.org/encyclopedias/bri/view.cgi?n=34709&search=bowyer#bowyer>).

20 The observant reader will have noted that, in contrast to modern English usage, all nouns are capitalized in Wotton's text, for example, "the poor **M**an reaches forth his **H**and into the **H**ouse" (emphasis added). David Crystal (*The Cambridge Encyclopedia of the English Language*, 1996, p. 67) explains that from the beginning

Wotton observes a difficulty under which he has labored is that "no Christian has commented upon these titles, that I have seen" and that the Jewish commentators are obscure because they wrote for a Jewish readership, assuming a knowledgeable public, but thereby unfamiliar to strangers. Wotton's remark that "no Christian has commented upon these titles, that I have seen" is surprising, given, as noted above, the attention of Christian-Hebraists in the late sixteenth and early seventeenth centuries to rabbinic works. It is reported that in Wales despite having a "great deal of leisure, he had a few books; but being of too active a genius to be idle, he drew up at the request of Brown Willis Esq.; who afterwards published them, the memoirs of the Cathedral Church of St. David in 1717, and of Landaff in 1719; and here he wrote his *Miscellaneous Discourses* . . ."[21]

Wotton, fluent in Latin, the language of the translations, and a prodigious scholar, was certainly aware of the European Hebraists' translations of and commentaries on several tractates of Mishnayot; indeed, even in Wales, distant from the centers of English Hebraists, he is known to have made use of the works of several of them, such as William Guise and William Surenhusius, even recording them and others in an appendix to the volume. In addition, he particularly mentions Edward Pococke, John Lightfoote, and John Seldon, referring to them in the text, thereby, as Ruderman remarks, "situating himself in a living tradition of Christian scholars, proudly regarding his own scholarship a direct continuation of all of theirs."[22] Wotton's remarks then most likely are addressed to these particular tractates only and the subject of the Jewish observance of the Sabbath, this despite the existence of Latin translations of both *Shabbat* and *Eruvin* by Sebastian Schmidt (Leipzig, 1661), for how else can they be understood?

---

of the eighteenth century, under Continental influence, all nouns considered important were capitalized, a practice extended to encompass all or most nouns. He suggests that it was done either for aesthetic reasons or "perhaps because printers were uncertain about which nouns to capitalize, and so capitalized them all." By the end of the 18th century grammarians were displeased by the lack of order and discipline so that the nouns that took a capital were dramatically reduced.

21 Bayle, Pierre, *A General Dictionary, Historical and Critical: in Which a New and Accurate TRANSLATION of that of the Celebrated MR. BAYLE*..., By the Reverend Mr. John Peter Bernard; the Reverend Mr. Thomas Birch; Mr. John Lockman; and other hands, vol. x (London, 1746), p. 206.

22 David B. Ruderman, "the Study of the Mishnah and the Quest for Christian Identity in Early Eighteenth-Century England: Completing a Narrative Initiated by Richard Popkin" in *The Legacies of Richard Popkin (International Archives of the History of Ideas Archives internationales d'histoire des idées)*, editor Jeremy D. Popkin (Dordrecht, The Netherlands: Springer, 2008), p. 137.

Towards the conclusion of the preface, Wotton expresses a positive view of rabbinic activity, noting the rationality of Mishnah, for "*I have endeavor'd to assign the Grounds upon which these Masters went in all these Constitutions; and where they are rational, as many of them are, I have given my Judgment in their Favor. . . .*"

There are two pages of foldouts illustrating various Sabbath activities, described in a section entitled "an Explication of the Two Figures." An example of this text is,

TAB. I

Fig. V. Here are two Balconies in the same house, with the Street underneath. One Man in one Balcony holds forth a Stick to another Man in the Second, who reaches out his Hand to take it from him. *Shabbath*, XI. 2.

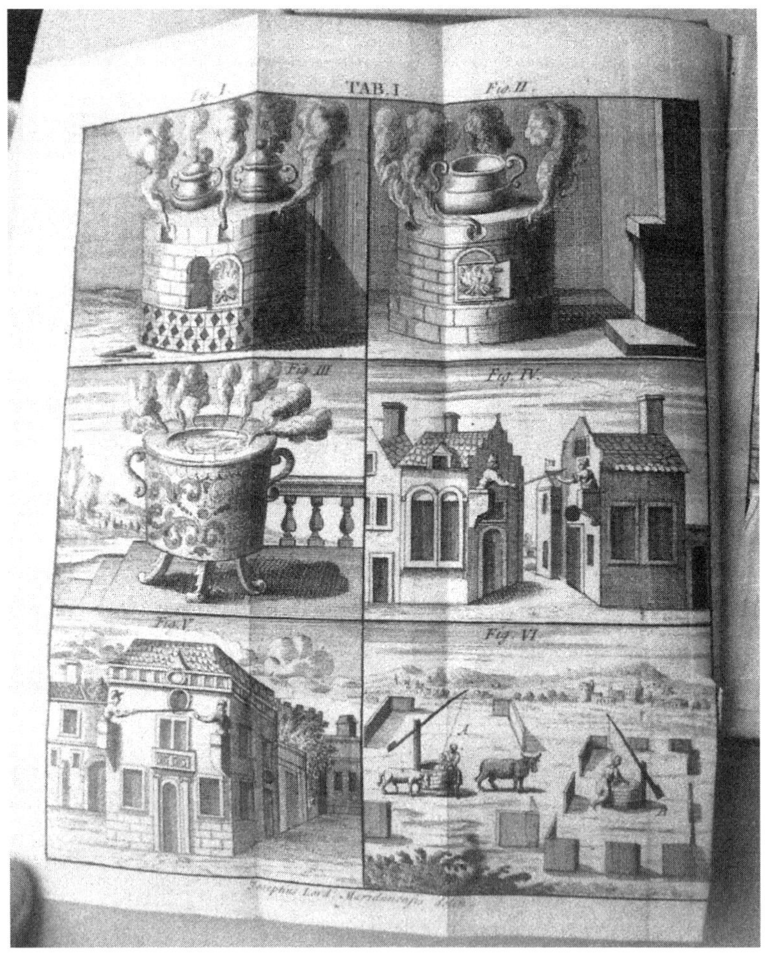

TAB. II

Fig. V. We have here a House broken through to one of its Corners, by which means part of the Wall on both Sides is fallen down. This Breach then could not be mistaken for a Door. *Eruvin*, IX. 3

Each volume begins with a brief description of the contents of the various chapters. For example, the first chapter of Shabbat is described as:

> REMOVALS, what, and how many Eighteen Constitutions chiefly Sabbatical, which were decided according to the Shammaeans. Other Constitutions wherein the Houses of Shammai and Hillel differ'd. Of giving Cloths to Dyers, Fullers and other Artificers, on the Sabbath Eve, when the Work could not be finished that Day. Of employing Gentiles to work for one on the Sabbath. Of baking and roasting the Evening before. Of Dressing the Paschal Lamb on the Sabbath Eve.

The text follows, in parallel Hebrew and English columns, accompanied by Wotton's extensive commentary. Below is Wotton's translation of the first Mishnah in *Shabbat* followed by a modern translation of the same text, that of Mesorah Publications (ArtScroll).

> **Wotton**
> Removals upon the Sabbath-Day are two, which within [a Place] are four; and two [likewise] which without [a Place] are four. How so: If a poor Man stands without, and the Master of the House within; the poor Man reaches forth his Hand into the House, and puts something into the Hand of the Master of the House, Or takes something out of his Hand, and carries it away; the poor Man [then] is guilty, and the Master free. If the Master puts his Hand out of the House, and gives [something] to the poor Man, or takes something from him, and draws his Hand in again; he is guilty, and the poor Man is free. If a poor Man reaches his Hand into a House, and the Master takes something out of it, or puts something into it, and the poor Man then goes off, they are both free. If the Master puts His Hand out, and the poor Man takes [something] out of his Hand, or puts any thing into it, and the Master draws his Hand in again, they are both free.

> **Mesorah Publications (ArtScroll)**
> The [types of] transfers on the Sabbath are two which are [in reality] four within, and two which are [in reality] four outside.
> How is this so? The poor man is standing outside, and the householder inside: If the poor man extended his hand inside and placed [an object] into the householder's hand, or if he took [an object] from it and brought [that object] out – the poor man is liable and the householder is exempt;

> if the householder extended his hand outside and placed [an object] into the poor man's hand, or if he took [an object] out of it and brought the [that object] in – the householder is liable and the poor man is exempt;
> if the poor man extended his hand inside and the householder took [an object] from it, or placed [an object] into it and he [the poor man] brought [that object] out – both are exempt;
> if the householder extended his hand outside and the poor man took [an object] from it, or placed [an object] into it and he [the householder] brought [that object] in – both are exempt.[23] [24]

Wotton's translation of the Mishnah is accompanied by a detailed commentary. In preparing it he utilized Jewish sources, referencing such authorities as Moses Maimonides (Rambam, c. 1135–1204) and Obadiah

---

23 *Mishnayot Seder Mo'ed 'im Perush Yad Avraham* (Brooklyn, 1979). Another example of the variations in the translation of this Mishnah can be seen from Soncino Publications, which states, "The carryings out of the Sabbath are two which are four within, and two which are four without. How so? The poor man stands without and the master of the house within: [i] if the poor man stretches his hand within and places [an article] into the hand of the master of the house, or [ii] if he takes [an article] from it and carries it out, the poor man is liable, and the master of the house is exempt. [again] [i] if the master of the house stretches his hand without and places [an object] in the poor man's hand, or [ii] takes [an object] there from and carries it in, the master is liable, while the poor man is exempt. [iii] if the poor man stretches his hand within and the master takes [an object] from it, or places [an object] therein and he carries it out, both are exempt; [iv] if the master stretches his hand without and the poor man takes [an object] from it, or places [an article] therein and he carries it inside, both are exempt" (Soncino Talmud, 1973).

24 A comparison of the first line of several translations of the same Mishnah (Shabbat 6:6) over time is provided at <http://onthemainline.blogspot.com/search?q=wotton>. The entries are: **1718**. Women may go out with a Piece of Money ty'd to a Sore. (Wotton); **1843**. Women may go out with a coin fastened on a swelling in their feet. (Raphall & de Sola); **1878**. A woman may go out with a coin on a sore foot. (Barclay); **1896**. Women may go out with a coin fastened to a swelling on their feet. (Rodkinson); **1927**. One may go out [on the Sabbath] with a sela on a corn. (Oesterley); **1933**. They may go out with the sela that is put on a bunion. (Danby); **1935ish**. She may go forth with the sela on a zinith [callus]. (Soncino); **1963**. A woman may go out with a sela upon a corn. (Blackman); **1982**. She may go out with the sela that is on the wound [on the sole of her foot]. (Artscroll); **1991**. She goes out with a sela coin on a bunion. (Neusner); **1996. [A woman] may go out** on the Sabbath **with a *sela* that is** bound **upon a *tzinis*.** (Artscroll); **1999.** A woman may go out with a Sela on a bunion. (Haberman). These entries are followed at onthemainline by more complete translations of the Mishnah.

Bertinoro (c. 1445 – c. 1515). Below is an example of Wotton's commentary on *Shabbat*, and facing it a reproduction of the text and commentary on *Eruvin*.

MISNA. Shabath 3

This Law was made capital afterwards upon a Man's gathering sticks on the Sabbath, (*Numb.* Xv. 32–36.) who was stoned for that Offense, because he did it *presumptuously*, as appears by what went before (V. 30.31.). i.e. he knew that he gather'd those Sticks on the Sabbath, and that such Work was then forbidden, and yet notwithstanding that his Knowledge, he was resolved to do it, let the Event be what it would. For whereas *Sins of Ignorance*, even in Sabbatical Cases, were expiable by Sacrifice, as appears in the Words foregoing, (*Numb.* xv. 27, 28, 29.) whatsoever was done *presumptuously* was threaten'd with *Excision. But the Soul that doth ought presumptuously, whether he be born in the Land or a Stranger, the same reproacheth the Lord: and that Soul shall be cut off from among his People: because he hath despised the Word of the Lord, and hath broken his Commandment; that Soul shall be utterly cut off; his Iniquity shall be upon him.* (V. 30, 31.) And then Immediately after this Commitiation comes the Account of the unfortunate Man that gather'd Sticks, wherin the Lord was Consulted, either because they did not know how far the Excision threaten'd (V. 30.) might extend; or, as it seems to me very probable, those Penalties threaten'd against *Sins of Presumption* in general were given at first upon that Account.

The Laws of Atonement in case of Sins of Ignorance committed by the Priest, by the Congregation, by a Ruler, or by One of the People of the Land, were at large set down before in the fourth Chapter of Leviticus. The punishment for *presumptuous Sins* in general is not there mention'd. The first flagrant Instance (probably) that happen'd in the Wilderness, was this of the Man that gather'd Sticks. . .

MISNA. *Eruvin.* 169

Cubits, (which comes to about nineteen Foot). it cannot well paſs for a Door or Gate, unleſs it be made expreſly of that Form, in which Caſe it is allow'd.

ט: מקיפין שלשה חבלים זה למעלה מזה וזה למעלה מזה ובלבד שלא יהא בין חבל לחבירו שלשה טפחים: שיעור חבלים ועוביין יתר על טפח כדי שיהא הכל עשרה טפחים:

§. 9. Theſe Encloſures [may be made] with three Ropes [ſurrounding the Camp in a parallel Order] one above another; only there muſt not be three Palms Diſtance between Rope and Rope. The Meaſure then and Thickneſs of the three Ropes [taken jointly] muſt be above a Palm, that the Height of the whole may be full ten Palms.

We are told, that *Moſes* left it as one of the *Conſtitutions* which he brought from *Mount Sinai*, that whatſoever wants of three Palms ſuperficial Meaſure, is only an Appendix of the thing that is next it: The three Ropes therefore being not three Palms aſunder from one another, are in the *Talmudic Style* joined together, and ſo conſtitute one entire Encloſure. Then if the *Breadth or Thickneſs* of the three Ropes together makes any thing more than a Palm, the whole Hedge will be full ten Palms high: I ſay, *Breadth or Thickneſs*. Whatſoever is three Palms in Circumference, though it be exactly circular, is ſuppoſed to be a Palm broad. *Maimonides* obſerves this is not geometrically true, the *Ratio* of a *Circle* to its *Diameter* being ſome ſmall matter more than three to one; which ſmall matter in Practice is generally overlook'd. *Bartenora*, who frequently owns that he cannot underſtand the Calculations of *Maimonides*, contents himſelf with telling us, that *Solomon*'s Brazen Sea was thirty Cubits in Circumference, and 10 Cubits from Brim to Brim, 1 *Kings* vii. 23. Hence it is that the Thickneſs of theſe Ropes, and of the Poſts, (by which they rectified their Entries) was to be taken.

§. 10. Theſe

At the end of the volume is "A list of those Learned Men who have translated the Mishna into Latin," arranged by *Seder* (Order), an Addenda, contents of the second volume, errata, and the final leaf reportedly being an advertisement, although lacking from the examined copy. The "list of those Learned Men" for *Seder Mo'ed* is reproduced below, indicative of the interrelationship and dependence of the commentaries of the Christian-Hebraists addressed in the previous chapter.

Seder Moëd, Order of stated Feasts.

1. *Shabbath*, The Sabbath. *Sebastianus Schmidius.*
2. *Eruvin*, Sabbatic Mixtures. *Idem.*
3. *Pesachim*, Paschal Laws. *Surenhusius.*
4. *Shekalim*, Shekels. *Johan. Henr. Ottho, Johannes Wulferus*, *
5. *Joma*, The Day of Expiation. *Robertus Sheringhamius.*
6. *Succa*, Feast of Tabernacles. *Surenhusius.*
7. *Jom-Tob*, Feast-Day. *Idem.*
8. Rosh Hashanah, Beginning of the Year. *Henricus Houtingius.*
9. *Taanith*, Fasts, *Daniel Lundius.*
10. Megilah, The Roll. *Surenhusius.*
11. *Moëd Katan*, Lesser stated Feast-Days. *Idem.*
12. Chagigah, Solemn Feasts. *Surenhusius*, Job. Henr. Hottingerus.*

There are also numerous varied head and tail-pieces.

IV

By mid-eighteenth century, the interest of Christian-Hebraists in rabbinic literature and studies had diminished. Observations as to the end of this period of Christian attentiveness to Jewish studies are noted by both Carlebach and J.W. Wesselius, the former writing that by the second half of the eighteenth century interest in the Talmud by Christians had waned but that "the preservation and study of the Talmud by Christian scholars in any measure might be regarded as one of the small miracles of the modern period." The latter comments, in a similar vein, that "for some time in the sixteenth century, and even more in the seventeenth century, a strong possibility had existed that the scholarly study of traditional Jewish literature would gain a permanent place in the universities of Europe. By the end of the first half of the eighteenth century, however, the attention of theologians and Hebraists had shifted away from rabbinic literature to other ways of studying the Old Testament. . . .[25]

Given the above, one might say that Wotton had come somewhat late to the study of rabbinic (Talmudic) literature. Nevertheless, it was still a period when such studies were valued. How was *Shabbat and Eruvin* viewed by Wotton's contemporaries? What, in retrospect, almost three centuries after its publication, was the impact of *Miscellaneous Discourses relating to the traditions and usages of the Scribes and Pharisees*?

---

25 Carlebach, pp. 85–88; Wesselius, p. 60.

Among Wotton's immediate and near contemporaries, both Bayle and Chalmers quote Jean Le Clerc's *Bibliothèque ancienne et modern* (Amsterdam, 1714–30), where we are told,

> that 'great advantage may be made by reading the writings of the Rabbins; and that the public is highly obliged to Mr. Seldon, for instance, and to Dr. John Lightfoot, for the assistances which they have drawn thence, and communicated to those who study the holy scripture. Those who do not read their works, which are not adapted to the capacity of every person, will be greatly obliged to Dr. Wotton for the introduction which he has given them into that kind of learning.[26]

Simon Ockley (1678–1720), a British orientalist, distinguished Cambridge professor and Adams professor of Arabic and vicar of Swavesy, endorsed Wotton's efforts in an unambiguous and warm letter dated March 15, 1717, which Wotton had made great efforts to obtain. In the letter Ockley emphasizes the importance of Hebrew learning for Christians. Indeed, Ruderman observes that Ockley stated bluntly that "Christians needed Jews and their religious traditions to understand themselves."[27]

A modern perspective is also positive. David B. Ruderman considers Wotton's greatest achievement in enhancing Jewish learning in England to be in *Shabbat and Eruvin*, which include a lengthy excursus on the value of rabbinic studies for Christians. Wotton, when examining these texts, was pleasantly surprised to find the Mishnah to be a most substantial work, notwithstanding the negativity of many learned men. He insists on its reliability. Wotton made substantial use of his predecessors, among them William Guise, William Surenhusius, and John Lightfoot.[28]

Wotton's translations of *Shabbat* and *Eruvin* are recorded in Erich Bischoff's *Thalmud-Übersetzungen*, a bibliography of translations of the Talmud, as, respectively, the third and second translations, of those tractates.[29] All of this is evidence that Wotton's work is known and remembered positively today.

26 Bayle, p. 207, Chalmers, p. 309.

27 Ruderman, "the Study of the Mishnah," p. 139. Ruderman considers the letter sufficiently important to reproduce it in the article.

28 Ruderman, David B. Ruderman, Connecting the Covenants: Judaism and the Search for Christian Identity in Eighteenth-Century England (Philadelphia, 2007), pp. 77–81.

29 Erich Bischoff, *Kritische Geschichte der Thalmud-Übersetzungen aller Zeiten und Zungen* (Frankfurt a. Main, 1899), pp. 37-38.

None of this, however, suggests that *Miscellaneous Discourses relating to the traditions and usages of the Scribes and Pharisees* was influential, reflected in the work of later scholars. Indeed, *Shabbat and Eruvin* was not reissued until 2010 and does not appear to be seriously referenced in later works. How to account for this relative neglect? I would suggest three possibilities. Firstly, as noted above, is the waning interest in such studies in the mid-eighteenth century, not long after *Miscellaneous Discourses* . . . was published; secondly, Wotton's translation is in English, at a time when the scholarly language of Hebraists was Latin; and thirdly, perhaps most importantly, Wotton was writing not for scholars, as suggested by Le Clerc, but "to give young divinity students a basic understanding of Jewish learning," who might not have been as interested in the subject as Wotton thought they might be.

All this notwithstanding, Wotton's achievement is not to be underestimated. A truly erudite scholar undertakes to translate and publish with commentary two lengthy and complex tractates. His translations, allowing for linguistic changes over the centuries, are consistent with accepted Jewish translations, and his commentary is erudite, utilizing accepted Jewish sources. Not a mean accomplishment for a Christian clergyman in Carmarthen, Wales. ☙

Tail-piece

Torah Authority

By: ASHER BENZION BUCHMAN

The Prohibition of Deviating—*Lo Sassur*

Rambam explains that the authority of the Rabbis to legislate is granted explicitly in both a positive (*mitzvas aseh* 174) and negative mitzvah (*lav* 312) that command the Jewish people to obey their legislation. This legislation includes their relating of traditions, their deductions of laws based on Biblical interpretation and also their own new "Rabbinic" legislation instituted as a fence around the Torah or for the needs of the time.

> The Supreme Sanhedrin in Jerusalem are the essence of the Oral Law. They are the pillars of instruction from whom statutes and judgments issue forth for the entire Jewish people. Concerning them, the Torah promises (*Devarim* 17:11): "You shall do according to the laws which they shall instruct you..." This is a positive commandment. Whoever believes in Moses and in his Torah is obligated to make all of his religious acts dependent on this court and to rely on them. Any person who does not carry out their directives transgresses a negative commandment, as it says (ibid): "Do not deviate[1] from any of the statements they relate to you, neither right nor left."... We are obligated to heed their words whether they:
>
> – learned them from the Oral Tradition, i.e., the Oral Law,
> – derived them on the basis of their own knowledge through one of the attributes of Biblical exegesis and it appeared to them that this is the correct interpretation of the matter,
> – instituted the matter as a safeguard for the Torah, as was necessary at a specific time. These are the decrees, edicts, and customs instituted by the Sages.
>
> It is a positive commandment to heed the court with regard to each of these three matters. A person who transgresses any of these types of directives transgresses a negative commandment. This is derived from the continuation of the above verse in the following manner: "According to the laws which they shall instruct you"—this refers to the edicts, decrees and customs which they instruct people at large

1 לא תסור.

Asher Benzion Buchman is the author of *Encountering the Creator: Divine Providence and Prayer in the Works of Rambam* (Targum, 2004) and *Rambam and Redemption* (Targum, 2005). He is the editor-in-chief of *Hakirah*.

> to observe to strengthen the faith and perfect the world. "According to the judgment which they relate"—this refers to the matters which they derive through logical analysis employing one of the methods of Biblical exegesis. "From all things that they will tell you"—this refers to the tradition which they received one person from another. (*Hilchos Mamrim* 1:1–2)[2]

Ramban is in agreement with Rambam's inclusion of these mitzvos in the *Sefer HaMitzvos*, but in the first *shoresh* argues vociferously against his use of them to include Rabbinic enactments, and limits them to Rabbinic interpretation. His objection is keyed by the argument, that if these mitzvos are so inclusive, then it makes no sense that *Chazal* distinguished between Torah laws where stringencies are applied in cases of *safek* (doubt) and Rabbinic laws where leniencies are applied in these cases, since in fact every time one violates a Rabbinic law, he is in fact violating two Torah mitzvos.[3] Ramban is well aware of the likely-to-be-proposed response and calls this proposal "twisted logic."[4] Indeed, what he suggests is the primary solution given by the majority of commentaries. *Tashbetz* is the first to apply it, saying "that such was the nature of each original *takanah,*that the Rabbis at the onset made a condition (תנאי) that should there be an issue of *safek* they allow it to be judged leniently."[5]

Rav Meir Simchah (*Meshech Chochmah, Shoftim*) couches this same explanation in the language of *lomdus.* Rabbinic prohibitions only[6] impose a stricture on a person from performing a specific act and there is a subjective element in this *issur*, while with Torah prohibitions the forbidden object or the act is innately tainted[7], and we must therefore protect ourselves from the harm that might come from them even in cases of *safek.* With Rabbinic infractions, no harm comes from the violation itself and thus the Rabbis have the leeway to permit in cases of *safek.*[8] To these explanations we should add, that Rambam's position is (see *Hilchos Issurei Biah*

---

2 The translations of *Mishneh Torah* are from the Chabad.org website, sometimes modified. The other translations are my own.

3 Why should we say ספק דאורייתא לקולא?

4 ואולי תתעקש ותאמר לדעת הרב כי מה שאמרו בכל מקום להקל בדברי סופרים הוא במחילה ותנאי וכו' ואין אלו דברים הגונים ולא של עיקר.

5 שכך היתה התחלת התקנה שהחכמים אסרו דבר זה בתנאי שיהא ודאי אסור אבל אם יש בו ספק הם מוחלין לדון בו להקל (זהר"ק בשרש הראשון).

6 אסור גברא.

7 אסורי חפצא.

8 (עיי"ש - וכעין סברא זה כתב ר"א וסרמן (בקונטרס ד"ס א:לב) בשם הגר"ח מבריסק בשטת הרמב"ן וכתב שסברת הרמב"ם אינו כן). He presents other arguments to bolster his stance and makes a strong case.

15:21, 17:18) that the very principle of[9] *Safek D'Oraissa l'Chumra*—that we need be stringent in cases of doubt when a Torah law is involved—is itself only a Rabbinic enactment, and certainly with this presumption it is easy to understand that this stringency need not be applied uniformly, and not on their Rabbinic enactments. Ramban apparently argues against this principle and this is part of the reason he found Rambam's position difficult.[10] [11]

Ramban's Source for *Mitzvos D'Rabbanan*

But, in fact, some latter-day scholars actually found the contention of Ramban that there is no Torah root to Rabbinic laws the more troubling position. If so, why do we have to follow them? Rav Elchanan Wasserman asked the question: "If so, why are we obligated to listen to them, and not transgress their words?"[12]

He answers with a fundamental principle, claiming there is such a thing as the "Torah's intent," which is the will of G-d, that the Rabbis are able to deduce from the Torah, and once discovered we are bound to follow it. "For all in which the Rabbis commanded, we know is the will of G-d, and doing the will of G-d is what all inhabitants of the world … were created for."[13]

---

9 ספק דאורייתא לחומרא.

10 מסתמא דדעת הרמב"ן כהרשב"א תלמידו (וכרש"י - עי' רשב"א קדושין עג., ותורת הבית שער התערובות דף 22) "דכשאמרו ספיקא דאורייתא לחומרא, דבר תורה הוא דספיקא דאורייתא כודאי מן התורה." ולכן טוען הרמב"ן דאי העיקר לאסורי דרבנן הוו גם כן מן התורה, היה חל גם עליהם הך כלל של "ספק כודאי".

11 Others argue the point that לא תסור should not apply except when one violates a law in protest to the enactment. Indeed, this is more severe and the direct violation is in זקן ממרא, still the underpinnings for all דרבנן must be לא תסור, thus this answer is not as compelling. See commentaries printed with the standard *Sefer HaMitzvos.*

12 ונראה...דקראי ד"ועשית ככל אשר יורוך", ו"לא תסור"; דלדעת הרמב"ם קאי קראי גם אמצות ואיסורין דרבנן...והרמב"ן סובר דלא קאי קרא ד"ולא תסור" רק על תורה שבע"פ שהיא דאורייתא ולא על של דבריהן כלל... אלא ע"כ צ"ל לכאורה לדעת הרמב"ן שלא נצטוינו כלל מן התורה לשמוע לדברי חכמים: ותימה גדולה לומר כן, דא"כ מאיזה טעם אנו חייבין לשמוע להן ושלא לעבור על דבריהן אחרי שאין לנו שום צווי בתורה ע"ז? (קונטרס דברי סופרים דף צ-צא).

13 והנה ביבמות דס"ב תניא ג' דברים עשה מרע"ה מדעתו והסכימה דעתו לדעת המקום פירש מן האשה ושיבר את הלוחות והוסיף יום אחד... ונראה דהא דהוסיף יום א' אינו אלא מדרבנן...ומ"מ הסכימה דעתו לדעת המקום דכן היה גם רצון השי"ת אלא שלא ציוהו ע"ז בציווי מפורש...ולדוגמא כשאסרו שניות לעריות גם רצון השי"ת היה כן שנגזור על עצמנו שניות אלא שלא צוה ע"ז בתורה מפורש...דכל מה שצוו חכמים אנו יודעין שכן הוא גם רצון ה' ודבר זה

Though he does not quote it, this logic echoes the understanding of *Ritva*, a follower of Ramban's school, in the concept of an *asmachata.*[14] "Whenever there is an *asmachta* from a Torah verse, G-d made us aware that it is proper to do this, but did not make it obligatory… and gave over to the Rabbis the obligation to make it set law should they wish to."[15] Ramban himself expresses a similar idea in defense of *B'Hag*'s counting Rabbinic mitzvos in the *Taryag Mitzvos* given to Moshe at Sinai. "Since the Rabbis are permitted via tradition to make *takanos* and place things in order, and they *darshan* in this hints and *gematrios.*"[16] Since the Torah hints to these ideas, therefore it is possible to say that they were given to Moshe at Sinai.

Nevertheless, were Ramban's position here based on Rav Elchanan's interpretation, we would expect to find it expressed in the words of Ramban himself. And even were we to consider that Ritva's position is essentially that of Ramban, there are considerable differences in it from what Rav Elchanan posits, extending the idea to *gezeiros* that have no textual basis at all, not just to *asmachtos* and laws based on "hints" and *gematrios.*

Acceptance by Israel

However, if we go back and read Ramban's argument in the *Sefer HaMitzvos* carefully, we can recognize that he actually introduced his objection to

---

לעשות רצונו ית"ש כל באי עולם מצווין ועומדין מתחל' ברייתן ע"ז דכל הנמצאים נבראו לעשות רצון קונם וכל פעל ד' למענהו (שם).

14 אסמכתא: When the Rabbis bring a verse from *Tanach* to support a ruling in which they still consider the law Rabbinic.

15 והא דקאמר אמר הקב"ה אמרו לפני מלכיות וכו' אינם מן התורה אלא מדרבנן... מ"מ ממה שאמרה זכרון תרועה יש ללמוד שראוי להזכיר פסוקי תרועה וכו' ומהכא סמכו רבנן לתקוני הני פסוקי דתקיעתא ומ"ה קתני ר"ע שאמר הקב"ה וכו' שכל **מה שיש לו אסמכתא מן הפסוק העיר הקב"ה** שראוי **לעשות כן אלא שלא קבעו חובה ומסרו לחכמים**... ולא כדברי המפרשים האסמכתות שהוא כדרך סימן שנתנו חכמים ולא שכונת התורה לכך ח"ו ישתקע הדבר ולא יאמר שזו דעת מינות הוא **אבל התורה העירה בכך ומסרה חיוב הדבר לקבעו חכמים אם ירצו כמ"ש ועשית ע"פ הדבר אשר יגידו לך** ולפיכך תמצא החכמים נותנין בכל מקום ראיה או זכר או אסמכתא לדבריהם מן התורה כלומר שאינם מחדשים דבר מלבם וכל תורה שבע"פ רמוזה בתורה שבכתב שהיא תמימה וח"ו שהיא חסירה כלום. **ריטב"א (ר"ה טז.)**.

16 מ"מ מנהג חכמים הוא לומר כלשון הזה לפי שהורשו מאתו ית' מפי הקבלה לתקן ולסדר והם דורשים בזה רמזים וגימטריאות. והתימה שתמה הרב מן תורה צוה לנו משה שירמוז למגלה ונר חנוכה בגימטריא איננו גדול. שכבר דרשו (מגיל' ז א) כתוב זאת זכרון בספר כתוב זאת מה שכתוב כאן ובמשנה תורה, זכרון מה שכתוב בנביאים, בספר מה שכתוב במגלה. כי התורה תצוה ותפרש ותודיע ותרמוז. וכבר רמזה לגלותנו בגימטריא כמו שאמרו (סנה' לח א) צדקה עשה הקב"ה עם ישראל שהקדים שתי שנים לונושנתם (סה"מ שרש א).

Rambam's use of *Lo Sassur*, with his answer to our question.[17] Basing himself on the Gemara in Shavuos (39a) that states that the mitzvah of reading the *Megillah* was based on their earlier acceptance at Sinai to obey the Rabbis,[18] he writes, "The Rabbis *darshen* with regard to mitzvos that will be initiated in the future, that they had accepted them upon themselves in Sinai...and thus the Rabbis are explicit that the reading of the *Megillah* was accepted at Sinai and accepted via a covenant[19] as were all the other [Torah] mitzvos and an oath was proclaimed on it with the consent of Moshe and G-d."[20]

Ramban explains that the alternative to having been commanded in the Torah to keep Rabbinic mitzvos is that Israel accepted upon themselves at Sinai to keep Rabbinic mitzvos just as they had accepted to keep the mitzvos of the Torah. In his essay *Mishpat HaCherem*,[21] he voices the opinion that a community can enact laws that are binding upon future generations, and explains his position by saying that this is the mechanism for the acceptance of the Torah at Sinai: "But of that it is binding on them and future generations, would seem to be true of every public acceptance as we find with regard to the acceptance of the Torah."[22]

(There is perhaps some difficulty in comparing the Torah laws of *Neder* and *Shevua* with the means by which the Torah became binding, and one can argue that this would make the acceptance of the Torah dependent on the binding force of the Torah law of oaths. But even before the Torah, mankind was bound by laws. The seven Noahide laws include

---

17 This was first pointed out to me by my friend Rav Shmuel Neuman, *shlita*.

18 קיימו וקבלו.

19 ברית.

20 ועוד שכיון שנאמר למשה בסיני שיקבלו עליהם ישראל מצות ב"ד הגדול ובאו הם ותקנו את אלו כבר נאמרו כלם למשה בסיני אין הפרש ביניהם באמירתם סיני אלא שזה בפרט וזה בכלל. וכבר הראית לדעת מדברי הרב שהחכמים דורשים במצות העתידות להתחדש שקבלו אותן עליהם בסיני, כאותה שהזכיר מפרק שבועת הדיינין (לט א) וכן מצינו כשהשביע משה את ישראל אמר להם הוו יודעים שלא על דעתכם אני משביע אתכם אלא על דעתי ועל דעת המקום שנ' ולא אתכם לבדכם אנכי כורת את הברית הזאת ואת האלה הזאת אין לי אלא מצות שנצטוו בסיני מצות העתידות להתחדש כגון מקרא מגילה מנין, כלומר מנין שהשביען משה עליהן על דעת המקום ועל דעתו ת"ל קיימו וקבלו היהודים עליהם ועל זרעם קיימו מה שקבלו עליהם כבר. הרי זה דבר מפורש להם שקריאת מגלה מקובלת מסיני ונכרת עליה ברית כשאר המצות ובאה בה שבועה על דעת משה ועל דעת המקום אם כן למה לא יאמרו עליה ועל כיוצא בה נאמרו למשה בסיני.

21 Page 298 in the Chavel ed.

22 אבל שהוא חל עליהם ועל זרעם נראה שאף לנדרים כן בכל קבלת הרבים כדאשכחן בקבלת התורה.

"civil laws"[23] and Ramban[24] contends that this includes the making of a civil system of laws for the conduct of business and oaths would be a part of this.[25])

Ramban, in commenting on the Covenant on the Plains of Moav, finds this principle explicitly expressed in the words of Moshe Rabbeinu, who even explains the conceptual reason for why the oath of the ancestors is binding on their children. The children are branches of a root that has bound itself to the *bris*:

> The covenant is the *shavua* and *alah* which follows, "to bind you by a covenant with the L-rd your G-d and his *alah*"…and with "he who is not here with us"—with the future generations that will exist … "lest you have a poisonous root"—and it mentions the root to express that He is able to bring future generations into this *alah,* for the root from which it grows is in front of Him today, and it is brought into the *alah* and covenant.[26]

No individual Jew may escape it even if he swore insincerely, since all of Israel committed themselves to it verbally in front of the entire nation:

> He will bless himself in his heart, saying that he will have peace… the L-rd will not forgive he who says he will have peace, because he did not accept the *alah*, "but His anger will burn against him, since he acceded to the Covenant in front of the entire nation of Israel."[27]

Ramban relies on a halachic principle. The Gemara[28] explains that Moshe swore the people "according to G-d's understanding and his own"[29]—and this was needed, so that the oath could never be annulled.[30]

---

23 דינים.

24 According to Rambam (see *Parashas Vayeshev*) this just means the enforcement of the other six laws, and there is room to argue that Rambam would indeed object to using the **נדר** as a source for the binding nature of the Torah.

25 He also holds that the *Avos* kept the whole Torah while in Eretz Yisrael; thus Torah law was already available.

26 והברית הוא השבועה והאלה אשר יזכיר, לעברך בברית ה' אלקיך ובאלתו (ט)... ואת אשר איננו פה עמנו - וגם עם הדורות העתידים להיות (יד)... פן יש בכם פרה ראש ולענה - והזכיר השורש לומר כי הוא יכול להביא באלה הדורות הבאים, שהשרש אשר הוא ממנו יצמחו הוא לפניו היום, והוא בא בברית ואלה הזאת (יז). (דברים כט)

27 התברך בלבבו לאמר שלום יהיה לי... לא יאבה ה' סלוח לו - לאומר יהיה לי שלום בעבור שאינני מקבל אלתו, אבל יעשן עליו אפו **כיון שבא בבריתו לפני עם כל ישראל** (יח)(שם).

28 ע' שבועת לט, כט.

29 על פי המקום ועל פי דעתו.

30 כי היכי דלא תהוי הפרה לשבועתייהו.

Ramban explains that G-d and Moshe together constituted a group and it is an "oath made according to the group that cannot be annulled.[31]

What emerges is that both the mitzvos of the Torah and mitzvos of the Rabbis are binding on Israel because their ancestors accepted them on *Har Sinai*.[32]

Ramban sees the Covenant the Torah describes as the force that binds Israel. Rambam, not depending on the oath as the source of obligation in Rabbinic laws, could theoretically not be completely dependent upon it for Torah laws either. *Chazal* put forward the concept that "The mountain was placed over their head as a barrel; if you accept it that is good, if not there will be your grave,"[33] and thus this acceptance was a bargain that could not be refused. The Torah was perhaps forced upon Israel at the moment it was given and the verse of *Lo Sassur* obligates them to obey the laws written by the Rabbis. *Chazal*'s understanding of the verse "We will do and we will listen,"[34] in which Israel committed themselves to perform the mitzvos before they even knew what they were, supports the position that the covenant was a product of free will. Both Rambam and Ramban must resolve this contradiction that *Chazal* also struggle with.[35] But at this point we only note that Ramban puts forth on a halachic basis, that democratic choice is the binding force behind all mitzvos.

---

31 Rashi explains that this is the concept of על דעת רבים. Ramban (*Shevuos* 39) brings one opinion that it is because it is G-d's command superimposed on their word that makes it eternally binding, but he personally agrees with Rashi that it is שבועה על דעת רבים, their public commitment that binds Israel forever: על דעת המקום וכנסת ישראל עמו כדאמרינן הוא ובית דינו, והוי דעת רבים.

32 In contrast, Rambam says that when the Talmud uses the principle of מושבע ועומד מהר סיני it does not even apply it to חצי שיעור אסור מן התורה, yet the laws are binding without the oath. See Appendix A where we address the difficulty presented by the fact that the Gemara refers to דאורייתא laws as מושבע ועומד מהר סיני and says explicitly that Rabbinic laws are not.

33 כפה עליהם הר כגיגית *Meshech Chochmah* and *Eshkol Hakofer* (introduction to *Megillas Esther*) explain that under the circumstances, there is no way that Israel could have refused. At that moment, the presence of G-d was so dominant over their existence they could not nor would they want to refuse, but this situation would not exist at any other moment in time and thus the pledge was of questionable legal status. *Chazal* thus say that the acceptance at the time of Purim is what binds Israel, since at that time G-d's presence was hidden.

34 נעשה ונשמע.

35 *Midrash Tanchuma* (*Noach*) says that their willing acceptance was for the Written Law, but for the Oral Law they needed to be compelled. Also see *Tosafos, Shabbos* 88a.

Democratic Choice

An even more democratic concept is put forth by a student of Ramban, Rav Dovid Bonfil. After quoting his teacher Ramban, that Rabbinic enactments are not based on *Lo Sassur*, he continues to explain:

> Now it becomes evident that the *takanos* of the Rabbis or their *mitzvos* are not Torah, but a man must follow them because the community is dependent on them and they and the *Nasi* of Israel prohibited themselves in what was permitted to them and it cannot then be permitted, just as one who accepts upon himself a prohibition in something that is permitted, that one must then commit himself to this prohibition and it is explicitly said in Talmud *Avodah Zarah* (36a) "that there is no obligation on a Rabbinic enactment unless the prohibition has spread throughout all of Israel" and this certainly is of the same nature. And in *Yevamos* (21a), with regard to the Rabbinic extensions of *Arayos*, it says that the Rabbis are commanded to make a fence around the Torah from that which is written "Guard my warnings"[36]—Make a fence around my prohibitions," [meaning] that a person is commanded to prohibit himself in things that are permitted to him. And elsewhere it says "Make yourself holy [by prohibiting] that which is permitted to you."[37]

Gezeiros and *takanos* are only binding because the people have decided to accept them and this is the meaning of "that it has spread throughout Israel." It would seem to be a collective *neder* of sorts made at the time of the decree, and it will not be binding if the people do not accept it. Another factor is that the Torah obligates the individual to elevate himself and thus the individuals are expected by the Torah to make such restrictions. Rav Dovid conflates the Ramban's concept of[38] *Kedoshim Tihiyu* with the Talmudic *drash* of *u'shamartam es Mishmarti.*

---

36 ושמרתם את משמרתי.

37 מעתה נתברר שתקנות חכמים או המצוות שלהם אינם תורה אלא שאדם חייב ללכת אחריהם מפני שהציבור תלוי בהן והם עם הנשיא של ישראל אסרו עצמן במותר שלהם ואין להתיר, כמו שקבל על עצמו אסור בדבר המותר שחייב לנהוג אסור. ובפי' אמרו בע"ז (לו.) שאין חיוב בשל סופרים אלא במה שפשט אסורו בכל ישראל והוא ודאי על זה הדרך, וביבמות (כא.) בענין שניות אמרו שחכמים מצווים לעשות סייג לתורה ממה שכתוב ושמרתם את משמרתי עשו משמרת וכו' שאדם מצווה לאסור על עצמו במותר לו. וכן אמרו במקום אחר קדש עצמך במותר לך. ומצות מגילה אין מכלל זה שאינה סייג לתורה, אלא מצוה בפני עצמה ואלולי שמצאו רמז בתורה לא היה כח בידם לעשות כדאיתא במס' מגילה. (סנהד' פז.)

38 See Ramban, beginning of *Parashas Kedoshim.*

Earlier we quoted from Ramban's lengthy essay *Mishpat HaCherem.* He explains there how the *Beis Din* of the city can enact laws and then he writes:

> The same law applies with regard to all or most of the people of the city, in the presence of the leadership of the city, should they make a *cherem,* as we see they are empowered to enact price controls (*Bava Basra* 8b) and enact a *cherem* [on violators of the controls]…. And the transgressor of the *cherem* is like one who has violated a *shevua* … and for this reason they said that the *cherem* cannot exist without ten people because [a smaller number] does not constitute a community (*tzibbur)* nor a *Beis Din* that stands in place of a community—moreover, a *cherem* applies to future generations."[39]

Here we find Ramban himself stating that this legislation is dependent on the will of the people and an oath-like commitment. Perhaps the most striking line here is that at least ten people are needed, for otherwise we lack "a community **or a *beis din* that stands in the place of a community.**"[40] What emerges is that the authority of the Rabbis to legislate new laws lies in their status as representatives of the nation at large. As Rav Dovid explains, Rabbinic authority begins with the obligation on the individual to elevate himself—*kedoshim tihiyu*—and to make a fence around

---

39 בחרם אע"פ שלא קבל עליו ואפילו לא היה שם בשעת גזרה כיון שב"ד רשאין להחרים כדכתיב ואשביעם ואקללם באלקים (נחמיה יג:כה) הרי החרם חל עליו ואסור לעבור על אותה גזרה כמושבע מפי עצמו, וכן הדין באנשי העיר אם הסכימו כולם או רובם במעמד טובי העיר והחרימו כיון שהן רשאין להסיע על קיצותם (ב"ב ח:) ולהחרים בדבר, חרם שלהם חל על כל החייבים לילך בתקנתם ונמצא העובר על קיצותם מכל אנשי העיר עובר על חרם והוא כעובר על שבועה וכו' ובזה אמרו שאין החרם מתקיים בפחות מעשרה לפי שאינן צבור ולא בי"ד שהוא במקום צבור וכו' ולא עוד אלא שהחרם חל אפילו על דורות הבאין אם החרימו ב"ד על אנשי העיר ועל זרעם ... כדכ' וישבע יהשע וכו' ארור האיש לפני ה' אשר יקום ובנה את העיר וכו' יכולין הם עצמן להתיר לו וכו' וכן אם מת הדור ההוא העומדין תחתיהן מתירין, והוא שיהיו גדולים כמותם בחכמה ובמנין כדין נדוי ושמתא כדמוכה במסכ' משקין (מ"ק יז.) וכו' וכשם שמתירים לעובר מהחרם שעליו כך מתירין החרם עצמו לנהוג בו היתר בלא שאלת חכם וכו' שהרי חכם מנדה לעצמו ומתיר לעצמו (משפט החרם).

40 Moreover he continues that should an annulment be done in future generations it requires those גדולים כמותם בחכמה ובמנין, exactly the mechanism needed for the annulment of laws passed by previous courts. He goes on to explain that these laws, such as price controls, differ from מגלה ותעניתים for in those cases, there was a נדר על דעת רבים and thus they can never be voided.

the Torah, and *Beis Din* thus acts as emissaries of the people to legislate laws that the Torah considers incumbent upon them.[41]

Yet another member of Ramban's school also expresses a viewpoint that aligns with this position. Ran contends that the principle of "*Beis Din* may execute lashes and other punishments, not in accordance with the law"[42] applies only when there is no king in Israel. When there is no king, then *beis din* is charged with his executive responsibilities and powers.[43] This position most likely reflects the view that the king gets his authority from the people.[44]

Rambam and the Authority of the People

However, the sources brought by Ramban's school to support the concept of a democratic principle behind Rabbinic authority are interpreted differently by Rambam and thus provide no evidence according to him for this principle. Rambam brings the concept of *gezeirah* needing to have spread (**נתפשטה**) to be binding in the following way:

> The following rules apply when a court issued a decree, instituted an edict, or established a custom and this practice spread throughout the Jewish people and another court arose and sought to nullify the original order and eliminate the original edict, decree or custom. The later court does not have this authority unless it surpasses the original court in wisdom and in its number of adherents. How is it possible that the later court will surpass the original court in number? For every Supreme Sanhedrin consists of 71 judges. **The intent is the number of Sages in the generation who consent and accept**

---

41 Both the Brisker Rav and the Rav (Rav Yosef Dov Soloveitchik, *zt"l*) attribute such an approach to Rambam as well, claiming that *Beis Din* has a second role as the representatives of the people. See Appendix B.

42 בית דין מכין ועונשין שלא מן הדין.

43 שמנוי המלך שוה בישראל וביתר אומות שצריכים סדור מדיני וכו' אבל השופטים והסנהד' היה תכליתם לשפוט העם במשפט אמתי צודק בעצמו שימשך ממנו הדבק ענין האלקי וכו' ואל תקשה ... שנראה ממנו שמנוי הב"ד הוא לשפוט כפי תקון העת וכו' **אבל כאשר לא יהיה מלך בישראל השופט יכלול שני הכחות. (דרשות הר"ן י"א)**

44 וזהו שכתב הרדב"ז (מלכים ג:ח) דאף דנאמר בספרי דמלך על פי נביא היינו על פי נביא או הסכמת כל ישראל. ועי' רמב"ן (שופטים יז:טז) דאם יענהו ה' על פי נביא יעשה על פי נביא ואם לאו יעשם בלי נביא. ונראה דאף עקר צורך בי"ד בדעתם במנוי מלך היא דעומדים במקום העם.

See also *Encyclopedia Talmudis*, *Dina D'Malchusa Dina*.

> **the matter stated by the Supreme Sanhedrin without opposing it.**[45]

The requirement of "having spread" is dependent on the acceptance of all *Chachmei Yisrael. Beis Din* is not a representative of all of the people, but of all the Rabbis.[46] Rambam further explains (*Halachos* 5–6) "that a *Beis Din* must first determine if most of the community is capable of bearing a particular [enactment], or if they are not able to bear it, and they may never decree a *gezeirah* on the community unless most of the community can bear it."[47] And then he continues:

> If a court issued a decree, thinking that the majority of the community could uphold it and after the decree was issued, the majority of the community raised contentions and the practice did not spread throughout the majority of the community, the decree is nullified. The court cannot compel the people to accept it.[48]
>
> It is not the acceptance of the people that makes the decree binding, but rather since there is no permission to make an overbearing law, once it is determined that this law is in that category the law is nullified on its own. The *gezeirah* was made in error. Still, the authority lies with the court, not with the people.[49]

As noted above, Ramban brings evidence to the concept of the community legislating from price controls[50] that the Gemara in *Bava Basra* (8b) says can be legislated by the community. Ramban says all the artisans of the city must be involved in the *takanah*. Yet the Gemara adds (9a):

---

45 ב בית דין שגזרו גזירה, או התקינו תקנה, והנהיגו מנהג, ופשט כל הדבר בכל ישראל, ועמד אחריהם בית דין אחר, וביקש לבטל דברי הראשונים ולעקור אותה התקנה ואותה הגזירה ואותו המנהג—אינו יכול, עד שיהיה גדול מן הראשונים בחכמה ובמניין.
ג היה גדול בחכמה אבל לא במניין, במניין אבל לא בחכמה—אינו יכול לבטל את דבריו; אפילו בטל טעם שבגללו גזרו הראשונים או התקינו—אין האחרונים יכולין לבטל, עד שיהיו גדולים מהם.
ד והיאך יהיו גדולים במניין, הואיל וכל בית דין ובית דין של שבעים ואחד הוא—זה מניין חכמי הדור שהסכימו וקיבלו הדבר שאמרו בית דין הגדול, ולא חלקו בו (הל' ממרים ב:ב).

46 We will bring further evidence to this later on.

47 אין רוב הצבור יכולין לעמוד בו.

48 הרי שגזרו בית דין גזירה, ודימו שרוב הציבור יכולין לעמוד בה, ואחר שגזרו אותה, פיקפקו העם בה ולא פשטה ברוב הציבור—הרי זו בטילה, ואינן רשאין לכוף את העם ללכת בה.

49 עי' בהלכה ז דכשנראה לעין שפשטה, מ"מ התוקף היא חלוש וב"ד דוקא נצרכין להתירו. אין הכח בשום מקום ביד הצבור. הכל מתחיל מאסור לעשות גזרה חמורה. עי' בלח"מ שחקר אלו פשטה היא אותו הדין של יכול לעמוד בהן. ונראה דאינם שוים, רק דטעם של אינם יכולים לעמוד בהם היא מציאות שבגללה ב"ד עוקרין.

50 במסיעין על קיצתן.

"Where there is an important person, then they are not trusted to do so."[51] [52] Rambam records the law as follows:

> The inhabitants of a city are permitted to establish fixed prices for any commodities they desire, even meat and bread. They may establish conditions stating that anyone who violates these guidelines will be punished in such and such a fashion. …When does the above apply? In a city where there is not a distinguished Sage (חכם חשוב) to correct the conduct within the city and improve the ways of its inhabitants. If, however, there is such a distinguished Sage, a condition established by craftsmen is not effective without the ruling of the Sage. They may not punish or inflict loss on anyone who does not accept their stipulation, unless that stipulation was made with the consent of the Sage. Whoever causes a colleague a loss because of a stipulation that was not made with the consent of the Sage is liable to pay.[53]

Even this legislation of commerce still required the *Chacham*. Ramban limits the need of this person to matters of where a financial loss is incurred by the purchasers.[54] And even so, Rashba says it is merely an important person rather than a *Chacham* and he has been appointed in an official capacity by the community[55]—his authority, too, comes from the people. Yet, even here, in issues that might be considered a matter for citizens and merchants to determine, Rambam says authority rests with the Rabbis.

The Mitzvah of *Kiddush HaChodesh*

Further insight into Rambam's and Ramban's positions on the basis for Rabbinic Torah authority can be drawn by investigating their views on the mitzvah of *Kiddush HaChodesh*. Rambam defines it in this way:

---

51 היכא דאיכא אדם חשוב לאו כל כמיניה

52 See commentary of Rabbeinu Gershom who explains that they should have waited for the אדם חשוב.

53 ח [ט] רשאין בני העיר לקוץ להם שער לכל דבר שירצו, ואפילו לבשר וללחם, ולהתנות ביניהם כל מי שיעבור על התנאי, יענשו אותו כך וכך. [י] וכן רשאין אנשי אומנייות לפסוק ביניהם שלא יעשה אחד ביום שיעשה חברו, וכיוצא בזה, וכל מי שיעבור על התנאי, יענשו אותו כך וכך.ט [יא] במה דברים אמורים, במדינה שאין בה חכם חשוב לתקן מעשה המדינה ולהצליח דרכי יושביה. אבל אם יש בה חכם חשוב, אין התנאי שלהן מועיל כלום; ואינן יכולין לענוש ולהפסיד על מי שלא קיבל מן התנאי, אלא אם כן התנה עימהם ועשו מדעת החכם. וכל מי שהפסיד לפי התנאי שאינו מדעת החכם, משלם.(הל' מכירה יד:ט-יא)

54 פסידא דלקוחות.

55 ממונה על הצבור.

To sanctify the months and to calculate the years and months in the court alone, as [*Shemos* 12:2] states: "This month will be for you the first of the months."[56]

Ramban (*Sefer HaMitzvos,* ibid.) objects to Rambam's counting of the setting of the month and the year as one mitzvah, and notes that *B'Hag* counts two independent mitzvos. Rambam's reasoning is clear from how he presents the mitzvah in *Mishneh Torah*. For example, he states:

> It is a positive commandment of the Torah for the court to calculate and determine whether or not the moon will be sighted, to examine witnesses until the moon can be sanctified, and to send forth [messengers] to inform the remainder of the people on which day *Rosh Chodesh* was observed, so that they will know the day [on which to celebrate] the festivals, as implied [by *Vayikra* 23:2]: "that you will pronounce as days of holy convocation," and as implied [by *Shemos* 13:10]: "And you shall observe this statute in its appointed season."[57]

The mitzvah is the establishment of a calendar and thus it incorporates the notification of the nation as well, so that the holidays will be uniformly observed by the entire nation of Israel.

Beis Din HaGadol and *Kiddush HaChodesh*

What role exactly does *Beis Din* play?

> G-d said, "This month will be to you the first of months" and the interpretation was given that "this testimony should be handed over to you"—in other words, that this mitzvah is not given over to every individual as Shabbos *Bereishis* where each person counts six days and rests on the seventh. We do not say similarly that each individual should observe the moon and declare a new month, etc., but rather this mitzvah should never be performed except by *Beis Din* and in Eretz Yisrael.[58]

---

56 לקדש חדשים ולחשוב שנים וחדשים בבית דין בלבד שנ' החדש הזה לכם ראש חדשים (סמ"ק מ"ע קנ"ג).

57 מצות עשה מן התורה על בית דין שיחשבו וידעו אם יראה הירח או לא יראה ושידרשו את העדים עד שיקדשו את החדש. וישלחו ויודיעו שאר העם באי זה יום הוא ראש חדש,כדי שידעו ואי זה יום הם המועדות שנאמר אשר תקראו אתם מקראי קדש ונאמר ושמרת את החקה הזאת למועדה. (הלכות קה"ח [א:ז])

58 אמר ית' החדש הזה לכם ראש חדשים ובא הפירוש עדות זה תהא מסורה לכם כלומר שמצוה זו אינה מסורה לכל איש ואיש כמו שבת בראשית שכל איש ימנה ששה ימים וישבות בשביעי עד שתראה לכל איש ואיש הלבנה שיקבע היום ההוא ראש חדש וכו' אלא מצוה זו לא יעשה אותה לעולם זולתי בית דין הגדול לבד ובארץ ישראל לבד. (סה"מ קנ"ג)

In fact, the new moon is an observable astronomical phenomenon just like the arrival of the seventh day, but rather than charging individuals to observe and follow nature, as is the case with Shabbos, the identification of these less than obvious lunar events is made the responsibility of *Beis Din.* Moreover, since different time zones will relate differently to the conjunction (*molad),* the evaluation must be made according to Eretz Yisrael time and in the place of the *Beis Din.* "This testimony is handed over to you"[59] does not mean that they are to proclaim the new month at their whim, but that it is their sighting of the new moon—as testified to them by witnesses[60]—that will be the determining factor.[61] So important is it that the new month be proclaimed at the day of the moon's actual appearance, that the witnesses are obligated to violate Shabbos in order to testify. Likewise, the *Mo'adim* must be aligned with the seasons, and *Beis Din* is charged with implementing rules based on astronomy and nature to ensure that this is so.[62] Thus *Beis Din* serves as the central authority for the entire Jewish people, whose sighting and observation is binding on the whole nation. One central authority had to be chosen, and who better than *Beis Din HaGadol.*[63]

However, Rambam emphasizes another reason for why *Beis Din* is entrusted with this responsibility. This reason emerges from Rambam's emphasis on establishing the *Mo'adim* at their proper time:

> As stated in the laws mentioned previously, the court made precise calculations and knew whether or not the [new] moon would be visible. Accordingly, we are assured that anyone with a proper spirit and heart, who desires words of wisdom and probes to grasp the mys-

---

59 עדות זו תהא מסורה לכם.

60 But if the court itself sees the new moon at the end of the day before nightfall, it may proclaim the month on its own.

61 This viewpoint is in contrast to what is more widely believed that in part the purpose in giving the authority to *Beis Din* is so that they would have the leeway to adjust the calendar to the convenience of the community. *Rosh Hashanah* 20 perhaps gives this impression. But see *Hakirah* 19 that *ADU* is not a function of community convenience but creating better calendrical accuracy. See also *Hilchos Kiddush Hachodesh* 3:15–19 where Rambam explains the application of איום differently than Rashi—its purpose is to cause the month to be proclaimed at its astronomical time.

62 See Appendix C.

63 Were this the only factor, one could argue that perhaps the king would have been better, but early on there was no king and also the monarchy declined far before the Sanhedrin disbanded, as we will see later.

> teries, will wish to know the methods of calculation used to determine whether or not the [new] moon would be visible on a particular night…for these methods are indeed abstract and deep matters. They constitute the mystery of the calendar, which was known [only] to great Sages, who would not convey these matters to [most] other people, but only to ordained and perceptive [Sages].[64]

It is only the most learned scholars, the *Chachamim,* who could be relied upon to know when the new moon would appear. The requirement of *smuchim*[65] is in all probability because they are the experts in the law who received the ancient traditions on matters related to these wisdoms[66] and who are the most qualified to judge on these issues and to determine the reliability of the witnesses. The law that witnesses were to be used is not some symbolic decree[67], but an application of the general halachic guideline in issues where certainty is required. In fact, even in ancient times when the moon was covered by clouds for consecutive months, the judges would use calculation and dispense with the requirement of witnesses. The making of such decisions could only be entrusted to the *Chachamim* of *Beis Din.*

Thus, two principles emerge on why *Beis Din HaGadol* was the arbiter of the calendar. 1) As a central authority, their acceptance would be binding on all of Israel. 2) As the assembly of the greatest Torah minds in the nation, they were the most fit to determine when it was the appropriate time for *Mo'adim* to be proclaimed.

Rambam explains:

> All the statements made previously regarding the [prerogative to] sanctify *Rosh Chodesh* because of the sighting of the moon, and [to] establish a leap year to reconcile the calendar or because of a necessity, apply to the Sanhedrin in Eretz Yisrael. [For it is they] alone, or a court of judges possessing *semichah* that holds sessions in Eretz Yisrael and that was granted authority by the Sanhedrin [who may authorize these decisions]. [This concept is derived] from the command given Moses and Aaron [*Shemos* 12:2]: "This month shall be

---

64 לפי שאמרנו בהלכות אלו שבית דין היו מחשבין בדקדוק ויודעים אם יראה הירח או לא יראה, ידענו שכל מי שרוחו נכונה ולבו תאב לדברי החכמות ולעמוד על הסודות יתאוה לידע אותם הדרכים שמחשבים בהם עד שידע אדם אם יראה הירח בליל זה או לא יראה ... **והוא סוד העבור שהיו החכמים הגדולים יודעים אותו ואין מוסרין אותו לכל אדם אלא לסמוכים נבונים** (קה"ח יא:א) עי' גם יז:כד.

65 סנהד' ה:ז, קה"ה א:א – סמוכים.

66 מומחים, בעלי הקבלה.

67 חק.

> for you the first of months." The Oral Tradition as passed down, teacher to student, from Moses our teacher [throughout the generations, explains that] the verse is interpreted as follows: **This testimony is entrusted to you and those [Sages] who arise after you and who function in your position.**[68]

The inheritors of the authority of Moshe and Aharon were given this role.[69]

The Fixed Calendar and Torah Authority

But, what if *Beis Din HaGadol* should disappear from the scene? Would the Jewish calendar cease to exist? Rambam addresses this issue both in *Sefer HaMitzvos* and in *Mishneh Torah* and explains what provisions the Torah made for that day.

> When, however, there is no Sanhedrin in Eretz Yisrael, we establish the monthly calendar and institute leap years solely according to the fixed calendar that is followed now. This concept is a halachah communicated to Moses on [Mount] Sinai: When there is a Sanhedrin, the monthly calendar is established according to the sighting of the moon. When there is no Sanhedrin, the monthly calendar is established according to the fixed calendar that we follow now, and the sighting of the moon is of no consequence.... When did the entire Jewish people begin using this calendar? At the conclusion of the Talmudic period, when Eretz Yisrael was in ruins, and an established court no longer remained there. In the era of the Sages of the Mishnah, and in the era of the Sages of the Gemara until the time of

---

68 כל שאמרנו מקביעת ראש החודש על הראייה, ועיבור השנה מפני הזמן או מפני הצורך, אין עושין אותו אלא סנהדרין שבארץ ישראל, או בית דין הסמוכים שבארץ ישראל שנתנו להן הסנהדרין רשות: שכך נאמר למשה ואהרון "החודש הזה לכם, ראש חודשים" ומפי השמועה למדו איש מאיש ממשה רבנו, שכך הוא פירוש הדבר—עדות זו תהיה מסורה "לכם", ולכל העומד אחריכם במקומכם (קה"ח ה:א).

69 This concept of במקומכם is in their role as those who received the position of בעלי קבלה from Moshe and Aharon and thus it would be the *Beis Din* of Yehoshua that accepted it from that of Moshe and Aharon. See the introduction to *Mishneh Torah* that one particular *Beis Din* is always considered the inheritor of this mantle. See introduction to *Peirush HaMishnah* that Aharon was the first to receive it from Moshe. See *Kovetz Chiddushei Torah* of *Mori V'Rebbi* Rav Yosef Dov Soloveitchik, *zt"l*, pg 46ff who expands on this concept and much of what I write here is based on his words.

Abaye and Rava, [the people] would rely on the establishment [of the calendar] in Eretz Yisrael.[70]

A *halachah l'Moshe miSinai* stipulated that once *Beis Din HaGadol* was no longer operable, the system of calculation[71] should be used.[72] Exactness was given up, but uniformity was preserved. Nevertheless, although the requirement of *Beis Din HaGadol* and *semuchim* was abandoned, a *Beis Din* in Eretz Yisrael was still required under this system.

Rambam, at the very beginning of *Hilchos Kiddush HaChodesh*, explains "that we do not calculate and establish months and intercalate years, but in Eretz Yisrael, as it is written, 'From Zion will the Torah go out and the word of G-d from Yerushalayim.'"[73]

Even calculation requires Eretz Yisrael—the source of the Torah. In *Sefer HaMitzvos* he writes as follows:

> And here there is a great principle amongst the fundamentals of our faith ... and it is that which we in the Diaspora keep count of the intercalation that we have by tradition ... it is not due to our calculations that [the calendar] is set, but because **a *Beis Din* in Eretz Yisrael have already selected this day** as *Rosh Chodesh* or a *Mo'ed*.[74]

---

70 ודבר זה הלכה למשה מסיני הוא שבזמן שיש סנהדרין קובעין על פי הראיה ובזמן שאין שם סנהדרין קובעים על פי החשבון הזה שאנו מחשבין בו היום ואין נזקקין לראיה... ומאימתי התחילו כל ישראל לחשב בחשבון זה? מסוף חכמי הגמרא, בעת שחרבה ארץ ישראל ולא נשאר שם בית דין קבוע. (קה"ח ה:ב)

We have been inexact in using the term בית דין הגדול as Rambam uses the term בית דין קבוע as well as סנהדרין in *Mishneh Torah* and only in *Sefer HaMitzvos* uses the term בית דין הגדול. We explain this in Appendix D.

71 חשבון.

72 ונראה כהחזו"א דאין חשבנינו חלק מההלמ"מ רק הא דעושין על פי החשבון The Chazon Ish says that the הלמ"מ is only that calculations must be made, but no set calculation is part of that הלמ"מ. This would accord with evidence discovered in the 20th century that the calendar has changed from first inception. See Adjler's essay on the history of the calendar in this volume.

73 אין מחשבין וקובעים חדשים ומעברים שנים אלא בארץ ישראל שנאמר כי מציון תצא תורה ודבר ה' מירושלים. (קה"ח א:ח)

74 אבל מצוה זו לא יעשה אותה לעולם זולתי בית דין הגדול לבד ובארץ ישראל לבד ולכן בטלה הראיה אצלנו היום להעדר בית דין הגדול וכו' ובכאן שרש גדול מאד משרשי האמונה וכו' וזה שהיותנו היום בחוצה לארץ מונים במלאכת העבור שבידינו וכו' לא מפני חשבוננו נקבעהו יום טוב בשום פנים אלא מפני שבית דין (כגירסת קאפח, ואין גורסין "הגדול" - עי' בהערות ר' חיים העליר ובלב שמח) שבארץ ישראל כבר קבעו זה היום יום טוב או ראש חדש.

There is a need for a *Beis Din* in Eretz Yisrael based on "From Zion the Torah shall go out, and the word of G-d from Yerushalayim."[75] Coupled with the *drash* of "All who stand in your place," the principle emerges that while *Beis Din HaGadol* is not necessary, still the Torah authority that they represent is indispensable. Torah authority of the *Chachmei Yisrael* is guaranteed in perpetuity and like *semichah* itself, is linked to Eretz Yisrael.[76] Remarkably, Rambam writes that Israel is guaranteed that it will always sustain a community in Israel—and this community will always have a *Beis Din* that will establish a Jewish calendar.

Rav Meir Simchah[77] writes that the principle that emerges from this analysis of present day *Kiddush HaChodesh* forms Rambam's stance on the reestablishment of *semichah:*

> It appears to me that if all the *Chachamim* in Eretz Yisrael agree to appoint judges and give them *semichah,* they will be *semuchim.*[78]

Both *Kiddush HaChodesh* and *semichah* are functions of "all who stand after you in your place," and since this power rests within the *talmidei chachamim* of each generation, the authority to grant *semichah* also remains with them.[79] The knowledge of Torah and the authority of Torah remains in *Chachmei Yisrael* and this enables the sustaining of a Jewish calendar, and in fact the sustaining of Judaism and the Jewish people.

Ramban's Explanation of *Kiddush HaChodesh*

Ramban saw the authority needed for *Kiddush HaChodesh* very differently. To him, the ability to perform *Kiddush HaChodesh* and *Ibbur Shanim* is dependent only on *semichah,* not the *Beis Din HaGadol,* and on the other hand

---

75 But whereas in *Sefer Hamitzvos* the authority is that of a *Beis Din* in Eretz Yisrael, in *Mishneh Torah* (5:13) he writes as follows: אנו מחשבין לידע יום שקבעו בו בני ארץ ישראל. Nevertheless, because the sourcing of the *halachah* is כי מציון and כל העומד במקומכם, we must assume that the intent is always to the Torah authority of the scholars of Eretz Yisrael.

76 ואף שבשעת הדחק היה גדול הדור קובע אף בחוץ לארץ (קה"ה א:ח, סה"מ), לא היה זה אלא משום "ונסמך בארץ ישראל" דעל ידי קבלת סמיכה בארץ ישראל היה לו כח הזה.

77 *Meshech Chochmah Parashas Bo.*

78 נראין לי הדברים, שאם הסכימו כל החכמים שבארץ ישראל למנות דיינים ולסמוך אותם, הרי אלו סמוכים (סנהד' ד:יא, וכן כתב בפיה"מ סנהד' א:ג).

79 As Rav Hershel Schachter noted in his article on "women rabbis" in *Hakirah,* Rabbi Shaul Lieberman assembled the early sources demonstrating that present-day *semichah* was a Rabbinic means of keeping alive original *semichah* until a qualified person arises who will be granted actual *semichah.*

this requirement can never be suspended.[80]

But if there is no requirement of *Beis Din HaGadol,* of one Central Court legislating for the entire nation, then what is the principle of "all who stand afterwards in your place" and why do we always find the proclamation in the hands of *Beis Din HaGadol* as long as it existed? He explains "that as long as *Beis Din HaGadol* existed the matter was handed over to them" (מסור להם) and:

> Permission of all of Israel was removed from any other court that existed with them and there was agreement that there would be no *Ibbur Shanah* unless the *Nasi* would agree.[81]

It is not absolutely clear from Ramban's language, who it is that hands over this authority to *Beis Din HaGadol.* But we know enough about Ramban's thinking to understand that it is the Jewish people as a whole who give them this authority, as the most straightforward reading of his words imply.[82] And although the agreement of the *Nasi* is needed, the authority only rests with him because the people grant it to him.

Later, Ramban suggests an amendment of which he is uncertain.

> It appears to me then when the Holy Temple existed, so that *Beis Din HaGadol* was in its proper place and permission was granted them from the *mikra* that states, "And you should do according to that which they tell you from that place which G-d chooses," there was no permission to any man to be *me'aber* or *mekadesh* except with their permission—and so it says in the *mechilta*: "Rav Yoshiyah says, 'How do I know that we are not *me'aber hashanah* except in *Beis Din HaGadol* in Yerushalayim? Because it says, "It will be the first to you. Speak to the entire congregation of Israel,"'" and this is the matter

80 He argues that *Beis Din HaGadol* was dissolved long before Talmudic times and *Kiddush HaChodesh* continued to be performed on the basis of testimony. Rambam clearly holds that in fact it functioned until the times of *Abaye* and *Rava.* We explain the two positions in Appendix E.

81 אל תשתומם בזה ממאמרם משה במקום שבעים וחד קאי וכו' אינו אלא למומחין ככם וכו' אלא בזמן שהיה להם ב"ד הגדול היה הדבר מסור להם והם היו מקדשים את החדש וכו' מפני שרשות כל ישראל נטולה מכל ב"ד אחר עמהם והיה מסכימין שאין מעברין השנה אא"כ ירצה הנשיא וכו' (סה"מ עשה קנ"ג).

82 According to this analysis, having a central calendar for all of Israel is not part of the mitzvah and opens the door to the possibility of there being different calendars in different places. See Appendix F.

we have explained, that they had the permission of all of Israel and the consensus of all of them, not that other *semuchim* are invalidated.[83]

On the one hand this language, based on the *mechilta,* confirms that the authority comes from all of Israel's consent. Simple logic demands that all of Israel have one calendar, and for this the consent of the people is needed. But here he introduces, as well, the idea that the *mikra* gives them exclusive authority in the same way they were given in *psak halachah* and based on the same verse. He apparently views this as a separate requirement, an expansion of the requirement of *semuchim*—viewing the declaration of the new moon as the establishment of a Torah *psak* and for this, of course, the authority must come from the Torah.[84]

Then he goes on to say that as long as there are *semuchim*, these two authorities—that of the appointed representative of all of Israel and that of the leading *posek*—are granted to the *Gadol HaDor.* [85] [86]

Thus, in his final evaluation, he requires central Torah authority akin to Rambam, but alongside of it sees the need of public consent, as a second element. But as central Torah authority is a required element embodied in *Semichah*, he is forced to say that *Kiddush HaChodesh* was done for future generations by Hillel in the year 356. Had he not acted, the Jewish calendar would have ended forever. In contrast, according to Rambam, Torah authority is indeed needed to establish the *Mo'adim*, but this authority remains forever within the hearts and minds of the *talmidei chachamim* of each generation.

---

83 יראה לי שבזמן שבית המקדש קיים שהיו ב"ד הגדול במקומם ולהם הרשות נתונה מן הכתוב שנ' (ר"פ שופטי') ועשית על פי הדבר אשר יגידו לך מן המקום ההוא אשר יבחר י"י לא היה רשות לשום אדם לעבר ולקדש אלא להם או ברשותם. וכך אמרו במכילתא (ר"פ החודש) ר' יאשיה אומר מנין אתה אומר שאין מעברין את השנה אלא בב"ד הגדול שבירושלם ת"ל ראשון הוא לכם דברו אל כל עדת בני ישראל. והוא העניין שפרשנו שהיה להם רשות כל ישראל והסכמה שלכלם, לא שיהיו שאר הסמוכין פסולין לזה.

84 וזו היא הרמב"ן לשטתו שהוא משוה הא דיש לב"ד הגדול כח להכריע ההלכה לכחם לקבוע ר"ח ד"כי על המשמעות שלהם הוא מצוה ונותן התורה" (שרש א דף יז ובפירושו על התורה). כמו שדיני מלאכה בימים טובים ניתן לפי דעתם כן זמני הימים טובים ניתן על פי דעתם. אבל בזמן שנתבטל כחם של בית דין הגדול, אין לשום בית דין היכולת לקבוע בעד כל ישראל.

85 אבל כיון שגלו ונטל כח המשפט מהם שהמקום גורם ואין להם כח אפילו כסנהדרי קטנה לדון דיני נפשות מאותה שעה תהיה הרשות ביד הגדול שבישראל לקדש ולעבר אפילו בחו"ל.

86 See *Chinuch* 495 who extends this to the *Gadol HaDor* of every generation, even in present times. See *Hakirah* 8, "Tradition! Tradition?" for a discussion of this.

Torah Authority

Ramban consistently contends that it is the acceptance of the people that gives authority to the Rabbis. Just as it is the source of the Rabbis' ability to establish *mitzvos d'Rabbanan*, it is the source for their ability to establish a universal calendar. According to Rambam, the authority for both *mitzvos d'Rabbanan* and for *Kiddush HaChodesh* comes from their position as the receivers of the *mesorah*[87], those who follow after Moshe and Aharon and stand in their place.

Ramban makes the point that the return of *Kiddush HaChodesh* via *Beis Din* will only occur with the reestablishment of *semichah* after the coming of Eliyahu HaNavi and with the rebuilding of the *Beis HaMikdash*. The importance of Eliyahu is perhaps the Aggadic tradition that Eliyahu never died and is able to pass on the *kabbalah* that had started with Moshe Rabbeinu, to a new generation. While Rambam quotes (end of *Mishneh Torah*) this statement of *Chazal* that Eliyahu himself will return, his own interpretation of the statement is that prophecy will return as a function of the same return of wisdom that will enable the reestablishment of the Sanhedrin by *Chachmei Yisrael*. ☙

87 בעלי המסורה.

Appendix A

והקשה התשב"ץ (זהר"ק לשרש הראשון) על רבינו "וענין מחלקותם בזה היא תימה בעיני הרבה, שדעתו של הרמב"ם היא הפך מה שהעלו בגמרא שבועות (כא:) ובאחרון מיומא (עז:) דהתם אקשינן עליה דריש לקיש דאמר חצי שיעור אסור מדרבנן ממתניתן דתנן שבועה שלא אוכל ואכל נבלות וטריפות חייב ור' שמעון פוטר והוינן עלה הא מושבע ועומד מהר סיני הוא? ואוקמוה ר"ל במפרש חצי שיעור ואליבא דרבנן ואי חצי שיעור אסור מדרבנן, מושבע ועומד מהר סיני הוא, ופרש"י משום האי לאו דלא תסור. ודחינן כיון דאית ליה היתר מן התורה לאו מושבע מהר סיני הוא. ובהכי סלקא שמעתא וא"כ איך אפשר לרבינו לומר שאיסורן דרבנן בכלל לאו דלא תסור הם? (עיי"ש) "ותירץ המג"א ד"מאחר שלא נאמרו בברור בסיני לא יאמר עליהם מושבע ועומד מהר סיני," אבל אין זה הוכחה שאינם נכללין בלאו דלא תסור. ואדרבא הביא ראיה (גם בלב שמח) מההוה אמינא דהגמרא דהיה עולה על דעתם דמשום לא תסור יהיה אסור דרבנן שוה לאסור דאורייתא דשניהם נקראים מושבע ועומד, אלא דמסיק הש"ס דאין דרבנן נקרא מושבע ועומד אבל עדיין חל לא תסור עליה. ומבואר שזהו שטת רבינו ממה שכתב בתשובה (פאר הדור ב) דלמסקנא "פחות מכזית אף שהוא אסור מדאורייתא אינו מושבע עליו מהר סיני," וכן פסק בהל' שבועות (ה:ז- ובאר הכס"מ שטתו כן). וזה לשון הרדב"ז "דנהי דחצי שיעור אסור מן התורה דחזי לאצטרופי אבל אין מפורש בתורה איסורו ובשבועה לא היתה אלא על הדברים המפורשים בתורה. תדע שהרי כתיב בתורה לא תסור מן הדבר אשר יגידו לך ואפ"ה חיילא שבועה אאיסורין דרבנן." (וכן הוא בר"ן בנדרים (ח:).) והקשה התשב"ץ על הרמב"ן, למה לא הביא הראיה שהביא הוא מן הש"ס. אבל לפי מה שראינו דהרמב"ן סובר דבאמת אף על מצוות דרבנן מושבעין אנו בהם מהר סיני אי אפשר להביא ראיה מהא דמצוות דרבנן אינן נקראין מושבע מהר סיני דאין מחוייבים הן מדאורייתא דאף על מצוות דרבנן כן נקראים הן מושבע ועומד. ועל כרחך לרמב"ן לשון מושבע ועומד 'לאו דוקא' היא וודאי אינו ענין של אסור תורה, ולכן מבואר כונת הגמ' בההו"א דאף על מצוות דרבנן מושבע ועומד הוא דהיינו על פי פירושו דקבלו ישראל לעשות כל אסורי דרבנן, ומסיק הגמ' "כיון דאית ליה היתר מן התורה" שאני דרבנן מדאורייתא. ומ"מ כבר כתב הרמב"ן דרבינו יטעון דמפורש בקרא שאני ממצווה דרבנן. ועוד דאף לפי הרמב"ן, מה שפרשו חז"ל בכונת התורה היא בכלל לא תסור וודאי בגדר השבועה היא.

Appendix B

והרי זה מסכים עם היסוד של הבריסקר רב (הל' סנהד' ה:א) דהקשה למה השמיט רבינו במנינו של בי"ד של ע"א הא דהעמדת כה"ג. ותירץ "שבהל' סהנד' איירי בב"ד בגדר "דבר הגדול" אבל כה"ג נתמנה (כה"מ ד:טו) משום "דבדבר השייך לכל ישראל הב"ד של ע"א הם הבעלים על זה." הרי חדש דב"ד יש להם גדר של שליח בעד כל ישראל. ועי' תוס' יומא יב: דסברי דהמנוי על ידי מלך ואחיו הכהנים. וזה הרעיון של הבריסקר רב מבוסס על דעת הרמב"ן ועל דעת ר' דוד דיש שני דינים

לב"ד, והדין השני היא דעומד במקום כל ישראל. והיא גם כן דעת מו"ר הגר"ד זצ"ל (קובץ חדושי תורה דף נא-נב) דמביא לשון רבינו בהל' תרומות (א:ב,ג) ומלכים (ה:ו) דמשם הוכיח דהא דבעינן ב"ד לכבוש הארצות הוא אותו הדין של "דעת רוב ישראל." ולכן הוכיח שיש שני חלותים בב"ד, של הוראה שלמדו ממשה דהיינו ויאצל מרוחו ושל זה של פרשת יתרו של דידעתם בם שהם שוטרי העם וכעין טובי העיר – "דכל היכא דאיכא הסכמת ב"ד הגדול, ישנן הסכמת ודעת רוב ישראל." מ"מ יש לפקפק על ראיות אלו ואין כאן מקומו להאריך.

Appendix C

ובאמת אצל עבור השנה יש שתי מיני טעמים שמעברים בשבילם דהיינו משום התקופה ועל האביב מצד אחד ועל צורכי עולי רגל מצד השני, ולכן כן משמע דנמסר הדבר לב"ד כדי שיוכלו לתקן המועדים לתועלת העם. אבל שאני עבור השנה מקדוש החדש דאין בקביעת עבור שנה שום סימן מובהק שבו תלוי האביב, דהרי אפשר דסימן אביב התבואה יסתור את סימן התקופה. אצל קדוש החדש המולד הוא עצמו התחדשות השנה אבל בעבור שנה אין לנו אלא "סימנים" שהשנה ראויה לעבור, ולכן יש חיוב על ב"ד לדון מעצמן מה הוא אביב ומה אינו אביב. ועוד מצינו דרבינו חלק בין שתי מיני טעמים שבעבורם מעברין (עי' חי' הגרי"ז בהל' קה"ח), ופירש (קה"ח ג:טז) דהא דאין מעברין בשעת רעבון לא נאמרה במקום שראויה החדש לעבר בשביל התקופה והאביב. דברים אלו הם סימני האביב וחיובא של תורה הוא לשמור את חדש האביב, דהיינו החיוב לסדר המועדים על פי שנת החמה (קה"ח א:א), והיינו עיקר החיוב שעל בית דין. אבל כיון שהתורה היה מוכרח למסור הדבר לבית דין מרכזי כמו שבארנו לעיל, אף דמגדר חיובם הוא לסדר הכל על פי הטבע במועדו, מ"מ כיון דממילא יש להם הכח לקדש או לעבר לכן בדיעבד ניתן להם הרשות לשנות הדבר קצת מסדר הטבע. ובכל זאת טעם החיוב הוא "שמור את חדש האביב," שתהא המועדים בזמנם.

Appendix D

דוקא בזמן סוף חכמי הש"ס נתבטל שם סנהדרין ולא מזמן חורבן הבית ורבינו קורא לסנהדרין בשם "בית דין קבוע" ועל "בית דין קבוע" תלוי קדוש החדש. המצות עשה (קעו) של מינוי שופטים הוא ב"דיינים הקבועין בבית דין" (הל' סנהד' א:א, וכתב בהלכה ג' "כמה בתי דינים קבועין יהיו.. קובעין בתחלה") ו"בית דין קבוע" היינו שהבית דין קבוע ועומד במקום מיוחד וזהו סנהדרין. ודוקא מזמן שנחרבה הארץ ונתבטל היישוב ונשלמה הגלות נתבטל בית דין קבוע. ומאז לא היה שייך עוד לקיים החלק השני של מצות קדוש החדש, שתהיו המועדים בזמנם בדקדוק, שהרי לא היה בית דין מרכזי קבוע בארץ ישראל לקבל את עדי הראיה, והראיה הקובעת והחשבונות שנמסרו לחכמים כולם מבוססין על ארץ ישראל (קה"ח יא:יז). ועוד בעינן לשם "סנהדרין" חכמים מוסמכים (סנהד' ד:א - על פי גירסת כת"י תימנים ועל פי פיה"מ סנהדרין א:ג), ואין שייך סמיכה אלא בארץ ישראל (סנהד' ד:ו), לכן

נראה עוד דכיון דנתבטל הסמיכה, לא היו יכולין לבטוח בהמחאת הדיינים לידיעת החשבון של המולד, שהרי באר רבינו (קה"ח יז:כד) שאף בזמנו כבר נאבד קבלת חכמים בחשבון המולד ומטעם זה הלוח בזמן הזה נקבע על פי חשבון העבור שאינו נעשית בדקדוק גדול (קה"ח ה:ב, ו:א, יא:ד). הרי משני טעמים האלו נתבטלו קדוש על ידי הראיה מזמן בטול סנהדרין.

Appendix E

כותב רבינו (עיין הל' קה"ח ה:ג, סנהד' יד:יב) דעדיין היה ב"ד הגדול וסנהדרין קיים עד ימי אביי ורבא. אבל טוען הרמב"ן דכבר נתבטל משגלתה סנהדרין מלשכת הגזית ארבעים שנה לפני חורבן הבית. ושטת הרמב"ן הוא ד"מאותה שעה בטלו כל הדינין התלוין בב"ד הגדול." וכבר תירץ המג"א דבזה פליגי רבינו על הרמב"ן, דלפי דעתו לא נתבטל אלא הכח לדון דיני נפשות. וכן הוא מבואר מדברי רבינו (סנהד' יד:יא-יב, סה"מ לאחר שרש יד) דהאי דין הוא הלכה בפני עצמו הנלמד מן "לבלתי שמע אל הכהן וגו' .. שבזמן שיש כהן מקריב על גבי המזבח יש דיני נפשות, והוא שיהיה בית דין הגדול במקומו," אבל לדברים אחרים עדיין שם ב"ד הגדול עליו. ובההקדמה למשנה תורה קרא רבינו לכל בית דין שלאחר ב"ד של מש"ר שם ב"ד הגדול ולכן נראה דאין שם ב"ד הגדול תלוי על קביעה במקום המקדש וכמו שהיה השם כן לפני הקמת הבית כן נראה דנשאר השם אחר חורבנו. וכך כתב רבינו (סנהד' א:ג) "קובעין בתחלה בית דין הגדול במקדש והוא הנקרא סנהדרי גדולה," דפירוש המלים הוא דכשקובעין הבית דין שהוא כבר בית דין הגדול במקום המקדש, אז נקרא בשם "**סנהדרי** גדולה." (והנראה דהרמב"ן מסכים דדנו דיני נפשות לפני הקמת הבית, והיה כבר שם ב"ד הגדול אבל מ"מ בכל מקום בעינן שהב"ד תהא במקום המקדש לשם ב"ד הגדול, ולפני בנין הבית היה שם המקדש על המשכן.)

והקשה הרמב"ן "ואפילו ביציאתם משם לטייל מעט ולחזור בטל כוחן ורשותן וכו' מלמד שהמקום גורם." אלא דעת רבינו דלא רק שם ב"ד הגדול לא נסתלק בגלותו אלא דגם שם סנהדרין - בית דין קבוע - היה עומד במקומו לאחר שגלתה. נקבעו אף סנהדריות הקטנות בארץ ישראל בשעת העמדת סנהדרי גדולה, ולא נסתלקה סדר הבתי דינים הקבועים בסלוק ב"ד הגדול ממקומו, רק דלא יוכלו עוד לדון דיני נפשות שתלוי בבתי דינים שנתעלו במדרגה על ידי קשירתם למקום המקדש. אבל בההקדמה להמצוות (סוף שרש יד) כתב רבינו "וכן דיני נפשות אין דנין בהם אלא בזמן שבית המקדש קיים ולשון המכילתא מנין שאין ממיתין אלא בפני הבית תלמוד לומר מעם מזבחי תקחנו למות הא אם יש לך בית אתה ממית אם לאו אין אתה ממית. ושם נאמר גם כן מנין שתהא סנהדרין סמוכה למזבח ת"ל מעם מזבחי." ומבואר בדבריו אלו וגם ממה שכתב שם להלן, דשתי ענינים נפרדים יש, דדיני נפשות תלוים בבית המקדש וגם דשם סנהדרין תלוי בקרבה להמזבח. והרי זה סותר מה שכתב בקה"ח (ה:ב-ג) דשם סנהדרין עדיין נשאר עד ימי אביי ורבא. והנראה פשוט, דכונתו דשם "סנהדרי גדולה" תלוי בקרבה להמזבח, כמו שכתב בהל' סהנדרין (א:א) דכשהוקם

ב"ד הגדול בירושלים נעשית סנהדרי גדולה. והך דין של סנהדרי גדולה הוא שפקע ממנו בגלות וכך הוא לשון הש"ס לפי גירסת הרמב"ן "גלתה סנהדרין גדולה."

ובזה ניחא קושית הרמב"ן מהא דהמרה בבית פאגי פטור דמשם הוכיח דאין זה רק גזה"כ השייך לדיני נפשות אלא דנסתלק שם סנהדרי גדולה ממנו. אלא בזה פליגי הרמב"ן ורבינו, דלרמב"ן נסתלק כל שם ב"ד הגדול ולרבינו לא נסתלק אלא שם סנהדרי גדולה, ורוב הדינים השייכים לב"ד הגדול אינם תלוים על שם סנהדרי גדולה התלוי במקום. ואיזה דין תלוי בשם סנהדרי גדולה? הדין דאיירי בה פשטה דקרא של "מן המקום ההוא" דהיינו דין זקן ממרא. ולפי רבינו רק לדין זה של סנהדרי גדולה נאמר "מקומן" ולא לשאר דינים של ב"ד הגדול. וכיון דלפי רבינו היה ב"ד הגדול עדיין קיים עד ימי רבא ואביי אין קשה עליו ממה שהביא הרמב"ן ראיות מבבלי וירושלמי שהיו מקדשין ומעברין לאחר החרבן. אבל, לפי רבינו, היו דוקא עושין כן בבית דין הגדול שבזמנם ולא "בשאר בתי דינין."

Appendix F

והעולה משטת הרמב"ן דלכל בית דין יש כח לקדש החדש, דלא חייבה הכתוב בחלק הראשון של המצוה שהגדיר רבינו, דחלק עקרי מהמצוה הוא שתהא רק קביעה אחת במועדים לכל ישראל - ולרמב"ן אין זה חלק מהמצוה כלל. ולפי דעת הרמב"ן מובן מה שכתב תוס' (ר"ה כא. ד"ה לוי - ותמה הריטב"א והטורי אבן על שטה זו) דלאחר חורבן הבית היה יכול בית דין בחוץ לארץ לקבוע יום אחר לר"ח מהא שנקבע בארץ ישראל ויהיה חלות לקביעותם. לפי הרמב"ן ניתן קביעת החדש לכל בתי דינים הסמוכים ולא היה תנאי בהמצוה שינהגו כל העם יום אחד. והא דהיו נוהגים כל ישראל בימי המקדש על פי קביעת ב"ד הגדול, זה היה דין היוצא מכחו של בית דין הגדול.

איני מחויב לתיאוריה המוצגת כאן. המקורות הנחקרים בגוף המאמר עומדות מצד עצמם, וכפי שכבר ציינתי, הן מהווים את נקודות המידע בשיטתו של רבי שמעון. התיאוריה חשובה בכך שהיא מסבירה את נקודות המידע בדרך פשוט וברור, ואם יימצאו עוד מקרים בהם דן רבי שמעון בעניין מידות ושיעורים בהלכה, ייתכן שהתיאוריה תיאלץ לעבור שינויים דרמטיים, או להיזרק לחלוטין. אך מהמידע הקיים לפנינו עת עתה, לפחות סביר לומר שרוב המקרים המנותחים במאמר זה הם דוגמאות טובות לכך שרבי שמעון פועל במישור הסטנדרטיזציה של מידות ושיעורים בהקשר רוב ההלכה – הדורשת מן העם היהודי לשמרה בבית, בשדה וברחוב, בחורין וסדקין של לבבות הפועמות לקצבה של התורה. אך במקרים שההחלטה על הלכה זו או אחרת מובאת בפני מערכת שיפוט של בית דין או המקדש, אזי רבי שמעון מגלה התנגדות עקשנית לסטנדרטיזציה זו. לפיכך, נראה הוא כדמות כה מעניינת וחשובה בשינוי אשר התהווה בהלכה בענין המידות והשיעורים.

☙

שיקח בשר בזול ויאכל, יין בזול וישתה." וצריך הוא לגנוב לא רק משל אביו, אלא גם משל אמו (דבר המצריך שיגנוב מדמים המיוחדים לסעודת אביו ואמו ביחד, או שאדם אחר ייתן מעות לאמו על מנת שאין לבעלה רשות בהן). ובהמשך הדברים, מופיעים דברי רבי יהודה:

> ר' יהוד' אומ' אם לא היתה אמו שוה לאביו בקול במראה ובקומה אינו נעש' בן סו' ומורה. מאי טעמ' דאמ' קרא "איננו שומע בקולנו". מדקול בענן שוין. במראה וקומה נמי בענן שווין.

צמצום המקרים בהם יכול נער להיחשב בן סורר ומורה, המגיע לפסגה בדברי רבי יהודה, מתבטאת בדרשות מגמתיות, אך מבחינה פורמאליסטית, הן מחריפות את הסטנדרטיזציה של ההלכה. רבי יהודה מחייב את הבן רק אם קיימת שויון מוחלטת בין קול, מראה, וקומה של ההורים, פורמאליות ש – כמעט או לחלוטין - מוציאה את דין "בן סורר ומורה" מכלל היישום. אך הסטנדרטיזציה נעשית בדברים הנוגעים להחלטות בית דין. רק לאחר הגעת ההורים והבן לבית דין, עולה השאלה, האם זה בן סורר ומורה, ואפילו בתחום הפעולה של בית הדין, רבי יהודה עושה סטנדרטיזציה.

לא כך שיטת רבי שמעון, המופיעה לאחר מדברי רבי יהודה:

> ...דתניא א"ר שמעון. מפני שאכל זה תרמיטר בשר ושתה חצי לוג יין באיטלקי אביו ואמו מביאין אותו לסקלו. אלא לא היה ולא עתיד להיות. ולמה נכתב. דרוש וקבל שכר.

רבי שמעון משתמש בציניות כאן. הוא אומר, בגלל שאדם זה אכל סכום זה של בשר, ושתה סכום כזה של יין, הוריו יביאו אותו לדין?! ברור שלא! מה שמסתתר כאן היא התזוזה: רבי שמעון מזיז את השאלה מחוץ לתחום בית המשפט, ומדבר על החלטת ההורים עצמם – בביתם - להביא את בנם לדין או לא. כמובן שהשיעורים של תרמיטר בשר וחצי לוג יין אינם אמורים להילקח כמדוייקים – אך עדין, בציניות, רבי שמעון משתמש במונחים של שיעורים ומידות. ובגלל שלשיטתו, שיעורים ומידות אינם מחייבים סטנדרטיזציה בתחום הפעולה של הבית דין, רבי שמעון בוחר להיות עקבי (על-אף שכמובן כאן הכל נאמר תוך מגמה כללית להפוך את דין בן סורר ומורה לאי-יישומי), ומעביר את הדיון למישור שיפוט ההורים, לפני הגעת השאלה לבית דין, בהחלטתם אם בכלל להביא את בנם למערכת המשפט.

ניפויים אלו נעשו? לפי המשנה במנחות פרק י, ד, קציר העומר הובא למקדש, שם הושטח לצורך ייבוש, ולאחר מכן, נטחן ומנופה. ובפרק יא, ב, גבי שתי הלחם ולחם הפנים, מובא מחלוקת: לפי תנא קמא לישתן ועריכתן בחוץ, ואם כן, מסתבר שאפילו הניפוי היה בחוץ. לפי רבי יהודה, כל מעשה שתי הלחם ולחם הפנים היה במקדש. ולשיטת רבי שמעון, כשרה כל תהליך שתי הלחם ולחם הפנים בעזרה, או בבית פאגי, שהוא מחוץ לעזרה. הרי ניפוי העומר נעשה בעזרה עצמה לכולי עלמא, וניפוי קמח שתי הלחם ולחם הפנים נעשה לפי רבי שמעון או בתוך העזרה, או מחוצה לה, אך עדיין בתחום הפעולה של הכהונה, בבית פאגי. עכשיו, במשנה שהובא לעיל בפרק ו, ז, מופיע תנא קמא (המובא כסתמא על ידי רבי, מסדר המשנה), שמחייב סטנדרטיזציה מאוד מדויקת לכל אחד מניפוים אלו, ואילו רבי שמעון פוסק רק "כל צרכה". לא רחוק מן הסברא לומר שרבי יהודה מחייב סטנדרטיזציה מסויימת אפילו תוך תחום הפעולה של הכהנים, אך רבי שמעון, אף על פי שבענייני האדם הרגיל ברחוב, מסכים ואף מחריף את מגמת הסטנדרטיזציה, מתנער מפורמאליות דוקא כאן, בתחום פעולה של המקדש, מקום ה"כהנים [ה]זריזים הם", כיון שאינו מקבל את הצעד הנוסף הכרוך בזה.[50]

בענין המזיק על ידי הדליקה, הדבר דומה. עצם שאלת חיוב או פטור לגבי נזק משריפה, רק תתישב בבית דין, כאשר המזיק והניזק באים לפני דיינים, מומחים בהלכות נזיקין; ההחלטה איננה ניתנת בידי המזיק עצמו, להחליט אם הוא חייב או פטור. רבי עקיבא, רבי אלעזר בן עזריה ורבי אליעזר נותנים שיעור קצוב, גם בתחום שיפוט הבית דין, אך רבי שמעון מתקומם נגד זה. שמא לפי רבי שמעון, דוקא כאן, בתחום פעולה של דיינים מומחים, חייבת ההלכה להשאיר את כל גמישות הפסיקה בידי הדיינים האמינים, ש"אין להם אלא מה שעיני[הם] רואות", ולברוח מסטנדרטיזציה.

ובענין שיעור אכילת הטבל, אכן רבי שמעון נמנע מלהפעיל סטנדרטיזציה, אך, כפי שראינו בבריתא, האפשרות סבירה מאוד שהוא רק נמנע "לעניין מלקות". מפליא איך הברייתא בבבלי תואמת את התיאוריה המוצגת כאן. לגבי ההחלטה של האדם הפשוט היושב בביתו ובטעות אוכל טבל, האם אני צריך עכשיו להגיע לירושלים ולהביא קרבן, הוא מסכים לסטנצרטזציה: חייבת ההלכה לתת גבול חד וחלק לאדם – האם אכלתי כזית או לא? אך לענין מלקות, החלטה אשר תתקיים אך ורק בבית דין של דיינים מומחים, אין שיעור חדש, אלא ההלכה נשארת כפי שהיא היתה במסורת הקדומה – כל שהוא.[51]

---

50 ממנחות פרק יב, ד, הובא לעיל סטנדרטיזציה של רבי שמעון בסכום המרבי שאפשר להביא בכלי אחד – ששים עשרון. שמה שונה הדבר מכאן, משתי סיבות: 1) רבי שמעון מסכים לתנא קמא שם ורק חולק על הסיבה לדין, שאולי היתה קיימת כבר קודם, ורק הובא מקור זה לעיל לדון בסיבתו של רבי שמעון. 2) מלשון המשנה שם מובן שהסולת כבר בכלי כאשר המקריב מביאו, כך שעצם השיעור חל על מעשה הקורה מחוץ לתחום הכהנים.

51 חברי, אריאל כהן, הפנה אותי לעוד מקרה מעניין, שנוגע לענייננו בעקיפין. בסנהדרין עא עמ' א, גבי בן סורר ומורה, הגמרא מביאה שורה של דברים הנלמדים בדרשה מן הפסוקים, המקטינים את הסיכוי שיוכל אדם להיחשב בן סורר ומורה ולהתחייב מיתה. "אינו חייב עד

מותר לאסור הינו אומדן סובייקטיבי, הנטייה "להקל על עצמי" מתחזקת, וקשה מאד לעמוד בפניה. ההלכה (ובאמת, כל תורת משפט של חברה תקינה) לא יכולה לפעול כשורה, כאשר ביום-יום, כל דקה, אנשים מחליטים להקל על עצמם מסיבות אישיות, ולהסתמך על זה ש"עדיין שדי לחה" או תירוץ אחר כל שהוא. רבי שמעון הוא חלק מתנועה הלכתית שהבינה את הפסיכולוגיה העומדת בין המשפט היבש לבין האדם החי ונתוני חייו, והחליטה שאנשים צריכים פורמאליזציה, גדרות חדים וחלקים בשיפוט הרגיל של החיים הדתיים והחברתיים. ולכן, הצורך להביא את החוקים וההלכות לסטנדרטיזציה ופורמאליות, חל קודם כל על האדם הפשוט, על החיים הפשוטים. כפי שמשה זילברג מבטא את הדבר:[49]

> המשפט העברי הוא – אם ניתן להאמר כך – משפט ללא שופטים. אין החוק מורה את הדיין כיצד לפסוק, הוא מורה את האדם כיצד לחיות. גם פריעת בעל חוב – זה היסוד המוסד של כל המשפט האזרחי – מצוה היא, וזכותו של הנושה אינה אלא רפלכס הנאצל מחובתו הדתית של החייב; השקפה ישראלית מובהקת, העומדת בניגוד דיאמטראלי להשקפתו הרכושנית הצינית של המשפט הרומאי, ואף להשקפה היותר ממוזגת של יורשיו המודרניים. פנייתו של המשפט העברי במישרין אל האזרח, היא יסוד וטעם או תוצאה הגיונית ממצוות לימוד התורה, ולפיכך הוכרזה מצווה זו שקולה "כנגד כולם". מעניין הדבר – ואיני יודע אם מישהו כבר שם לב לכך – כי השם "פסק דין" במובן הכרעה קונקרטית, מצוי בכל התלמוד כולו רק פעם אחת בלבד. והלא דבר הוא!

ההלכה מתכוונת להיות מערכת משפטית בלי שופט – האדם דן את עצמו בכל רגע, לפי מצפונו. במקרים אלו, סטנדרטיזציה חשובה למדי. אך, במקומות שוודאי הדבר צריך להגיע לתחום הפעולה של הבית דין או של בית המקדש, אינו דבר המובן מאליו שהצורך ליישם סטנדרטיזציה חל. יכול חכם להאמין שאדרבא, במקרה כזה, רצוי להעמיד את המצב כפי שהיא כבר קיימת בהלכה הקדומה, ולתת את הדבר לפני הדיינים או הכהנים. הם אינם נתונים לאותם הלחצים הפנימיים כמו האדם הפרטי. ההחלטה להרחיב את יישום הסטנדרטיזציה לתחומים אלו הינה צעד הגיוני נוסף מעל ומעבר להחלטה לעשות כן במקרים שתחום ההחלטה היא דעת האדם הרגיל ברחוב. ייתכן שתנא יישם סטנדרטיזציה באחרון בלי לעשות כן גם בראשון. מתוך התמודדות באפשרות זו, נבדוק את כל מקרה היוצא מן הכלל בדברי רבי שמעון, כשלעצמו.

המקום הראשון בו הוצבע על יוצא מן הכלל בדברי רבי שמעון הוא ניפוי הסולת ללחם הפנים (או שמא אפילו ניפוי לשתי הלחם ולקרבן העומר), ועולה השאלה: איפה

49 מ. זילברג, כך דרכו של תלמוד. בית ההוצאה של הסתדרות הסטודנטים של האוניברסיטה העברית, ירושלים. 1964, עמ' 52.

מסופק אם בכלל אפשר להסיק מסקנה חדה בשיטת רבי שמעון, בתמונה המתבררת, קיים איחוד הדוק במקומות בהם רבי שמעון מתנגד לסטנדרטיזציה, ואציע בפני הקורא את התיאוריה שלי.

הרי העבודה של היהדות הרבנית היתה ליצור מערכת חוק או משפט מתוך קבוצת "מצוות" – התחייבויות דתיות. התחיבות דתית, כמו אדיאל אתי או מוסרי, יכולה להיאמר בסגנון "הוי מקבל את כל אדם בסבר פנים יפות" או "מדבר שקר תרחק". כך מתלבשות התחיבויות מוסריות, פתוחות, ואפשר לעבוד כל החיים לחתור ליעד, ולא להשיגו. כך פועלות מעלות המוסריות של רבי פנחס בן יאיר, למשל. אבל מערכת משפטית חייבת נורמות מחייבות, שאפשר לדעת מיד, בבירור, אם אני חייב או פטור, טמא או טהור.[48] לכן, בעידן של התפתחות היהדות במישור המשפטי-הלכתי, התחילו להביא לסטנדרטיזציה של מידות ושיעורים כדי שהעולם היהודי יוכל לדעת מפורשות, מה חובתו בעולמו ההלכתי. בדיוק כמה צריכים לאכול מן המצה בפסח? כמה זמן צריך אדם לעמוד במקום טמא ולהיטמא? וכן בכל פרט ופרט בדיני התורה. ספרות התנאית והאמוראית מרמזת לעידן הישן, בה הסטנדרטים היו אורגאניים וטבעיים, בלשונות שונות: "בראשונה", "בתחילה", ו"משנה ראשונה", ובכך החוקר יכול לראות מעבר לממסד מונוליתי ולגלות את הרבדים השונים בהתהוות ההלכה. המגמה הנגלית על ידי המחקר מורה על כך שבית הלל בפרט פעלו בתחום הפורמאליזציה, והוסיפו בכך תלמידי האסכולה.

רבי שמעון, כאמור, נצר לאסכולת בית הלל, והשקפתו ההלכתית גדלה על רקע זה. לכן צפויים פסקיו הדוגלים באיחוד וסטנדרטיזציה בשיעורים ובמידות. במקומות בהם רבי שמעון הופך את המגמה הכללית שלו, מתעוררת השאלה – מה שונה במקרים אלו, במוקדים ההלכתיים האלו, שמצדיק דוקא שיעורים טבעיים ולא פורמאליים? ודוקא במקומות אלו, כפי שנוב̇ע מהמקורות, קיימים ברי-פלוגתא על רבי שמעון, היוצרים סטנדרטיזיה בדיוק במקומות שרבי שמעון בורח מזה. מוכח מכך שאין רבי שמעון פוסק בשיטה פחות פורמאלית בלית ברירה – ברור אם כן שרבי שמעון בוחר במתכוין באי-סטנדרטיזציה.

כל המקורות בהם ראינו שרבי שמעון דוגל בשיטת הפורמאליזציה (ויותר מכל חבריו, בהרבה מהם), יצויין שמדובר במקרים בהם האדם הפשוט, היהודי ברחוב, חייב להחליט בשביל עצמו אם הוא חייב קרבן או לא, אם הוא טמא (ולכן מטמא וחייב טהרה וקרבנות) או לא, אם מותר או אסור, אם הוא נתן מספיק או לא. אלו דברים שכמעט ואי אפשר לדמיין שיגיעו לדיין אחר ממצפון היחיד. עניינים אלה, בגלל זה, מייצרים מצב אינטימי בין ההלכה ובין שומרה, והסודיות של מצב זה נוטה להתנערות מסויימת מהתחייבות. אדם שעומד להפסיד ממון רב אם השדה שלו אסור כבר בחרישה, וכדומה, כאשר אין עין מפקחת, יכול לכפוף את הכללים ולהצדיק את מעשיו. כאשר הקו הדק בין

48 ואכן, בפילוסופית המשפט, קיימת קונצפט, void for vagueness, הפוסלת חוקים שאינם מספיק ברורים ומפורשים - שאינם סטנדרטיים מספיק.

השאלה כאן היא, כמה צריך אדם לאכול מפירות שלא הופרשו מהן תרומות ומעשרות, לחייבו? רבי שמעון כאן אוחז בשיטה הטבעית, הפחות פורמאלית, שאדם שאוכל אפילו טיפה, יתחייב. חכמים, לעומתו, אומרים שיטה פורמאלית, כזית, שיטה הידועה מהרבה מידות ושיעורים מאכליים. משמע מכאן שרבי שמעון מחייב בכל מובן של המילה את האוכל כל שהוא, בין אם מדובר בחיוב קרבן, בין אם מדובר בחיוב מלקות. אך בבבלי,[46] מובאת ברייתא האומרת, "רבי שמעון אומר, כל שהוא למכות, לא אמרו כזית אלא לענין קרבן." דברי הברייתא הזו שופכים אור על שיטת רבי שמעון[47] בשני דרכים אפשריות שונות: לשיטת רב ירמיה - היא מעמידה אוקימתא בדברי רבי שמעון במשנה. שיטת רבי שמעון הטבעית, הלא פורמאלית הזו, רק שייכת בענין מלקות. אבל לחיוב חטאת, מסכים רבי שמעון לסטנדרט של כזית. ולדברי רב ביבי, הברייתא לא מעמידה את דברי רבי שמעון באוקימתא, אלא מציגה שיטה אחרת בשמו, ואם כן, הברייתא שומרת מסורת שבה רבי שמעון פועל בסטנדרטיזציה יותר ממה שמופיע בשמו במשנה. מאיזה זוית שיוקח הדבר, הברייתא למעשה מביאה את רבי שמעון קרוב ככל האפשר לעמדה המצויה שלו בענין מידות ושיעורים. אך אין מנוס מכך ששיטת רבי שמעון במשנה בהחלט בולטת כמו המקורות האחרים בחלק זה, בזה שהיא מעמידה את רבי שמעון כמנוגד לסטנדרטיזציה שאחרים מקיימים.

ז. דברי סיכום

ברורה מגמתו הרגילה של רבי שמעון מרוב המקרים בהם רבי שמעון מתבטא בענין מידות ושיעורים. מדבריו בפאה, ביכורים ושמיטה, ופסקיו בשבת ואונאה, ודעותיו במעשה הקרבנות, נראה לעין שרבי שמעון פועל לסטנדרטיזצית המצב המשפטי של מידות ושיעורים בהלכה. אך למעשה, יש מדבריו שלא מתאימים למהלך זה, על פניהן. נפיית סולת ללחם הפנים (ואולי לעומר ולשתי הלחם), דין חיוב מדליק דליקה שהזיקה, וחיוב חטאת (ואולי גם מלקות) לאוכל טבל, הם מקומות בהן רבי שמעון לוקח את הצד הפחות פורמאלי, וזה בניגוד לתנאים אחרים, שדוקא כן פועלים לפורמאליזצית המידות האלו.

בתיאור הדברים, ובהבאתם יחד לצורך מחקר, העבודה החשובה נעשתה. הרי תיאוריות, תמיד אפשר ליצור, והם לרוב נשארות בבחינת השערות גרידא. אך כאשר הדברים עקביים, אפשר לבסס תיאוריה יותר חזקה, שעל-אף העובדה שהיא איננה וודאית כמו נקודות המידע שהתבררו בלימוד, שווה תשומת לב והתחשבות. אף-על-פי שאני

46 מכות יז עמ' א, דפוס וילנא. ניסיון רבי שמעון לשכנע את חכמים שהוא צודק, ותשובתם לו, ותגובתו האחרונה, בענין הברייה, וכן שני המסורות בגמרא המובאות בשם רב ביבי ורב ירמיה בדברי ר"ש בן לקיש בענין הקמח והחיטה, אינם לענייננו. ראה מ. כהנא, ספרי זוטא, עמ' 206, גבי העניין הראשון.

47 וכן נראה מדברי אפשטיין (מבוא לנוסח המשנה, עמ' 578).

התוספתא פירשה אותה כמאמר בפני עצמו, המסביר את סיבת החיוב או פטור של הדין הכללי.[43]

מצד שני, ליברמן[44] לא רואה את הדברים כך, אלא לוקח את דברי רבי שמעון בתוספתא כחולקים על התנאים הבאים אחריו, בדיוק כפי שנובע מדבריו במשנה ובמכילתא. קשה לקבל את דברי ליברמן כאן, כי דברי רבי שמעון נמצאים במיקום שקשה לומר שהם פשוט כותרת – הם מובאים כניגוד לדברי תנא קמא. לכן נראה שדברי רבי שמעון כאן מוסבים על קביעת תנא קמא שאם יש באדם מספיק כח להעביר את האש עד היכן שהוא הגיע, חייב אפילו אם למעשה הרוח עזרה לפשיטת האש. על זה רבי שמעון אומר שאפילו בלי הרוח, אם האש עצמה היתה מגיעה לשם, אזי יהיה המדליק חייב, אפילו אם הוא לא ניבה, ולא המנבה. זו הדרך הסבירה ופשוטה ביותר שאפשר להבין את רבי שמעון - כחולק על תנא קמא.[45] אם הצעה זו מתקשה להתקבל על הדעת, אפשר לאמץ את הפירוש היוצא לפי גולדברג, וכפי שהצעתי לעיל, שמגמת דברי רבי שמעון בתוספתא היא להוות כותרת והקדמה למחלוקת התנאים, כמאמר כללי, ולא חולק הוא עליהם.

לא באמת משנה איזה הסבר בדברי רבי שמעון ניקח, לפי שניהם, רק אחרי דברי רבי שמעון מגיעה מחלוקת התנאים האחרים. לפי כל האמור לעיל - ובניגוד להסבר ליברמן - נדמה שהתוספתא עורכת את דברי רבי שמעון לפני המחלוקת כדי לקבוע שאין רבי שמעון חולק על הסטנדרטיזציה של התנאים הבאים מאוחר יותר. אם כן, נראה שהתוספתא משמרת מסורת ברבי שמעון שאינה גורסת אותו כפוסק נגד מגמת הסטנדרטיזציה שדוגל הוא ברוב המקרים. מה שלא נאמר גבי התוספתא, כמובן ברור הדבר ששיטת רבי שמעון במשנה שונה מהסטנדרטיזציה שרבי שמעון רגיל בה, וכל תיאוריה לגבי שיטתו הכללית תצטרך לקחת את ענין בבא קמא פרק ו, ד בחשבון.

המקור האחרון בו רבי שמעון שונה ממגמתו ברוב המקרים נמצא במסכת מכות. המשנה בפרק ג, ב, אומרת:

> כמא יאכל מן הטבל ויהא חייב. ר' שמעון או'. כל שהוא. וחכמ' אומ'. כזיית. אמ' להן ר' שמעון. אין אתם מודין לי (כ)[ב]אוכל נ!(מ)[ב]!לה כל שהוא !(שהוא)!חייב. אמרו לו. מפני שהיא כביריתה. אמ' להן. אף חיטה אחת כבירייתה.

---

43 כמובן, גם יכול להיות שמדובר שתי מסורות בענין דברי רבי שמעון.

44 תופסתא כפשוטה, נזיקין, עמ' 61.

45 האפשרות השניה היא לומר שלפי רבי שמעון, לא מתחשבים כלל בשום הפחה או נבייה שעושה המנבה, ורק מתחשבים בגודל הדליקה. אם גדולה מספיק להגיע למקום שהגיע בלי ניבוי, יהיה חייב המדליק, ואם לא, רק אז נתחשב במנבה או ברוח. אך אפשרות זו כל כך פשוטה שאין צורך לאומרה, ואפילו תנא קמא יסכים לרבי שמעון אם זה כל מה שהוא אומר. האפשרות השלישית היא לומר שלפי רבי שמעון, אין מתחשבים כלל באדם או רוח הבאים להפיח על האש, אלא בעצם האש עצמה, אך זה לא הגיוני: למה לא נחייב אדם המפיח על שרפה ומעבירה יותר ממה שהיתה עוברת בלי נפיחתו? לכן הבאתי את האפשרות הפשוטה והכי הגיונית להבנת דברי רבי שמעון, אם הוא חולק על תנא קמא.

את הדבר כספציפי לכל דליקה. אך בתוספתא,[41] שיטת רבי שמעון ממוקמת לפני המחלוקת התנאית:

> ?נ?יבה וניבתו הרוח. אם יש בשלו כדי ל?נ?בות הרי זה חייב. ואם לאו הרי זה פטור. ר' שמעון או' "שלם ישלם המבעיר את הבערה". הכל לפי הדליקה. המדליק בתוך שלו כמה תעבר הדליקה. ר' לעזר בן עזריה אומ' שש -עשרה אמה דרך רשות הרבים. בשעת הרוח שלשים אמה. ר' יהודה או'. שלשים אמה ובשעת הרוח חמשים אמה. ר' עקיבא או'. חמשים אמה ובשעת הרוח שלש מאות אמה. מעשה בערב שקפץ האור יתר משלש מאות אמה והזיק. מעשה שעיברה הדליקה את הירדן שהיתה קשה. במי דברים אמורים. בזמן שקפצה. אבל אם היתה מסכסכת והולכת או שהיו עצים מצוין [להר] <לה> אפי' עד מיל הרי זה חייב. עברה נהר או ?ג?דר או שלולית שהן רחבין שמונה אמות. פטור.

גולדברג[42] מסביר את ההבדלים בין רשימת התנאים הנמצאת במשנה לבין הרשימה בתוספתא, ואת הוספת עניין הרוח לכל שיטה ושיטה בתוספתא. אך הדבר הכי מעניין לעניינו הוא מיקום שיטת רבי שמעון. גולדברג מציין שדברי רבי שמעון הם "הבאה מילולית מסוף מ"ד", ומסביר ש:

> במשנה סודרו דברי ר' שמעון אחרי המחלוקות בקשר לדיון 'עד כמה תעבור הדליקה'. התוספתא מסדרת את דבריו כאן מפני שהם מסבירים את ה'חיוב' וה'פטור' של הקטע הקודם. ונראה שאין מי שחולק עליו כאן. דברי ר' שמעון גם משמשים כהקדמה למחלוקת תנאים שמביאה התוספתא תיכף בסמוך.

מדבריו, משמע שהוא מבין שכמו שבתוספתא, דברי רבי שמעון מנותקים ממחלוקת התנאים הבאה לאחריהן, כך גם במשנה. קשה לקבל את דבריו במשנה, כי דברי רבי שמעון בהחלט נובעים וקריאים כחולקים על התנאים האחרים, אך בתוספתא, נראה שהוא צודק. הלא דברי רבי שמעון נזרקים אחורה (בהשוואה למקומם במשנה) – או המשנה או התוספתא החליטה להעביר את דבריו, ובכך לשנות את המשמעות שלהם. כנראה גולדברג קושר את תפקיד דברי רבי שמעון בתוספתא ובמשנה, כי ברור לו שמקור משותף לשניהם, אך אין צורך להבין כן. שני המקורות יכולים בהחלט לינוק ממקור קדום אחד, מימרא של רבי שמעון, ועורך המשנה פירשה כעוד דעה במחלוקת התנאים, בעוד

41 תוספתא בבא קמא, פרק ו הלכה 22-23.

42 גולדברג, א. פירוש מבני ואנליטי לתוספתא מסכת בבא קמא, הוצאת מגנס, ירושלים. 2001. עמ' 133-134.

כי תצא אש. למה נאמר, עד שלא יאמר יש לי בדין, הואיל וחייב ע"י קנוי לו לא יהא חייב על ידי עצמו, אם זכיתי מן הדין, למה נאמר כי תצא אש, אלא בא הכתוב לעשות את האונס כרצון ושאינו מתכוין כמתכוין ואת האשה כאיש לכל הנזקין שבתורה. – ומצאה קוצים. הא לא באו קוצים אלא ליתן שיעור, אם יש קוצים יש שיעור ואם אין קוצים אין שיעור, מכאן אמרו עברה הנהר והדרך והגדר שהוא גבוה מעשרה טפחים והזיקה, פטור מלשלם; כיצד עומדים על הדבר, רואין אותו כאלו הוא עומד באמצע בית כור ומדליק, דברי רבי אלעזר בן עזריה, רבי אליעזר אומר שש עשרה אמה כדרך הרבים, רבי עקיבא אומר חמישים אמה; רבי שמעון אומר שלם ישלם המבעיר את הבעירה, הכל לפי הדלקה, מעשה שעברה דליקה הירדן והזיקה, מפני שהיא מרובה; אימתי בזמן שקפצה, אבל אם היתה מצפצפת ומהלכת אפילו עד מיל, הרי זה חייב.

המכילתא היא דבי רבי ישמעאל, ובדרך כלל לא מביאה את משנת רבי. אך כאן, מובאת המשנה שלנו כפי שאנו מכירים אותה, אך באמצע הדיון על קוצים, שהיותם באזור מחייבת את המדליק אפילו יותר מהשיעור המסויים. בנוסף לכך, תחילת הדרשה, על הקוצים, אינה כלל במשנתנו, וסוף הדרשה גם כן לא נמצאת במשנה. מחלוקת התנאים גם מובאת במקום מוזר – הלא רבי שמעון מביא דרשה על פסוק הנדרש בעוד שני פסקאות במכילתא, וכאן אין מקומו של דרשה על "שלם ישלם המבעיר את הבערה", ואם התנאים האחרים חולקים על דברי רבי שמעון בדרשה זו, למה לא הביאה המכילתא את דבריהם בפיסקא הנכונה? למה כאן, על קוצים?

המכילתא אומרת שני דינים: 1) אם יש קוצים, או דבר אחר דליק, שיאפשר לשרפה לשרוף רחוק יותר, אז מתחשבת ההלכה בשיעור הריחוק ממקור הדלקה, ויהיה חייב המדליק בנזק עד מרחק זה. 2) אך אם יש דברים שדרכם לכבות שרפה, כגון נהר או גדר חזק, אז אפילו במרחק קצר יהיה פטור. מיד לאחר מזה, הוכנסו דברי התנאים למכילתא, בגלל דמיון ענייני בדבריהם. ואז מביאה המכילתא מעשה שעל פניה תומכת בדברי רבי שמעון: "מעשה שעברה דליקה הירדן..." אך משמע מהאוקימתא "אימתי", שפסק המכילתא ב"מפני שהיא מרובה" שהוא "פטור", וזה סותר את מה שרבי שמעון היה פוסק במקרה זה. לפי רבי שמעון, הכל לפי הדליקה, ודליקה מרובה שעברה את הירדן היתה מחייבת את המדליק, בין מצפצפת, בין קפצה. אם כן, יכול באמת להיות שבמכילתא, דברי התנאים ומחלוקתם תקועה באמצע ענין הקוצים, והם לא חלק מקורי מהדיון.

על-אף אפשרות זו במכילתא, ברור שהמכילתא כאן משמרת עדות לשיטת רבי שמעון, ומפגינה מסורת חזקה שרבי שמעון לא הולך בשיטתו הסטנדרטית בהלכה זו – לעומת תנאים אחרים, שכן. רבי שמעון מנוגד לחכמים שעושים פורמליזציה, והוא משאיר

בתוספתא המקבילה[38] למשנה זו, כתוב:

העומר היה מנפהו בשלש עשרה נפה. שתי הלחם בשתים עשרה. לחם הפנים באחת עשרה. בדקה ובגסה. בדקה שתהא קולטת את הסלת ובגסה שתהא קולטת את הסובין. ר' שמעון בן לזר או' שלש עשרה נפה היו זו על גבי זו זו על גבי זו. תחתונה שבכולן עשויה שתהא קולטת את הסלת.

בתוספתא, אין זכר לשיטה הלא-פורמאליסטית. מובאת שיטת תנא קמא, והסבר מפורט יותר של רבי שמעון בן אלעזר, אך אין הד לשיטה הטבעית "כל צרכה" של רבי שמעון. קשה לשער אם התוספתא לא הכירה את שיטת רבי שמעון במסורתה, והעלימה אותו משום שלדבריה, אין המסורת במשנה נכונה, או אם הכירה את דברי רבי שמעון ופעלה במכוון כדי להדיר את השיטה הזו.[39] אי-אפשר, איפוא, לנטרל את עדות המשנה לשיטת רבי שמעון המשתמש בשיעור טבעי כאן, על ידי התוספתא. כל תיאוריה כללית בענין שיטת רבי שמעון תצטרך להתמודד עם מקור זה במשנה.

במשנת בבא קמא פרק ו, ד, כתוב:

המדליק בתוך שלו. עד כמה תעבר הדליקה. ר' לעזר בן עזריה או'. רואין אותה כילו היא באמצע בית כור. ר' אליעזר אומ'. שש עשרה אמה, כדרך הרבים. ר' עקיבה או'. חמשים אמה. ור' שמעון אומ'. "שלם ישלם, המבעיר את הבעירה". הכל לפי הדליקה.

כאשר אדם מדליק שרפה בשדה שלו, עד איזה מרחק יתחייב המדליק על נזקי האש? התנאים נותנים מרחקים קצובים, אך רבי שמעון חולק על כולם, ונותן שיעור טבעי, אינדיבידואליסטי, לדבר – הכל לפי הדליקה. אם שרפה קטנה איך-שהוא הגיעה למרחק גדול יותר ממה שהיה יכול אדם לצפות, יהיה המדליק פטור, וגבי שריפה גדולה, יכול להיות גבול החיוב הרבה יותר אפילו ממה שפסק רבי אלעזר בן עזריה.

מחלוקת זו נמצאת גם במכילתא דר' ישמעאל,[40] אך כאן, הדבר מעלה שאלות.

---

38 מנחות פרק ח הלכה 14.

39 בענין השיעורים, הובאה לעיל כבר האפשרות שתוספתא מנחות "מחריפה" את עמדת רבי שמעון לעומת המשנה. אם כן, שמא גם כאן קורה דבר דומה, ושיטת רבי שמעון לא הוכנסה לתוספתא משום שהתוספתא "מעוניינת" בהחרפת שיטתו. אם כן, מעניין לשים לב שבמקום שיטת רבי שמעון המקילה, מובא בתוספתא שיטת רבי שמעון אחר, הנותן אומץ לסטנדרטיזציה של הנפות עם סברא התומכת בשיטת תנא קמא. האפשרות מפתה, אך שמא אני קורא יותר מדי לתוך התוספתא, שסוף סוף ידועה בהרבה כמסורה מקבילה למשנה, ולא צפויה התאמה בינה לבין המשנה.

40 מהדורת הורוביץ-רבין, עמ' 297.

המקורות האלה, ולוודא שהם אכן מקורות סותרים לגישתו של רבי שמעון שהתברר עד כה. לאחר שהמקורות ינותחו כפי שראוי להם, הם יהוו נקודות מידע על שיטתו של רבי שמעון, ושמא דוקא מקורות אלה היוצאים מן הכלל, יהיו אלה שירמזו על שיטה מחושבת ומתוכננת של רבי שמעון. כמובן כל תיאוריה חייבת להתבסס על המקורות כפי שהם לאמיתם, ובעצם, ליבון שיטותיו של רבי שמעון בכל מקום שאפשר, חשוב יותר מתיאוריות המנסות לעשות סדר בדבריו. אך שמא בגמר העבודה במקומות בהם נראה שרבי שמעון יוצא מן הכלל, יהיה אפשרי להציע תיאוריה לפרש את הרעיון שעומד מאחורי פסקיו של רבי שמעון.

בענין קרבן העומר, המשנה[36] מביאה מחלוקת לדבר ניפוי הקמח, כדי שיהיה נחשב סולת.

> העומר היה מנופה בשלש-עשרה (י)[נ]פה. שתי הלחם [ב]שתים-עשרה. לחם הפנים באחת-עשרה. ר' שמעון או' לא היה לה קיצבה אלא סולת מנופה כל צ(ו)רכה היה מביא. שנ' "ולקחת סלת ואפית אתה" "שתים מערכות". שתהא מנופה כל צ(ו)רכה.

לפי תנא קמא, הניפוי להכנת קמח ללחם הפנים, שתי הלחם וקרבן העומר צריך להיעשות במספר מסויים של נפות. העומר צריך להיות הסלת הכי נקייה, ולכן מנופה בשלש-עשרה נפות, ושתי הלחם מספיקה בשתים-עשרה, ולחם הפנים באחת-עשרה. אך לפי רבי שמעון, אין שיעור למספר הנפות, אלא הדבר נתון לשיפוט המנפה – "כל צרכה" – שיהיה הקמח דק לדעת המכין. בניגוד לרוב המפרשים הקלאסיים, אלבק בפירושו למשנה מצמצם את רבי שמעון רק ללחם הפנים,[37] ואומר שרבי שמעון מסכים לדברי תנא קמא בעניין העומר ושתי הלחם. לדבריו, המגמה הנראית הפוכה בדברי רבי שמעון, שכאן הוא מתנגד לסטנדרטיזציה ודוגל בשיעור טבעי לחלוטין, מוגבלת רק ללחם הפנים. עדיין, דברי רבי שמעון בענין לחם הפנים (וגם בעומר ושתי הלחם למפרשים האחרים) הם, על פניהם, מנוגדים לשיטתו הנראית עד כה. האם שיטה זו מוכרת כדברי רבי שמעון לכולם?

36 מנחות פרק ו, ז.

37 למשל, רבי עובדיה מברטנורא כותב: "דאפילו לכתחלה לא נתנו חכמים קצבה מכמה סאין חטין או שעורין מביאין עומר ושתי הלחם ולחם הפנים..." לדבריו רבי שמעון חולק על כל דברי תנא קמא. וגם בבבלי, בסוף פרק ז (עו עמ' ב), הדפוס אפילו שונה מכתבי היד, ובמקום "לה" בדברי רבי שמעון, יש "להן" שכנראה מהווה "תיקון" על פי הבנה פרשנית שרבי שמעון חולק על כל הניפויים. כמובן, מבחינת כתבי-היד, אלבק צודק. גם בכתבי-היד של התלמוד וגם בכתבי-היד של המשנה, דברי רבי שמעון הם "לה" ולא "להן", וגם הפסוק שמביא כהוכחה מויקרא כד 5 רק מדבר על לחם הפנים. אך אפילו לר' עובדיה מברטנורא היתה הגירסה הנכונה "לה" ועדיין שייך את דברי רבי שמעון לחלוק גם בעומר ושתי הלחם, וכן משמע מפירוש המשניות של הרמב"ם, שבדברו על "י"ג נפות", אומר ש"אין הלכה כר"ש", ושלש-עשרה נפות רק שייך בעומר. ר' שלמה עדני ב<u>מלאכת שלמה</u> מסכים לפשט הנובע מהגירסא הנכונה, וכדברי אלבק, אומר שרבי שמעון, "אלחם הפנים קאי, ואין צריך י"א נפה..."

חכמים, ולא דין דאוריתא. בטומאת נבלה, מופיעים דברי רבי שמעון בתוספתא,[30] על סיבת ההבדל בין שיעור טומאת בהמה וחיה לבין שיעור טומאת שרץ.

> ...אמ' ר' שמעון. מה ראו לומ' בבהמה חיה בכזית טמא ובשרץ <בכעדשה>. אלא בהמה וחיה בריתן בכזית. שרץ תחילת ברייתו כעדשה.

עצם עניין התוספתא מורכב[31] ואין כאן מקומו. רצוני רק להעיר על כך שרבי שמעון, כאשר הוא מסביר את סיבת השיעור המבוסס על תחילת בריית בעלי-החיים השונים, משתמש במילים "מה ראו לומר" – שסגנון לשון זה מורה על העובדה שהשיעור הינו קביעה של חכמים, ולא דין מן התורה. הבבלי מביא את דרשת רבי שמעון, פעם[32] בעילום שם, ופעם בשם רבי יהודה מדיסקרטא.[33] וגם בירושלמי[34], "מפני מה אמרו", מורה על אותו מקור רבני לעומת מקור דאוריתא לשיעור. בירושלמי, שמו של רבי שמעון נשמר עם הסיומת "בן יוחי", לעומת העדרתו בתוספתא, דבר המורה על זה שהירושלמי משמר כאן מסורת דבי רבי ישמעאל, וברור אם כן שגם בדבי רבי ישמעאל ודבי רבי עקיבא, שמרו את מסורת רבי שמעון בענין סיבת השיעור לטומאת נבלה, ואין החרפת דבריו כדברים הנובעים הישר מן התורה.[35]

ו. יוצאים מן הכלל? רבי שמעון בקרבן העומר, נזקי אש ואכילת טבל

עד כאן, הוראה שרבי שמעון בהחלט חלק מהותי ואולי קיצוני (בכך שדבריו לא מובאים להלכה בחלק מהסטנדרטיזציות שלו) של המהפך העובר משיעורים ומידות טבעיים וסובייקטיביים, לקצובים, אובייקטיביים ופורמאליסטים. אך קיימים כמה מקומות שאין סטנדרטיזציה בשיטת רבי שמעון, ואדרבא, פועל הוא נגד שיטות אחרות פורמאליסטיות, ומקורות אלה חשובים לא פחות מהמקורות שלעיל. הדבר הכי חשוב הוא לתעד את

30 שבועות א, הלכה 7.

31 ראה י.נ. אפשטיין, מחקרים בספרות התלמוד ב', "שרידים מדבי רבי ישמעאל".

32 חגיגה יא עמ' א, זה לענין טומאה. וראה מעילה טו עמ' ב וטז עמ' א לחילוק אפשרי בין שיעור אכילה לשיעור טומאה. אך אין זה נוגע לענייננו.

33 נזיר נב עמ' א.

34 נזיר נו ע"ב, הלכה ב. "תני ר' שמעון בן יוחי או'. מפני מה אמרו. השרץ מטמא בכעדשה. מפני שהשרץ תחילת ברייתו בכעדשה."

35 מעוררת תשומת לב העובדה ששיטת תנא קמא בתוספתא מבינה את שיעור כזית לטומאת נבלה של בהמה וחיה, כנובע מפסוק: "בכזית מנא לן ת"ל "או בנבלת חיה". מה ת"ל 'טמאה' להביא את כזית." תיאום שיעור עם דרשה מעניינת כאן דוקא כי היא דומה מאוד למה שהתוספתא במנחות עושה בשם רבי שמעון, דבר שלא היה קיים במשנה בדברי רבי שמעון. כאן למעשה, בשבועות, התוספתא מונעת את עצמה מ- (או אין לה מסורת ל-) החרפת שיטת רבי שמעון בשיעורים להיות ענין דאוריתא, אף-על-פי שאולי, כפי שהצענו, עשתה התוספתא כן במנחות.

השרירותיות המסויימת הקיימת בשיעור, היא היא שיטה רגילה בדרך עיצוב ההלכה על ידי החכמים.

דברי המשנה המוזכרת לעיל מובאים בפירוט יתרה בתוספתא (פרק יב, 9-8):

> אמרתי להן. ת'ל "סלת בלולה בשמן" מנחה ששולט בה לבוללה. אמרו לי. בששים שולט בששים ואחד אין שולט. אמרתי להן. כל השיעורים שבתורה קצובין הן. <בארבעים סאה הוא טובל>. בארבעים סאה חסר קירטוב אינו יכול לטבול בהן. כביצה מטמא טומאת אוכלין. חסר אפי' שומשום אינו מטמא טומאת אוכלין. שלשה על שלשה טמא מדרס. שלשה על שלשה חסר נימא אינו טמא טומאת מדרס. הוי כל השיעורין שבתורה קצובין הן.

מקור זה בולט בכך שהוא מוסיף עוד מקרים של פורמאליזציה רבנית, שרבי שמעון לא המציא, אך ברור שהוא מאמץ, ומביאם כדוגמאות והוכחה שאכן, ההלכה בנויה בשיטה זו של פורמאליות בענין מידות ושיעורים. כאן רבי שמעון מזכיר את השיעור של טומאת אוכלים ואת שיעור טומאת מדרס של בגד, בנוסף לשיעור מי מקוה. רבי שמעון מבליט את ענין הפורמאליזציה בכך שהוא מדגיש את האבסולוטיות של השיעורים: "חסר אפילו שומשום אינו מטמא טומאת אוכלים".

בעוד שני דרכים שונה התוספתא מהמשנה. בתוספתא, רבי שמעון מביא פסוק לתמוך בשיעור ששים עשרונים למנחה, ובלשון התוספתא, רבי שמעון מבטא את הכלל אחרת – במקום "כל מידות חכמים כן", הוא אומר "כל השיעורים שבתורה קצובים הן". במשנה, הכלל של רבי שמעון לא אומר במפורש שיש פורמאליזציה בשיעורים, הכל נאמר בעקיפין – "כל מידות חכמים כן". אבל בתוספתא, המילה "קצובים" מופיעה, והיא מפרשת במפורשות את הפורמאליזציה. אם כן, רבי שמעון מעודד אפילו יותר מקרים של סטנדרטיזציה הלכתית במישור השיעורים, ובטון יותר חריף, ממה שידוע מהמשנה עצמה.

אפשר להשאיר את שני המקורות האלו כשתי מסורות בדברי רבי שמעון. אך בגלל שבתוספתא, רבי שמעון מופיע עם פסוק, שמחזק את אפיון המידה של המנחה לרמה של דאורייתא, האוזן הקושבת גם שמה לב לכך ש"מידות חכמים" של המשנה הופכות ל"שיעורין שבתורה" בתוספתא. במקרה רגיל, המילה "תורה" לא צריכה לרמוז לדין דאוריתא, ואכן, בספרות התנאית כמעט ולא נכנסים להבדל שבין דאוריתא לדרבנן. אך כאן, בגלל הבאת טקסט-סימוכין, כבר נשמע הדבר כהחרפת השיעור והפורמאליזציה לגדר של דאוריתא. ואם כן, שמא עדים אנו להבדל מהותי שבין דברי רבי שמעון במסורת התוספתאית לבין המסורת המשנית (או אפילו להבדל מגמתי של עורכי הקבצים), שבה, כדי לחזק את הפורמאליזציה של המידות והשיעורים, רבי שמעון אפילו מבטא את הדינמיקה כדין דאוריתא.

על-אף אפשרות זו בדברי התוספתא במנחות בשיטת רבי שמעון, עדיין, רוב המקורות בהסבר רבי שמעון מורים על כך שהסטנדרטיזציה היא פרי-מעשיהם של

שתות לאונאה ומשתמש בכלל זה גם במטבע. הסטנדרט לאונאה קצוב לפי רבי שמעון לא רק במטלטלין, אלא גם בכסף בו קונים, והרי נמצא אחדות בשיטת רבי שמעון בפורמאליזציה בענין שיעורים ומידות גם בענין זה.

ה. קדשים וטהרות: סיבת הפורמאליזציה – רבי שמעון במילים שלו

בענין קרבן מנחה המובאת נדבה, מלמדת המשנה במסכת מנחות, פרק יב, ד:

> ומתנדב אדם מנחה שלששים עישרון ומביא בכלי אחד. אם אמ'. הרי עלי ששים ואחד. מביא ששים בכלי אחד ואחד בכלי [אחד]. שכן הציבור מביא ביום טוב הראשון של חג שחל להיות בשבת ששים ואחד. דיו ליחיד שיהא פחות מן הציבור אחד. אמ' ר' שמעון, והלא אלו לפרים, ואלו לכבשים. אין נבללין זה עם זה. אלא עד ששים יכולין להיבלל(ן). אמרו לו. ששים נבללין וששים ואחד אינן נבללין. אמ' להן. כל מיד( )[ו]ת (כ) חכמ' כן. בארבעים [סאה הוא טובל. ארבעים] סאה חסר ק(ו)רטוב אינו יכול לטבול בהן. שאינן מיתנדבין לוג שנים וחמשה. אבל מיתנדבין שלשה וארבעה וששה [ו]משׁשה ולמעלן.

לפי תנא קמא, המקסימום שאפשר להביא בכלי אחד זה ששים עשרונים, ואם נדב נדבן ששים ואחד, מביא בשני כלים. הסיבה לכך הוא רעיון מעמדי, שבו וודאי צריך להיות שסך כל העשרונים הבאים משל ציבור, אם נחשבים ביחד, צריך לעלות על המניין המרבי של עשרונים שמותר ליחיד להביא בבת אחת.[29] לעומת שיטה זו, רבי שמעון אומר ששיעור ששים נבחר כיון שיותר מששים לא נבללים. כאשר חבריו מקשים עליו שבאמת, לא ברור שששים זה גבול מוחלט, רבי שמעון עונה עם כלל חושפני: כל מידות של חכמים הם כך, שיש גבול שתוחם את ההלכה, גבול סטנדרטי. אף על פי שאולי יש מצב שאדם חזק יכול לבלול יותר מששים עשרונים, הדרך של חכמים במידות הוא לעשות סטנדרטיזציה, ולשים גבול ברור על הסכום המרבי. כמו כן, ארבעים הסאה הנצרכים לטבילה. רבי שמעון חולק על הסברה ההגיונית של תנא קמא בשיעור, ומסביר שעצם

29 דברי תנא קמא ודאי צריכים ביאור – הלא רבי שמעון צודק שאין כל העשרונות של יו"ט הראשון של חג שחל להיות בשבת נבללות יחדיו. למה, אם כן, לחבר בין המספר הזה, שחלקיו בהחלט יבואו בנפרד, לבין הסכום המקסימאלי שיכול יחיד להביא **ביחד**? על-אף שלשיטת רבי שמעון באנו עד הלום, רק נשים לב שגם רבי שמעון וגם תנא קמא נותנים סיבות לסכום שהם לוקחים כמובן מאליו – ששים. כנראה שיעור זה של עשרונות כבר היה ידוע, ובעוד שרבי שמעון, כפי שמיד נראה, נותן סיבה פורמאלית לסכום, תנא קמא (שכנראה משקף שיטת החולקים על רבי שמעון) צריך לעגן את השיעור בסברא. יוצא מכך שאף על פי שרבי שמעון והחולקים עליו מסכימים הלכה למעשה, עדיין השאלה של פורמאליות וסטנדרטיזציה עומדת ביניהם.

שוב בענין הלכות שבת העדות ברורה למגמת רבי שמעון לסטנדרטיזציה של השיעורים, ושוב בשני רבדים: הוא מציע שיעור פורמאלי לכל המשקים לגבי מלאכת הוצאה, ובאוקימתא שלו להסבר השיעורים האינדביואליסטים, הוא שוב מביא פורמאליזציה לענין הוצאת דברים שאין רגילים בני האדם להצניעם – ובדברים אלו הוא מעמיד שיעור לכל דבר, לעומת התנא קמא, שאוחז שהשיעור למצניע הוא כל שהוא. דין חיוב הוצאה בשבת שוב נותר כמעט בבלעדיות במישור הדברים שבין אדם לעצמו, כמו הדינים בחלק הקודם, בזרעים.

ד. שתות לאונאה – סדר נזיקין

כאשר מוכר דורש יותר מהמחיר המקובל לחפץ מסויים, הוא נכנס לגדר דיני אונאה. המשנה פוסקת[25] שעד לשישית יתרה על המחיר ההוגן, המקח קיים, אך יתר מזה, רשאי הלוקח לחזור בו (תוך זמן מסויים). כל זה בנוגע למטלטלין, אבל במטבעות עצמן, גושי המתכת האמורים לשקול את המשקל המתאים לשמם, קיים מחלוקת לגבי כמה הם יכולים לשקול פחות ממשקלם הרשמי ועדיין להיחשב מטבע כשרה. בפרק ד', ה, כתוב:

> וכמה תהא הסלע חסירה ולא יהי בה הוניה. ר' מאיר אומ'. ארבעה אסרות מאסר לדינר. ר' יהודה אומ'. ארבעה פונדיונות מפונדין לדינר. ר' שמעון אומ'. שמונה פונדיונות משני פונדיונים לדינר.

לפי רבי מאיר, הסלע יכול להשתחק מרוב השימוש בו 1/24 ממשקלו, ועדיין להיחשב מטבע סלע כשר.[26] לפי רבי יהודה, הגבול הוא 1/12. לפי רבי שמעון, לעומתם, הסכום הוא סכום רבי יהודה כפול שתים,[27] דהיינו, 1/6. יוצא לפי רבי שמעון, שהאונאה במטבעות שווה לאונאה במטלטלין, וכן מעירים ר' עובדיה מברטנורא, תפארת ישראל וח. אלבק. וגם בתוספתא[28] מופיעים שלש התנאים האלה באותן השיטות, וליברמן שם מעיר על שיטת רבי שמעון, "ואין חילוק בין מטבע למטלטלין."

שוב עדים אנו לפסק הלכה של רבי שמעון המיישר קו בין שיעורים שלדעת אחרים, שונים: מטבע טיבו שונה מהותית ממטלטלין, שהרי אינו סחורה, אלא מעות, וערכו מבוסס בהרבה על יכולתו לקנות דברים אחרים. לפיכך, היה אפשר לומר ששויו צריך לתאום את הציפיות של הסוחרים ברמה יותר מדוייקת. אך רבי שמעון לוקח את הגבול ההלכתי של

25 בבא מציעא פרק ד, ג.

26 כפי שמסביר אלבק, הסלע ארבעה דינרים, ודינר 24 איסרים. לכן לפי רבי מאיר, הסלע יכול להשתחק משקל של ארבעה איסרין, שהם ששית הדינר – וששית הדינר שווה 1/24 מארבע דינרים, שהם סלע אחד. ולרבי יהודה, החישוב הוא ארבע פונדיונות. כל דינר הינו 12 פונדיונות, ולכן ארבע פונדיונות הן שלישית הדינר. כיון שיש ארבעה דינר בסלע, שלישית הדינר שווה ל1/12 מתוך הסלע.

27 רבי יהודה אומר ארבע פונדיונות, ורבי שמעון פוסק שמונה (4x2).

28 פרק ג' הלכה 17.

בירושלמי לאחר שגולדברג משבץ לתוכו את גירסת המלאכת שלמה, ואת תיקוניו לצלע השנייה:

> ותני כן על דר' שמעון. לא נאמרו כל השיעורין האילו אלא **למצניעיהן**. הא **למוציאיהן ברביעית**. ותני כן על דרבנן. לא נאמרו כל השיעורין האילו אלא **למוציאיהן**. הא **למצניעיהן** ברביעית.

(אני מציין את שלש המקומות שבו הנוסח שונה ממה שקיים בכת"י ליידן.) גולדברג טועה כמעט בוודאי, כי לפי תנא קמא, שככל הנראה אוחז בשיטת פרק ז, ג, מצניעיהן יהיו חייבים בכל שהן, ולא ברביעית.

מדרך ציטוטו של גולדברג את דברי הירושלמי על פי המלאכת שלמה, ברור שהוא הבין שהגירסה שהיתה לפני ר' שלמה עדני היתה בנויה כמו הנוסח הקיים בידינו – רבי שמעון קודם, ואחר-כך תנא קמא. לגירסה זו, גולדברג מכניס את הנוסח של ר' שלמה עדני בצלע הראשונה – בדברי רבי שמעון. בזה, נוצר הקושי בהבנת דברי רבנן (תנא קמא). רצוני להציע תיקון יותר פשוט, שמתקן את הנוסח בלי הקשיים של גולדברג, וגם בלי הצורך להחליף בצלע של רבנן את המילים "מוציאיהן" ו"מצניעיהן". אם בנוסח שקיים בידינו, נחליף רק את "רבי שמעון" ו"רבנן", כל הבעיות נופלות מאליהם: נוסח הצלע השניה, השייכת עכשיו לרבי שמעון, תואמת בשלמות לנוסח של מלאכת שלמה (ובעצם הוא הביא בפירושו רק את הצלע השניה ולא הראשונה), וגם הצלע הראשונה השייכת עכשיו לרבנן (תנא קמא) תואמת את פרק ז, ג וגם את שיטת תנא קמא בפרק ח, א. והנה הנוסח המשוחזר:

> ותני כן על **דרבנן**. לא נאמרו כל השיעורין האילו אלא למוציאיהן. הא למצניעיהן כל שהן. ותני כן על **דר' שמעון**. לא נאמרו כל השיעורין האילו אלא למצניעיהן. הא למוציאן ברביעית.

נוסח מתוקן זה[23] עדיף: במקום שלשה תיקונים לעומת הנוסח בכת"י ליידן, החילוף שאנו מציעים רק משקף שינוי אחד. בנוסף לכך, שיטת רבנן (תנא קמא) מובנת כשיטה המוכרת מפרק ז, ג והרישא של פרק ח, א, במקום שיטה משונה, לא ידועה משום מקור תנאי. ובאמת, אחרי כתבי דברים אלו, ראיתי שגם לליברמן[24] היה ברור שלפני מלאכת שלמה היתה הגירסא שהצעתי.

---

23 בהוצאת תלמוד הירושלמי של האקדמיה ללשון העברית, מופיעים סימני קריאה סביב "רבנן" ו"ר' שמעון". בהקדמה שלו להוצאה, מסביר בנימין אליצור ש"סימני קריאה באים להצביע על נוסח תמוה ולהסב את תשומת לב הקורא שאכן כן הוא הנוסח בכתב היד (sic!), אבל נוסח זה צריך עיון." סביר מאוד שמה שהפריע לעורכי המהדורה היתה הצרימה בין השיטות האלו לידוע לנו משיטתם במשנה, וההצעה שלי בוודאי מתקנת את ה"צריך עיון".

24 בירושלמי כפשוטו, עמ' 155, סוף הלכה א'.

הידועה. במקום זה, הוא משתמש בהלכה הידועה, ומבטיח שהוא מכיר ומבין את ההלכה הזו היטב, אך מפעיל אותה בחיזוק מגמתו לסטנדרטיזציה ופורמאליזציה, גם בנושא פרק ז, ג.

כיון שהגענו עד הלה, ברצוני לטפל בעוד דבר המובא בדברי גולדברג, על דברי רבי שמעון במשנת שבת ח, א. גולדברג מביא את דברי הירושלמי (יא ע"ב), אלא שמביאם בתיקון הנוסח של ר' שלמה עדני במלאכת שלמה. גולדברג מודע לכך שדברי הירושלמי עמומים. הירושלמי אומר:

> ותני כן על דר' שמעון. לא נאמרו כל השיעורין האילו אלא למוציאיהן. הא למצניעיהן כל שהן. ותני כן על דרבנן. לא נאמרו כל השיעורין האילו אלא למצניעיהן. הא למוציאן ברביעית.

הירושלמי כאן נותן הסבר לדברי רבי שמעון ודברי התנא קמא. לפי רבי שמעון, השיעורים נאמרו למוציא את הפריטים, אך המצניע אותם, יהיה חייב בכל שהוא. ולתנא קמא (חכמים בלשון הירושלמי), השיעורים נאמרו למצניע, אך מי שמוציא, יהיה חייב רק ברביעית. כמובן, ניסוח זה של הירושלמי חולק על אותה המשנה שהוא מנסה להסביר. דוקא תנא קמא מסביר את השיעורים הרבים על מלאכת הוצאה, לא רבי שמעון. "כל שהן" בכלל לא עולה על הפרק לשיטת רבי שמעון, האומר שאפילו למצניע, הוא רק חייב לפי השיעורים של תנא קמא. ברור שהנוסח לא תקין.

גולדברג מפנה את הלומד לדברי ר' שלמה עדני. יצויין שהמלאכת שלמה לא מתקן את גירסת הירושלמי, אלא מצטט את הירושלמי בנוסח התקין בעיניו, שכנראה עמד לפניו, ובכך משמש עד נוסח חשוב לקטע ירושלמי זה. לפי המלאכת שלמה, הגירסא של החלק הראשון בירושלמי היא: "ותני כן על דרבי שמעון. לא נאמרו כל השיעורים הללו אלא למצניעיהן, הא למוציאיהם ברביעית." גירסא זו בירושלמי מובנת וסבירה בכך שהירושלמי מסביר את שיטת רבי שמעון בפרק ח, א לעומת פרק ז, ג: רבי שמעון אומר שבמלאכת הוצאה רגילה, המוציא יהא חייב על משקים רק בשיעור רביעית. ובמצניע (כלומר, אדם שמחשיב אפילו שיעור קטן יותר, על ידי זה שהוא מצניעו), יהיה חייב אם הוציא, רק בשיעורים של תנא קמא (כדי גמיעה, כדי מזיגת הכוס, וכו').

בפירושו, גולדברג[22] תיקן את הצלע הראשונה והשנייה של מאמר הירושלמי, על פי מלאכת שלמה, שמביא רק את הצלע של רבי שמעון במימרא. אך גולדברג ממשיך ומתקן את הצלע השנייה של הירושלמי, על דעת עצמו, וכותב: "ותני כן על דרבנן, ולא נאמרו כל השיעורין האילו אלא למוציאיהן (כצ"ל); הא למצניעיהן ברביעית." זה תיקון של גולדברג עצמו, ואינו מופיע בדברי ר' שלמה עדני. מובן למה גולדברג מתקן: השיטה של תנא קמא לא תואמת לדברי הירושלמי כפי שמופיעה לפנינו – הרי "כל השיעורין הללו" נאמרו דוקא למוציאיהם (דהיינו, בפרק ח, א), ולא במצניעיהן (ז, ג). הנה טקסט הקטע

---

22 שם, ד"ה "ר' שמעון או' כולם ברביעית...". שוב, עושה כן גולדברג על פי ליברמן, שם.

עקיבא עצמו. לכן מפרש גולדברג שרבי עקיבא אמר את הרישא של פרק ז, ג, ונחלקו תלמידיו בפירוש דברי רבם. תלמיד אחד (כנראה רבי מאיר) מסביר את דברי רבי עקיבא בסיפא של פרק ז, א, כפי שמובן מפירוש ר' יוסי בר חנינא בבבלי, ש"הוציאו" מדבר על כל אדם, בעוד רבי שמעון חולק על הבנה זו, ושיטתו מובאת בפרק ח, א.

דברי גולדברג בעצמם קשים, כי הוא מניח שפרק ז, ג, באמת ניסוח רצוף של שני תנאים שונים, רבי עקיבא ורבי מאיר. אם אכן כך, העיקר חסר מן הספר, כי המשנה זורמת בקול אחיד, ואין זכר לשינוי השיטות בין רבי עקיבא לתלמידו. המשנה נשמעת כשני צדדי מטבע, ולא כמימרא ופירוש. זאת ועוד, הרבה כללים נאמרו במשנה, וברור שלא כולם נאמרו על ידי רבי עקיבא.[20] בנוסף על כך, אין קושי כלל לקבל את ההצעה שכל המשנה בפרק ז, ג היא אכן רבי עקיבא, שאוחז בדרך אחת, ורבי שמעון הבא אחריו, חולק על רבו מפורשות, ומרבה בפורמאליזציה. ויותר מזה: כבר מקבל גולדברג את הייחודיות של רבי שמעון מתוך כלל תלמידי רבי עקיבא, כממציא חומרה (וסטנדרטיזציה) בפרק ח, א, בכתבו "ונוסף על מחלוקת עיקרית זו, שכל שאר תלמידי ר' עקיבא חולקים על דעתו של ר' שמעון..."[21] קשה אם כן לקבל פיצול כירורגי כזה דק בפרק ז, ג, כי כל מה שמרוויח גולדברג על ידו זה שלא תהיה משנה פרק ז, ג כאחד תלמידי רבי עקיבא, החולק על רבי שמעון. אם כבר מקבל גולדברג את העיקרון שכל תלמידי רבי עקיבא חולקים על רבי שמעון, אזי אפשר באותה דרך לומר שרבי שמעון חולק על רבי עקיבא עצמו.

אם צודקים אנו בביקורת העדינה כלפי גולדברג, אז בהחלט, סתמת המשנה בפרק ז, ג, כולה דעת תנא אחד (אולי רבי עקיבא ואולי לא), ומלמדת ששיעור שאינו כשר להצניע, דהיינו, כל שהוא, רק מי שמצניעו חייב עליו. לפי המשנה, אם ראובן מצניע שיעור חלב מזערי, הוא יהיה חייב על הוצאתו, אף על פי שרוב העולם לא מצניעו, ולא מחשיבו. ראובן יהיה חייב במקרה שרוב העולם פטור. אך בפרק ח, א, רבי שמעון נותן שיעור בדיוק ב"כל שהוא" הזה, ואומר שרק יתחייב ראובן אם זה לפחות שיעור מינימלי. והשיעור המינימלי הזה, מוצא רבי שמעון בשיטת תנא קמא בפרק ח, א. כך רבי שמעון, באוקימתא שלו, מייצר עוד סטנדרטיזציה חדשה תוך כדי התחשבותו בהלכה הקודמת. התחשבות זו חשובה, כי על ידה, רבי שמעון לא חייב להיתפס כתנא היוצר מהפכה בהלכה

20 למשל, במשנה בבא קמא ח, ו, רבי עקיבא חולק על כלל המובא בעילום שם. (אף שבכת"י קויפמן אין את המילים "זה הכלל", עדיין ברור שיש כאן הכללה). נוסף על כך, מנחות פרק יא, ג, פסחים פרק ו, ב, שביעית פרק ו, ב ושבת פרק יט, א, הם כל המקומות שכלל נאמר בשם רבי עקיבא, דבר שמורה על כך שכללים אחרים לאו דוקא רבי עקיבא אמרם (וודאי, אנו עדים לכללים אחרים במשנה המופיעות בשמות של תנאים אחרים). ובמקרה שלנו הספציפי, הכלל נאמר על ידי רבים: "כלל אמרו" – ניסוח שלא נשמע כמו כלל בשם תנא אחד.

21 שם, עמ' 164.

החיוב במלאכה זו בין פריטים שונים. והלא צודק הירושלמי (יא ע"ב) בשואלו על שיטת רבי שמעון, "איפשר לומ' דבש ברביעית וחומץ ברביעית." הלא דברים אלו, כפי שמסביר קרבן העדה, שונים בחשיבותם, ואיך ייתכן שיהיו שיעוריהם שווים? אך עד כדי כך מפליג רבי שמעון בסטנדרטיזציה, שאפילו פריטים שונים במהותם, שהיה הגיוני וסביר לחלק בשיעורם לחיוב הוצאה בשבת, עדיין, רבי שמעון רואה סיבה לאחד בם את שיעורם. אך כאן רבי שמעון נתקל ככל הנראה בשיעורים ידועים לדורות; הרי שיעור כדי גמיעה לחלב, ומזיגת הכוס ליין, והאחרים, ידועים הם לו מדורות קודמים. איך יכול רבי שמעון להתעלם מהשיעורים המוכרים?

ובזה, כאן, אנו עדים לא רק למהלך רבי שמעון כעוסק בפורמאליזציה בשיעורים ומידות, אלא גם בדרך בו הוא מתייחס לרובד הקודם, הפחות פורמאלי. רבי שמעון יוצר אוקימתא שתאפיין את השיעורים הקודמים כשייכים רק למצניע. רק במקרה שבו האדם המוציא את המשקה מקנה חשיבות סובייקטיבית לשיעור פחות מרביעית, על ידי זה שהוא מצניע את המשקה (דהיינו, שומר אותו – דבר שרוב בני האדם לא היו עושים), אזי חלים על המשקים השיעורים שמפרט תנא קמא. לרבי שמעון, אם כן, הדין הקודם מקויים במקרה מיוחד, בו האדם מוכיח את חשיבות המשקה שהוא מוציא, מעל ומעבר לחשיבות שרוב בני אדם מייחסים למשקה זה. מהלך זה מעיד על התמודדות רבי שמעון במציאות הישנה, בו בזמן שהוא דוחה את האי-פורמאליות הקיימת במצב הקדום.

אך גם באוקימתא של רבי שמעון, מסתתרת עדות נוספת המורה על עקביות במגמתו לפורמאליזציה ואיחוד מידות ושיעורים. כדי להבינה במלא כוחה, קיים צורך להבין את המשנה בפרק הקודם, ז, ג, ששם כתוב:

> ועוד כלל אחר אמרו. כל הכשר להצניע [?ו?]מצניעים כמוהו. הוציאו בשבת חייב עליו חטאת. וכל שאינו כשר להצניע [ו]אין מצניעים כמוהו. הוציאו בשבת אינו חייב אלא למצניעו.

גולדברג[18] מזכיר שר' יוסי בר חנינא לומד שמשנה זו חולקת על רבי שמעון בפרק ח, א, והיא כאחד מתלמידיו האחרים של רבי עקיבא. לפי ר' יוסי בר חנינא בבבלי, בפרק ז', הכוונה היא שדבר שרגילים בני אדם להצניע (דהיינו, לשמור עליו), בשיעור מסויים, אם הוציאוהו בשבת, חייב חטאת. אם זה דבר שאנשים לא מצניעים, או מדובר בשיעור קטן ממה שרוב אנשים מחשיבים ושומרים, אזי רק האדם שבפועל מצניעו, מגלה את דעתו ש"אחשביה", ולכן יהיה חייב עליו. כמובן, אנשים אחרים, לא יהיו חייבים בשיעור כזה.[19] אך גולדברג מוצא חולשה מסויימת בזה שמשנה המתחילה ב"כלל", שלדבריו הינו סגנון המתאים לרבי עקיבא, תהיה לפי אחד מתלמידיו החולקים על רבי שמעון, ולא לפי רבי

18 שם, עמ' 155-156.

19 וכך מפרש י.נ. אפשטיין במבוא לנוסח המשנה, עמ' 105. דברי אפשטיין תומכים בקריאה שאני מציע, שפרק ז, ג לעומת פרק ח, א, מפגינה עוד סטנדרטיזציה בדברי רבי שמעון.

שמעון לא רק נותן שיעור קצוב לדבר שברובד קדום יותר היה ללא שיעור, אלא הוא גם משווה את השיעורים של דברים אלו – שכולם בסדר זרעים -אחד לשני. זה רובד נוסף של פורמאליזציה, בו התנא לא רק מעמיד שיעור קשוח, אלא גם מאחד עניינים שונים לאותו שיעור. בהלכות שבת, יעלה שוב פורמאליזציה משנית זו של רבי שמעון.

מדבריו של רבי שמעון בהלכות שמיטה, פאה וביכורים, עולה שהוא מתעסק במכוון בהפיכת סטנדרטים טבעיים, גמישים ואינדיבידואליסטים לנורמות קשוחות, אחידות ופורמאליות, הן בשיעורים מסויימים, והן ביישור קו שיעור אחיד לאורך כמה וכמה נושאים נבדלים. כמובן, עניינים אלו של חקלאות הם ניתנים לכל איכר ופועל בעצמו; קשה מאוד לדמיין מצב בו ההחלטות האלו - אם נבחרו מספיק פירות לביכורים, או נותרה מספיק מן התבואה לפאה, או אם השדה הזה לח - או יבש - מספיק להחשיב את עבודתו כצורך שנת השמיטה – יגיעו למחליט חיצוני יותר ממצפון האדם עצמו.

ג. בהלכות שבת – סדר מועד

בפרק שמיני (משנה א) של מסכת שבת, עדים אנו להתייחסותו של רבי שמעון למצב הקדום, הפחות פורמאלי.

> המוציא יין כדי מזיגת הכוס. ח( )[לב], כדי גמייה. דבש כדי ליתן על הכתית. שמן כדי לסוך אבר קטן. מים כדי לשוף את הקלורית. ושאר כל המשקין ברביעית וכל השופכים ברביעית. ר' שמעון או'. כולם ברביעית. לא נאמרו כל השיעורים האילו אלא למצניע[י]הם.

כהמשך לפרק הקודם, המשנה שלנו דנה בשיעור המחייב במלאכת הוצאה בשבת. תנא קמא (כפי שאברהם גולדברג[17] מעיר, הוא רבי יהודה של התוספתא, פרק ח' הלכה 10) מביא שיעורים שונים לכמה וכמה מיני משקים, שהמוציאם יתחייב חטאת, ובעניין שאר המשקים, שיעור הוצאתם הוא רביעית. לעומת הפירוט של תנא קמא, רבי שמעון אוחז שכל המשקים שיעורם ברביעית כדי להתחייב בהוצאתן בשבת. במקום שתנא קמא מייחס שיעור מיוחד ומפורט לכמה מינים, רבי שמעון קובע שיעור קצוב, ומשווה את

רבי שמעון מחלק בין ביכורים עצמם ל"תוספת" ביכורים, שהם עדיין מין במינו. קיימת רמה של תוספת ביכורים שהיא מובדלת מ"עיטור ביכורים" (מין בשאינו מינו). חשוב לשים לב שתוספת ביכורים וביכורים עצמם הם אותו מין, כך שההבדל היחיד שיכול להיות ביניהם הוא השיעור. אכן, שיטת רבי שמעון, שכל משנה זו דבריו, היא שחייב להיות שיעור לביכורים, ושיותר מזה, זה כבר "תוספת ביכורים". עדות זו, לפחות כך נראה לי, מחזקת באופן מה את הגירסה שמאמץ ליברמן בירושלמי, ששורת הדברים ששיעורם "ששים", הם דברי רבי שמעון.

17 גולדברג, א. <u>פירוש למשנה מסכת שבת</u>, בית המדרש לרבנים שבאמריקה, ירושלים, תשל"ו. עמ' 161-164.

הולך מעל ומעבר לסטנדרטיזציה רגילה זו, ומחייב גם פורמאליזציה במיקום השיעור בשדה, ובמעשה הקצירה. השיעור המינימאלי של פאה צריך להתמקד בחלק האחרון בו קוצרים.

המשנה במסכת ביכורים, פרק ב, ג, אומרת:

> יש בתרומה ובמעשר מה שאין בביכורים. שהתרומה והמעשר אוסרין את הגורן. ויש להם שיעור. ונוהגין בכל הפירות. בפני הבית ושלא בפני הבית. ובאריסים ובח( )[כ]ורות ובסיקריקון ובגוזל( )[ן]. הרי אלו בתרומה ובמעשר מה שאין בביכורים.

המשנה מצהירה שלתרומה ולמעשר יש שיעור, דבר שאינו כן בביכורים. עובדה זו מסכימה להלכה הקדומה בריש פאה, שאין לביכורים שיעור. אך הירושלמי (סה ע"ג) משווה את הפאה והביכורים, על ידי הבאתו את הפיסקא הבאה:

> תני ר' ישמעאל. הביכורים אחד מששים. פיאה אחד מששים. ראשית הגז אחד מששים. תרומה טמיאה אחד מששים. תרומה שאין הכנהים מקפידין עליה אחד מששים...

פה מובא בשם ר' ישמעאל רשימת דברים ששיעורם אחד מששים, ובתוך הרשימה נמצאים פאה וביכורים. ליברמן[14] מפנה לגירסת המהר"י בן מלכי צדק והר"ש, שמעידים[15] על נוסח הירושלמי שהיה לפניהם, ובמקום "ר' ישמעאל" הם מביאים את "ר' שמעון". עדות זו על עד נוסח לא מוכר של התלמוד הירושלמי חשובה מאד, שאין בידינו יותר מכתב-יד אחד, וכל שריד עדות לגבי נוסחתה עשוי להורות על נוסח אחר שהיה קיים – במיוחד במקרה זה ששני הראשונים מסכימים לגירסא שאינה תואמת את המופיע בכת"י ליידן. בעדות זו לנוסח הירושלמי בביכורים, תפקיד רבי שמעון כתנא הדוגל בפורמאליזצית השיעורים בולט. גם בפאה וגם בביכורים[16] (ובראשית הגז ותרומה), רבי

---

14 תוספתא כפשוטה ביכורים עמ' 852, הערה 88.

15 בתחילת פרק ג' של מסכת ביכורים.

16 הערכה שהגירסא הנכונה בירושלמי היא "רבי שמעון" ולא "רבי ישמעאל" מקובלת כהנחה על ידי ליברמן. ובאמת, רבי שמעון מתעסק בשיעורם של הביכורים בעוד כמה נושאים. למשל, בתחילת פרק ג' במשנה ביכורים, רבי שמעון פוסק שאף על פי שאדם קורא שם לביכורים בתחילת גידולם, חייב הוא שוב לקרוא להם שם ביכורים מאחר שייתלשו מן הקרקע. שיטה זו מאוד קרובה לרעיון שראינו בפסקו של רבי שמעון גבי פאה, שאדם חייב לתת בסוף השדה כשיעור – בשני העניינים, רבי שמעון מקטין את שיעור הזמן הכשר לעשיית החלק הפורמאלי של המצווה – קריאת שם הביכורים, ולקיטת השיעור המינימאלי של פאה. נוסף על כן, במשנה ביכורים פרק ג' משנה י' (וגם בתוספתא פרק ב' הלכה 12-13 עמ' 292 במהדורה ליברמן):

> ר' שמעון או'. שלוש מידות בביכורים. הביכורים ותוספת הביכורים ועיטור הביכורים. (מין בשאינו מינו). תופסת הביכורים מין במינו. [ועיטור הביכורים מין בשא[י]נו מינו]. תוספת הביכורים נאכלת בטהרה ופטורה מן הדמיי. ועיטור הביכורים חייב בדמיי.

בוודאי יש לה שיעור מלמעלה.[11] ל. גינצבורג מסכים למעשה עם השיטה הזו, ומנסה לקשר את המשניות שלנו לרבדים שונים שמקורם ב"קובץ הלכות עתיק" שהיווה מקור גם למשנה וגם למכילתא.[12]

ברור שיש כאן צרימה במשנה, בגלל הרכבת מקורות מרבדים שונים. הסברים של התלמודים והחוקרים הם תוצאה של דרכים שונות ליצור הרמנוזציה בין הרבדים הסותרים. אך נראה ברור שבמצב הקדום (שאליו משנה א' תואמת), לא היתה לפאה שיעור כלל. אך לאחר מכן, יש רובד שבו כבר יש לפאה שיעור (רובד המשתקף ממשנה ב'), והמשנה מעידה על תהליך סטנדרטיזציה בהתהוות ההלכה. תהליך זה, לפי דרך אחת, מוסברת כאוקימתא, ש"אין לה שיעור" רק מדבר מלמעלה אך לא מלמטה, ולפי דרך שנייה, מובנת בפשטות כהחמרה וסטנדרטיזציה של חכמים על דין התורה הבסיסית האינדיבידואלית. חשוב לציין שכמו בהלכות שביעית, כאן שוב יש כעין "משנה ראשונה" ו"משנה אחרונה" – ובשני המקורות, ההלכה הקדומה התאפיינה בשיעור טבעי, או בלא שום שיעור, כל עוד הרובד השני של ההלכה עסקה בפורמאליזציה וחיזוק שיעור קצוב.

כפי שנראה במקור הבא, בביכורים, יש עדות לכך ששיעור המשנה "ששים" - לפאה וגם לביכורים - הם דברי רבי שמעון. לפני זה, רצוני לברר את פאה א, ג, שבו מפורשות מופיע רבי שמעון:[13] "נותנין פיאה מתחילת השדה [ו]מאמצעה. ר' שמעון אומ' ובלבד שיתן בסוף (ב)[כ]שיעור." לפי התנא קמא, אפשר לתת פאה מכל מקום בשדה, ובסוף, אם מה שניתן מגיע לסכום אחד מששים, יצא ידי חובתו. אך לפי רבי שמעון, חייב הקוצר להשאיר שיעור פאה בסוף השדה דווקא. הלכה זו מתווספת לסטנדרטיזציה של רבי שמעון לגבי השיעור של פאה, ומרחיקה לכת, לחייב שלא רק השיעור יהיה ששים, אלא שבנוסף לכך, כל הששים ישויירו בסוף השדה. פורמאליזציה זו מראה איך רבי שמעון נוטל חלק בסטנדרטיזציה של שיעור טבעי לשיעור פורמאלי, שבו כל בית הלל יכולים להסכים, כך שהשיעור נשנה במשנה כהלכה סתמית. אך לא בכך מסתפק רבי שמעון; הוא

---

11 אלבק הבין דרך התוספתא והירושלמי את המשנה, ומפרש גם את המשנה על ידי חילוק בין הלכה דאוריתא להלכה דרבנן. אך כפי שכבר הערתי לעיל, ליברמן מבין את התוספתא דרך הבנתו את המשנה, ומבסס את החילוק בין מלמעלה למלמטה.

12 גינצבורג, ל. <u>על הלכה ואגדה</u>, הוצאת דביר, ירושלים, 1960. עמ' 93-90. אודות מחלוקת זו בין ליברמן וגינצבורג, למדתי מפרופ' כהנא, בעל פה. לא שוכנעתי מדברי גינצבורג, כי בונה הוא גירסא בפאה המתאמת את המוטיב "אין פוחתים...אבל מוסיפים עד עולם" הנמצא עשר פעמים בערכין פרק ב'. אך למעשה, פאה לא מופיעה כאחד מהדברים הרשומים בערכין, וגירסת גינצבורג נותרת כהשערה ספקולטיבית. קיימים קשיים אחרים בדברי גינצבורג, אך אין כאן המקום להאריך, וגם שם, דבריו על פאה הם אגב הניתוח המרכזי, דברי המשנה בערכין פרק ב', והמקור המשותף לה ולמכילתא (בא ה').

13 וכן מופיעים דבריו בתוספתא פרק א' הלכה 5: "נותן אדם פיאה (מ)[ב]תחילה ובאמצע(ה) ובסוף ואם נתן בין בתחילה בין באמצע בין בסוף יצא. ר' שמעון או'. אם נתן בין בתחילה בין באמצע בין בסוף הרי זו פאה. וצריך שיתן בסוף כשיעור."

"נתת תורת כל אחד ואחד בידו"! הירושלמי[5] מסביר, "זה או': כל[ת] (ת)לחה שלי. וזה או' לא כל[ת] (ת)לחה שלי." כל אחד יצטרך להחליט אם הגיע שדהו לסף האיסור או עדיין לא. על-אף העובדה שמצב זה שרר לאורך דורות,[6] בית הלל או מקדימיהם ההלכתיים החליטו בשלב מה שמערכת משפטית צריכה אחידות ושוויון בעיני החוק כלפי כל אחד ואחד. הצדקת החוק ואכיפתו כרוכים בתיאום החוק ל"משפט אחד יהיה לכם – משפט השוה לכולכם."[7] מגמה זו ברורה מדברי בית הלל, ורבי שמעון, תלמיד האסכולה הזו, מבטא את הסיבה למגמת ההסטנדרטיזציה של המידות והשיעורים.

רבי שמעון לא רק אוחז בשיטת בית הלל; הוא גם מחריף את הפולמוס ההלכתי נגד אי-פורמאליזציה משפטית. בתחילת מסכת פאה, כתוב: "אלו דברים שאין להן שיעור. הפיאה והביכורין..." אך מיד לאחר מכן, במשנה ב', כתוב, "אין פוחתין לפיאה מששים. אף-על-פי שאמרו. אין [ל]פיאה שיעור." אף על פי שאמרו שאין לפאה שיעור במשנה א', מסבירה משנה ב', עדיין, יש מינימום שחייבים לתת. בחולין,[8] הגמרא שואלת, הלא אין לפאה שיעור, איך אפשר לומר שפאה שיעורה אחד מששים? ועונה, שמדאוריתא, אין לפאה שיעור קצוב, אבל מדרבנן, חייבים לתת אחד מששים.[9]

מהבבלי יוצא שההבדל בין מצב בו ניתן לפאה שיעור והמצב שלא ניתן לה שיעור הוא אם מדובר בדין התורה או תקנת חכמים. אך בירושלמי[10] כתוב:

> הפיאה יש לה שיעור מלמטן ואין לה שיעור מלמעלן. [הביכורי' וראיון אין להם שיעור לא מלמעלן ולא מלמט'. אית תני תנא. הפיאה והביכורים וראיון אין להם שיעור לא למעלן ולא למטן...]

קיימות פה שתי אפשרויות להבנת התוספתא בפאה פרק א' הלכה 1: לפי האפשרות הראשונה, תמיד לפאה היה שיעור מלמטה, וזה ש"אין לה שיעור", מכוון לשיעור מלמעלה (שאי-אפשר לעשות את כל השדה פאה). אך לביכורים וקרבן ראיה, אין שיעור מינימאלי או מקסימאלי. לאפשרות השנייה, גם לפיאה אין שיעור מזערי או מרבי. בשתי אפשרויות אלה, ההבדל בין המשנה הראשונה לשניה במסכת פאה אינו אם מדובר בדאוריתא או דרבנן, אלא אם מדובר בשיעור למטה או למעלה. וכך באמת יוצא מהתוספתא עצמה, "העושה כל שדהו פיאה אינה פיאה." אין לפאה שיעור מלמטה, אך

---

5 שביעית לג ע"ד.

6 ראה הערה 4.

7 בבא קמא פג עמ' ב, דפוס וילנא.

8 בבלי קלז עמ' ב.

9 ואם נתן פחות מאחד מששים, ולא היה בדעתו להשלים, אינו פאה, ועדיין חייב בפאה. וכך בעצם מפרש ש. ליברמן את התוספתא, ראה תוספתא כפשוטה עמ' 126. אך בירושלמי משמע אחרת, כפי שנראה עתה.

10 פיאה טו ע"א.

[עד] ()אימתי חורשין שדה האילן ערב שביעית. בית שמי אומ'. כל זמן שהוא יפה לפרי. בית הלל אומ' עד העצרת. וקרובים דברי אלו להיות כדברי אלו.

בפרדס, לפי בית שמאי, החרישה מותרת כל זמן שהיא מיטיבה לפירות שכבר קיימים בשדה בשנה הששית. לאחר זמן זה, נחשבת המלאכה כהכנה לשנת השמיטה, ואסורה מטעם "תוספת שביעית" – הוספה באיסורי שנת השמיטה על השנה הקודמת לה. אך לפי בית הלל, אין המלאכה נחשבת לטובת פירות שביעית עד חג שבועות, ומכאן ואילך, אסורה מטעם תוספת שביעית. המשנה מעידה שדברי בית שמאי ובית הלל מאוד קרובים, ולכן, עצם המחלוקת היא על הרעיון של השיעור. בית שמאי מסתכלים על סף ההלכתי כגבול אינדיבידואליסטי, לא קבוע. ייתכן שבשדה פלוני, המלאכה תותר עד לג' סיון, ובשדה של אדם אחר, בח' סיון. מגיע לכל שדה הערכה משלו, בביסוס על אבן-דרך טבעית, וייתכן שהתאריך המדויק ישתנה עקב המצב המימי של הקרקע. אך לבית הלל, דבר זה לא סביר, ומחייבים את כל החקלאיים לתאריך קצוב, שבו - לא משנה מה מצב השדה מבחינה מעשית - אסור לחרוש.

במסכת שביעית (פרק ב, א), רבי שמעון מציג את עמדתו הפורמאליסטית, התואמת את שיטת בית הלל:

עד אימתי חורשין בשדה הלבן ערב שביעית. עד שתיכלה הלחה כל זמן שבני אדם חורשין ליטע ( )[במקשאות ובמ]דלעות. א' ר' שמעון. נתתה תורת כל אחד ואחד בידו. אלא בשדה הלבן עד הפסח ובשדה האילן עד העצרת.

משנה זו מדברת על שדה של תבואה או קטנית, שסף חרישתו ההלכתי לפי תנא קמא[4] הוא רטיבות הקרקע מחמת הגשמים. כאשר הקרקע רטובה מספיק לגדל קישואים, החרישה בשדה נחשבת לטובת השנה הששית, ומותרת. לאחר מכן, כאשר הקרקע יבשה משיעור זה, כל חרישה תתיחס לשנה הבאה, ותיאסר משום תוספת שביעית. אך לשיטת רבי שמעון, הזמן לא נקבע על ידי מדד טבעי, אלא תאריך מלאכותי-קשוח, חג הפסח. דברי רבי שמעון תואמים את דברי בית הלל מפרק א' משנה א' לא רק בתיאום הקיים בשיטתם גבי שדה אילן, אלא גם ברעיון העומד אחר שיטת שניהם, אותה מנסח רבי שמעון כעיקרון מנחה בסיסי בכל ענין מידות ושיעורים: אם השיעור אינו סטנדרטי, אזי

4 שהוא, לפי הירושלמי, רבי מאיר, עיי' ירושלמי שביעית לג ע"ג. הירושלמי מגיע למסקנה שאין רבי מאיר ורבי שמעון חולקים באותה המחלוקת של בית שמאי ובית הלל, כי הלא ההלכה כבית הלל. אלא רבי מאיר מזכיר כאן את המשנה הראשונה ורבי שמעון מזכיר את המשנה האחרונה. מוכח מהירושלמי שאין מחלוקת בית שמאי ובית הלל מחלוקת סטאטית, אלא מהלך היסטורי: בראשונה ההלכה היתה לפי מדדים טבעיים, כפי שמנסח בית שמאי את המצב, וכפי שרבי מאיר מזכיר. אך בית הלל תיקנו מדד סטנדרטי, ובזה השיעור של תוספת שביעית נהפך למידה קשוחה ואובייקטיבית.

ממוסדים, מפורשים ואי-אורגניים. רבי שמעון בר יוחי היה תנא מבית מדרשו של בית הלל מהדור הרביעי, ותלמידו של רבי עקיבא. גם מחוץ לתחום מידות ושיעורים, ידועה נטייתו לשיטות ייחודיות, המנוגדות לקונסנזוס התנאי.[3] שיטותיו לפעמים כל-כך משונות וחלוציות, שאינן נפסקות להלכה, אך נשארות במקורות התנאיים כשיטות-יחיד. תוך-כדי עיון בשיטותיו הנוגעות לעניין כמויות הלכתיות, יוצע שרבי שמעון הוא דמות מכריעה בתנועת הסטנדרטיזציה. בנסיון לאסוף את כל המימרות של רבי שמעון שבמשנה, בתוספתא ובמדרשי ההלכה, הנוגעות לענין מידות ושיעורים בהלכה, יוצגו מקורות השופכים אור על שיטתו הייחודית גם בענין זה, והמגמה לסטנדרטיזציה בקרב חז"ל בכלל. על פי מקורות אלו, תיבחן שיטת רבי שמעון בסוגיות שונות הנוגעות לעניין שיעורים ומידות, דרך מסורות הנוסח הקיימות בידינו, והשוואה בין דבריו בתחומים השונים של ההלכה בם הם נמצאים. דברי רבי שמעון עקביים במידה רבה, ומפסקיו היוצאים מן הכלל, אולי יתבהר העיקרון דרכו מחליט רבי שמעון אם לפעול לפורמאליזציה, או להתנגד לכך.

ב. בענין החקלאות – סדר זרעים

בתחילת מסכת שביעית, מופיעה מחלוקת בין בית שמאי ובית הלל לענין המועד הסופי בו מותר לחרוש בשדה אילן בשנה הששית למחזור השמיטה.

בבסיסו, אורגאני. לכן, החוק יחול מן הסתם על כל מקרה שבו הוא יקדם את הטובה או ירתיע את הרעה (בטרמינולוגיה של הארט, מקרה ה"core", העיקרי של החוק). תחום החוק, אם כן, בשלב ראשוני זה, הוא אורגאני. אדם המבין מה מונע את המחוקק יבין ברגש אינטואטיבי אם החוק חל על מקרה פלוני. אך לאחר מכן, תחום החוק חייב מיסוד, להגביל את הפרמטרים של יישומו, לתחום מפורש. הארט מציין שקיימות כללים משפטיים משניים, secondary legal rules, הנצרכות, דרכם הכללים הבסיסיים (primary legal rules) נאכפים. אחד מהם הוא כלל ההכרה (the Rule of Recognition), המצביע על דרך שבה כל חבר בחברה יוכל ללמוד את החוקים הבסיסיים, ואחד הוא כלל השפיטה (the Rule of Adjudication), הנותן לחברה דרך לדעת אם אחד החוקים הופר, ואיך להעניש את המפר. שני כללים משניים אלו מצריכים פורמאליזציה מסויימת בחוק הנידון. למשל, קשה מאוד להחליט אם אדם עובר על חוק האומר, "אל תיסע בכלי-רכב במהירות מסוכנת", בגלל עירפול התחומי: כמה זה מהירות מסוכנת? לעומת זה, קל יותר להחליט אם אדם עבריין, אם החוק אומר, "אל תיסע בכלי-רכב במהירות היתרה על מאה קמ"ש." עלות הפורמאליזציה היא שיהיו מקרים בהם מאה קמ"ש הם לא מהירות מסוכנת, וגם מקרים שאפילו תשעים קמ"ש הם מהירות מופרזת (לדברי הארט, מקרים אלו הם "penumbra", מקרים שלא היו בתודעה של יוצרי החוק); אך ברוב המקרים, החוק המפורש ישרת את הציבור נאות, בזמן שהחוק האורגאני אי-יישומי. אין כוונתי בכל זה לומר שכל חוק עובר את שני השלבים האלו במפורש, ייתכן והשלבים יקראו בו-זמנית, אך מבחינה מושגית, הם נבדלים, ועליהם המחקר הנוכחי מדבר.

3 ראה את שיטתו למשל במוקצה, ובדבר שאינו מתכוין.

שיטת רבי שמעון בשיעורים ובמידות*

מאת: דניאל וולטמן

א. פתיחה

חקר ההלכה בכלל, ושיטות הפוסקים והמחוקקים בפרט, מאפשר ניתוח מהלך התפתחות מערכת החוק היהודי לאורך דורות. מבנה המשפט היהודי הינו מערכת הדורשת ממחזיקיה ונושאיה לא רק נאמנות לכלליה מן העבר, אלא גם פיתוח ייעודי וכנה שמטרתו לבנות בהווה מערכת העונה על צרכי הדור, וממשיכה בעתיד לבנות את עצמה, בשיכלול וחידוש, לצמיתות.[1] ובכן, מערכת ההלכה של עם ישראל, מימות תורת משה והלאה, מציגה את עצמה כאחת מהמורשות הרציפות והארוכות ביותר של התפתחות משפטית הידועות לאנושות. ההלכה הרבנית והתורה שבעל-פה, כפיתוח של - ובנייה על – התורה הכתובה, וכחלק בלתי-נפרד ממנה, נותנת לעולם הצצה לתהליך התבגרות משפטית של המערכת מיוזמת רועיה, התנאים והאמוראים. מחקר זה יתמקד בחלק חשוב של מהלך התפתחות זה, הפורמאליזציה והאובייקטיביזציה של החוקים[2] מגבולות וסייגים טבעיים, לסטנדרטים

* מאמר זה התהווה והתפתח בתוך מסגרת הסמינר "מידות ושיעורים בספרות התלמודית" באוניברסיטה העברית, ירושלים, בתשע"ה, בהנחיית פרופ' מנחם כהנא. כמה מן המקורות המובאות הוצגו על ידו, ודיונים סביבם עובדו על ידי לתוך המאמר. תודות לפרופ' כהנא וחברי לסמינר, וגם לחברי מחוצה לו, על הערותיהם לטיוטה ותרומתם למאמר הסופי. כל טעות הנמצא בו נשאר שלי בלבד. באשר למהדורות: אם איני מציין למהדורה מיוחדת לציטוטים מתוך ספרות חז"ל, אפשר להניח שהשתמשתי במהדורה שנבחרה על ידי האקדמיה ללשון העברית.

1 לפיתוח מפורט של רעיונות אלו, ראה א. ברקוביץ, ההלכה: כוחה ותפקידה, מוסד הרב קוק, ירושלים. תשס"ח. עמ' רי-ריח. רעיון זה מנוסח גם כן על ידי ר' משה גלזנר, בהקדמה לספרו דור רביעי על חולין: "...מה שנמסר פירוש התורה על פה ונאסר לכתבה, הוא כדי שלא לעשות קיום לדור דורות, ושלא לקשור ידי חכמי דור ודור לפרש הכתובים כפי הבנתם, כי רק על אופן זה נכון לנצחיות התורה, כי שינוי הדורות ודעותיהם, מצבם ומעמדם הגשמיי והמוסרי, דורשות שינוי דיניהם תקנות ותיקונים."

2 מהלך זה אינו מיוחד להלכה, וגם במערכות משפטיות אחרות, קיימת מגמה זו. לפי התיאוריה הפוזיטיביסטית של החוקה (ראה ה.ל.א. הארט, Positivism and the Separation of Law and Morals. Harvard Law Review 71 (4) 593-629), החוק הוא בעצם קונצרוקציה סוציאלית. המניעים של חוקה יכולים להיות רבים: תועלתניות, שמירה על המשטר, מוסריות, שיקולים דתיים ועוד רבים. היוזמה לחוקק נובע מצורך מסויים, והצורך

דניאל וולטמן למד לתואר ראשון בישיבה אוניברסיטה, והוסמך לרבנות על ידי הרבנות הראשית לישראל. בעוד הוא עובד כמתכנת מחשבים, הוא לומד לתואר שני בחוג לתלמוד והלכה של האוניברסיטה העברית בירושלים. הוא מתגורר עם אשתו ושלשת בניו ביד בנימין.

עשרים או שלשים, יכול לומר אילולא שסילקתני הייתי עוסק בתורה, לפיכך אמר שמה אם מעט ואם הרבה יאכל, שמתן שכרן שוה", ע"כ. ונמצא לפ"ז שבהלקח ת"ח צעיר לימים שיגע בתורה כ' שנה בלבד, אין זה חסרון לו, כי הוא יקבל שכרו משלם כאילו עסק בתורה פ' שנים, השמש עדיין זורח במקום אחר, אבל ההפסד הוא לנו, בעולם הזה, שנלקח מאתנו ת"ח גדול צורבא מרבנן דנבט, שעדיו היה לגאון ולתפארת בישראל, היה מיועד לגדולות ונצורות ממש, הרי זה בגדר בא השמש בצהריים, הוא הלך למנוחות ואותנו עזב לאנחות.

תהא נשמתו צרורה בצרור החיים, הרופא לשבורי לב יחבוש ויחזק אותנו ואת משפחתו, אבי היתומים יחוס וירחם על ארבעה העוללים הקטנים שנשארו יתומים מאב ומאם ויסייעם שיגדלו ויפרחו לתפארת בית אבות, ומי שאמר לעולמו די יאמר לצרותינו די ובא לציון גואל יקיצו וירננו שוכני עפר. ☙

ע"כ, בדרך כלל כשפוגעים באיש מכירים בו מיד שהוא מאיזה סוג, יש לו רצונות וחשבונות אישים, אבל אסתר היתה נושאת חן בעיני כל רואה, שלכל אחד ואחד נדמתה לו כאומתו, כל מי שראה אותה חשב שהיא חושבת כמותו, שהיא שייכא לסוג שלו. וכך היה אצל הג"ר איתם, כל מי שפגע אותו הרגיש ידידות עז ואהבת אח, לכל אחד נדמתה לו כאומתו.

במו"ק כה: שנינו "והי' ביום ההוא והבאתי את השמש בצהריים, אמר ר' יוחנן מאי ביום ההוא, זהו יומו של יאשיהו שנהרג בצעירותו, כדכתי' בן ל"ט שנים היה במותו" ע"כ, ופי' המהרש"א דביאת השמש בצהריים אינה הפסד וחסרון לשמש עצמו, כי השמש עדיין מזריח ועולה במקום אחר, אלא ההפסד הוא לאלו שהיו נהנים עד אז מאורו ומתחממים ממנו, והיינו בא השמש בצהריים.

והנראה להעמיק בביאור הענין ע"פ הא דאיתא בירו' דברכות (פ"ב ה"ח) "כד דמיך ר' בון בר ר' חייא, על ר' זעירא ואפטר עילוי' 'מתוקה שנת העובד כו' אם מעט אם הרבה יאכל, למה היה ר' בון בר' חייא דומה, למלך ששכר פועלים הרבה והיה שם פועל אחד והיה משתכר במלאכתו יותר מדאי, מה עשה המלך, נטלו והיה מטייל עמו ארוכות וקצרות. לעיתותי ערב באו אותם פועלים ליטול שכרן ונתן לו שכרו עמהן משלם, והיו הפועלים מתרעמין ואומרים אנו יגענו כל היום וזה לא יגע אלא שתי שעות, ונתן לו שכרו עמנו משלם. אמר להן המלך יגע זה לשתי שעות יותר ממה שלא יגעתם אתם כל היום כולו, כך יגע ר' בון בתורה לכ"ח שנה מה שאין תלמיד ותיק יכול ללמוד למאה שנה" ע"כ. וכעי"ז בתנחומא פרשת כי תשא (סי' ג) "רבי תנחומא בר אבא מתוקה שנת העובד אם מעט ואם הרבה יאכל, והשבע לעשיר איננו מניח לו לישון, אמרו לו לשלמה, אילו אחר אמר הפסוק הזה היינו שוחקין עליו, אתה שכתוב בך ויחכם מכל האדם תאמר מתוקה שנת העבד אם מעט ואם הרבה, אין הדבר כך, שכל מי שהוא רעב אכל קמעא שינתו מתנדנדת ממנו, אכל הרבה שינתו מתוקה. אמר להם איני מדבר אלא בצדיקים ובעמלי תורה. כיצד, אדם שכל שנותיו ל' שנה, ומעשר שנים ואילך הוא עמל בתורה ובמצות, ומת לשלשים שנה. ואדם אחר חי שמונים שנה, ומעשר שנים ואילך עמל בתורה ובמצות עד שמת, אתה אומר הואיל ולא יגע הראשון אלא כ' שנה בתורה, וזה יגע ע' שנה, שהקב"ה מרבה לזה שכר יותר ממי שעסק בתורה כ' שנה. לפיכך אני אומר אם מעט ואם הרבה יאכל, שיכול בן כ' שנה לומר לפני הקב"ה, אילולא שסלקתני מן העולם בחצי ימי הייתי מאריך שנים ומרבה בתורה ובמצות, לפיכך אני אומר אם מעט ואם הרבה יאכל, שמתן שכרו של זה כמתן שכרו של זה וכו'. אמר רבי לוי משל למה הדבר דומה, למלך ששכר פועלים למלאכתו, עם שהן עושין נטל המלך אחד מהם וטייל עמו, לערב באו הפועלים ליטול שכרן, בא אותו הפועל שטייל עם המלך ליטול עמהן, שמא יכול המלך לומר לו אתה לא עשית עמהם אלא שתי שעות טול כפי מה שעשית, אף הוא יכול לומר למלך אילולא אתה שביטלתני וטיילתני עמך היה שכרי מרובה. וכך הקב"ה יתברך שמו - המלך זה הקב"ה, והפועלין אלו עמלי התורה, מי שיגע בתורה חמישים שנה ומי שיגע בתורה

במקצועות קשות שבתורה, הל' קו התאריך, טריפות, טהרות, ריבית ועוד, ותמיד היה מוכן ליכנס לעומק הענין והעלה דבר ברור, בדעת ובשכל הישר, ונתפעלתי מכוחו העצום לירד לעומקן של דברים ולהוציא מרגניתא טבא.

לפני כמה שנים הוציא לאור מאמר מקיף על זקנו הגרי"א, והדפיסו בקובץ ישורון, שם משתקף ידיעה רחבה והבנה עמוקה בכמה מקצועות בתורה וכן ידיעה מקיפה בהיסוטריה ועוד ענינים. כבר שמעתי מכמה ת"ח שכשקראו את המאמר חשבו לעצמם שהדברים ודאי נכתבו ע"י ת"ח מבוגר שכבר הגיע לבן חמשים וכדו', והופתעו לשמוע שהמאמר נכתב כשהמחבר היה אברך צעיר בן כ"ב שנים בלבד.

הג"ר איתם הי"ד הוציא לאור ספר לכם יהיה לאכלה על הל' תולעים, בו הוא פורש את השמלה ומציע סוגיא דתולעים ומטייל בו ארוכות וקצרות. גם הספר הלזה עמוק הוא, מלאכת מחשבת הראוי לת"ח זקן ויושב בישיבה וכולו אומר כבוד, וכמעט ולא יאומן שהספר יצא לאור כשהיה אברך בן כ"ה שנים בלבד - אבל כך היה עוצם חכמתו וגדולתו בתורה.

מלבד גדולתו בתורה, היה גם בקי במקצועות אחרות, תכנון היסטוריה ועוד, אני שמעתי מכמה מורות במקצועות שונות שעמדו בקשר עם הג"ר איתם הי"ד, וסיפרו שהיו מתפעלים מעומק ידיעותיו וחכמתו עד שחשבו שבודאי כל מגמתו היה המקצוע המדובר, ומה גדול היה הפתעתם כששמעו שבאמת לא היה זה עיקר משימתו כלל אלא היה אברך העוסק בתורה והוראה ואסוקי שמעתתא אליבא דהלכתא, והעיון והטיפול במקצועות הללו היו דברים שעשה 'בין הסדרים'.

כן היה הג"ר איתם הי"ד עמקן גדול, בעל פנימיות גדולה, שהבין עומק ופנימיות של כל דבר ודבר, והיה לו היכולת להבין ולהסביר נקודות פנימיים בפשטות נפלאה. דבר נדיר הוא למאד, בדור שאינו רואה אלא לפָנים (סוטה מז:), שיהא אחד הרואה עומקן של דברים, ולא רק פני הדברים בלבד. תמיד עמדתי משתומם על תפיסתו העמוק, איך שהוציא דברים עמוקים ומסובכים ופירשם בפשטות ובשכל הישר. כן היה מבקש האמת בכל דבר, ללא סטיות ורצונות עצמיים, אלא ביקוש האמת, האמת היה אהוב עליו יותר מכל.

אבל הגדול ביותר מגדולתו בתורה וחכמה, היה גדולתו במדות ודרך ארץ בין אדם לחבירו. נעימותו היה להפליא ממש, מדותיו התרומיות, וותרנותו וענוותנותו היו לאות ולמופת לכל מכיריו. שנינו בסנהדרין כד. "ואקח לי שני מקלות לאחד קראתי נועם ולשני קראתי חובלים, נועם אלו ת"ח שבא"י שמנעימים זה לזה בהלכה כו'" ע"כ, הג"ר איתם הי"ד היה מנעים לחבירו בהלכה, אף כשהיה חולק היה בענווה ונעימות יתירא. לא פעם עלו חילוקי דיעות בינינו בהלכה כדרך כל העוסקים באסוקי שמעתתא אליבא דהלכתא, ותמיד הייתי מתרגש מדרכו הנפלא להציע הדברים בענווה, בפשטות, ובדרכי נועם.

כל מי שהכיר את הג"ר איתם הרגיש בו ידידות ואהבה, כל מי שעבד אתו יחד באיזשהו מקצוע הרגיש כאילו המקצוע הלזה הוא הדבר היחיד שתופס מקום בראשו. במגילה יג. שנינו "ותהי אסתר נשאת חן אר"א מלמד שלכל אחד ואחד נדמתה לו כאומתו"

בא השמש בצהריים: רב איתם שמעון הנקין הי"ד

מאת: דניאל אשר קליינמאן

צר לי עליך אחי כי נעמת לי מאד (שמואל ב, כו)

בגשתי לחקוק עלי נייר קוים לדמותו של ידיד נפשי הרה"ג ר' איתם שמעון הנקין זצ"ל הי"ד, חם לבי בקרבי בהגיגי תבער אש, קול נהי נשמע בציון איך שודדנו, מי יתן ראשי מים ועיני מקור דמעה לבכות מעין הפוגות על שבר בת עמי.

קשה לתאר גודל האסון הנורא ועוצמת הכאב הגדול שנחתה עלינו כי עלה המוות בחלוננו, בהילקח מאתנו ידידי עז מאח אציל המידות כליל המעלות איש האשכולות. שנינו בשבת קנג. "אמר ר"י ברי' דרב שמואל בר שילת משמיה דרב, מהספדו של אדם ניכר אם בן עוה"ב הוא אם לאו", ופירש"י שאם כשר היה הכל בוכין עליו ומורידין דמעות ומספרין בשבחו עיי"ש. ועוד שם "בעא מיניה ר' אלעזר מרב, איזהו בן עוה"ב, א"ל ואזניך תשמענה דברך מאחריך לאמר זה הדרך לכו בו כי תאמינו וכי תשמאילו" ע"כ. מהספדו של ידידי הג"ר איתם הי"ד ניכר שהיה בן עוה"ב ממש, כשהייתי בא"י בימי השבעה השתוממתי מהמראה הגדולה אשר לפני איך שנקבצו אנשים מכל הגוונים ומכל המפלגות וכל הנביאים מתנבאים בסגנון אחד, מעידים על גדולתו והשגתו בתורה וחכמה, ועוד יותר מגדולות במדות טובות והנהגה נפלאה בין אדם למקום ובין אדם לחבירו, כולם מורידין עליו דמעות ומספרין בשבחו, ואומריו עליו זה הדרך לכו בו, והוא הסימן המובהק שהיה בן עוה"ב.

שנינו בתענית ד. "אמר רבא האי צורבא מרבנן דמי לפרצידא דתותי קלא דכיון דנבט נבט", ופירש"י "בחור חריף כו' כיון דנבט נבט, שמתחיל לבצבץ ולעלות עולה למעלה, כך ת"ח כיון שיצא שמו הולך וגדול למעלה", ע"כ. וכוונתו, דת"ח צעיר שלן בעומקה של הלכה, מכיון שמתחיל לעלות ויצא שמו, ה"ה פורץ וגדל ועולה מעלה מעלה עד שנעשה גאון ומאור לישראל. כולנו ראינו האי צורבא מרבנן ידידי ר' איתם הי"ד, שהיה מבצבץ ועולה, הולך וגדל ולן בעומקה של הלכה וקונה ענינים ומקצועות שלימים בהיקף בכללותיהם ופרטיהם וחותר לשרשים ויסודות ויורד לעומקם להבין טעמי הדברים ולהעמיד יסודותיהם ולאסוקי שמעתתא אליבא דהלכתא עד שמשנתו ברורה וההלכה ברורה. מאמריו הנפלאים תמיד עשו גלים בעולם התורה, כל מאמר שנתפרסם ממנו באיזה מקצוע שיהיה היה קולע אל המטרה, והיה ניכר עליו שזהו מעשה ידי אמן, אב בחכמה שהוא רך בשנים.

בתקופה האחרונה עסקנו יחד להוציא לאור תשובות וחידו"ת של זקנו מרן הגאון מוהרי"א הענקין זצוק"ל, וכמה פעמים עלו שאלות מסובכות הנוגעים לבירור הלכה

דניאל אשר הכהן קליינמאן רב דקהל נחלת דוד דפלטבוש ומחבר ספר קובץ הלכות פסקי הרה"ג הרב שמואל קמינצקי שליט"א.

חקירה

כרך כ' – שנת תשע"ו

תוכן עניינים

זכור

הלכה

חקירה

כרך כ' – שנת תשע"ו